The Promise of Reason

Studies in
The New Rhetoric

Edited by John T. Gage

Southern Illinois University Press / Carbondale and Edwardsville

Copyright © 2011 by the Board of Trustees,
Southern Illinois University
Chapter 3 copyright © Barbara Warnick; chapter 4 copyright © Jeanne Fahnestock; chapter 7 copyright © Alan G. Gross; chapter 9 copyright © Roselyne Koren; chapter 12 copyright © Jean Nienkamp (all rights reserved); chapter 13 copyright © American Forensic Association (reprinted with permission); chapter 15 copyright © Paula Olmos Gómez
All rights reserved
Printed in the United States of America

14 13 12 11   4 3 2 1

Library of Congress Cataloging-in-Publication Data
The promise of reason : studies in The new rhetoric / edited by John T. Gage.
    p. cm.
Includes bibliographical references and index.
  ISBN-13: 978-0-8093-3025-6 (cloth : alk. paper)
  ISBN-10: 0-8093-3025-3 (cloth : alk. paper)
  ISBN-13: 978-0-8093-8628-4 (ebook)
  ISBN-10: 0-8093-8628-3 (ebook)
1. Rhetoric. 2. Academic writing. 3. Reasoning.
  4. Language and logic. I. Gage, John T., 1947– II. Perelman, Chaïm New rhetoric.
PE1431.P76 2011
808—dc22   2011005359

Printed on recycled paper. ♻

The paper used in this publication meets the minimum requirements of American National Standard for Information Sciences—Permanence of Paper for Printed Library Materials, ANSI Z39.48-1992. ∞

Contents

Acknowledgments   vii

INTRODUCTORY ESSAYS

1. Introduction   1
   John T. Gage

2. Chaïm Perelman: A Life Well Lived   8
   Noémi Perelman Mattis

SECTION ONE

CONCEPTUAL UNDERSTANDINGS OF *THE NEW RHETORIC*   19

3. Empiricism, Securement, and *The New Rhetoric*   21
   Barbara Warnick

4. "No Neutral Choices": The Art of Style in *The New Rhetoric*   29
   Jeanne Fahnestock

5. The Function of the "Universal Audience" in Perelman's Rhetoric: Looking Back on a Theoretical Issue   48
   Loïc Nicolas

6. Lucie Olbrechts-Tyteca's New Rhetoric   55
   David A. Frank and Michelle K. Bolduc

SECTION TWO

EXTENSIONS OF *THE NEW RHETORIC*   81

7. Solving the Mystery of Presence: Verbal/Visual Interaction in Darwin's *Structure and Distribution of Coral Reefs*   83
   Alan G. Gross

8. Kenneth Burke's "Identification" and Chaïm Perelman and Lucie Olbrechts-Tyteca's "Communion": A Case of Convergent Evolution? 103
   Richard Graff and Wendy Winn

9. Language and Axiological Rationality: The "Non-thought" of French Linguistics in the Mirror of *The New Rhetoric* 134
   Roselyne Koren

SECTION THREE

THE ETHICAL TURN IN PERELMAN AND *THE NEW RHETORIC* 145

10. Perelman on Democracy as a Confused Notion 147
    Ray D. Dearin

11. Philosophical Art or Rhetorical Skill: How Perelman's Ethical Pluralism Makes McKeon's Analytical Pluralism Ethically Conscientious 162
    Linda Bensel-Meyers

12. RhETHorICS 171
    Jean Nienkamp

SECTION FOUR

USES OF *THE NEW RHETORIC* 183

13. Awakening the *Topoi:* Sources of Invention in *The New Rhetoric*'s Argument Model 185
    James Crosswhite

14. Analogical Reasoning in the Teaching of Science: The Case of Richard Feynman's Physics 206
    Maria Freddi

15. From Laconic Apothegms to Film Quotations: Rhetorical Advantages of Shared *Paroemiai* 223
    Paula Olmos

16. A Timeless Attack: Essence and Definition Arguments in Leo Tolstoy's *The Kingdom of God Is Within You* 236
    Mark Hoffmann

Contributors 247
Index 253

Acknowledgments

James Crosswhite's essay "Awakening the *Topoi:* Sources of Invention in *The New Rhetoric*'s Argument Model" appeared in *Argument and Advocacy* 44.4 (Spring 2008): 169–84. Grateful acknowledgment is made to the publisher for permission to reproduce this essay. "Lucie Olbrechts-Tyteca's New Rhetoric," by David A. Frank and Michelle K. Bolduc, *Quarterly Journal of Speech* 96.2 (May 2010): 141–63, is reprinted by permission of the publisher (Taylor & Francis Group, http://wwwinformaworld.com), copyright © National Communication Association, and by permission of Taylor & Francis Ltd. (http://www.tandf.co.uk/journals) on behalf of The National Communication Association. Richard Graff and Wendy Winn's essay "Kenneth Burke's 'Identification' and Chaïm Perelman and Lucie Olbrechts-Tyteca's 'Communion': A Case of Convergent Evolution?" was originally conceived as a follow-up article to their essay "Presenting Communion in Chaïm Perelman's New Rhetoric," published in *Philosophy and Rhetoric* 39 (2006): 45–71, and some parts of that essay are summarized in their essay here. Quotations from Perelman's letters are reproduced in "The Function of the 'Universal Audience' in Perelman's Rhetoric: Looking Back on a Theoretical Issue," by Loïc Nicolas, with the kind authorization of the Fondation Perelman (Brussels) and its president, Guy Haarscher. Excerpts from "Evidences," published in *Le Monde*, 19 April 2003, are used, with permission, in "Language and Axiological Rationality: The 'Non-thought' of French Linguistics in the Mirror of *The New Rhetoric*" by Roselyne Koren.

For assisting me in organizing the 2008 University of Oregon conference that inspired this collection, "The Promise of Reason: *The New Rhetoric* after Fifty Years," I wish to thank especially Teresa Coronado, James Crosswhite, Susan Dickens, David Frank, Ian Jensen, Anne Laskaya, Carolyn Bergquist, Suzanne Clark, Kathleen Horton, Marilyn Reid, Nicole Tabor, Steve Shankman, Henry Wonham, and Lesley Wallace Wooten, among many others. Among the University of Oregon organizations that provided support for that conference were The Carleton and Wilberta Savage Endowment for International Relations and Peace, The Harold Schnitzer Family Program in Judaic Studies, the UNESCO Center for Intercultural Dialogue, the Robert D. Clark Honors College, the College of Arts and Sciences, the English department, and the president's office. For assistance in preparing this edited collection, I am grateful also to Megan Benner, Sarah Stoeckl, and Stephen Summers.

My gratitude, as always, goes to Robin Gage for her support in many ways. For generosity of spirit and mind, as friends of this project, honor is due also to Noémi and Danny Mattis.

One of the keynote speakers at "The Promise of Reason" conference was Michael Leff, to whom I wish to pay tribute with this offering. All of us feel the terrible loss of his voice of reason, his brilliant scholarship, and his friendship.

Introductory Essays

1

Introduction
John T. Gage

Chaïm Perelman and Lucie Olbrechts-Tyteca published *Traité de l'argumentation: La nouvelle rhétorique* in 1958, over fifty years ago. In that work, known to English readers as *The New Rhetoric*, they forged a new place for reason in a postwar world in which logical positivism and science seemed to some to have demonstrably failed to fulfill the promise of freedom. The kind of reason they sought was not the pure form desired by analytic philosophers but the less formal modes of reasoning, and their attendant modalities of speech, described for centuries by rhetoricians. They sought an understanding of rhetorical reasoning, or argumentation in the broadest sense, to resist the brute force of violence on the one hand and the brute force of validity equations on the other. "Only the existence of an argumentation that is neither compelling nor arbitrary," they wrote,

> can give meaning to human freedom, a state in which a reasonable choice can be exercised. . . . It is because of the possibility of an argumentation that provides reasons, but not compelling reasons, that it is possible to escape the dilemma: adherence to an objective and universally valid truth, or recourse to suggestion and violence to secure acceptance for our opinions and decisions. (514)

The promise to be found in a theory of argumentation based on a philosophical reinterpretation of the principles of classical rhetoric was no less than a human community capable of overcoming difference without recourse to either the superiority of transcendental truth or the strength of willfully subjective power. It would be, rather, a foundation for active justice based on the strength of reasons actually given in specific situations in which agreement is sought, not Reason in an absolute, transcendent sense. "The theory of argumentation," they wrote, "will help to develop what a logic of value judgments has tried in vain to provide, namely the justification of the possibility of human community in the sphere of action when this justification cannot be based on a reality or objective truth" (514). The phrasing is hopeful. It looks forward to—it promises—a way out of the dilemma created by a belief that human reasoning operates according to definable and dependable rules and self-evident facts: if true reasoning belongs only to science, differences in human values are solved only by one or another form of coercion. Thomas Conley, speaking of the statement quoted above, has said that when it is "read against the background of the experiences that gave rise to it," that is, World War II and the Holocaust in Europe, "there can be no mistaking . . . [its] tone of urgency" (299).

A half century later, the intricacies, the implications, and the urgencies of *The New Rhetoric* are still being studied. The present volume represents some of the directions of these investigations. Insofar as a large number of scholarly works have appeared in the past fifty years dealing with *The New Rhetoric* or with Perelman's work in general or situating Perelman among the other major figures of the twentieth century who have contributed to theories of human communication (for example, Martin Heidegger, Jürgen Habermas, Hannah Arendt, Emmanuel Lévinas, John Dewey, Kenneth Burke, Stephen Toulmin, and Wayne Booth), the richness and complexity of *The New Rhetoric* is amply demonstrated. What will be the trajectory of such work into the next fifty years? Perhaps this volume will help point the way.[1]

The rich diversity of issues taken up by essays in this volume suggests that scholarship on *The New Rhetoric* will continue to explore the meaning and implications of its theory in an attempt to understand more completely the practical and ethical dynamics of the human performance faculty we call argumentation. But these essays also suggest strongly that such scholarship will embark on new trajectories. These include the extension of *The New Rhetoric*'s model of argumentation to account for argumentative phenomena in the visual, electronic, and new media realms and in scientific, religious, and literary texts; the use of *The New Rhetoric* in theorizing education or in providing specific techniques for teaching rhetorical invention; and the study of the interconnections among the ideas of Perelman and Olbrechts-Tyteca and thinkers from closely related or vastly different realms, such as those treated (in depth or in passing) in essays here: Kenneth Burke, Thomas Kuhn, Martha C. Nussbaum, Stephen Toulmin, Richard Weaver,

Richard McKeon, Charles S. Peirce, Paul Ricoeur, Emmanuel Lévinas, and Hans-Georg Gadamer, as well as Philipp Melanchthon, Giambattista Vico, Plato, and of course Aristotle. In addition to indicating such trajectories, it is among my hopes for this volume that it will help to promote an understanding of the need for scholars in different national and educational cultures and languages to be in dialogue rather than to work solely in their separate traditions of inquiry. It illustrates, more so than other studies of *The New Rhetoric*, perhaps, that scholars of argument must and do write for what that text calls "a universal audience."

The New Rhetoric was intended by Perelman and Olbrechts-Tyteca to rehabilitate forms of reasoning believed to be "extraneous to the purely formal" study of logic. Although these forms had been thought to "elude reason" (2), Perelman and Olbrechts-Tyteca held that they must be seen as the substance of reason, given the overly restrictive framework within which formal logic needed to operate in order to provide rules for validity. Formal logic could not account for the manifold ways people attempt to persuade or are actually persuaded, nor for the possibility of degrees of adherence to ideas based on provisional and situated arguments, and it required a univocal language as the modality of reasoning and a conception of the "self-evident" that are both imaginary. "A narrow conception of proof and logic," they wrote, "has led to a constricted view of reason" (510). Rather than base a theory of argumentation on such a model, Perelman and Olbrechts-Tyteca defined their project as "the study of the discursive techniques allowing us to induce or increase the mind's adherence to theses presented for its assent" (4). With this redefinition of the realm of reason came an enlarged field of discursive techniques—in fact, anything that might be uttered (or otherwise made present) for the purpose of strengthening adherence to an idea. They acknowledged that this had always been the terrain of rhetoric, and they drew heavily from the rhetorical tradition with the objective of creating a *"rapprochement"* between rhetoric and philosophy. The result was a study that attempted to provide a comprehensive description of the forms arguments take, from the general level of genre to the smallest level of locution. Their book might be said, then, to provide a grammar—or perhaps an anatomy—of argument as it exists rather than as it should exist, normative only insofar as the appeal to reason can be weaker or stronger. But it is more than that. It also provides a defense of reason as a matter of responsible human interactions in contrast to both skepticism and violence. It provides a theory of justice as embodied in these interactions. It validates a community of minds in which freedom is paramount: "The use of argumentation implies that one has renounced resorting to force alone, that value is attached to gaining the adherence of one's interlocutor by means of reasoned persuasion, and that one is not regarding him as an object, but appealing to his free judgment" (55).

It establishes, in the context of the failure of formal logic to provide justification for statements of value and preference, not only that values *are* argued about but also that they *must* be. Reason, then, is not opposed to emotional commitment. Reason, as Perelman and Olbrechts-Tyteca understand it, is justified not because it can be reduced to normative definitions but because it is a living, dynamic activity performed among people who seek an alternative to violence in the realm of their disagreements. To exercise this faculty requires making free choices from among innumerable ways to argue, and these choices in turn imply responsibility, on the part of both the speaker and his or her audience. "Only rhetoric, and not logic," Perelman wrote in 1949, almost ten years before the appearance of *Traité de l'argumentation*,

> allows the understanding of putting the principle of responsibility into play. In formal logic, a demonstration is either convincing or it is not, and the liberty of the thinker is outside of it. However, the arguments that one employs in rhetoric influence thought, but never force ... agreement. The thinker commits himself by making a decision. His competence, sincerity, integrity, in a word, his responsibility are at stake. (qtd. in and trans. by Frank and Bolduc 187)

Only a rhetoric that justifies, rather than compels, puts human freedom and responsibility on the line. These, in turn, place a higher value on the process of being reasonable than on any truth one might allegedly own by "winning," as if the goal of winning an argument were to overcome the freedom of thought of one's audience in the exercise of one's own. During a 2008 conference devoted to *The New Rhetoric*, from which the essays in this book derive, I heard Chaïm Perelman's daughter, Noémi Perelman Mattis, respond to a paper in which the presenter had described argument as a search for the truth. "My father," Mattis said, "cared more for finding common ground through compromise of the truth," and to illustrate she related a story about when she was eleven years old and full of "certain knowledge." She had told her father confidently that the Sistine Chapel is in Florence. No, he said, the Sistine Chapel is in Rome. No, she said, it is in Florence. After a few rounds of contradictory assertions, Chaïm finally said to her, "All right, then, let us split the difference and agree that the Sistine Chapel is really in Siena." Mattis's story compels us to ask under what circumstances agreement matters more than truth—only a small variation on the ancient conflict between eloquence and wisdom. But perhaps here wisdom consists not in knowing correctly for its own sake but in judging the consequences on human relations of having "certain knowledge." It seems that the absence of objectively and universally valid truth that is posited in *The New Rhetoric* entails the acknowledgment of a higher motive than being right. So what if the Sistine Chapel is in Rome, if that fact separates child from father? The goal of argumentation is peace in the family. And is this not *like* the search for truth?[2]

The contents of *The New Rhetoric* provide a seemingly exhaustive framework for the study of discursive means of gaining adherence. Some of its key terms have been and will continue to be scrutinized, complicated, and applied. These include *presence*, the essential bringing to consciousness of ideas; *communion*, the bond between speaker and audience necessary to effect a meeting of minds; *quasi-logical* argumentative devices or the use of what has sometimes come to be called "informal reasoning"; arguments *based on the structure of reality* and arguments *establishing the structure of reality* as forms of discursive argument, which are pragmatic characterizations of rhetorical *topoi* and figures of thought; *philosophical pairs*, or the lexilogical resources of dialectical terms that give weight to arguments by association and dissociation according to the underlying opposition of *appearance and reality*; and—a term that has perhaps prompted the most critical inspection and controversy among scholars—*universal audience*, a conception designed to provide a defense of reason derived from, and perhaps analogous to, the role of universalizing in Kant's ethical system. In the course of justifying and examining these and other features of the deep structure of argument, Perelman and Olbrechts-Tyteca offer a thorough treatment of the classical *loci* and figures of speech, analogy, probabilities, and, in stark contrast to most of the classical rhetorical tradition, the role of laughter and ridicule in argument.

The essays collected here take up several different kinds of questions raised by Perelman and Olbrechts-Tyteca's monumental treatise. I have grouped them into topical sections and attempted, in introductions to each section, to suggest relationships among the essays that go beyond the section divisions. The essays begin, however, with a reflection by Noémi Perelman Mattis, who is not a scholar of Chaïm Perelman's work but whose understanding of its place in his life is unmatched. Her brief memoir provides a human and historical context for the essays that follow. This is the first occasion she has had to tell in print about her father and his work.[3]

I trust that the diversity of issues treated and raised by these essays demonstrates that research inspired by *The New Rhetoric* thrives—in Europe, the Middle East, and the United States—and that it does so because of the urgency of the issues it raises. Each of these essays presents theses for our assent and attempts to earn that assent by a variety of discursive means. Argumentation *about* argumentation can itself be assessed according to various theories of argumentation, and Perelman and Olbrechts-Tyteca seemed to understand that their own argumentation could itself come under scrutiny. There is no last word. The best that one can hope is that our humanity is engaged. As Perelman put it at the conclusion of *The Idea of Justice and the Problem of Argument*, "And, as in all argument, the solutions adopted will not be irresistible in themselves; their adoption is a matter of one's being ready to answer for them when one has, in all honesty and sincerity, weighed the pros and cons" (207).

And so it is up to the audience, for whom honesty and sincerity of consideration is as much an ethical principle as honest and sincere argumentation. It is up to us as members of audiences, as well as arguers, to fulfill the promise of reason.

Notes

1. The essays collected here are revised versions of papers and addresses given at a conference, "The Promise of Reason: *The New Rhetoric* after Fifty Years," held at the University of Oregon in May 2008. Over 120 scholars from thirteen countries gave papers at this conference. In addition to the present collection, other essays given as papers at the conference have been collected for special issues of journals: *Argument and Advocacy* 44.4 (Spring 2008), edited by David A. Frank, and *Philosophy and Rhetoric* 43.4 (2010), edited by James Crosswhite. Another conference commemorating the fiftieth anniversary of *The New Rhetoric*, "From Perelman and Beyond: From the Rhetorical Tradition to Argumentation Studies," was held in January 2008 at Tel-Aviv University, and selected papers from that conference appeared in the journal *Argumentation* 23.3 (December 2009), edited by Ruth Amossy. Together, these conferences and collections of essays do not indicate a sudden flourishing so much as they represent a coalescing of ongoing research in the field of argument studies from linguistic, pragmatic, rhetorical, and philosophical perspectives. But such work itself suggests that international and interdisciplinary interest in *The New Rhetoric* and the study of argumentation will continue to grow.

2. In documenting and discussing the alleged disagreement between Perelman and Henry Johnstone over the question of whether rhetoric should be considered "a technique or ... a mode of truth," Alan G. Gross and Ray D. Dearin conclude that Perelman (in showing how philosophers argue) and Johnstone (in making this dissociation) are both exemplifying rhetoric as "aimed at universal truth without equivocation" (81, 97).

3. An unpublished interview with Noémi Perelman Mattis is cited in the essay by Frank and Bolduc in this volume, and two unpublished reminiscences are cited by Gross and Dearin in their bibliography (195). The text here is edited from a transcription of a talk Mattis delivered on 17 May 2008 to the assembled scholars at the opening session of the "Promise of Reason" conference (see note 1 above). Her audience was moved by the talk, which many agreed helped provide a human dimension to the proceedings—

rare in such academic gatherings. She attended the entire conference, offering specific criticism of papers, insisting often, for instance, that her father was not a rhetorician but a philosopher who used rhetoric to solve a philosophical problem. Her insights were indispensable. I am grateful to Noémi Mattis for her participation in this project and to David Frank for arranging her visit to the conference.

Works Cited

Conley, Thomas M. *Rhetoric in the European Tradition*. Chicago: U of Chicago P, 1994.

Frank, David, and Michelle Bolduc. "Chaïm Perelman's 'First Philosophies and Regressive Philosophy': Commentary and Translation." *Philosophy and Rhetoric* 36.3 (2003): 177–206.

Gross, Alan G., and Ray D. Dearin. *Chaïm Perelman*. Albany: State U of New York P, 2003.

Perelman, Chaïm. *The Idea of Justice and the Problem of Argument*. Trans. John Petrie. London: Routledge and Kegan Paul, 1963.

Perelman, Chaïm, and Lucie Olbrechts-Tyteca. *The New Rhetoric: A Treatise on Argumentation*. Trans. John Wilkinson and Purcell Weaver. Notre Dame: U of Notre Dame P, 1969.

2

Chaïm Perelman: A Life Well Lived

Noémi Perelman Mattis

I'm the daughter of Chaïm Perelman and Fela Perelman. I am not a scholar of rhetoric or a historian of my father's life. My father had hoped that I would work with him in the philosophy of law, so I studied law and some philosophy. Had I stayed in Belgium, he would have been disappointed, as I fully intended to be an attorney, to enter the bar and practice law, and not to go into academia at all. But life took a different turn. I married, came to the United States, and wound up being a psychologist. This happens to be the one field of human endeavor and humanistic sciences where my father's shadow does not extend. David Frank asked me if it was rebellion: no, absolutely not. Without a doubt, I don't think anyone could ever rebel against my father, the kindest, most loving, and easiest person to get along with whom I've ever known. But it's just that this is where my interests took me. Because he and I and our family all lived through the dark hours of the Holocaust, I have tried to understand the human mind, the human spirit, and what makes human beings do things that go completely against what we think of as reason.

Now, having been both very close and very far from my father, both in fields and in continents, I had the chance to ask him questions that others have wondered about. One of them is, why did he not pay attention to propaganda, to forms of speech that are absolutely not rational? It is not that he didn't know about that. We had lived through Hitler and Goebbels and had heard the darkest speeches that could be uttered—the most unreasonable, irrational speeches. But his answer to me was: *I am a philosopher. As a philoso-*

pher, I am only working—it's not that the other things are not important—but I am only working in the field of rational argument. The way one philosopher would talk to another philosopher in an effort to reach the truth, to understand what is truth—what is the truth in a world that refuses "revealed" truth?

Brussels University was founded in response to the reopening of the Catholic University of Leuven, and the motto of Brussels University is "free inquiry," *le libre examen*. And its song, which is quite irreverent, is "À bas la calotte," which means "down with the skullcap" or, basically, down with a religion that accepts a given, absolute authority and tells you what to believe; in that case, it was the Catholic church. Now, my father was not anti-Catholic (my husband, Danny, remembers that at our wedding, the first row was entirely cardinals and bishops—these were my father's friends). But he shared in the idea that revealed truth is not acceptable to a free mind; one has to have a right to inquire freely and search freely for the truth.

We live in a terrible time right now with the rise of fundamentalisms of all kinds and with grave dangers to rationalism. My father lived through similar or even worse dangers and worse irrationality. I admire the optimism in the title of this book, and I think that Perelman would have approved and would have felt very much that indeed "reason" is where we need to turn when the world seems like such a dangerous place.

My father was born in Poland in 1912 at a time of fierce anti-Semitism and turmoil. His father had married a poor girl and had not gone to the university but started looking for a way to make a living. And finding that it was not easy for a young man to make a living at that time in Poland, he sought a better place and came to Antwerp, in Belgium, where a group of Jewish people involved in the diamond trade welcomed newcomers. So he stayed in Belgium and put my father, then twelve years old, in charge of his own mother and his three siblings. One of my aunts told me, "Chaïm was very much in charge. He was the one who made sure that we survived, that we came to Belgium a year later; he arranged everything." One of the extraordinary things to me about my father is always how *young* he was. The things he did as a twelve year old! How precocious and competent he was!

So my grandfather found a job in the diamond trade. (Jews at that time always liked diamonds because you can put them in the lining of your coat in case you have to run away very fast.) He was not a diamond dealer; he was a poor man, a broker. He would take a stone from one person and sell it to somebody else, and he barely eked out a living. The apartment where they all lived was small, and they were all crowded one on top of another. When my father wanted to study, he went to the corner café, the only place where he would have a little peace. When my father left for Belgium at thirteen, he spoke only Yiddish and Polish, but very shortly he learned French and Flemish, which was what he needed to learn in order to be a student in the high school in Antwerp. He earned pocket money, supporting himself by teaching Latin to his classmates; he told me he would read the book one week ahead and then tutor his classmates.

Despite all of that, he managed to graduate early and went to Brussels University to study philosophy, of all things. He was immediately recognized as somebody really special, a really great intellect. He met my mother when he was nineteen. They were classmates. My mother was almost three years older than he was, but they were classmates because she had come from Poland (the gymnasium in Poland lasts a year longer) and my father was ahead—so they were classmates even though three years apart in age. He lied to her about his age, fearing that she would not be willing to be his girlfriend. She found out his real age only when they needed to show their papers to get married.

When he first introduced himself to her, she said, "You're Perelman? You don't look it." His reputation had preceded him, and she expected something very different. Anyway, he fell madly in love with her, and theirs was an extraordinary love affair: they fought, they loved, they lived vibrant lives in a true partnership. There is absolutely no way to overestimate how much my mother contributed to who my father was, to what my father did, and certainly to everything other than his purely intellectual pursuits. They had an extraordinary life together. My father would not have had that life with anybody other than my mother.

She was quite an amazing woman, the granddaughter of the grand rabbi of Bedzin. At that time, a grand rabbi in Poland in a Jewish community was, the way I understand it, something like "the Godfather" without the crime. People came over all the time to request favors or ask for advice. There was a constant flow of people coming in and asking: "Please, help," "Please, do this," "Please, advise," "Please, do that." Interestingly, that was exactly the way my parents' home became later on. There were oodles of people there all the time. When I would get up in the morning, I had to be fully dressed to go to breakfast because there would be all these people, people everywhere. I still remember a time when a colleague and friend of my father, Boris Chlepner, came to the house and asked me, "Is your dad home?" I said, "No, he's at the university." "Where's your mom?" I answered, "She's taking a nap." He asked, "She's taking a nap, with all these guests here?" And I looked around and indeed there were twelve people there. And I said, "Those are not guests; they just grow here!" That's the way it was. There was a young pianist rehearsing on the piano in one corner. A painter had an easel in another corner. There were people who were waiting to talk to my mother because they needed help with one thing or another. One group was in one room and another group was in another room, and they were just waiting for the time when they would have an audience—not with my father but with my mother. *She* was the grand rabbi. In addition, the phone rang constantly, and she would run and answer—it was usually for her—in any of four or five languages, fluently going from one to the other. This house was truly alive. It was not always easy for me because once in a while she would also give away my room. I would come home, and she would announce to me that I had better find another place to go because my room had been given to some visitor from abroad.

Getting back to my story line: my father met my mother—a great love affair—he finished at Brussels University, and so did she. (She, with a doctorate in history, would later write a couple of books.) They were married in 1935, and I was born the next year. Then came the dark years. Terrible things were happening in Poland (where my mother's family still lived), the darkness gathering all around. My father was in the military at the time, and, as the war started, he was involved in battle. But when he heard that the Belgian army was about to surrender, he went AWOL in order to avoid capture and came back to Brussels. At that time, my mother and I, with my grandparents and aunts (my father's family), were trying to escape to France, but with the bombing all around we did not succeed and came back to Belgium. During the war, after a short while, I was no longer with my parents because they started doing very dangerous work in the underground, and I became a foster child, hiding in foster homes.

My father was twenty-eight when the war started. A year or so later, the Nazis asked the grand rabbi of Belgium to get together a group of the leaders of the Jewish community in Belgium in order to organize the Jewish community. This became the Association des Juifs en Belgique (AJB). Despite his youth, my father was one of the leaders of the Jewish community and was asked to join the group. But after awhile, he and others in the committee realized that the AJB was actually going to be used by the Nazis, not to help the Jews but to facilitate the Nazis' work of death—my father and those in the community didn't yet know about extermination, only about deportations. So my father and three others created a different committee, a clandestine committee (Le Comité de Défense des Juifs, CDJ), and decided that they were also going to remain part of the AJB, because officially resigning would tip off the Nazis that they knew what was going on. And, in fact, they managed to subvert some of the resources of the AJB in order to be helpful to the CDJ.

It is significant that all the pictures of the partisans from that time show a dozen men and my mother. My mother was always there; she was the equal partner, involved in every bit of the resistance, though she never took much of the credit because she was of another age—where the credit always went to the husband. But she was absolutely central in all of these endeavors. My father may have been the more intelligent in some ways, but my mother had savvy and smarts, the likes of which I've never seen. So she was part of the group that did partisan work—dangerous, underground resistance work.

A few years ago, I had a rather extraordinary experience. A friend of mine told me that she had lunch with a woman who was visiting from Los Angeles. The visitor told her, "My sister has just written a book about my father's life called *Escape to Life*. It's about how my father escaped from Buchenwald where his wife and two babies were exterminated. When he returned to Belgium and tried to tell the story of what was really going on at Buchenwald, in the concentration camps, nobody believed him." My friend interrupted, "If your father was from Belgium, would he know the parents of my friend Noémi?" And the woman said, "The book is *dedicated* to Professor Perelman!" Indeed, when nobody would believe him, somebody sent this escapee, Mr. Herskowitz, to my father, who *did* believe him. My father got a group of people together, and somebody played the piano in order to ensure that if there were bugs, nobody could hear their conversation. And so Herskowitz told his story to the assembled group. For the first time, the resistance knew that people were not being sent to a labor camp; they were being sent to concentration camps. And, after that, the most heroic deed of the Belgian Underground happened, which was blowing up the rails to stop a deportation train and help the passengers escape.

That story has always been very special to me because in my work, I feel it is so important to believe my patients—and sometimes believe the unbelievable. So I felt such a kinship with my father because he also was willing to believe the unbelievable. My father knew about the ugly deeds of which human beings are capable. And, if he didn't write about it, it's not because he didn't think it was important.

The underground was a strange marriage of ideologies. Some people were communists or communist sympathizers. Everybody was united in fighting the Nazis, but the communist sympathizers were hoping to defeat fascism in order to establish communism in Western Europe. And, on the other hand, there were people like my parents, who were Zionists and wanted very much to see the Jewish people survive, not only as individual human beings but also as a *people*, the Jewish people, that the Nazis had been so intent on destroying. Notably, the Holocaust was the only war primarily directed against children, because the Nazis wanted to destroy the Jewish seed. They wanted the Jews to be erased from the face of the earth, so the Zionists felt it was essential to ensure that the Jews would survive as a people. My parents were not religious; they rarely set foot in a synagogue or worshiped in any way. My father was trained in Talmudic studies as a youngster and understood the religion very well, but neither of them was religious. In Western Europe, most people are not religious (it's an American peculiarity that people either are religious or pretend to be, in very large numbers). But the Jews, *as a people*, needed to survive. The conflict between the communists and the Zionists in Belgium is one that has been perpetuated through the years. And, actually, it's still going on. There was a communist historian who hated my mother (and my mother hated him) and who, until his recent death, was trying very hard to change history—to hijack this history and give all the credit to the communists and to erase or minimize the role of the Zionists. This is a different story altogether, but it's interesting that this feud is going on long after the death of many of the participants.

After the war, my father went back to his studies, and my mother became very involved with the Mossad. She was coordinating the illegal immigration of people coming back from camps who wanted to go to Israel. Our home was a strange place at that time because we saw so many people returning from concentration camps and brought to refugee camps, and my mother would take the children home. When I came home after having been in hiding, I found that in my parents' home there were forty other children and I had to take my turn. This house was everybody's house.

In one of her lectures, my mother told a funny story about this time. After the war, she was organizing groups of people going to Palestine, which was illegal because Palestine was a British mandate and Jews were not allowed to go there. At the time, a lot of stateless people were coming from concentration camps and were put in refugee camps. But they wanted to go to Palestine, and if one were to wait to ascertain everybody's name and vital statistics, it would take forever. Those people were in refugee camps and needed to be able to leave *now*. My mother didn't obey rules; she did what needed to be done and did it *now*. So a group of people got together and made up a list of names and ages and other information—Goldberg, Rabinovich, and so on, a series of Jewish names—then they signed the papers for these people. I was enlisted as an eight-year-old to help forge some signatures because they couldn't have only PhD's signing all these documents; they needed somebody who was still a little illiterate. So I became a forger at the age of eight.

Then, with the lists, my mother went to talk with the consul of Panama to request visas, ostensibly to send these people to Panama. The consul really wanted those people to immigrate. My mother told how she visited him in a hotel in Antwerp, but he had the flu and couldn't come out of the hotel room. So he received her in his bathrobe in the hotel room. She had an assistant, and so did he. At some point, they wanted to talk privately and adjourned to the only private place: the bathroom. The consul offered my mother the toilet, he sat on the bidet, and there they negotiated the fate of hundreds of people! My mother got those visas for Panama, and on the basis of the visas she got transit visas for the refugees through Belgium; as they later arrived, their picture was taken and each was given made-up identity papers.

Then came the moment when they were all brought to the harbor, and the Belgian officials were checking them off (Goldberg and Rabinovich and so on). Suddenly a mistake was discovered: one page had been erroneously copied twice, and two groups of people had the same identity. There had already been a Mr. Rabinovich, and suddenly there was a second Mr. Rabinovich. That's possible, but the second Mrs. Goldberg? And the second Mr. Schwartz? So obviously, something was wrong, and the officials didn't know what to do. My mother placed herself in the middle of all the officials, saying, "I represent the International Association of Refugees." She was now one of the officials. Knowing the minds of bureaucrats, she told the officials, when they discovered this problem, "Why don't we all go to the corner café, have a cup of coffee, discuss what we should do, and then we'll come back with a decision." And as she and the officials left, she told her Mossad associate, in Hebrew, "Get them all on board." When my mother and the officials came back half an hour later, all the refugees were on the ship, and the ship was sailing. An official said, "My God! What's going on?" My mother said, "Let's not worry about it. You know, this is Panama's problem. They're going to Panama; the Panamanians will figure it out." And the bureaucrats didn't want to bother. Everybody was ready to go home. And at that moment, as the ship was about two hundred feet away, those refugees, filled with joy, started singing "Hatikvah" ("The Hope"), the Hebrew national anthem. They started singing "Hatikvah" in the loudest voice ever, and from the shore everybody could hear those people singing "Hatikvah." The custom officials looked at Mother and said, "What's that?" Without blinking, my mother replied: "That's the Panamanian national anthem; they have been rehearsing it for weeks."

After my father went back to his studies, he refused every kind of medal for his resistance work. In Belgium, you have to sign a request to get a medal, and he sent back a letter saying, "I only did what I had to. My house was on fire; I took a pail of water to extinguish the fire. I don't need medals and I will not accept medals except for academic achievements." (My mother didn't mind the medals. She wore them with her feathered hat!) But my father went back to his work. Actually, he had never really interrupted his work because while in the underground, in the darkest hours, he was writing his book on justice. My mother always said that she is responsible for one line in that book. Perelman had written, "The Nazis are saying that..." and my mother said, "You should say, 'The Nazis *were* saying...' because this book will not be published as long as the Nazis *are* saying." So with the Nazis vanquished, the book got published, and my father was soon promoted to full professor, the youngest in the history of Brussels University. During the war, by the way, he could not teach. The children could not go to school; the professors could not teach. If you were Jewish, you were crossed out of society. But Brussels University continued to pay his salary and kept him alive through the war years, which is why my father would never leave Brussels later as he felt a deep debt of gratitude toward the university.

I think back again to how young he was. I remember, when I was ten years old, he came with me to register me for secondary school. He was thirty-four and a dashing young man. We went to the room where some young teachers were on duty to register the new students, and as we walked in the door, all of them rose to their feet. It was such a shock for me: there was my young father, and everybody rose when he walked through the door.

While he went back to his studies and writings, my mother continued her work for the state of Israel. This is around the time when he started *The New Rhetoric* and where Lucie Olbrechts comes into the picture. Lucie Olbrechts was the very opposite of my mother. My mother was flamboyant, funny, savvy, and smart; she was adored or hated, but nobody had anything but extreme feelings about her. People who have known her have a devotion to her that goes on years and years after her death. I went to a memorial ceremony ten years after her death, and over two hundred people attended, including young people who had been children when she died—people who could not let go of what my mother had meant to them. Lucie Olbrechts was the very opposite. She was transparent; she had pale skin and wispy blond hair; she seemed to have always been old. She was very close to me because I was the only child in her world, so she gave me the doll that had been hers as a child. She gave me things that were very precious to her. Lucie and her husband had been social friends with my parents, even though they were much older, and Lucie had actually worked with my mother in the underground.

One day, during a dinner party, my father was talking about his big project, and she got really excited about it. He was saying that he needed an assistant because he wanted to have examples, and a whole lot of legwork would be required. Most of the work he did usually came just from his head and didn't need research. But for this book he wanted examples; he was looking for an assistant, and she volunteered. She was the daughter of a well-known psychiatrist who was dead by the time I met her. She and her husband were not rich but very comfortable. She had gone to the university and had finished her bachelor's degree, a *licence*, but she didn't do what most women in her station would be doing at the time. Most women at the time would have been involved in an active social life or would have pursued hobbies. She really didn't do any of that. Her husband was very reclusive; he spent most of his time in his office. He was a statistician (and everything that this implies in terms of fun and games). And she was basically very, very lonely with nothing much to do except read; she read a lot. And so she volunteered to work with my father, and they worked together for a long time. My mother had objections to this collaboration; she would say, "If you want to establish a school in Brussels, it's important that you spend more time with your students."

Anyhow, they produced a book that started out two thousand pages long. The publisher was adamant that they needed to cut it down to eight hundred pages, so they did, and there was a lot of extra material that never got published. They streamlined most chapters and excised others. Some joint articles were published from the excised material, and one chapter, "Le comique . . . ," was published years later by Lucie under her own name after my father yielded to my mother's entreaties and discontinued the collaboration. I remember that when the book was being published, my father and mother were discussing the question of authorship. They explored the possibility of crediting authorship as: "Chaïm Perelman, with the collaboration of Lucie Olbrechts-Tyteca." But my father said, "No, she really should have her name as the coauthor because she has worked for ten years, she has never been paid, and this is the only payment that I could ever give her." My mother said, "But, you know, people will wonder about who did what." He said, "Don't be ridiculous. Everybody knows. Everybody knows who the philosopher is, and, you know, my name is first in reverse alphabetical order. Everybody knows." And my mother said, "Well, maybe there might be a day when everybody won't know." That's the conversation that I overheard . . . and my mother was always right.

Though he called the book *The New Rhetoric*, my father, first and foremost, was always a philosopher. He was a good orator and had a lot of energy. He always had something to say; he would lecture to anybody he met. That included the queen of Greece or the cardinal of Venice before he became Pope John XXII, whom he met at a philosophy meeting. Every time you would see him, he was lecturing—to anybody he met. But he didn't know about the field of speech or rhetoric in America, had never heard of it. He didn't pay very much attention to American scholarship. Western Europeans at that time didn't have the highest respect for America in the humanities. I like to think that I'm responsible for establishing a link to America because once he had a daughter on this continent, he had to figure out a way to come and visit me![1]

My father went on to write many books and many articles and to get honors—honors galore. Several honorary doctorates, the Francqui Prize, anything there was to earn. He seemed to be president of all kinds of organizations. And he pursued many different projects, such as a project with lawyers and judges on the topic "How do lawyers or judges reason?" and another with a group of historians around the topic "How do historians decide what is a historical fact?"

At the end of his life, he was made a baron by the king of Belgium. He told his friend Maneli that he had considered not accepting that title because he was profoundly democratic; it bothered him a bit to have a title of nobility. On the other hand, it kind of tickled him: there he was, a Jewish kid from Poland who becomes ennobled in the Belgium kingdom. My mother was thrilled, lapped it up. My father liked that it was a hereditary title and he could pass it on to me, but I have made no use of it. I don't know what I would do with it—unless I wanted to sell cosmetics. My cynical son, when I called him to say, "Your grandfather was just made a baron by the king of Belgium," replied, "Is there any land that goes with it?"

Unfortunately, this was the last honor to come my father's way because he died very shortly after that. He had to choose the *devise* for his coat of arms. The motto he chose was "*Tzedek, Tzedek, Tirdov*": "Justice, justice, you will pursue." *Tzedek* is an interesting word because it's both "justice" and "equity." In Hebrew, there is one word for straight, narrow justice, the rule of law, and there is another word for justice that embraces equity and charity—because if it is not charitable, it's not just. Charity is really giving people what they're due, what they're owed. So this became the motto on his coat of arms. The Belgian parliament had to pass a special law to allow Hebrew on a coat of arms in Belgium because previously they had allowed only French, Flemish, or Latin. So Hebrew was added for the first time.

My mother took great pride in her Jewishness. She told me the story of how one day, many years earlier, when she and my father were newlyweds, a landlady wanted to know whether she was Jewish and started a conversation with, "I notice you don't go to church on Sunday." My mother's response was, "No, we're Jewish, but we don't mind at all if you go to church on Sunday."

This was my mother's absolute pride of who she was; no shame, no hiding, never allowing anybody to condescend to her. My father, who had been known as Henio in Polish schools, was always Chaïm in his parent's home. Henio in Polish became Henri in Belgium, until after World War II. After the war, he proudly took on the name Chaïm, even though it is unusual in Belgium or in France to use a Hebrew name. He proudly went back to the name Chaïm to affirm his Jewishness.

My father died in 1984. At the funeral, there were throngs for blocks and blocks. I don't know many college professors who have a funeral like a president or a prime minister. He was a rock star; he had a funeral where people for hours and hours and hours were coming to pay their respects.[2] My father's honors continued after his death: a street was named after him. (My mother made sure it was after *him*, never *them*; but it should have been named after *them*.) The borough placed a plaque on their house identifying it as a high place of the Belgian Resistance. The honors were many, but they really had not mattered that much to him. What would have mattered to him is the knowledge that many people were still interested in his life and work. He was speaking to posterity; he wanted his work to continue. He wanted future scholars to dialogue with him just as he had been dialoguing with Aristotle, Kant, and others. And so the work being done around his legacy is the greatest honor and the greatest gift he could have received, and I'm forever grateful for that.

Notes

1. Editor's note: For a description of Chaïm Perelman's relationship with American rhetoricians and philosophers and the arrangements for his first visit to the United States, see Alan G. Gross and Ray D. Dearin, *Chaïm Perelman* (Albany: State U of New York P, 2003), 9–11.

2. Lucie's end was quite different. I last visited her some years after my father's death. She had sold her house for an annuity. When she lived longer than the buyers had planned on, they insisted on moving in to "take care" of her; she appeared to be restricted to a small part of her house. During my next trip to Belgium, I was told that Lucie had "disappeared"; it seems that she had been absconded by her caretakers. Her will was probably amended; she had repeatedly told me that she had written me into her will for an artwork that she loved, yet I was never notified of her death.

SECTION ONE

Conceptual Understandings of *The New Rhetoric*

The four essays in this section are devoted primarily to questions about how to understand the specific intentions and key concepts of *The New Rhetoric*. Such questions range from the empirical status of its methodology, to the role of style in its analysis of argument, to the function of the concept of the universal audience, to why and how the work gains strength from Lucie Olbrechts-Tyteca's theory of the comic. Some key concepts taken up in other sections of this collection include discussions of "presence" by Alan G. Gross (in section 2), "communion" by Richard Graff and Wendy Winn (in section 2), "confused notions" by Ray D. Dearin (in section 3), "pluralism" by Linda Bensel-Meyers (in section 3), and *topoi* by James Crosswhite (in section 4).

Barbara Warnick's essay here provides an appropriate beginning for the scholarly studies in this volume because it argues for the epistemological integrity of *The New Rhetoric*. In contrast to an empirical basis for argumentation, she claims, the theory is "adaptive" to cultural contexts. Criticisms of the book as relativist, she argues, misunderstand its goal of developing "a heuristic method for analyzing arguments in use." The question of the book's philosophical integrity as an empirical heuristic arises again in the essay by Roselyne Koren (in section 2). Specific argumentative techniques are described in many other essays in this volume—for example, see the essays by Koren (again) and Jean Nienkamp (in section 3) and all of the essays in section 4.

Jeanne Fahnestock offers here the most detailed examination to date of the reasons Perelman and Olbrechts-Tyteca emphasized style in their theory of argumentation and included figures of speech among the techniques of reasoned argumentation, concluding that *The New Rhetoric* offers a theory of language in response to prevailing views of the function of figurative language. She provides an extensive review of the sources of Perelman and Olbrechts-Tyteca's comments on language, both historical and contemporary. Other essays in this volume that describe specific stylistic techniques in argumentation include Gross's, Graff and Winn's, Maria Freddi's (in section 4), and Paula Olmos's (in section 4).

Loïc Nicolas reflects here on the reciprocal relations between speaker and audience indicated by *The New Rhetoric*'s use of the term "interlocutor" to show how its concept of argumentation is fundamentally dialogic. This analysis enables him to connect the idea of the "universal audience" to Lévinas's concept of the "other" as internal audience. The universal audience is also discussed in the essays by Warnick, Bensel-Meyers, and Nienkamp.

David A. Frank and Michelle K. Bolduc provide us here with an extensive study of the collaboration between Perelman and Olbrechts-Tyteca, based on their other individual and collaborative writings as well as information from the Perelman Archives at the Université Libre de Bruxelles. In the process, they offer a vivid reminder that The New Rhetoric cannot be understood properly without its many discussions and examples of the role of humor in argumentation. Another essay in this collection that makes reference to the role of the comic is Olmos's.

3

Empiricism, Securement, and *The New Rhetoric*
Barbara Warnick

The intent of this essay is to address recurring issues in the literature on the new rhetoric project (NRP) and to propose a way of thinking about the project that is responsive to some of the objections raised by its critics. In short, these issues revolve around questions of argumentation's relationship to formal and informal logic. The charge against it is that the NRP lacks a viable criterion or set of criteria for establishing the validity of argumentative reasoning and that therefore its system enables the perpetuation of "baneful relativism" (Govier, *Problems*, qtd. in Boger 214).

Criticisms such as this one have been circulating since *The New Rhetoric* was first published, and Chaïm Perelman attempted to respond to some of them in 1984 when he noted that the philosopher "addresses himself to the universal audience *as he conceives it*, even in *the absence of objectivity* which imposes itself upon everyone. The philosopher develops an argumentation thanks to which he aspires to convince any competent interlocutor whatsoever" ("New Rhetoric and the Rhetoricians" 191). This and many other statements in *The New Rhetoric* emphasize that the universal audience is a construction of the speaker, who is in the process of forming and articulating the best possible argument regarding a question that is open to deliberation and decision in a context in which the arguer's goal is to increase the adherence of the audience to theses presented for their assent.

Perelman and Lucie Olbrechts-Tyteca's position has consistently made uneasy those who seek an objectively valid truth criterion for the acceptance of situated argument. In a 2005 article in the journal *Argumentation*, for example, George Boger charges that the incorporation of the background assumptions of audiences into the universal audience construct is problematic because it introduces an unstable criterion for judging the worth of an argument and can be viewed as a "useless fiction . . . that has nothing to do with the messy world of multivocality" (212). Boger concludes his critique by wondering whether the vulnerabilities in the universal audience construct are "a fault with argument or with some sample of mature adult human beings" (212). This rhetorical question reveals a misconstrual of the universal audience that occurs frequently in the critical literature—the tendency to equate the universal audience with a materially existing group of potential listeners or readers rather than to view it as a moderating construct in the composing of arguments.

Later in his article, Boger proceeds to wonder whether "an appeal to a universal audience seems to devolve to the question 'whose universal audience'?" (208). A question such as this implies that what is needed is a perspective *outside* of context to which we can have recourse in making judgments *in context*. But when it comes to argumentation intended to influence opinion and action in such situations as choosing the best candidate or making the best political decision in uncertain contexts, pure objectivity is not really possible. Perelman and Olbrechts-Tyteca ask whether it is "good enough to say that one has merely to adopt the viewpoint of someone in [the constellation] Sirius, and be perfectly disinterested, in order to be able to provide an objectively valid opinion? The inevitable reaction of the parties to the controversy in the face of such an intrusion would be surprise, if not indignation" (60). The implication of this statement is that one must be a stakeholder in a controversy in order to be so positioned as to have a say in its outcome. Therefore, true objectivity in the contexts of quotidian argumentation is not possible.

Boger's reactions exemplify some of the criticisms leveled against the NRP's epistemological position. Other problems include a failure to distinguish between a prescriptive perspective on the study of argumentation (such as is found in formal logic) and one that is descriptive, along with a failure to appreciate that Perelman and Olbrechts-Tyteca's system was designed and intended to study argument practices as embedded and contextualized forms of communicative action.

The purpose of the remainder of this essay is to examine the ways in which the epistemological viability of *The New Rhetoric* is secured, not by formal principles of logical consistency or decontextualized truth standards, but instead by a confluence of empirical findings based on its authors' examination of argument structures and practices. When I speak of these elements as "securing" *The New Rhetoric*'s account of argumentation, I mean that, taken together, they furnish the means by which its account is supported, tied down, or warranted and thus capable of functioning as a linchpin in the study of argumentation as a force in society.

These empirical findings consist of three dimensions of the NRP:

(1) its extensive use of arguments *as presented* to develop an account of how they are designed to increase audience adherence to the theses presented for their assent,
(2) its attention to the *field specificity* of arguments as used, and
(3) its *cataloging of recognizable argument scheme types*—a system that subsequently influenced a good deal of argumentation research on the use of schemes in context.

I will now explain how each of these dimensions of the NRP functions to support the epistemological integrity of its system for studying and analyzing argument in use.

Let us begin by considering the process that *The New Rhetoric*'s authors used when they set about their task. Instead of devising a formalist account of the workings of argumentation, Perelman and Olbrechts-Tyteca studied arguments in use, scrutinized their features, identified their components, and developed a general account of how they function to promote audience adherence. They studied arguments as used in such fields as law, philosophy, natural science, and politics to establish how public arguments function to provide a basis for public knowledge. Perelman himself noted that what was needed was "an extensive inquiry into the manner in which the most diverse authors in all fields do in fact reason about values." He and Olbrechts-Tyteca therefore set about "analyzing political discourse, the reasons given by judges, the reasoning of moralists, [and] daily discussions carried on in deliberation about making a choice or reaching a decision or nominating a person" (Perelman, "New Rhetoric" 1083).

Through close analysis of argument texts drawn from many fields, Perelman and Olbrechts-Tyteca identified specific elements—such as facts, truths, and presumptions—that served as starting points for arguers seeking audience adherence. The NRP is laced through with examples in use in which arguers and their audiences took as true the same elements as a basis for agreement. Through these examples, *The New Rhetoric*'s authors established that such elements operate functionally to provide a foothold for shared understanding and consensus in contexts in which arguments are made.

For example, agreed-upon facts can increase audience adherence so long as they conform to the structures of the real accepted by an audience and are not challenged (Perelman and Olbrechts-Tyteca 68). Truths function in much the same way. In *The New Rhetoric,* Perelman and Olbrechts-Tyteca note that whereas "facts" are generally used to designate objects of precise, limited agreement, "truths" are applied to more complex systems involving relations between facts (69). Truths include scientific findings, disciplinary techniques, and principles of practice. In a given cultural context, facts and truths will retain their status so long as they are "considered as valid for a universal audience" (131).

In addition to facts and truths, a third element contributing to the formulation of premises is presumption. *The New Rhetoric* notes that, while presumptions enjoy presumptive universal agreement, adherence to them falls short of being maximal, since audiences will expect them to be reinforced. Presumptions may be said to benefit from inertia, which is explained in the following way: "Inertia makes it possible to rely on the normal, the habitual, the real, and the actual and to attach a value to them, whether it is a matter of an existing situation, an accepted opinion, or a state of regular and continuous development. Change, on the other hand, has to be justified; once a decision has been taken, it cannot be changed except for sufficient reason" (106).

Inertia, therefore, plays a role in what can be assumed, insofar as audience adherence is concerned. Common presumptions that rely on what is accepted include, for example, the idea that the quality of an act reveals the quality of the person responsible for it; our tendency to initially believe that what someone tells us is true; and, I would add, presumptions of convention, such as that a person accused of a crime in U.S. courts is presumed innocent until proven guilty beyond a reasonable doubt.

A second major means of securing the integrity of the NRP's approach to argumentation is its emphasis on field specificity in describing argument practices. Perelman and Olbrechts-Tyteca emphasize the usefulness of considering how argumentation occurs differently in specific fields so as to illustrate and establish the regularities of its practice and thereby evaluate its functionality as a mode of proof. As *The New Rhetoric* notes, a discipline or field "often determines . . . the level at which the argumentation must be presented, laying down what is beyond dispute, and what must be regarded as irrelevant to the debate" (465).[1]

Knowledge in specific fields rests on conventional presumptions and criteria for evaluation of proofs and claims. For example, Perelman and Olbrechts-Tyteca note that scientific proofs generally rely on a system of measurement in which findings are viewed as free of values and are based upon observable, quantifiable facts (74). Rationalism also plays a role in science, since certain propositions are set apart as axioms and hold a privileged place within the larger system. In contrast, the law is bound by conformity with the principles of the legal system in which precedents function as examples that establish rules that then serve as general principles to regulate adjudication. In contrast, the field of philosophy as a discipline at mid-twentieth century valued reasoning modeled after forms of proof in mathematics and assumed that philosophical arguments should be addressed to the universal audience and should "avoid . . . the use of arguments that would be valid only for particular groups" (110–11). Of course, different strains of philosophy proceed differently, since empiricism, rationalism, and nominalism each proceed from a different and contrasting set of assumptions (465).

A third and final means of empirical support for *The New Rhetoric*'s epistemological integrity comes from its careful consideration of the associative and dissociative schemes of argument and their uses. By studying and cataloging the patterns of argument structure across contexts and disciplines, the NRP offered a useful typology of scheme types based on actual argument practices that has subsequently served as a resource for studying the workings of arguments in use. Perelman and Olbrechts-Tyteca's breakdown of scheme types has expanded our understanding of how argument works by elaborating on the role of audience adherence in the acceptance of specific types of scheme-based reasoning links. Furthermore, through their study of the role of values in argument, Perelman and Olbrechts-Tyteca have shown how quotidian argument forms rely on values, as in arguments from dissociation and double hierarchy. As I have demonstrated with Susan L. Kline in "*The New Rhetoric*'s Argument Schemes," the schemes as described in the NRP form the basis of an expanded system of *topoi* that can be used to study many argument practices in contemporary society.

Support for this system of scheme types grows out of the method used by the NRP to develop it. As Perelman noted, he and Olbrechts-Tyteca culled through arguments used in a number of fields at the time of their research, collected them, and studied their structure. These argument samples made up the "quotes on file cards" to which Noémi Perelman Mattis has referred in her description of their work. The scheme types they identified have been subsequently studied and further cataloged by argumentation scholars (for example, Warnick, Measell, Schiappa, Gross and Dearin, and Warnick and Kline). They include quasi-logical schemes, argument forms based on the structure of reality (that is, what the audience views as "real"), schemes used to establish the structure of reality, and dissociation. All of these argument forms are indigenous to the cultural contexts of the West that are European in origin. They function well generally in those contexts because they draw upon values, beliefs, and presumptions subscribed to in those cultures.

Perelman and Olbrechts-Tyteca believed that patterns of audience adherence and the attributes of the "universal audience" were specific to the culture in which they were used, and they noted that each culture has its own conception of what is to be "regarded as real, true, and objectively valid" (33).[2]

If we consider the factors that predispose Western audiences to accept the various scheme types, we can see how this might be the case. As *The New Rhetoric* notes, quasi-logical schemes such as transitivity, reciprocity, and disjunction function similarly to the syllogism by transferring audience allegiance from an accepted premise through an intermediary term to a conclusion. Their persuasiveness therefore derives from their resemblance to formal logic (193). Reciprocity arguments rely on a perceived and conditional symmetry between two terms. Contradictions depend on the idea that simultaneously asserting "x" and "not x" is absurd. Transitivity as a scheme has the structure of categorical syllogisms that convert nonformal to formal expression through reduction and thus has the appearance of formal logic. By making use of recognized and habitual practices of association, then, quasi-logical schemes exploit the cultural and cognitive predispositions of audiences as construed by arguers. In our study of arguments as used in extended discussions on specific ethical issues, Kline and I found that, of 1,037 argument schemes in our sample, 386 or 37.2 percent were quasi-logical. While this finding was based on a limited sample in a series of mediated discussions, it does indicate that in contexts of deliberation in the West, quasi-logical schemes are used frequently.

Arguments based on the structure of reality make use of liaisons and relations that are already accepted by the assumed audience. For example, causal arguments are grounded in culturally held beliefs, not the least of which is that events generally must have a cause rather than be the result of random chance. Coexistential schemes such as are found in act-person relations and arguments from sign derive their persuasiveness from audiences' predisposition to accept what is concrete and empirically accessible. The schemes in this category were the ones most frequently used in my and Kline's sample. Of the 1,037 schemes used in the discussions that we studied, there were 542 instances of this scheme type, accounting for 52.2 percent of the total.

Arguments establishing the structure of reality seek to create new perceptions and to cause the audience to see things differently. This category includes example, illustration, model and anti-model, analogy, and metaphor. Analogies and metaphors bring together two structures—a better-known structure (the *phoros*) and one that is lesser known (the *theme*). They thus facilitate the development and extension of thought by giving the *theme* a structure and a conceptual setting. Examples are generally used to address disagreement over a particular rule or principle that the example is invoked to establish. As Perelman and Olbrechts-Tyteca note, regardless of how the example is presented or the field in which it is used, "the example must, in order to be accepted as such, enjoy the status of a fact, at least provisionally" (353). Otherwise, it cannot function to resolve the uncertainty that the arguer is using it to address. In a similar manner, arguments from model and antimodel present a person or group as a model to be imitated or avoided. In contrast, instead of reforming reality, illustrations function to strengthen adherence to a known rule or principle by providing particular instances. Illustrations serve to provide a vivid picture of an abstract matter and thus to increase its rhetorical presence for the audience (360). In my study with Kline, arguments establishing the structure of reality numbered 63, or 6 percent of the total sample of 1,037 schemes.

Dissociation—the fourth major scheme category—was a newly identified category occurring in *The New Rhetoric*. Dissociation is designed to remodel or reshape audience perceptions by disengaging incompatible notions that had originally been unified and by using the valued term of a hierarchized pair to produce a value reorientation (Warnick and Kline 122). Dissociations rely on the recognition of the appearance/reality hierarchy ubiquitous in Western society. Dissociations occur infrequently (making up only 4.4 percent of the schemes in my study with Kline), but when they are used, they often have a noticeable impact since they function to resolve incompatibilities and contradictions.

It is my opinion that concerns about the epistemological viability of *The New Rhetoric* have been misplaced. Preoccupations about the need to establish an "objective ideal" of what makes a good argument (Boger 234) elide a central accomplishment of *The New Rhetoric*, which was to develop a heuristic method for analyzing arguments in use. Following its model by developing analytic frameworks for judging modes of influence that are not confined to the approaches of conventional logic can enable us to better understand how discourse operates in alternative cultural settings. By using a descriptive, empirically based approach to consider modes of influence in those contexts, we can deepen our understanding of how culturally and disciplinarily situated individuals do in fact reason about values and reach consensual decisions about matters that do not lend themselves to definite resolution. Perelman and Olbrechts-Tyteca's approach to studying argument as enacted can thus enable us to better understand modes of influence that are not grounded in a conventional logical framework but instead rely on other situated conventions specific to the social context in which they occur.

Notes

1. The field in which the argument occurs is thus closely related to audience expectations native to that field. These expectations develop within the epistemological context of that field that, in Stephen Toulmin's work, functions as backing. See Toulmin, *Uses of Argument*.

2. For examples of how mutual influence occurs in various cultural contexts, see Fitch, "Cross-Cultural Study," and Warnick and Manusov, "Organization."

Works Cited

Boger, George. "Subordinating Truth—Is *Acceptability* Acceptable?" *Argumentation* 19.2 (2005): 187–238.

Fitch, Kristine L. "A Cross-Cultural Study of Directive Sequences and Some Implications for Compliance-Gaining Research." *Communication Monographs* 61.3 (1994): 185–209.

Govier, Trudy. *Problems in Argument Analysis and Evaluation*. Dordrecht, the Netherlands: Foris, 1987.

Gross, Alan G., and Ray D. Dearin. *Chaïm Perelman*. Albany: State U of New York P, 2003.

Mattis, Noémi Perelman. "Perelman and Olbrechts-Tyteca: A Personal Recollection." Presented by Ray D. Dearin. Speech Communication National Convention. New Orleans, LA. November 1994.

Measell, J. S. "Perelman on Analogy." *Journal of the American Forensic Association* 22 (1985): 65–71.

Perelman, Chaïm. "The New Rhetoric and the Rhetoricians: Remembrances and Comments." *Quarterly Journal of Speech* 70.2 (1984): 188–96.

———. "The New Rhetoric: A Theory of Practical Reasoning." *The Rhetorical Tradition: Readings from Classical Times to the Present*. Ed. Patricia Bizzell and Bruce Herzberg. Boston: St. Martin's, 1990. 1077–1103.

Perelman, Chaïm, and Lucie Olbrechts-Tyteca. *The New Rhetoric: A Treatise on Argumentation*. Trans. John Wilkinson and Purcell Weaver. Notre Dame: U of Notre Dame P, 1969.

Schiappa, Edward. "Dissociation in the Arguments of Rhetorical Theory." *Journal of the American Forensic Association* 22 (1985): 72–82.

Toulmin, Stephen. *The Uses of Argument*. Cambridge: Cambridge UP, 1958.

Warnick, Barbara. "Two Systems of Invention: The Topics in the *Rhetoric* and *The New Rhetoric*." *Rereading Aristotle's* Rhetoric. Ed. Alan G. Gross and Arthur E. Walzer. Carbondale: Southern Illinois UP, 2000. 107–29.

Warnick, Barbara, and Susan L. Kline. "*The New Rhetoric*'s Argument Schemes: A Rhetorical View of Practical Reasoning." 1992. *Readings on Argumentation*. Ed. Angela J. Aguaya and Timothy R. Steffensmeier. State College, PA: Strata, 2008. 114–28.

Warnick, Barbara, and Valerie Manusov. "The Organization of Justificatory Discourse in Interaction: A Comparison Within and Across Cultures." *Argumentation* 14.4 (2000): 381–404.

4

"No Neutral Choices": The Art of Style in *The New Rhetoric*

Jeanne Fahnestock

Writing in *Policy Review* in 2000, journalist Mark Bowden closed his discussion of Western involvement on the African continent with the following claim: "The problems in Africa must ultimately be solved by Africans, not because the rest of the world shouldn't care, but because only Africans can" (64). In 2005, Prime Minister Tony Blair set up a commission on African issues, and the BBC ran a series featuring an activist's question, "Can Africa's problems be solved by Africans themselves?" ("Africans"). Taking a defensive stance with the same language, Mark Dybul, U.S. Global AIDS coordinator, defended the preferred ABC method of HIV prevention in 2007 because "the ABC approach was developed in Africa by Africans." During his March 2008 trip to Africa, President George W. Bush held a joint news conference with President Kagame of Rwanda where the issue of Darfur and other regional conflicts was raised. Kagame, whose nation had sent troops to Darfur, was asked specifically who should address such issues; he answered, "If it is in Africa, by Africans" ("Remarks").[1] This comment was echoed in subsequent editorials, sound bites, and blog snippets: "Tragedy of Africa" is just one example where the same phrasing appears (Williams). Perhaps the source, if there could be one source, for this repeated perspective and phrasing is a book published in 1992 by the Africa Policy Information Center and edited by William Minter, contributor to the *Nation* and a senior analyst with Africa Action. This collection of three policy documents has, angled in bold letters across the cover, a summarizing title that distills this form/content pair: *Africa's Problems / African Initiatives*.

In all these examples, a linguistic formula has come to express and at the same time justify a policy principle, that the problems of a region are best addressed by that region's people. Independent users chose the same stylistic device to express and indeed epitomize this argument. In fact, their position seems indissociable from its form, though the form can be isolated and filled with other content. It occurs in such gnomic observations as "When in Rome, do as the Romans do" or "It is easy to praise Athens to the Athenians." The prototype is perhaps the advice given by Jesus: "Render therefore unto Caesar the things which are Caesar's; and unto God the things that are God's" (Matthew 22:21). The linguistic device used in all these examples is the figure polyptoton, the reappearance of the same lexical root through different derivational or inflectional forms, a stylistic tactic identified by both Aristotle and Cicero and linked by both to what dialectical manuals called the *argument from conjugates*. Cicero's example in the *Topica* is, "If a field is 'common' [*compascuus*] it is legal to use it as a common pasture [*composcere*]" (391). Philipp Melanchthon's example of the same topic, 1,500 years later, expresses the doctrine of heat or caloric as a substance: "The water is hot; therefore there is heat in the water" (670). *The New Rhetoric* calls this device the "argument from flections," the argument based on similar word roots, though it does not name the figure (Perelman and Olbrechts-Tyteca 151); Lucie Olbrechts-Tyteca devotes a section to "Les Derivations," word play based on repeated roots in *Le comique du discours* (75–76). The ultimate source of the appeal in this epitomizing figure is probably the pattern of similar phonemes it offers to our pattern-seeking brains, but each instantiation involves other choices as well. The African policy version, for example, constructs continental, geographical identities for a Western perspective and presents implicit objects of agreement based on classification (those residing on the continent of Africa are Africans) and on level of interpretation (continental versus regional or national or religious). It can be difficult to prize apart this kind of figurally expressed argument that offers a sensible (that is, a hearable or visible) linguistic pattern as part of its cogency.

This opening example helps to illustrate certain foundational points about the language of argument made throughout *The New Rhetoric*: language choices encode selected objects of agreement and constitute techniques of argument, in this case a scheme of association. Such language/argument links occur throughout a treatise that dedicates itself, after all, to the "*discursive* means of obtaining the adherence of minds." Chaïm Perelman and Olbrechts-Tyteca were well aware of other means, conditioning by dimming the lights or draping the set with flags, but they limited themselves: "Only the technique which uses language to persuade and convince will be examined" (8). This attention to "discursive means" is attention to how an argument is actually expressed. The authors abandon the logicians' practice of rephrasing or formalizing arguments in order to purge them from their particular wording. Instead, *The New Rhetoric* assumes that the actual wording is significant, and it devotes a considerable part of its ample space to issues of language. I want to discuss first the place of language attention in the arrangement of *The New Rhetoric*—the global nature and advantages of its approach—especially on neutral language and invisible figures. Next, the sources, or potential sources, of Perelman and Olbrechts-Tyteca's insights will be reviewed in order to assess, overall, what they avoid and successfully emphasize.

The Place of Style in *The New Rhetoric*

The New Rhetoric's attention to language may not be salient in most readers' impressions of the book. First off, where does *The New Rhetoric* comment on language? To answer that question requires comparing it with other rhetorics in its treatment of style. Aristotle seems to leave style and arrangement, matters of presentation, as a final issue in a fragmentary Book 3. The influential *Rhetorica ad Herennium*, which first sets up the pedagogical canons of invention, arrangement, style, memory, and delivery, also separates style into a final separate section (Book 4). Cicero, master of style who yet has relatively little to say on it, offers brief catalogs, reflecting his sense that his audience already knows "this stuff" thoroughly. Quintilian comes to stylistic issues per se in Books 8 and 9 of the *Institutio oratoria*, and his discussions of now-lost treatises show the attention devoted to stylistic issues in the preceding centuries. These are all examples of treating style after invention has been treated. Later antiquity offers the dedicated treatises on style of Hermogenes, Dionysius of Halicarnassus, Demetrius, and Longinus. And this pattern of detailed attention continues in the rhetorical texts collected by Karl Halm. During the early modern reconstruction project, with new access to the Byzantine tradition, the philologically acute humanists expanded their sections on style in general rhetorics (for example, George of Trebizond and Philipp Melanchthon) and with treatises dedicated only to the figures by Petrus Mosellanus, Joannes Susenbrotus, Henry Peacham, John Hoskins, and many others, not to mention with the various supporting scholia and tabular epitomes.

But the dispersion of the art of rhetoric into five parts never actually sealed off one part from another. Quintilian's observations on lines of argument in Book 5, for example, are filled with digressions on appropriate language for certain lines of argument, and Cicero's *De inventione*, while it methodically catalogs arguments in the different stases, lapses into comments on strategies and passages of illustrative phrasing. Similarly, Susenbrotus or Peacham, who produced dedicated figure manuals, nevertheless constantly observed the argumentative effects of various devices.

The New Rhetoric also has, in effect, a separate, inserted treatise on style in part 2, covering agreement, what an audience will accept as a foundation on which the arguer can build. Part 2's chapters concern the objects of agreement, choices from among them, and their presentation (see the overview, 65–66). Chapter 3 is the most obviously concerned with language, but since, as the authors stress, choice and presentation are inseparable, much of chapter 2 belongs as well. Unfortunately, these chapters, in their very titles and throughout, contain translation problems in the English version. For example, the usually reliable translators chose "data" as their translation of the French term *données*. This choice has a certain Latin authenticity, but to an English speaker, "data" suggests only facts, and quantitative ones at that. But the *givens* in an argument can include any accepted premise from the objects of agreement, including truths, presumptions, values, hierarchies, loci. Thus the title of part 2, chapter 3, translated "Presentation of Data and Form of the Discourse" would be better rendered as "Presentation of the Givens and the Form of the Discourse."[2]

Perhaps these misleading titles have put English readers off. The notion of presence offered in the beginning of chapter 2 has received attention; Alan G. Gross and Ray D. Dearin, for instance, have elevated it into an architectonic rhetorical principle (135–52), and Richard Graff and Wendy Winn have written on figures of Presence and Communion. Keith Grant-Davie, Ruth Amossy, Robert Tucker, and others have also discussed *The New Rhetoric*'s language commentary. But otherwise, these sections are among the most neglected parts of the treatise.

Nevertheless, this separate section on style matches the pattern of having a separate section in a manual devoted to expression, but in *The New Rhetoric* this section does not come after a full discussion of invention. Nor does it contain everything the authors have to say about style. Far from it. *The New Rhetoric* also deliberately breaks the pattern of isolation and disperses observations on language choices throughout the treatise, occasionally stopping for paragraphs or even pages to concentrate on a given device. And of course in the case of the figures of speech, Perelman and Olbrechts-Tyteca declare their intention not to discuss them in isolation but to redistribute the figures among the arguments they best express. This dispersal highlights the functions of choices but downplays their formal identification and salience. Gross and Dearin call it "correct conceptually" but "indefensible as an expository strategy" (115). This problem of how to present the argument/language connection has no easy solutions.

All-Inclusiveness

Nevertheless, the innovation in arrangement in *The New Rhetoric* corresponds to an innovation in the material covered. The authors understand that any study of persuasive language is a study of choices among possibilities, a point familiar to all students of style, then and now, and a point completely in accord with their observation that any individual arguer must select from among potential objects of agreement and potential argument schemes. However, they are uncomfortable with the notion, a reigning assumption in literary stylistics, that only deviant expressions are of interest. No, as they emphasize, "unnoticed expressions are still argumentative" (151). This observation, though, gives the analyst of rhetorical style an enormous problem, since, as Perelman and Olbrechts-Tyteca note, "any study concerned not with divergences but with what goes unnoticed will be of a global nature" (151). "Global" is the term used in the French original. Perelman and Olbrechts-Tyteca understood that once analysts begin to consider the linguistic choices that go into a persuasive text, they can be overwhelmed. Anything, absolutely anything that comes into view under some method of analysis can count in the persuasive dynamic of a text.

To offer an example of the explosion of potentially significant features, the eclectic section 39, "Modalities in the Expression of Thought," covers the following subjects: negative expressions and negative words; subordinating and coordinating conjunctions; subordination in adjective/noun pairings; prepared phrases; concession markers; hypotactic and paratactic passage patterns; sentence types such as statements, questions, commands, and wishes; verb tenses; generic third person and indefinite pronouns; singular versus plural nouns; and demonstratives such as "this" and "that." All these linguistic variables can affect the "certainty, possibility, and necessity of a proposition" (163).

Classical and early modern rhetorical manuals typically ignore most of these preliminary choices of representation or encoding. But *The New Rhetoric* sets the precedent for a rhetorical stylistics that combines attention to the arguer's basic semantic and syntactic choices and to the high-end devices labeled as figures. Perelman and Olbrechts-Tyteca's arrangement decision shows that they *tended* to correlate basic encoding decisions with the objects of agreement and more noticeable features with the techniques of association and dissociation.

To illustrate what their attention to the basics brings into view: in section 32, "Choice of Qualifiers," the authors discuss the role of adjectives and the insertion into a class that comes with the act of naming and qualifying in establishing the objects of agreement (126–27). The "epithet," they note, "results from the visible selection of a quality which is emphasized and which is meant to complete our knowledge of the object" (126). In short, we can pay attention to the adjectives and to whether terms are modified or not in the effort to understand how prior agreements are being invoked. Cases in the history of science illustrate this point. In the eighteenth century, when the nature of electricity was under debate, the objects of agreement about apparently related phenomena were less stable. Luigi Galvani, Alessandro Volta, and others rarely referred to what they thought they were observing without a qualifier. It was always "natural," "artificial," or "animal" electricity, depending on whether it was observed in lightning, friction, or frog muscles. But eventually these phenomena were unified, the adjectives disappeared, and as historian George Johnson puts it, "electricity is electricity" (74). The opposite has happened in the case of genes. The evolution of this term, a concept before there was any experimental evidence for it, has been thoroughly traced by historians and rhetoricians of science, from Charles Darwin's "gemmules," to Hugo De Vries's "pangenes," to Wilhelm Johannsen's 1909 clipping to "genes," decades before Erwin Chargaff or James D. Watson and Francis Crick's chemical and structural discoveries. But in the last decade, the term has grown problematic as an object of agreement, thanks to the discoveries of exxons, introns, embedding, overlapping, and RNA control of the genome. The term "gene" is now often accompanied by a descriptor, and as Francis Collins, director of the National Institutes of Health's human genome sequencing program, noted two years ago, "We almost have to add an adjective every time we use that noun" (Pearson 401).

The Advantage in All-Inclusiveness

There is a unique advantage in this burdensome all-inclusiveness. Most important, it licenses the incorporation of the analytical methods of discourse analysis, pragmatics, and sociolinguistics to the study of language in argument, especially those versions like the Systemic Functional Linguistics initiated by M. A. K. Halliday or the Critical Discourse Analysis of Norman Fairclough and his adherents, who harness their version of discourse analysis to institutional critique. Discourse analysis in all its varieties pays methodical attention to the options of semantic and syntactic representation briefly mentioned in part 2 of *The New Rhetoric*. But discourse analysts are usually concerned with uncovering unconscious patterns of usage, with decoding representation to reveal underlying ideologies. They operate like cryptographers and seldom see texts as arguments that do not compel adherence. Yet, for those interested in argument, they do often elicit patterns with undoubted persuasive consequences, if the analyst also has available some parallel concepts about the constituents of argument such as *The New Rhetoric* so richly provides.

The New Rhetoric was written well before these approaches were formulated (in the 1970s and 1980s). But with the attention in chapters 2 and 3 of part 2 to the basics of word choice and sentence construction, *The New Rhetoric*'s treatment of style can accommodate the quantitative methods of the discourse analysts to yield a much fuller rhetorical stylistics than one will find in the older manuals. In all the categories it opens, it provides striking observations and directions for further study.

No Neutral Choices

To cite just one, in keeping with the global extension of stylistic choice at the level of word choice, is *The New Rhetoric*'s well-known observation that, among the spectrum of choices for a concept, there are no neutral choices. Living in (or have we just lived through?) the era of postmodern language anxieties, this declaration of the tendentiousness of all language choices comes as no surprise. Once the analyst knows enough about the options to realize that even the simplest determiner "the" carries implications of ostensive reference and definiteness, every text becomes a minefield of covert tendencies. It is easy to find examples of the persuasive loading that can come from simply shifting a participial phrase to the front of a sentence or from using a series with one loaded term that infects the other items sharing its grammatical slot.

But there is another half to that statement about neutral choices: "There is no neutral choice—but there is a choice that appears neutral, and this can serve as a starting point for the study of modifications for the purpose of argument. What term is neutral clearly depends on the environment" (149).[3] There follows an example of how, during the World War II German occupation of Belgium, the term "*boche*" was the usual label for the occupiers among Belgians, so that the term "*allemand*" indicated something else. The issue *The New Rhetoric* touches on here is what linguists would call the difference between a marked and an unmarked term, the unmarked term being the default and therefore unnoticed choice, depending indeed on context, the marked term being the less expected choice that can draw attention to itself and initiate a Gricean implicature to detect intentions behind its use. The *boche/allemande* example is a fascinating one because it is just the opposite of what one expects in the usual discussions of connotation where a term like *boche* would be considered the marked term and *allemand* the unmarked or "neutral."

If there are no neutral choices, how does one yet identify the choice that seems neutral? The usual procedure assesses the connotations that a competent language user would assign to a series of synonyms, lining them up on a kind of Likert scale according to their negative to positive connotations. (Other scales such as formality or familiarity would be possible.) Perelman and Olbrechts-Tyteca cite elsewhere an example from Arthur Schopenhauer that what a "neutral observer" would call a "phenomenon of worship," a supporter would call an "expression of piety" and a detractor "a superstition" (a discussion of question-begging in adjective choice; see 114). So there is "background radiation" in assessing the "more neutral" choice, coming from a term's widely accepted connotation (140), though once again the situation and the argument itself are influences.

The versions of almost any national or international news story offered in the press and online news services provide options for judging the relative neutrality of a term. Headline and lead, like figural epitomes, compress attitude and interpretive context in their succinct choices. The 2008 election of Silvio Berlusconi's party, and hence his selection as prime minister in Italy, offers a convenient example. Headlines on April 14 and 15 like "Third Term for Berlusconi" (*New York Daily News*), "Berlusconi Is Back as Italian PM" (*New York Post*), "Berlusconi Wins Third Term in Italy" (*Los Angeles Times*), and "Berlusconi Sweeps Back to Power" (*Boston Globe*) display a typical spectrum of degrees of intensity. Most readers would find the headline with "Sweeps" less neutral than the others, but even these have their differences since "Third Term for Berlusconi" gives no one agency for the event, compared to "Berlusconi Wins." But even the headlines giving Berlusconi agency are off somewhat, since in a parliamentary system it is more correct to say that a prime minister's party has won. Yet most of the headlines use this conventional and probably invisible synecdoche, so it is tempting to call this "heroic" choice, crediting the "win" to Berlusconi, as conventional and neutral in this context.

Even the obviously less neutral "Sweeps" headline is itself more neutral than another version, "Berlusconi Sweeps Back into Power as Left Concedes Defeat in Italian Elections" (*Guardian* [UK]); this headline names the defeated as well as the victor, so the triumph is stronger. But is it more or less neutral than this version: "71-Year-Old Billionaire Regains Power in Italy" (*San Francisco Chronicle*)? The two most influential newspapers in the United States added a context for the election: the wording "Berlusconi

Poised for 3rd Term as Economy Stalls" (*Washington Post*) creates stasis in "Poised," resonant with "Stalls"; the entire situation is frozen. Last and certainly least neutral of all is "Economy Ailing, Frustrated Italy Picks Berlusconi" (*New York Times*). This headline contains an opening modifier to provide the interpretive setting ("Economy Ailing") and personifies an entire country as a single agent acting in unison, like a disappointed shopper picking the last available tomato.

The more or less neutrality of the headlines continues throughout the stories as the contrasting choice of epithets demonstrates: Berlusconi is a "media billionaire" who "won a decisive victory" (*Boston Globe*), a "flamboyant billionaire politician" who "scored a comeback victory" (*Washington Post*), and an "idiosyncratic billionaire" who "snatched back political power" (*New York Times*). Reading these versions, you may have said to yourself that "to snatch back power" is more negative than "to score a comeback victory" or that "to sweep" an election is better than "to win" it. In making these mental ratings, you were probably confident that other English users would agree with your relative weighting. If someone thought that "to win an election" was stronger than "to sweep to victory," you might question his or her competence. Only an unusual context, or argument, could alter these default weightings.[4] What we do in assessing the neutrality of terms is exactly what is done in the case of other objects of agreement. We construct provisional connotations from our personal sense of how the typical/normal/universal reader would respond. The "more neutral" choice is the choice transcending the saliently non-neutral choices.

By paying attention to apparently neutral choices, Perelman and Olbrechts-Tyteca go on to make two of their most memorable observations on style: that the apparent absence of technique can be the technique of "being natural," and that unremarkable, ordinary language facilitates a transfer from the acceptability of the language to the acceptability of the content. "The relationship between ordinary language and admitted ideas," they write, "is not fortuitous: ordinary language is by itself the manifestation of agreement, of a community of thought, by the same right as the received ideas. Ordinary language can help promote agreement on the ideas" (153). The authors suggest that the way to advance new and shocking value judgments would be to use a style that was not shocking (152).

The Figures of Speech

Perhaps the knottiest discussion on style in *The New Rhetoric* concerns the figures of speech. Here the authors reach for a new understanding, and where they eventually come out is a clear gain: they recapture the role of figures in argumentation. In recovering this perspective, they are really being faithful to the actual discussions of the devices in the ancient manuals where they are typically tied to certain lines or strategies of argument. And they are also reinventing what was apparently unknown to them: Melanchthon and other early modem rhetorician/dialecticians had already fused certain figures with the arguments they achieved. But how Perelman and Olbrechts-Tyteca get to this conclusion, and how they negotiate the problems, is certainly problematic.

The authors begin by acknowledging two characteristics required in a figure: first, a discernible structure independent of content (which they say modem logicians distinguish as syntactic, semantic, or pragmatic), and second, a use distanced from the normal manner of expression, which for that reason can attract attention (168, 227). These characteristics set up impossible or difficult conditions. A figure should be formally definable or distinct, but under that definition, anything formally definable could be a figure, a position they find unacceptable (169). The second criterion is as problematic: a use distanced from a normal manner of expression. As an unusual locution, a figure would be noticeable, but to notice it would introduce a potentially damaging form/content dissociation.

To address these difficulties and to redeem the figures from their relegation to the status of mere ornamentation, *The New Rhetoric* proposes the following effect: "The whole of the argumentative significance of figures arises at the moment when this distinction, which was immediately noticed, is dissolved through the effect produced by the speech" (169). So presumably the audience notices the device but then immediately forgets that it is a device. "We consider a figure to be argumentative, if it brings about a change of perspective, and its use seems normal in relation to this new situation. If, on the other hand, the speech does not bring about the adherence of the hearer to the argumentative form, the figure will be considered an embellishment, a figure of style" (169). This point is later restated as follows: "In order to perceive its [a figure's] argumentative aspect, it is necessary to conceive of a step from the common to the uncommon, and a return to another order of commonness, that created by the argument at the moment of its completion" (171).

To complicate this characterization even further, Perelman and Olbrechts-Tyteca specify that a figure can be argumentative without necessarily bringing about adherence to the overall conclusions of the discourse; the audience just has to see the individual move or premise "in its full value" (170). If a figure fails to deliver its individual argument, it "will fall to the level of a stylistic figure." After this point about three stages—common to uncommon back to a new order of common—the authors offer what they label as their most important point:

> It is necessary to understand that the normal [like the "neutral"] expression is relative not only to a milieu, an audience, but to a particular moment in the discourse. If one admits, on the contrary, that there is a way of expressing oneself that is the good, authentic, true, and normal way, then one can conceive of a figure only as something static: an expression is or is not a figure, depending on the hearer's reaction. Only a more flexible conception, which considers the normal in all its changing facets, can do full justice to the place argumentative figures occupy in the phenomenon of persuasion. (171)

They then claim to concur "by the relativization of the normal" with Longinus's observation that figures should be hidden. The final line in this section is their own attempt at an invisible figure, normalized at this point in the discourse: "Party dresses are in order in certain surroundings, and do not attract attention" (171), a switch to metaphor, or even allegory, which is pretty difficult to ignore.

The position they have sketched out is difficult to defend. First of all, the notion that one notices a device and then has a lapse of memory or is distracted and ceases to find it remarkable because one accepts the individual point or argument asks for quite a bit of cognitive processing and seems to flatly contradict Longinus's point about invisibility, with which they claim to concur, and also to contradict their own concluding observation about what can seem normal at a particular point in a discourse. In addition, their bottom line—if you notice it, it's a figure of style; if you don't notice it, or if you cease to notice it, it's a figure of argument—is difficult to support. Is it warranted by introspection into one's own reading processes? Supporting evidence might someday come from a functional MRI conducted while someone reads an argument with a trenchant metaphor to see if there is a sudden activation of a secondary response that is then muted. Or perhaps this issue would be better addressed by the authors' typical sensitivity to differences in degree. You may notice a figure and still find it convincing *as a figure*, or notice it and then forget it is a figure, or not notice it at all. At any rate, anyone who spends time studying the figures is going to notice many more of them than does the untrained listener.

Is *The New Rhetoric* any better in dealing with the systematics of the figures? Perelman and Olbrechts-Tyteca dismiss the traditional divisions, especially that between figures of thought and speech, which they consider to have damaged the whole subject (172). If the traditional divisions are useless, how should one go about organizing the figures? The manuals, beginning with the *Rhetorica ad Herennium* in rough fashion, categorize according to grain size, looking at figures that involve words, sentences, and passages and distinguishing tropes, schemes, and pragmatic figures. Some later manuals go by manipulations (omission, addition, permutation) and see these same moves operating at the word or sentence level. Thus, one can omit a letter from a word or a word from a phrase. Still other manuals go roughly by function: Melanchthon has three orders of figures—concerning word choice and meaning, concerning action (pragmatic dimension), and concerning amplification.

The New Rhetoric actually inverts the categorization problem by identifying functions first and then, as appropriate, the linguistic choices expressing those functions. As a result, as the authors note, the same figure can appear more than once because it can fulfill different functions. Section 42 is devoted to illustrating, with a "quick survey," this principle of organization by taking the three preliminary functions—choosing objects of agreement, giving them presence, and establishing communion with the audience—and identifying the kinds of devices that can accomplish these effects (172). Then, throughout the techniques of argument in part 3, the authors disperse traditional devices according to the arguments they express, covering, as the index indicates, some sixty-nine traditional devices. There are, however, many holes; the entire discussion of the quasi-logical arguments of reciprocity, for example, cites many arguments expressed in perfect antimetaboles, but the figure is never identified at this point, nor is the gradatio named in the discussion of transitivity, although the authors again cite a perfect instance. So the intended program is laudable but the execution incomplete, as they concede.

The Sources

In both the interpolated section on style and the dispersed discussion of devices, Perelman and Olbrechts-Tyteca reach for new characterizations of the argumentative significance of choices and figures. What were the sources of their views, and how do their views compare with those of other language theorists available in the 1950s? To pay attention first to part 2, chapter 3, the inserted section, the sources cited show that the authors consulted, as expected, canonical classical rhetorics. Of these latter, they frequently reference the most detailed Roman treatments of style, the *Rhetorica ad Herennium* of 80 B.C.E. and Quintilian's *Institutio oratoria* of 90 C.E. They were aware of later extensions, of Longinus, of Omer Talon from the sixteenth century, and of Giambattista Vico's complete rhetorical manual and Cesar Chesneau

Du Marsais's treatise on the tropes, both from the eighteenth century. But they also read literary criticism, notably Yves Gandon's *Le démon du style*, historical studies of rhetoric in French and German, works in semantics and philology, and some contemporary rhetorical works, including Kenneth Burke and even Richard Weaver, whose *Ethics of Rhetoric* contains a section on the rhetorical force of the parts of speech.[5] Another important reference is to Max Black's article on "Vagueness," cited on page 130; Black is the actual source of the notion, put forward on the following page, of a "fringe of indefiniteness" (131) surrounding certain words, a contribution worth further study (Black 434–35).

Three sources not just cited but discussed in the text are worth special notice. First, Perelman and Olbrechts-Tyteca knew the General Semantics movement, initiated by Alfred Korzybski in the 1930s (*Science and Sanity*) but popularized by his followers like Stuart Chase and S. I. Hayakawa, whose *Language in Thought and Action* is still in print (148). The General Semanticists believed that improved language practices would address social problems, especially those stemming from bias. They were adamant foes of generality in language, recommending as an extreme measure that all abstract terms be given subscripts to limit their reference. *The New Rhetoric* does not follow their characterization of absolute levels of generality in words but points out instead that an impression of concreteness is really a product of the presence given to a term/concept (148), certainly a just corrective.

The authors also discuss I. A. Richards, who, summarizing a late-nineteenth-century trend (as represented by Alexander Bain and Brainerd Kellogg), redefined rhetoric as the study of misunderstanding and its remedies. For Richards (in both *The Philosophy of Rhetoric* and in his work with C. K. Ogden), so far as interpretation was concerned, recourse to context was the answer. But while always calling for attention to the argumentative situation, *The New Rhetoric* points out that choosing the relevant context of interpretation is also a matter of interpretation. Overall, *The New Rhetoric* does not follow the prescriptive approach endorsed by the General Semanticists or Richards and taken up by the many language engineers, the Strunk and Whites of the postwar years. Perelman and Olbrechts-Tyteca do not believe in salvation through an impossible linguistic purity.

Another important source for the authors, as David A. Frank and Michelle K. Bolduc show, is Jean Paulhan, cited by both Olbrechts-Tyteca and Perelman in later retrospectives as their window into classical rhetoric (Frank and Bolduc 182). Paulhan is referenced throughout *The New Rhetoric*, but his contribution to a 1949 issue of *Les Cahiers du Sud*, "Treatise on the Figures; or Rhetoric Decrypted" ("Traité des figures ou la rhétorique décryptée"), is mentioned at the critical point of redefinition in the chapter on figures (168). There are certainly differences between this piece and *The New Rhetoric*'s account of language. Paulhan retains classifications of the figures, at least as a point of departure; sees "figures of reasoning" as a small subcategory (203–4); and is ultimately concerned with encoding, with how well language choices express a writer's thoughts and emotions (234). But there are also striking similarities or premonitions. Notably, Paulhan finds that in some contexts, figures can often seem completely normal; in his terms, they fall below the level of a figure. Other expressions seem to him to exceed that level when a text draws attention to its own linguistic choices. Paulhan even has a passage imagining the questions of a reader who notices the language—who is, in other words, dissociating form from content. In keeping with his levels of figural transparency (212), Paulhan describes figures as sometimes falling asleep but capable of being revived (211), a notion memorably applied to metaphor in *The New Rhetoric* (407–8). Paulhan believes finally that rhetoric allows or even promotes a certain hesitation between whether an expression is spontaneous or studied (236). Many of *The New Rhetoric*'s observations certainly follow these points; Paulhan is the likely source of the book's disappearing figures. His final contribution, however, may have been his overall attitude toward rhetoric. He does describe language as an "exterior necessity," like natural or social laws, the winds on the sea, or, notably, the walls of a prison (237). But he believes that rhetoric can, as he says, dig a break in this wall by "making language . . . vacillate before our eyes" ("*fasisant en quelque façon à nous yeux vaciller le langage*," 237). Thanks to the vocabulary provided by rhetorical treatises, he believes readers can always see an expression as both what it expresses and as a linguistic choice.

Also worth considering, though this may be a surprising tack to take, are the sources not cited in *The New Rhetoric*. Some were simply too recent. For example, the authors probably did not know Noam Chomsky's *Syntactic Structures* published in 1957, but Perelman observed in a later article that human language ability is not limited to the syntactic competence described by the generative grammarians ("Rhetorical Perspectives" 83). In 1958, they evidently did not know J. L. Austin's *How to Do Things with Words*, not surprising since the book version of the lectures did not appear until 1962, though the lectures were delivered in 1955 and their insights were offered in earlier articles (Austin vi). But passages certainly suggest that they understood what we now call the speech act dimension of an utterance. In the opening of part 3, they observe that a discourse can be construed as an act, a sign, or a means (189). Perhaps more surprising, the authors also do not cite Roman Jakobson, whose groundbreaking article on selection and combination, the paradigmatic and syntagmatic dimensions of language choice, appeared in 1956 in English (Jakobson 98–100). Yet they in effect rehearse the paradigmatic axis in section 38, "Verbal Forms and Argumentation," when they discuss the "family" of terms that serves as the background against which any selected term stands out (151). Olbrechts-Tyteca went on to use Jakobson's famous "Two Aspects of Language" in her 1974 study of humor. In the same year that *Traité de l'argumentation: Le nouvelle rhétorique* was published, Jakobson was one of the distinguished participants in a conference at Indiana University that brought together linguists, psychologists like George Miller, and literary critics like Rene Wellek to inaugurate a research program into stylistics and psycholinguistics. However, this group paid virtually no attention to persuasive language or to the contributions of rhetoric (Sebeok); they took language study in another direction, away from the functional and persuasive.

A perhaps more surprising absence, one certainly not accounted for by recency, is *The New Rhetoric*'s neglect of the great dialectical manuals of the fifteenth and sixteenth centuries, though Perelman and Olbrechts-Tyteca were certainly aware that they were reviving older dialectic practices. In his 1970 retrospective and synthesis written for the "Great Ideas" series, Perelman sketched a history of rhetoric and noted the reforms of the sixteenth century, but, apparently following Walter Ong, he blamed Peter Ramus and Talon for destroying the classical rhetorical heritage and beginning a fruitless preoccupation with style. Had the authors looked into the dialectical manuals of Agricola or Melanchthon or Johann Sturm or Ludovico Carbone or Gerardus Vossius, they would have discovered projects analogous to theirs, quite successful at offering systems of practical reasoning and melding attention to style and argument.

The point of citing these missing sources is not to complain that Perelman and Olbrechts-Tyteca did not read every rhetorical manual or contemporary scholar of language that they might have or could have. The point instead is to suggest that even though *The New Rhetoric* does not mention these other great traditions of language analysis, the cognitive approaches, speech act theory, and later discourse analysis, it is in fact compatible with them all and even some sense completes them. The anticipation of these approaches underwrites the possibility of what we might call a much needed "grand unifying theory" of persuasive language.

Conclusion

Separately, there may be nothing completely new, or unthought of before, in the sections on language in *The New Rhetoric*; but then the authors claim recovery, not novelty, for their project. Presence, aptly psychologized, is essentially a version of amplification; even the wording of part of its definition recalls the passage in Quintilian on forcing the judge's attention. Linking topics to figures of speech was also not new: classical rhetoric and early modem dialectical manuals tied the figures to lines of argument. But it is nothing short of a miracle that the whole of these lost teachings was recaptured at once, synthesized into a single bolus and delivered into the middle of the twentieth century.

The New Rhetoric's achievement in 1958 can also be appreciated in terms of the prevailing views that it overcomes. It wrests attention from language as decoration or as the badge of unique literary merit in an exclusively aesthetic dimension. It does not reduce rhetorical stylistics to effective communication, as in Richards and the General Semanticists' reduction of the art to textual tinkering to prevent misunderstandings. And while Paulhan is certainly an enormous influence, *The New Rhetoric* ultimately abandons his ambiguities, playfulness, and emphasis on consumption for the ethically serious business of choosing to argue (see Perelman, "New Rhetoric" 416–17).

There is one more dragon to slay, and that is suspicion or perhaps even fear of the "prison house" of language leading to a fanatical intolerance of "mere words" or to a skeptical dismissal of mere form (a dismissal still evident in commentaries on *The New Rhetoric*). As a radically analytical text, *The New Rhetoric* could "almost" be taken to reinforce "language skepticism," since it unmasks so many deep and consequential choices. But the authors' faith in argumentation and their emphasis on the ethical commitment required of the arguer really extends to the arguer's language. Overall, their attitude toward language is positive. There may be no neutral choices, but there are choices. In *The New Rhetoric*'s fuller definition: "Language is not only a means of communication: it is also an instrument for acting on minds" (132). Perelman repeated this definition emphatically in an article published in 1974, refuting philosophical requirements for an idealized language: "The rhetorical approach," he wrote, "considers language as an instrument enabling one mind to act upon another" ("Rhetorical Perspectives" 82).[6] Given this high valuation, it is no wonder that *The New Rhetoric* devotes an ample portion of its capacious space to how we say what we argue. Attention to language is a constant subtext so that, of all the classifications and categories that *The New Rhetoric* can be placed into—philosophical, sociological, legal, ethical—it should also be considered as a treatise on language.

Appendix: The New Rhetoric's *Major Insights/Points/Claims about Style*
- There are no neutral term choices, though there are choices that count as neutral (unmarked) in a certain context, and stylistic analysis is based on an awareness of options. To generalize this point: characteristics that are attributed to words are in fact products of their use.
- Concrete diction and abstract diction are not fixed categories. Presence determines the degree of abstraction and not the reverse.
- There are no indifferent substitutions of synonyms.
- Ordinary, unremarkable language represents a set of agreements, a community of thought (153). Ordinary language promotes agreement on ideas, and an apparently neutral style increases credibility.
- Clichés (section 40) may promote agreement, as may prepared phrases, slogans, and catchwords that are developed de novo and require frequent reinforcement.
- Rhetorical style is a matter of manipulating presence and lack of presence (amplification and minimization or *auxesis* and *meiosis*).
- Rhetorical style concerns much more than the figures; it involves constitutive choices of any kind. This emphasis reveals the persuasive or argumentative consequences of small-scale choices (section 39), especially in the expression of the objects of agreement.
- Many language choices construct or encode the rhetorical situation (communion with the audience is one aspect).
- The figures themselves are best understood as expressions of certain objects of agreement and of individual arguments, though any one-to-one exclusive pairing of figure to argument is not possible (a point amply understood by Quintilian, George of Trebizond, Melanchthon, and others).
- Any dissociation of form and content, any awareness of device, can damage a persuasive case.
- Through stylistic means, the status of "elements" as objects of agreement can be altered; personal tastes can be presented as standards or values; values can be presented as facts; judgments of fact as values.

Notes

1. President Bush made a trip to Africa in February 2008, creating the occasion for a news conference with President Kagame. In his remarks, President Bush repeated the same sentiment but used *ploche*, not *polyptoton*: "President [Kagame] mentioned something that I agree with, and that is, the role of the United States and others is to help African nations deal with African problems" ("Remarks").

2. Similar problems plague the title of section 37, translated "Technical Problems in the Presentation of Data." The adjective "technical" in English, especially in combination with "data," also has misleading associations. It would be more correct to say "Problems of Techne/Technique in the Presentation of Givens."

3. "Il n'existe pas de choix neutre—mais il y a un choix qui parait neutre et c'est a partir de celui-la que peuvent s'etudier les modifications argumentatives. Le terme neutre depend evidemment du milieu" (Perelman and Olbrechts-Tyteca, *Traité* 201).

4. There are exceptions with highly polarized terms: the label "conservative" was applied to Berlusconi in some AP reports that ran in several venues, such as on newsmax.com (headline: "US Friend Returns to Power in Italy"). To call Berlusconi a "colorful conservative" in that context is laudatory; in the *San Francisco Chronicle* less so; in the UK *Guardian*, definitely not.

5. The following list shows the range of their citations: Burke, *Rhetoric of Motives* (135 as well as several more times); Saint-Aubin, *Guide pour la class de rhétorique* (152); Gandon, *Le démon du style* (153 as well as several more times); Morris, *Signs, Language and Behavior* (154); Brunot, *La pensée et la langue;* Rostand, *Grammaire et affectivité* (several times); Weaver, *The Ethics of Rhetoric* (158); Longinus, *On the Sublime* (160); Klemperer, *L. T. I. Notizbuch eines Philologen* (162); Porzig, *pas Wunder der Sprache* (163); Laswell, *Language and Politics*, quoting Paechter, *Nazi-Deutsch* (164); Estève, *Études Philosophiques sur l'expression littéraire* (166); Paulhan, *Les hain-tenys*; Paulhan, "Traité des figures ou la rhétorique décryptée"; Talon, *Audomari Talaei Rhetoricae libri Duo P. Rami Praelectionibus Illustrati*; Volkmann, *Hermagoras oder Elemente Rhetorik* (169); Baron, *De la rhétorique* (173); Du Marsais, *Des tropes* (174); Chaignet, *Le rhétorique et son histoire* (175); Britton, *Communication* (179); and Caillois, *Poetique de St-John Perse* (182).

6. Perelman's definition is worth quoting at length:

To this reductionist conception of language, which is entirely defined by its syntax and by semantic rules of a purely formal nature, I wish to oppose the rhetorical approach which considers language as an instrument enabling one mind to act upon another. If we consider language in this light, we can show that it is as unsuitable to call a language "ideal" when it possesses properties mentioned by Professor Church as it would be suitable to call glass an ideal material because it is transparent and cannot lose its shape. Just such qualities are needed for the fabrication of window-panes, but it does not mean that anyone would think of using this material to make a shirt or a pair of trousers. ("Rhetorical Perspectives" 82–83)

Works Cited

"Africans on Africa." *BBC.com*. BBC, 7 July 2005. Web. 5 July 2010.

Aristotle. *On Rhetoric: A Theory of Civil Discourse*. Trans. George A. Kennedy. New York: Oxford UP, 1991.

Austin, J. L. *How to Do Things with Words*. Cambridge, MA: Harvard UP, 1962.

Black, Max. "Vagueness: An Exercise in Logical Analysis." *Philosophy of Science* 4.4 (1937): 427–55.

Bowden, Mark. "African Atrocities and 'The Rest of the World.'" *Policy Review* 101 (2000): 51–64.

Cicero, Marcus Tulius. *De inventione; De optimo genere oratorum; Topica.* 1960. Trans. H. M. Hubbell. Cambridge, MA: Harvard UP, 1976.
Dybul, Mark. Interview with John Testrom. *HIVPolicy.net.* Global Business Initiative, September 2007. Web. 6 July 2010.
Fairclough, Norman. *Analysing Discourse: Textual Analysis for Social Research.* London: Routledge, 2003.
Frank, David A., and Michelle K. Bolduc. "Chaïm Perelman's 'First Philosophies and Regressive Philosophy': Commentary and Translation." *Philosophy and Rhetoric* 46.3 (2003): 177–206.
Gross, Alan G., and Ray D. Dearin. *Chaïm Perelman.* Albany: State U of New York P, 2003.
Halliday M. A. K. *An Introduction to Functional Grammar.* 3rd ed. Rev. by Christian M. I. M. Matthiessen. London: Oxford UP, 2004.
Halm, Karl. *Rhetores Latini Minores.* Leipzig: Teubner, 1863.
Jakobson, Roman. *Language in Literature.* Ed. Krystyna Pomorska and Stephen Rudy. Cambridge, MA: Harvard UP, 1987.
Johnson, George. *The Ten Most Beautiful Experiments.* New York: Knopf, 2008.
Melanchthon, Philipp. *Erotemata Dialectices. Corpus Reformatorum.* Ed. Carolus Gottlieb Bretschneider and Henricus Ernestus Bindseil. Vol. 13. New York: Johnson Reprint, 1855. 508–759.
Olbrechts-Tyteca, Lucie. *Le comique du discours.* Brussels: Université de Bruxelles, 1974.
Paulhan Jean. "Traité des figures ou la rhétorique décryptée." 1944. *Oeuvres complètes.* Paris: Cercle dus livre précieux, 1966–70. 196–237.
Pearson, Helen. "Genetics: What Is a Gene?" *Nature* 441 (May 2006): 398–401. Web. 6 July 2010.
Perelman, Chaïm. "The New Rhetoric: A Theory of Practical Reasoning." *The Rhetoric of Western Thought.* 1978. Ed. James L. Golden, Goodwin F. Berquist, and William E. Coleman. Dubuque, IA: Kendall Hunt, 1989. 391–419.
———. "Rhetorical Perspectives on Semantic Problems." *The New Rhetoric and the Humanities: Essays on Rhetoric and Its Applications.* Dordrecht, Holland: Reidel, 1979. 82–90.
Perelman, Chaïm, and Lucie Olbrechts-Tyteca. *The New Rhetoric: A Treatise on Argumentation.* Trans. John Wilkinson and Purcell Weaver. Notre Dame: U of Notre Dame P, 1969.
———. *Traité de l'argumentation: La nouvelle rhétorique.* Paris: Presses Universitaires de France, 1958.
Quintilian. *Institutio Oratoria.* Vols. 1–4. Trans. H. E. Butler. Cambridge, MA: Harvard UP, 1920–22.
"Remarks by President Bush and President Kagame of Rwanda in Joint Press Availability." *Business Wire.* Allbusiness.com. 19 February 2008. Web. 20 July 2010.
Sebeok, Thomas, ed. *Style in Language.* Cambridge, MA: MIT P, 1960.
Williams, Walter E. "Tragedy of Africa." *Washington Times* 28 February 2008. Web. 6 July 2010.

5

The Function of the "Universal Audience" in Perelman's Rhetoric: Looking Back on a Theoretical Issue

Loïc Nicolas

This essay deals with two notions that lie at the heart of the Perelmanian rhetorical system and that link it to Aristotelian thinking: the nature of support and, above all, its correlate, the audience.[1] As such, we must not forget that for Chaïm Perelman, in nonformal argumentation, there is always an essential "contact of minds."[2] By this, he means a prior and reciprocal representation that an agreement is possible with a fantasized other, an agreement grounded on a cognitive and intellectual structure known to be shared by both parties. Thus, arguing is a singularly purposeful activity guided by the common aim of finding a rationally acceptable solution, capable of overcoming a conflict of meaning, in order to perpetuate the community. Therefore, the initial disagreement fulfills the function of a *kairos*: it becomes the opportunity, as Emmanuelle Danblon puts it, "to discuss norms, principles and conventions that structure social reality" (100). By saying this, she actually extends the Perelmanian analysis. This initial disagreement requires multiple viewpoints about good and justice and demonstrates that "the nature of public good cannot be settled by science or by dogma" (Ricoeur 167). It justifies the use of language to bring about a *common sense*. Beyond "evidence and irrationality" (Perelman, *Rhétoriques* 255), it can rightfully be regarded as the expression of community. From there, the issue of discrimination is raised or, more precisely, that of "acknowledging" understood as the ability to determine the conditions under which a potential option may become a decision that each and everyone will make.

For this reason, the argumentative process takes the form of a negotiation, depending on the discursive proofs that condition how the speech will be received and eventually justify and legitimize taking action. As Perelman puts it: "Speech affects its audience in such a way that, as it continues, the way the audience reacts, the way it digests information changes. Hence the chosen order of elements in an argumentation is of the utmost importance. This is a true conditioning of the audience" (*Rhétoriques* 451). For all that, this is not a one-sided influence but, on the contrary, an interdependent relationship in which the speaker adjusts to his or her audience thanks to the external constraint that the organization of the speech represents. This guarantees the rationality of the argumentative approach and the sphere of its application. "Thus the nature of the audience to which arguments can be successfully presented will determine to a great extent both the direction the arguments will take and the character, the significance that will be attributed to them" (Perelman and Olbrechts-Tyteca 30).

Consequently, I shall examine this idea through the lens of dialogism and anticipation that are particularly relevant when addressing the "universal audience." The goal of this essay is to examine in what sense the moment of discursive production can be analyzed as an *interlocutive* relationship. The role of a person as speaker and as capable of speech is necessarily subordinated to his or her position in a real or an imagined interlocution. The understanding of this special process of projection and anticipation is essential when the universal audience is the horizon of the discourse.

First, I would like to summarize the notion of universal audience as Perelman understood it and which "put his readers through much difficulty," especially because of unjustified associations between "the idea of reason and the idea of truth."[3] In other words, the problem raised by such a notion is that of its relationship with the rhetorical system, which deals with what is contingent, ambiguous, and mainly revocable—it has nothing to do with what can be implied generally. However, according to Perelman, the issues raised by rhetorical argumentation are not different when the speaker (or the author) addresses the universal audience. In this sense, there is no exception in the system, nor does the possibility to have a "unique truth" emerge. What is sought in the speech directed to the universal audience is no more obvious, nor is the structure more restrictive, than it is with a particular audience. As Perelman explains, "What characterizes a formal argumentation is its singular meaning whereas social, juridical, political or philosophical argumentation cannot get rid of every ambiguity" (*Rhétoriques* 91) because the premises upon which it relies are only plausible, thus unsure and temporary. In this way, there is always a legitimate possibility of objecting to the argument put forward because support is "a fact, not a right" (87), even though the speaker tries to turn this support into a "right" by presenting the reasons given *as if* they were an intrinsic constraint. Thus, as a discursive process, the nature of rhetoric is not altered because the speaker addresses the "universal audience." It does not become "positivism" and "rationalism," approaches that Perelman condemns. But this movement does change the status and the value of the argumentation of the speaker. What is upheld is more "sensible" and aims to convince rather than to persuade, but the conclusion that the speaker comes to is not therefore indisputable or immune to discussion. It would deny individuals the possibility to doubt that cannot be taken from them. Against Descartes and his concept of clear and distinct ideas, the persistence of doubt is strongly highlighted in Perelman's theory of rhetoric. "More sensible" is thus an especially important concept because resorting to reason and to a person's consciousness allows, according to Perelman, "going beyond the idea of truth" (*Rhétoriques* 220). Coexisting disagreements about "value judgments" such as good or justice become acceptable and intelligible.

Indeed, in order to acknowledge the value of disagreement and to offer it to debate, it is necessary to postulate that there are always several ways to be reasonable, that is, to accept a variety of understandings of the universal audience. This is not the shadow of skeptical relativism looming here but only the condition that explains the existence of juridical or "philosophical controversy." As Perelman says: "As a result, in my opinion, what is sensible is not . . . always the solution everyone will agree on because there is not always a guarantee of a single solution." There might be a single solution when it does not raise any sensible objections: what is considered as a "fact" or as a "truth" is validated by the actual agreement given by the universal audience. Yet, such an argumentative approach aims to convince. Therefore, it can never "content itself with a majority"[4] without trying to confront every argument likely to be put forward, with the purpose of reaching the best solution.

Addressing the universal audience depends on the way the speaker, relying on the call to reason, imagines the rationality of others. Such a stance thus implies that the speaker's primary challenge is to imagine the conditions in which the argument will be received by all competent and honest listeners and to anticipate and examine closely every likely criticism. There is, in particular for Alan G. Gross and Ray D. Dearin, a confrontation with the standards of rationality that are present in the mind of the speaker. Consequently, as a member of the audience, the speaker must necessarily support the argument he puts forward, which means being himself convinced.

For Perelman, "the impossibility to convince" and "the impossibility to convince oneself" go together. The first listener is first of all the speaker himself asking for justification. Resorting to reason is resorting to one's own reason and generalizing one's own concept of rationality and objectivity while disregarding social and temporal contingencies. In that sense, this hypothesis about the others' reason or, let's say, the reason of all that allows one to address the universal audience comes from a double model: the model of an individual as a would-be contradictor and representative of a common reason and the model of argumentative ethics that sets up the relationship to the other characterized by the use of justification. The "call to reason" is what gives to nonformal argumentation its ethical dimension, because the speaker goes beyond the pursuit of an impact at all costs and "conforms to Kant's categorical imperative that may be applied to thinking," to use Perelman's words.[5] As George C. Christie says, "If the relationship between the judge and the universal audience that he has constructed imposes certain general moral constraints on that audience, it imposes even more such moral constraints on the judge himself. In a sense, such requirements can be grouped under the heading of 'honesty'" ("Universal Audience" 48). Of the same mind, James Crosswhite explains that "[t]he universalising interest of reason" when the speaker invokes the universal audience is "essentially an ethical one" (154).

Consequently, in the case of particular audiences, the creation of a model is de facto very different from the one that is created when addressing the universal audience. In the first case, the speaker is somehow forced to bring the multitude back to unity. The speaker creates a fictive being who represents the essential characteristics that are thought to be in the audience facing the speaker, whom he must convince. This *reduction* process aims at selecting, on the basis of what is represented as "dominant opinions and unquestioned beliefs" (Perelman and Olbrechts-Tyteca 20), what would be the most persuasive *hic et nunc* without worrying about the criticism likely to come from the other audiences. The speaker pays attention to the majority, which offers an evaluation of his argumentation. In the second case, everything is more difficult as it concerns a hypothesis about the nature of humanity. From an ontological point of view, the principle of "majority" is unsatisfactory, as I mentioned earlier. In his article "Rhétorique et philosophie," Perelman describes the speaker as having de facto a moral duty: he has to present only intellectual constructions, arguments, and conclusions that can be valid as such as well as for everyone (*Rhétoriques* 217–20). We find ourselves in front of an opening movement toward reason that is able to include anyone's act of support or, in other words, even "this man" who stands for us all and whom the speaker himself embodies in the first place. That is why Perelman says it is "hard to control... the idea of universal audience,"[6] since it is above all intimate. However, I believe that this idea gives meaning to the parallel between rhetoric and dialectic, at least considered as a mental stance. Addressing the universal audience amounts to debating with oneself, that is, to undergo the necessary trial of contradiction and justification allowing for no possible loophole. The particular agreement is eventually only a particular case of the agreement with others, as Perelman and Olbrechts-Tyteca explain in the beginning of *The New Rhetoric*. Here they also explain that the precondition to debate with oneself consists in conceiving of oneself "as divided into at least two interlocutors, two parties engaging in deliberation" (14). This means picturing oneself in a speech interaction in which the participants argue and justify their respective points of view. Although Perelman's commentators have barely referred to it, the term "interlocutor" is pervasive in his philosophy and theory of rhetoric. It will be particularly relevant in the last part of my essay.

Programming the reception of the speech by this universal audience—and, to a lesser extent, by any kind of audience—implies, before the start of the speech, the setting up of a device based on the fiction of a dialogue and on the principle of anticipation. However, there is a distinction to be made here, again. In the case of a particular audience, anticipating consists above all in "controlling [its] reactions,"[7] according to what is known about its *habitus*, its *pathos*, and its psychological and sociological conditions. In the case of a universal audience, there is no point in "controlling," as it cannot be done. It is rather an "answer in advance" that is possible thanks to a dialogue with a constructed Other who is at the same time and above all oneself, as mentioned earlier. To be open to the universal audience is thus to let the Other speak within the context of a fictive dialogue. It boils down to endangering one's own speech by putting it to the test of confrontation with a would-be contradictor. To put it in another way, it is a "dialogue" that the speaker acknowledges as virtually likely within the context of another speech. It may be called an opening to interpellation, since in this process the speaker reaches toward the principle of the dialectic reciprocity.

Therefore, it is not the audience that the speaker has to imagine but what we could call the "generalized interlocutor," by reference to George Herbert Mead's phrase the "generalized other" (see Christie, *Notion of an Ideal Audience*). Indeed, to a certain extent, thinking about the Other only as a listener is to deny the Other any status in interlocution. Turning into a fiction this relationship to this "generalized interlocutor"[8] allows one to contemplate or, even better, prevent any remarks and objections that could rightfully be made by any honest interlocutor. To put it in a different way, there can be no speech meant for an audience without the ability to make the first move, to anticipate contradictions. To be gifted with the sense of this rhetorical dialogue is not only knowing how to answer but knowing how to answer *in advance*, even before doubt can emerge within any individual endowed with reason and recognized by the speaker as a potential interlocutor.

In this sense, the rhetorical process consists in a never-ending anticipation of objections, criticism, or protests that "everyone" may make at any moment of the development and that the speaker seeks to thwart in advance. Thus, the oratorical stance may be said to consist in not saying as much as in saying, in keeping silent—provided the argument is relevant—to avoid ruining the strength of conviction. Based on a dialogue, anticipation must then be considered as a means to shape the Other's position, to program his judgment and then his action, but also as the act of uttering itself. Somehow, the speaker finds himself responsible for and thus, as it were, "bearing the Other," as Emmanuel Lévinas puts it (133, my translation), with whom he struggles to negotiate a meaning through the use of rhetoric. He tries to discriminate the arguments that would be the most likely to win his own support if he were in the place of this Other, whom he tries to convince with an argument that he claims to be universal.

To conclude, I would say that addressing the universal audience is, in a certain sense, very similar to Kant's transcendental dialectic: the argument and the counter-argument do not come from two different interlocutors but are both put to the test by the trial of reason. Yet, Perelman and Olbrechts-Tyteca's theory of argumentation must be first regarded as a "new philosophical criticism but much more flexible than Kant's,"[9] insofar as it includes the possibility of different moral concepts that may rationally be subject to debate.

Notes

    1. French excerpts were all translated by Gersende Guingouain unless otherwise mentioned. I am sincerely grateful to her for her work, as well as to Florian Alix, who proofread my original text.
    2. See Perelman and Olbrechts-Tyteca, *New Rhetoric*, 14–17.
    3. Letter to Paul de Loye, 6 August 1970, Chaïm Perelman Archives.
    4. Letter to Georges Kalinowski, 2 April 1973, ibid.
    5. Letter to J. P. Weber, 29 January 1960, ibid.
    6. Letter to Professor Henry W. Johnstone Jr., 21 March 1972, ibid.
    7. Ibid.
    8. See in particular Todorov (70).
    9. Letter to Raymond Ruyer, 12 July 1958, Chaïm Perelman Archives.

Works Cited and Consulted

Amossy, Ruth. "Nouvelles rhétoriques et linguistique du discours." *Après Perelman: Quelles politiques pour les nouvelles rhétoriques? L'argumentation dans les sciences du langage*. Ed. Roselyne Koren and Ruth Amossy. Paris: L'Harmattan, 2002. 153–71.

Canivet, Michel. "Le principe éthique d'universalité et la discussion." *Chaïm Perelman et la pensée contemporaine*. Ed. Guy Haarscher. Brussels: Bruylant, 1993. 381–99.

Christie, George C. *The Notion of an Ideal Audience in Legal Argument*. Boston: Kluwer Academic, 2000.

———. "The Universal Audience and the Law." *Chaïm Perelman et la pensée contemporaine*. Ed. Guy Haarscher. Brussels: Bruylant, 1993. 43–67.

Crosswhite, James. *The Rhetoric of Reason: Writing and the Attractions of Argument*. Madison: U of Wisconsin P, 1996.

Danblon, Emmanuelle. "La *Nouvelle Rhétorique* de Perelman et la question de l'auditoire universel." *Perelman: Le renouveau de la rhétorique*. Ed. Michel Meyer. Paris: Presses Universitaires de France, 2004. 21–37.

Dominicy, Marc. "Perelman und die Brüsseler Schule." *Die Neue Rhetorik: Studien zu Chaïm Perelman*. Hrsg. Josef Kopperschmidt. Munich: Wilhelm Fink, 2006. 73–133.

Golden, James L. "The Universal Audience Revisited." *Practical Reasoning in Human Affairs: Studies in Honor of Chaïm Perelman*. Ed. James L. Golden and Joseph J. Pilotta. Dordrecht, Holland: D. Reidel, 1986. 287–304.

Gross, Alan G., and Ray D. Dearin. *Chaïm Perelman*. Albany: State U of New York P, 2003.

Haarscher, Guy, ed. *Chaïm Perelman et la pensée contemporaine*. Brussels: Bruylant, 1993.

Koren, Roselyne, and Ruth Amossy, eds. *Après Perelman: Quelles politiques pour les nouvelles rhétoriques: L'argumentation dans les sciences du langage*. Paris: L'Harmattan, 2002.

Lévinas, Emmanuel. *Du sacré au saint: Cinq nouvelles lectures talmudiques*. Paris: Éd. de Minuit, 1977.

Nicolas, Loïc. *La Force de la doxa: Rhétorique de la décision et de la délibération*. Diss. Paris: L'Harmattan, 2007.

Perelman, Chaïm. *Le champ de l'argumentation*. Brussels: Presses Universitaires de Bruxelles, 1970.

———. *Logique et argumentation*. Brussels: Presses Universitaires de Bruxelles, 1971.

———. *Rhétoriques*. Brussels: Presses Universitaires de Bruxelles, 1989.

Chaïm Perelman Archives. Université Libre de Bruxelles, Brussels, Belgium.

Perelman, Chaïm, and Lucie Olbrechts-Tyteca. *The New Rhetoric: A Treatise on Argumentation*. Trans. John Wilkinson and Purcell Weaver. Notre Dame: U of Notre Dame P, 1969.

Ricoeur, Paul. "Langage politique et rhétorique." 1970. *Lectures I: Autour du politique*. Paris: du Seuil, 1999. 161–75.

Tindale, Christopher W. *Rhetorical Argumentation: Principles of Theory and Practice*. Thousand Oaks, CA: Sage, 2004.

Todorov, Tzvetan. *Mikhaïl Bakhtine: Le principe dialogique, suivi de Écrits du Cercle de Bakhtine*. Paris: du Seuil, 1981.

Vannier, Guillaume. *Argumentation et droit: Une introduction à la* Nouvelle rhétorique *de Perelman*. Paris: Presses Universitaires de France, 2001.

6

Lucie Olbrechts-Tyteca's New Rhetoric
David A. Frank and Michelle K. Bolduc

Between 1947 and 1984, Chaïm Perelman and Lucie Olbrechts-Tyteca, both alone and in collaboration, crafted the new rhetoric project. Rhetorical scholars have wondered what contributions Olbrechts-Tyteca made to their 1958 collaboration *Traité de l'argumentation: La nouvelle rhétorique*, a work translated into English in 1969 under the title *The New Rhetoric: A Treatise on Argumentation*.[1] Some believe her contributions to the project have been obscured, overlooked, and neglected. Joseph Marchal argues: "Typically, Perelman is credited with the work of *The New Rhetoric* to the exclusion of Olbrechts-Tyteca. Though all indications lead to their full partnership in the conception research and writing of *The New Rhetoric*, Olbrechts-Tyteca's name and role are literally being written out of the history of rhetoric" (10). He then rectifies this perceived injustice, informing his readers that he will "list the authors in the reverse order to the title page, following the usual alphabetical order of the last names" (10).

In an earlier rendition of Marchal's concern, Robert Scott conducted a rhetorical analysis of Perelman's 1984 reply to the critics of *The New Rhetoric*. Scott faults Perelman for centering on his reputation rather than on ideas (90). In counting the number of "I" pronouns in the reply, Scott observes:

> In the short essay, ten of the forty paragraphs begin with the word "I"; five begin with a very short phrase followed by "I." With an occasional reference to Madame Olbrechts-Tyteca, twice in the opening

pages and the use of the first person plural five times, the focus of the essay becomes *my* work. For example, after beginning a short paragraph with *our* in reference to *The New Rhetoric*, Perelman follows with another short paragraph—a single sentence—that claims that the concept of the "universal audience" from the co-authored book has caused the most misunderstanding among "*my* rhetorical readers." (90, our emphasis)

Alan G. Gross and Ray D. Dearin also note, "For a man so deeply imbued with a sense of justice, [Perelman] may . . . have done an injustice to his long-term collaborator . . . by not specifying her role in the creation of *The New Rhetoric*" (xi).

Others, such as Perelman's successor, Michel Meyer, and Perelman's daughter, Noémi Perelman Mattis, argue that he established the philosophical agenda for the project and should be given credit for the originality of *The New Rhetoric*. Mieczyslaw Maneli, one of Perelman's closest friends, acknowledges Olbrechts-Tyteca in his encomium to the new rhetoric but features Perelman as the prime mover. Barbara Warnick takes a third perspective, holding that Olbrechts-Tyteca played a major role in the development of the examples and middle range theory in their collaboration. There is evidence to support various judgments about the Perelman and Olbrechts-Tyteca collaboration. We devote this essay to a consideration of the roles played by Perelman and Olbrechts-Tyteca in the new rhetoric project, with a focus on Olbrechts-Tyteca's contributions. We also consider the issues raised by scholarly collaborations more generally, a topic neglected in the discussion of Olbrechts-Tyteca's contributions to the new rhetoric project and in the rhetoric literature more generally.

In the first section of this essay, we turn to archival materials on the creation of *The New Rhetoric*, Lucie Olbrechts-Tyteca and Chaïm Perelman's respective histories of the new rhetoric project, and other evidence to suggest there were three new rhetoric projects: one belonging to Perelman, the second to Olbrechts-Tyteca, and the third to the collaboration. The second section of the essay is devoted to Olbrechts-Tyteca's new rhetoric project and builds from Warnick's findings, offering evidence that Olbrechts-Tyteca's major philosophical contribution is an understanding of "the comic of rhetoric." We conclude by suggesting that Perelman and Olbrechts-Tyteca shared a commitment to the rescue of reason in the wake of World War II, that Perelman brought to the collaboration an expertise in philosophy and logic, and that Olbrechts-Tyteca contributed her command of literature, literary criticism, and the comic.

The Nature of Scholarly Collaborations: The New Rhetoric Project

In their definitive treatment of scholarly collaboration, Lisa Ede and Andrea Lunsford avoid casting collaborative writing in binary terms. Indeed, they find "it is not possible or desirable . . . to develop a set of binary opposites that would neatly characterize collaborative writing situations as either hierarchical or dialogical, conservative or subversive, masculine or feminine" (134). In the case of the Perelman and Olbrechts-Tyteca collaboration, Marchal, Gross, Dearin, and Scott do adopt a binary in which Perelman is dominant in the hierarchy. Meyer, Perelman Mattis, Maneli, and others endorse this hierarchy. Gross, Dearin, and Scott question if this hierarchy is just. To move beyond the binary frame, we study the collaboration diachronically and synchronically.

Scholars have relied almost exclusively on *The New Rhetoric* for their speculations about the collaboration, freezing the text as the primary evidence of the collaboration. Even here, the evidence offered by critics about the collaboration is weak. Marchal asserts that "all indications lead to their full partnership" but offers no proof (116). Perelman, Scott argues, overemphasizes his persona, diminishes the role played by Olbrechts-Tyteca in *The New Rhetoric*, and takes credit for the concept of the universal audience. But Scott offers no evidence that the notion of the universal audience was a result of the collaboration and fails to detail the role Olbrechts-Tyteca played in the collaboration or why Perelman, who had published over 130 articles and five books on the new rhetoric when he wrote the reply to his critics in 1983, should not assume a significant persona. Neither does Scott explain why Perelman needed to engage in a significant rehearsal of notions he had developed in a fifty-year career. More telling is Scott's failure to consider the trajectory of Perelman's public scholarship—that Perelman had published many articles and a groundbreaking book before his collaboration with Olbrechts-Tyteca. Nor does he place Perelman in his rhetorical situation or consider the exigencies prompting him to set forth the new rhetoric.

Our criticism of Marchal and Scott does not diminish the importance of Olbrechts-Tyteca's contribution to the new rhetoric project or the significance of the articles and book extending the ideas of the new rhetoric she wrote on her own. We do believe, however, it calls for critics to extend the temporal and contextual frames used in their judgments of collaborations. Warnick has conducted the most careful study to date of the Perelman–Olbrechts-Tyteca collaboration. She found that the Free University of Brussels had very little it could share with her on Olbrechts-Tyteca's background or work on the new rhetoric project. Our research has confirmed her finding. Consequently, Warnick was left with Olbrechts-Tyteca's scholarly texts as the primary source of her analysis. In the analysis of these texts, she came to a more nuanced sense of the collaboration. Perelman, Warnick concluded, did bring to the collaboration an overarching vision of a philosophically grounded rhetoric. Olbrechts-Tyteca brought her understanding of the social sciences and literature and an interest in the comic. Our effort here is meant to build from Warnick's insights but to do so with a consideration of the rhetorical situations in which Perelman and Olbrechts-Tyteca collaborated.

Those who have made judgments about the Perelman and Olbrechts-Tyteca collaboration have remained within a synchronic frame, bracketing the *Traité* as the evidence for their claims. Perelman and Olbrechts-Tyteca both had independent scholarly careers. Both published independent articles and books on the new rhetoric project. To address the questions raised by their collaboration, we need to provide diachronic studies of both scholars, alone and in collaboration. We believe the study of scholarly collaboration should be supplemented with research on the trajectories of the ideas and publications of those involved in collaboration and, when possible, complemented by ethnographic and archival research designed to unveil how a particular collaboration worked. To understand the nature of the Perelman and Olbrechts-Tyteca collaboration, we have their articles and books, the Perelman papers in the archives at the Free University (unfortunately, no files in the archives are dedicated to Olbrechts-Tyteca), and reports about the nature of the collaboration.

To understand the scholarly trajectory of Perelman's, one must appreciate his context, topics addressed in his publications, and his temperament. Perelman's exigencies included the crisis of twentieth-century anti-Semitism and totalitarianism. The Nazis murdered 23,000 Belgian Jews, a fate Perelman narrowly escaped. Perelman helped to found the Comité de Défense des Juifs (Committee for the Defense of the Jews—CDJ) and was a major leader of this group, which was responsible for saving the lives of many Belgian Jews. That Perelman, a Jew, contributed to the defeat of Hitler and National Socialism and then achieved public success and international fame as a scholar after the war may have served as an existential claim for him that Judaism had not only survived but also triumphed. Indeed, Perelman was significantly influenced by Jewish thought. The new rhetoric project draws on Talmudic reasoning to develop a counter model to Western rationalism.

Perelman sought out and accepted leadership roles in the Belgian Resistance, Jewish and scholarly organizations, and the United Nations Educational, Scientific and Cultural Organization and also administrative positions within his university. King Baudouin of Belgium awarded Perelman the title "Baron." The ambition driving him to achieve public attention and recognition cannot be reduced to raw egotism, for he saw himself as representing the intellectual vitality of the Jewish people and an enactment of philosophy of "dual loyalty," that European Jews could be faithful citizens of European nation-states and committed Jews. Perelman's acceptance of tokens of esteem and his claim on the new rhetoric project might be explained by his need to triumph, as a representative of the Jewish people, over the Holocaust and the Nazis. Regardless, a close reading of his scholarship suggests that he introduced the philosophical framework of the new rhetoric project and many of its key notions as a response to the traumas of the Holocaust and World War II. And it could be that Olbrechts-Tyteca was his first audience for these notions: her responses might have influenced the development of the new rhetoric's touchstones.

Perelman published over 150 single-authored articles between 1931 and 1984, many in major scholarly journals. These works respond to questions raised by European and American scholars in the first part of the twentieth century. They span a host of topics and reflect the trajectory of his thinking. Perelman reports that his intellectual development began with an embrace of logical positivism in 1929, the same year the Vienna Circle's manifesto was published (*New Rhetoric and the Humanities* 55). His articles between 1931 and 1947 reflect this philosophical frame, although there are clear hints that he was ready to critique and move beyond logical positivism.

Between 1931 and 1947, Perelman wrote on a multitude of topics, including paradox, antinomies, axiology, judgment, knowledge, definitions, methodology, liberty, democracy, freedom, choice, and justice; he devoted monographs to Friedrich Nietzsche, Eugène Dupréel, and Bertrand Russell; he penned a dissertation on Gottlob Frege's logic and articles on the Jewish question in Europe. His first book, *De la justice*, which he wrote while in the underground during the war and finished in August 1944, embraced logical positivism and stipulated that reason did not play a role in value disputes. Perelman was "deeply dissatisfied" with the conclusion he reached in this book that logical positivism could not inform the *vita activa* but was limited to the *vita contemplativa*, leaving value choices to the irrational and violence. With the tragedy of the Holocaust and the Nazi movement in mind, Perelman wrote that it "was . . . difficult to be resigned to positivism which declared equally arbitrary all value judgments, when our whole being revolted against totalitarian ideologies, which scoffed at the dignity of man, and the fundamental values of our civilization, liberty and reason" (*New Rhetoric and the Humanities* 55). Perelman's dissatisfaction with the conclusions in *De la justice* was the exigence for the new rhetoric project, and Perelman embarked on a search for a system of nonformal reasoning appropriate for values (see Frank).

Small spiral notebooks in the archives at the Free University, dated 1944 to 1947, contain notes Perelman took of the books and articles he read as he sought to address the limitations of logical positivism. Perelman decided to "follow the method adopted by . . . Frege," who studied the reasoning used by mathematicians, and to do the same in the analysis of those who reason about values. Perelman sought to examine the reasons used by judges, moralists, and others who had to deliberate on issues related to policy and action. Olbrechts-Tyteca joined him in his project in 1947. Soon after, she and Perelman made their "rhetorical turn."

Perelman and Olbrechts-Tyteca's ten-year collaboration effectively ended in 1958, with a brief reprise in 1983. After 1958, Perelman aggressively promoted the new rhetoric, securing after much effort Italian and English translations of the *Traité*. In his post-1958 work, he continued to develop the new rhetoric as a system of reasoning analogous to that found in law. He sought a nonformal system of logic and viewed his work as squarely in the philosophical tradition. Unlike in Olbrechts-Tyteca's writing, Perelman's solitary writings did not draw from literature in any significant manner. The footnotes in his solitary works are to authors familiar to continental philosophers, including Aristotle, Kant, Spinoza, Vilfredo Pareto, Henri Bergson, and the like. His solitary work after 1958 lacks the blending of the philosophical with the literary and the emphasis on the comic, both traits marking his collaboration with Olbrechts-Tyteca. The Perelman archives demonstrate that he assumed sole responsibility for establishing the case for and seeking an English translation of the Traité, a long and protracted process that lasted over eight years. Olbrechts-Tyteca did not seek the limelight, nor does her solitary work concern itself with the philosophical or legal orientation taken by Perelman. Her path to the *Traité* was from literature, with some background in statistics.

Olbrechts-Tyteca was ten years older than Perelman and married to Raymond Olbrechts, head of the statistics department at the Free University of Brussels. Her family was affluent, and her father was a noted psychiatrist. Both Perelman and Olbrechts-Tyteca had Eugène Dupréel as an instructor at the Free University. Olbrechts-Tyteca was a licentiate in the social sciences, which is equivalent to a master's degree in the United States. Perelman and Olbrechts-Tyteca met during World War II, and their first collaboration was against the Nazi occupiers. Olbrechts-Tyteca assisted Fela Perelman (wife of Chaïm) and the CDJ as a committee "godmother" for displaced Jewish children. During the war, Olbrechts-Tyteca worked at the Brabant division of the Belgian League Against Tuberculosis where, according to Lucien Steinberg, she employed a member of the CDJ. Noémi Perelman Mattis reports that Olbrechts-Tyteca falsified positive reports of tuberculosis to protect Jewish children.

With the exception of an article Olbrechts-Tyteca wrote in collaboration with P. Fonteyne in 1950 on radioscopic examination, her scholarly productivity begins with her collaboration with Perelman. Perelman had fifty articles and a book before he and Olbrechts-Tyteca published their first collaborative article in 1950. Olbrechts-Tyteca published four single-authored scholarly articles and one book, which all flowed from the agenda set by the new rhetoric project. It is clear as well that Olbrechts-Tyteca developed an independent trajectory of thought within the larger constellation of the new rhetoric project, although one emanating from an agenda and framework established by Perelman.

Warnick provides ample evidence that Olbrechts-Tyteca's "contribution to *The New Rhetoric* was that of analyst and conceptualizer" (82). She brought to the collaboration a keen interest in literature drawn from German, French, English, Italian, Spanish, and Jewish literary sources, including Laurence Sterne's *The Life and Opinions of Tristram Shandy*, Miguel de Cervantes's *Don Quixote*, Lewis Carroll's *Alice's Adventures in Wonderland*, Virgil Gheorghiu's *The Twenty Fifth Hour*, Marcel Jouhandeau's *Un monde* and *De la grandeur*, and François Mauriac's *Le mystère frontenac* and *Les maisons fugitives*, all of which found their way into the *Traité*. Indeed, the rhetorical turn of the collaboration was a result of Olbrechts-Tyteca's familiarity with the work of literary theorist Jean Paulhan. Perelman and Olbrechts-Tyteca's first publication appeared in 1950, in *Revue philosophique*, under the title "Logique et rhétorique."

After the war, sometime in 1947, Perelman and Olbrechts-Tyteca were at a dinner party where Perelman discussed his postwar research on the discovery of an expression of reason for the *vita activa*. She joined him at that point. Over a thirty-three-year period, Perelman and Olbrechts-Tyteca published seven articles and two books. All but one article and both books were published between 1950 and 1958. Their last article, published in 1983, was a celebration of the career of Vilfredo Pareto, the Italian economist, from whom Perelman and Olbrechts-Tyteca borrowed freely for their theory of argument. Olbrechts-Tyteca recounts how she and Perelman began the new rhetoric project:

> Memories are also a confession: Ch. Perelman and I were, at the beginning of our research, almost as ignorant of rhetoric as learned men of the twentieth century could be. Philosopher and logician, a doctor in law as well, Perelman had dedicated the best of his scholarly activity to

> formal logic and analytical philosophy. As for me, I had a background based in the social sciences, economic sciences, rather good notions of psychology, and I had practiced statistical research. If I insist on what we were, it is because it seems to me sometimes important to remind myself that we were neither classical philosophers, nor historians, nor literary critics, and that our enthusiasm cannot have been at any moment that of a specialist happy to enlarge the import of his discipline. Let us say that to no degree, neither by profession nor by taste, was rhetoric dear to us. ("Rencontre" 3)[2]

Olbrechts-Tyteca then describes the problem they were trying to solve:

> In reality, toward the end of the war Perelman had written his study on *Justice* where he extended, as far as was possible, the distinction between formal logic and value reasoning. To do such an analysis for other confused notions attracted him greatly. But it seemed to him, on the other hand, that the vast domain of values and norms that these analyses would certainly highlight would remain vague and unexplored so long as we limited ourselves to affirming that values have a role in our lives without knowing how to talk about them or how to adhere to them. (3)

Here, Olbrechts-Tyteca explains Perelman's role in setting the agenda for the new rhetoric project: the exigence for their scholarly collaboration was Perelman's dissatisfaction with logical positivism.

Olbrechts-Tyteca then describes how Perelman, "struck by the success" of Frege's methodological empiricism, thought it proper to study the logic of value judgments in a similar manner. She notes: "The research Perelman proposed was not a concern of experimental psychology," a field that had intrigued Olbrechts-Tyteca. Like Perelman, she was interested in rational behavior. Their collaboration was designed to seek an expression of nonformal reason intended for a world of ambiguity and incomplete information.

In search of literature on nonformal logic, they read or reread Théodule Ribot's *Logique des sentiments*, Gabriel Tarde's *Logique sociale*, Edmond Goblot's *Logique des jugements de valeurs*, Boris B. Bogoslovsky's *The Technique of Controversy*, Frédéric Paulhan's *La logique de la contradiction*, André Lalande's *La Raison et les Normes*, Ferdinand Gonseth's *L'idée de dialectique*, and the work of Harold Lasswell on propaganda. This literature was useful, but Perelman and Olbrechts-Tyteca found that it constituted "only a relaxing of logic, not the exploration of a domain" (Olbrechts-Tyteca, "Rencontre" 4–5). They purchased editions of the *Moniteur*, the record of debates in the Belgian parliament, in search of examples and illustrations of the logic used in argumentation. The first concrete study of argument conducted by Perelman and Olbrechts-Tyteca was their close reading of MP Richard Crossman's 1 July 1945 speech, delivered before the British parliament. "Desiring a way to put our hands in the dough," Olbrechts-Tyteca wrote, "and in the name of preliminary experience, we had proceeded to the minutely detailed discourse of Crossman relative to English politics in Palestine" ("Rencontre" 4). Crossman, who had spent 120 days as a member of the Anglo-American Committee of Inquiry in study of the British Mandate, used this speech to urge Parliament to allow more Jewish immigration into Palestine and to condemn Foreign Minister Ernest Bevin's British policy of severely restricting Jewish immigration. Crossman, Olbrechts-Tyteca continued,

> seemed excellent to us; the material was sufficiently well known so that we could seize the intentions. The foreign idiom offered the danger of creating illusion: one knows that the sleeping metaphor often appears too alive to the novice reader. But these illusions were born, undoubtedly, from too much attention. They had, for an exploratory attempt, more advantages than disadvantages.
>
> We were also convinced that there were in this text many arguments [that were] not concerned with formal logic that should have a certain weight with listeners—indeed for a strict logician like Perelman, [there was] not a single one.
>
> One could discern, in addition, that no nuance of expression was immaterial, nor no disposition of statements. It seemed thus certain that important factors relative to the order, to the person, to the use of concepts, analogies, were taken *rationally* in the consideration of the listening of such a discourse. ("Rencontre" 5)

The choice of Crossman and his speech on Palestine was not a coincidence as Perelman and his wife were deeply involved in activities designed to promote Zionism, although they were aligned with the more moderate expressions of the movement, in particular that of the Anglophile Chaïm Weizman. Crossman made use of a number of claims in his address that Perelman and Olbrechts-Tyteca would later use to develop the notions of pragmatic argument, composite audience, and quasi-logical expressions of reason.

After this study, Olbrechts-Tyteca records:

> It was almost chance that, at this moment, put before us classical rhetoric. I liked the books of Jean Paulhan, *Les fleurs de Tarbes*, notably. There in its appendix were some extracts of Brunetto Latini, which showed an ancient author who also wondered about problems relative to arguments of discourse. And if he wondered about them, it was not

in a private capacity, but because others had done it before him. From there, to go back to the great classical tradition and notably to the Aristotle of the *Topiques* and the *Rhétorique*, there was only a [single] step.

But if the idea of drawing our research on non-formal logic—what we began to designate "argumentation" so as to oppose it to "demonstration"—closer to the rhetorical tradition did not put us off from the beginning, it is probably because our teacher E. Dupréel had brought to light the value of the Sophists and had familiarized us with the worth of the opinable. Beyond Aristotle, we were not ashamed to rejoin Gorgias. ("Rencontre" 5–6)

Perelman corroborates Olbrechts-Tyteca's account, calling their reading of *Les fleurs de Tarbes* a "revelation" prompting his rhetorical turn. From Paulhan, Perelman and Olbrechts-Tyteca derived the need for a "reinvented" or a new rhetoric, the value of clichés and commonplaces (which in turn lead to the recovery of Aristotle's epideictic), and the two key topoi in the new rhetoric project, the classical and romantic.

Their turn to rhetoric was intended to redeem the promise of reason, one that had been unduly restricted by logical positivism, and to affect a rapprochement between rhetoric and reason. Their first article, "Logique et rhétorique," provides a justification for and an outline of their 1958 magnum opus. After the publication of "Logique et rhétorique," Perelman and Olbrechts-Tyteca collaborated on their first English-language article in 1951, "Act and Person in Argument," which was published, at the suggestion of Richard McKeon, in the University of Chicago journal *Ethics*. They published their first book, *Rhétorique et philosophie: Pour une théorie de l'argumentation en philosophie*, in 1952. The book consisted of five chapters, the first being the "Logique et rhétorique" article and the second "Act and Person in Argument." The other chapters were based on articles Perelman had published in the aftermath of the war.

The six journal articles Perelman and Olbrechts-Tyteca wrote between 1947 and 1958 were either folded into the two books or served as significant elaborations of themes introduced in the books. Over this eleven-year period, Perelman and Olbrechts-Tyteca worked toward the completion of their major work dealing with rhetoric and argumentation. Perelman set forth the purpose of this work in a 1952 article titled "Raison éternelle, raison historique," observing: "A treatise of argumentation, that would attract attention to the argumentative use of reason, will allow one to show that the criticism directed at strict rationalism, that which recognizes only analytical proofs, is worth nothing for a rationalism that makes a place for dialectical proofs as well" (353). This treatise, he continues, would develop Aristotle's dialectical proofs, doing so by assuming that human beings are endowed with reason and are essentially reasonable beings. Perelman saw rhetoric capable of achieving the aspirations of the philosopher. The philosophically grounded rhetorician

> would follow the prescriptions of Kant's categorical imperative: he wants his premises and his reasoning to be valid for the community of reasonable minds, for the universal audience. Even if the theses of the philosopher are mystical, their philosophical defense aims at the universal. This aim is the sole criterion of rational argumentation, of which one finds the most beautiful models in philosophical thought. In his argumentation, the philosopher addresses the universal audience, whose historical characteristic we have seen. The theses that this audience is supposed to accept, the places that it prefers, the examples and the analogies that inspire it, vary in time. And if philosophers summon this audience, it is always in order to modify one or the other accepted theses by depending on other accepted theses that serve as a lever in argumentation. It is in this way that philosophy is doubly precious for historical reason, both because philosophy reveals it to us, in formulating it, and because philosophy modifies it. ("Raison éternelle" 353)

This article is the first citation in *Traité de l'argumentation*, for it establishes the philosophical touchstones for the book and the new rhetoric project.

Perelman and Olbrechts-Tyteca devoted ten years to the *Traité*. Perelman's daughter, who witnessed the collaboration, reports that her father's relationship with Olbrechts-Tyteca was formal, with Perelman addressing her as Madame Olbrechts-Tyteca and Olbrechts-Tyteca calling him Professor Perelman. Olbrechts-Tyteca gathered many examples of argumentation, placing them on note cards. Perelman, in an August 1973 letter to Italian scholar Letizia Gianformaggio Bastida, described how the *Traité* was written (Mattis). Perelman wrote the first draft, and Olbrechts-Tyteca followed with her editing and contributions. In a 22 May 1969 letter to Perelman, Ray Dearin, who wrote the first dissertation on *The New Rhetoric*, asked, "I would like to know exactly what role your colleague, Madame Olbrechts-Tyteca, played in the writing of the *Traité de l'argumentation: La nouvelle rhétorique*. Did you and she collaborate on the whole treatise, or did each of you contribute certain sections independently? If so, which sections did each of you write?" Perelman responded on 27 May with this answer: "Mrs. Olbrechts-Tyteca, who is no philosopher but who studied sociology and literature, [wrote] the Treatise together with me, most of the sections having been re-written by both of us." In an earlier letter, Perelman recommended Olbrechts-Tyteca's history of the new rhetoric project to Dearin.

The evidence in the text of the *Traité* is strong that the philosophical rhetoric Perelman developed in a host of single-authored articles between 1948 and 1958 established the foundation of the new rhetoric project. In particular, "First Philosophies and Regressive Philosophy" is the linchpin for the approach taken in their larger work. The four articles he wrote in collaboration with Olbrechts-Tyteca were also of great importance. Warnick celebrates the role played by Olbrechts-Tyteca, finding that her input as an analyst and conceptualizer allowed her to make a contribution to the analysis of argument structure and to provide the examples Perelman needed for a grounded philosophical rhetoric (71, 82–83). In fact, based on her examination of Olbrechts-Tyteca's use of dissociation and philosophical pairs in *Le comique du discours* and in her article "Les pairs philosophiques," Warnick declares that Olbrechts-Tyteca "was a major contributor" to the *Traité* (70).

However, Warnick's analysis may understate Olbrechts-Tyteca's contribution: her conclusions that Olbrechts-Tyteca's analysis of discursive comic schemes is "painstaking" and "often overworked" (73) and that Olbrechts-Tyteca is "a middle-level theorist" (83) may not give sufficient weight to the notion of the "comic," one we believe she contributed to the new rhetoric project, suggesting she was deeply involved in the global philosophy of that project. We believe that if Olbrechts-Tyteca's post-*Traité* work on the comic is considered, she might be recognized as having developed a major philosophical pillar in the new rhetoric project, one that was underdeveloped in the *Traité*.

The Comic in Argumentation

Olbrechts-Tyteca worked ten years on *Le comique du discours*, which was published in 1974 by the Free University of Brussels.[3] Perelman wrote a short preface. Our reading of her *Comique* offers a snapshot of Olbrechts-Tyteca's contribution to the new rhetoric project, particularly in the *Traité*. Perhaps more important, *Le comique* also unveils how Olbrechts-Tyteca's elaboration of the comic broadens the new rhetoric project.

The significance of the comic for both the *Traité* and *Le comique du discours* reflects the importance of Henri Bergson, the profoundly influential French philosopher. Perelman and Olbrechts-Tyteca imported key Bergsonian notions into the new rhetoric project, including his ideas on time and, moreover, on the meaning of the comic.[4] Bergson locates the essence of the human in the comic, endorsing the definition of human as "an animal which laughs" (3). Bergson here distinguishes the inanimate landscape, which is incapable of laughter and the comic, from the human, which is capable of humor. Following this Bergsonian insight, we might say that if the human being reasoning is the linchpin of the *Traité*, the human laughing is the complement developed by Olbrechts-Tyteca in *Le comique*.

Olbrechts-Tyteca's notion of "*le comique de la rhétorique*" (the comic of rhetoric) follows the distinction made previously in the *Traité* and differentiates a comic *of* rhetoric, which is the object and thesis of her study, from a comic *in* rhetoric ("*le comique dans la rhétorique*") (Perelman and Olbrechts-Tyteca, *Traité* 188). The comic *in* rhetoric, she notes, may be a result of how the speaker establishes a rapport with the audience—how a speaker might animate his or her speech for a tired audience, relax a tense atmosphere, or make a speech whose content is unpleasant pleasant for the listeners. While this comic in rhetoric can combine with rhetorical processes, it is not itself concerned with the schemas of argumentation. On the other hand, the comic *of* rhetoric can be discerned by its object: the conditions and frames of argumentation, the schemas of argumentation that can be discerned by the audience (*Comique* 7). The essential point of the comic of rhetoric is, then, argumentation and, more precisely, its form (structures, schemas, and processes) rather than its content (29). Moreover, marked by ambiguity, temporality, and unrestrictive conclusions, the comic is a matter of argumentation rather than demonstration (42–43).

That Olbrechts-Tyteca's definition of a comic *of* (rather than *in*) rhetoric derives from the *Traité* provides an initial clue to the way in which her collaboration with Perelman was significant for her own work. Olbrechts-Tyteca is careful to detail the important influence of the new rhetoric project on her own. She points to her collaborative work with Perelman frequently: forty-four references to the *Traité* and four references to their collaborative article on temporality appear both within the body and in the notes of *Le comique du discours*. (By contrast, she makes only twelve references to Perelman's work and even fewer—only five—to her own work.) She asserts that the new rhetoric project invites further research: "As regards the theory of argumentation, this study has shown that the schemas of analysis that we drew out in our *Traité* lend themselves to closely related research" (*Comique* 393). Moreover, she very clearly lays out how her *Comique du discours* follows the argumentative exposition of the *Traité*:

> Our plan of study will also be an exposition. For the reader who knows *Traité de l'argumentation: La nouvelle rhétorique,* it will be an advantage. It seems to us now that the regressive method (many others of which could have been used instead) we used there responded—perhaps without our being completely aware of it—to an imperative felt by all the sciences at that time to adopt a genetic classification, meaning in the broadest sense a classification in which the different types of

> objects are produced, as it were, from each other. Our chapters correspond to a successive deepening of what is given. We do not see at the current time any valid reason to adopt another method. (22–23)

This passage amplifies the immense influence that her collaboration with Perelman had on Olbrechts-Tyteca, so that even the very structure of her book seems informed by their collaborative work. It is no surprise, then, that such statements as "argumentation is always likely to become comic" and "all the elements of rhetoric can be and are comical objects" derive from their *Traité*, where she and Perelman declare, for example, that every procedure, including those of rhetoric, can easily become a source of the comic (*Comique* 43, 393; see also *Traité* 253; *New Rhetoric* 188).

In his preface to Olbrechts-Tyteca's *Le comique du discours*, Perelman explicitly declares it to be an outgrowth of their collaboration. He begins by stressing that while *Le comique du discours* can be viewed within the context of theories on laughter, it makes an essential contribution to the theory of argumentation. He writes, "Indeed, the present study is essentially a contribution to the general theory of argumentation; if it undoubtedly contains interesting material for a general theory of comedy, it is only in addition to the former" (5). He also declares *Le comique du discours* to be a continuation of the *Traité*: "The present work thus constitutes an extension of the *Traité de l'argumentation*, the enumerations, classifications, and terminology of which it resumes, all the while enriching it by numerous analyses, always accompanied by concrete and delightful examples" (5). What we learn from this is twofold: that Olbrechts-Tyteca made use of the system of argumentation and its structural, lexical, and classificatory devices developed in their *Traité*, and that Olbrechts-Tyteca's work, according to Perelman, enriches their new rhetoric project.

Olbrechts-Tyteca's description of the comic of rhetoric in *Le comique* allows us to better grasp just how Perelman and Olbrechts-Tyteca's new rhetoric project features the comic as a rhetoric that confuses, denies the search of clear definitions and categories, and allows notions that appear to be in contradiction to coexist. The comic, they assert in a striking passage of the *Traité*, is an important key to understanding argumentative processes:

> We will resort to comic examples to clarify our analysis. We do not believe that a study of the comic in the art of oratory is a direct matter of our topic—even though the comic may be a very important factor for winning over the audience or more generally for affirming a likeness between the speaker and the listener, for reducing value, notably to ridicule the opponent, to bring about timely distractions.

But our interest will not be brought to bear so much on the comic *in* rhetoric than on the comic *of* rhetoric. We mean by this the comical use of some types of argumentation. If, as we believe, there is a comic of rhetoric, the comical elements can help us to uncover certain argumentative processes, which in their ordinary and common form are more difficult to discern. Every procedure can easily become a source of the comic; the procedures of rhetoric certainly cannot avoid this. In some cases, does not the comic effect result precisely from finding what one believes to be usual processes of reasoning distorted for the occasion, or from the use of such an argumentative scheme, whether it is untimely, excessive, or clumsy? (*Traité* 253; *New Rhetoric* 188)

That the comic appears here as they explain their methodology is suggestive. We cannot be but struck by the abrupt nature of the shift as they move from declaring that they will use humorous illustrations as examples directly into a discussion, seemingly digressive, of the comic of argumentation. This is a salient point: although they pronounce the comic as ostensibly tangential to the new rhetoric project, they simultaneously suggest that it is the comic that can disclose processes of argumentation otherwise hidden in customary—that is, serious—rhetoric. This sudden move reveals both the underlying importance of the comic in their work and, moreover, how the comic serves as a key marker of their collaboration.

A quick glance at the table of contents of the *Traité* would hardly signal the significance that the comic plays therein; only "The Ridiculous" figures as a chapter heading. And yet, if the comic is somewhat ancillary to the schemes of argumentation in the *Traité*, a potential outcome of argumentative *praxes* (*Traité* 253; *New Rhetoric* 188), Perelman and Olbrechts-Tyteca nevertheless make frequent reference to how the comic can arise by means of various argumentative techniques in the *Traité*.

The easiest and most expansive place to find the comic in the *Traité* appears in Perelman and Olbrechts-Tyteca's discussion of the use of "the ridiculous" in quasi-logical arguments (see *Traité* 276; *New Rhetoric* 205). The discussion of the ridiculous and irony in the *Traité* serves as a bridge between the general theory of argument techniques outlined in chapter 3 and the introduction of an informal logic. This bridge is key, as it enacts both the theory of rhetoric and the praxis of argumentation that Perelman and Olbrechts-Tyteca develop.

Tellingly, they declare that "it is the ridiculous . . . which is the principal weapon of argumentation," continuing that "[t]he ridiculous is what deserves to be greeted by laughter" (*Traité* 276; *New Rhetoric* 205). They then cite Dupréel's notion of exclusive laughter, "a response to the breaking of an accepted rule," to flesh out the definition of the ridiculous (*Traité* 276; *New*

Rhetoric 205). Ridicule leads to action—laughter that can endorse or punish rule-breaking. Recall that rhetoric for Perelman and Olbrechts-Tyteca deals with the vagaries of time—Bergson's *durée*. This theme yokes freedom to reason and confronts the pretensions of ideological thinking through ridicule and irony. An argument can earn ridicule, Perelman and Olbrechts-Tyteca note, if it challenges without good reason a well-accepted opinion. Ridicule can be used as well for those who do not accept the reasonable premise held by the audience. The audience might also dismiss the arguments of an advocate because his or her conclusions are ridiculous. As an example of this, Perelman and Olbrechts-Tyteca cite Richard Whately's ridicule of the methods of biblical criticism as a comic attempt at a *reductio ad absurdum*: in an anonymous pamphlet, Whately deduced ridiculously that if the same standards used to assess the historical veracity of the Bible were used to determine the historical existence of Napoleon Bonaparte, one could prove that even Napoleon did not exist (*Traité* 278–79; *New Rhetoric* 207).

One prominent expression of ridicule, Perelman and Olbrechts-Tyteca continue, is irony. They illustrate irony with a statement made by Paul Reynaud in 1950 that neutrality had "twice served Belgium so well" (*Traité* 279; *New Rhetoric* 208). In context, Reynaud meant the exact opposite—that Belgian neutrality in both wars had not saved the country from war and occupation. The juxtaposition of the historical reality with the proposition invites a comical response.

In addition, the use of the comic also allows the collaborators to ridicule the pretensions of apodictic logic. They draw from Laurence Sterne's eighteenth-century comic novel *Tristram Shandy* to illustrate how abuse or ignorance of rules can lead to the ridiculous. A key illustration taken from Sterne's novel was an argument made by a grandson that he was justified in sleeping with his grandmother:

> "But whoever thought," cried Kysarcius, "of lying with his grandmother?"
>
> "The young gentleman," replied Yorick, "whom Shelden speaks of, who not only thought of it, but justified his intention to his father by the argument drawn from the law of retaliation. 'You lay, sir, with my mother,' said the lad. 'Why may not I lie with yours?' 'Tis the argumentum commune," added Yorick. (qtd. in *Traité* 304; *New Rhetoric* 226)

Perelman and Olbrechts-Tyteca use this exchange to note that the validity of an argument of reciprocity is dependent on a rhetorical situation, not on the decontextualized abstractions of principles and rules favored by analytic philosophers.

The "comic of rhetoric" motif is underdeveloped in the *Traité*, and yet it does capture the philosophical theme Perelman and Olbrechts-Tyteca use to differentiate demonstration from argumentation, apodictic logic from nonformal reasoning, and the *vita contemplativa* from the *vita activa*. Olbrechts-Tyteca, some sixteen years after the publication of the *Traité*, published her work on the rhetoric of the comic and made use of the argumentative schemes she and Perelman developed in the *Traité* to offer a robust analysis.

More important, if *Le comique du discours* derives from their collaborative work, both Perelman and Olbrechts-Tyteca describe *Le comique du discours* as expanding the frame of the new rhetoric project. Perelman, for example, concludes his preface by suggesting that the comic is tied to rhetoric as a man to his shadow; as he writes, "the comic accompanies, as its shadow, the whole field of discourse" (*Comique* 5). Perelman's statement is instructive, and not only because one may be tempted to read in his evocative description of the comic as the "shadow" (*ombre*) of rhetorical study an example of Perelman's "inclination to assume ownership of the [new rhetoric] project," as Warnick has described their collaboration (69). First, by declaring that the comic accompanies rhetoric, he acknowledges the important role that the comic has to play in the study of argumentation generally and in the new rhetoric project more specifically. Moreover, he also implies that *Le comique du discours* may be seen as a companion piece to the *Traité*.

Olbrechts-Tyteca thus surprises the reader with the frank avowal of how in her methodology the comic came first and was then followed by its connection to rhetoric: "We do not hide from ourselves the fact that quite often laughter at random in meetings and lectures came first, and then its association with a rhetorical scheme" (*Comique* 23). Just when the reader may be tempted to attribute this initial attraction for the comic to a simple lack of rhetorical gravitas, Olbrechts-Tyteca continues with an implicit criticism of how the comic is infrequently an object of study for rhetoric. For Olbrechts-Tyteca, theorists of rhetoric have too often disregarded the importance of the comic of rhetoric (23). Indeed, she wonders if the first studies of rhetoric were not in fact offshoots of the comic, speculating that the "first rhetorics" might have been "born of the comic" (398).

What is striking about these assertions is just how much she sees her study as not only extending but indeed transforming the conclusions of the *Traité*, and even the new rhetoric project more generally. While again affirming how the structure of her work takes up that of the *Traité*, Olbrechts-Tyteca seems to expect the latter to be modified by her *Comique du discourse* by returning to an

> argumentative framework, argumentative schemes—that we described in our treatise on argumentation, to see the hold that the comic has on them. Doubtlessly, this will tie our study to a theory of argumentation, itself subject to revision.... The existence of these schemes and their classifying is not certain. But the study of their comic use will have as an effect a clarification of rhetoric, just as pathology can clarify what is normal. And if our previous work must find itself modified from it, so much the better. (*Comique* 22)

Olbrechts-Tyteca underscores how the comic is integral to the new rhetoric project, indicating that her work shores up the *Traité* by suggesting that a reader might laugh even while reading a treatise on argumentation: "Even a treatise on argumentation can provoke laughter" (44).

Olbrechts-Tyteca's elaboration of the comic may be seen as broadening the *Traité*'s philosophical conclusions. Examining the *Traité* in light of *Le comique*, we find that the conception of audience is one rhetorical notion that finds itself expanded under Olbrechts-Tyteca's influence: the focus on ridicule, exclusive laughter, and irony highlights the role of the audience in argumentation. The audience is free to laugh at those who either break or follow rules, as argumentation, unlike demonstration, allows for ambiguity and free play within the paratactic structure of discourse. The "comic of rhetoric" pervades the *Traité*'s conceptualization of audience. For example, the authors turn once again to *Tristram Shandy* to develop their theory of audience. They write:

> In *Tristram Shandy*—since argumentation is one of the main themes of this book, we shall often refer to it—Tristram describes an argument between his parents, in which his father wants to persuade his mother to have a midwife: "He ... placed his arguments in all lights; argued the matter with her like a Christian, like a heathen, like a husband, like a father, like a patriot, like a man. My mother answered everything only like a woman, which was a little hard upon her, for, as she could not assume and fight it out behind such a variety of characters, 'twas no fair match: 'twas seven to one." (*Traité* 29; *New Rhetoric* 22)

The more serious point they derive from this humorous example is the need for the speaker to develop several lines of argumentation for the composite audience, one made of disparate groups.

Although the universal audience—rhetoric's equivalent to Kant's categorical imperative—was Perelman's idea, Olbrechts-Tyteca's work on the comic broadens the *Traité*'s premises on the universal audience (*Traité* 40–46; *New Rhetoric* 31–35). In the *Traité*, the universal audience is already a nuanced idea: their concept of such an audience recognizes that individual audiences might have different values. "Every argumentation that aims at a particular audience has the disadvantage that the speaker, insofar as he adapts to the views of his listeners, risks depending upon arguments that are unfamiliar or even clearly opposed to those accepted by people other than those that he is presently addressing" (*Traité* 40; *New Rhetoric* 31). However, in *Le comique du discours*, Olbrechts-Tyteca realizes that her theory of the discursive comic complicates even the very definition of the universal audience, and she posits that our understanding of the universal audience would be enriched by a consideration of it in terms of the rhetoric of the comic (see also Warnick 78).

In answer to her question, "Does the universal audience laugh?" she answers:

> We conclude that the more that the universal audience is made accessible by means of the comic of rhetoric, the richer our perspective of this audience will be. When we have an example of laughter released by the comic of rhetoric, we would do well to ask ourselves often to what extent we think that the universal audience would laugh about it. This would perhaps help us to have a better idea of this audience. (*Comique* 412)

Olbrechts-Tyteca not only develops and extends the concept of the universal audience but also, through the comic, offers a vision of argumentation that hinges on a deep sense of humanity. This is not altogether absent in the *Traité*; however, in the view of Olbrechts-Tyteca, the concept of the universal audience hinges on arguments *ad humanitatem*. She suggests that laughter itself comprises a wish for universalization and human communion that is also inherent to the concept of the universal audience. As a result, she argues, we can understand the whole of the rhetoric of comedy in the universal audience: "The human desire for the universality of laughter causes us to attribute to the universal audience the whole of the rhetoric of comedy. . . . It is perhaps our pure impulse for human communion that spurs us to laugh" (*Comique* 407–12, esp. 410).

The philosophical agenda Perelman established, the search for a sense of reason beyond formal logic, finds an answer in the sense of the comic suggested and developed by Olbrechts-Tyteca. For her, laughter procures the willingness of the listener to listen and, potentially, to adhere to the speaker's argument: "One of the primordial aspects that distinguishes argumentation from demonstration is that argumentation assumes a minimum of good will on the part of the listener. . . . Laughter reminds us that this good will is the very condition of dialogue" (*Comique* 415–16). The comic thus provides the framework necessary for true dialogue and the creation of the universal audience, and consequently for the effective practice of argumentation.

We can trace literary monuments of the comic as important markers of Olbrechts-Tyteca's role in, and expansion of, the collaborative new rhetoric project. She declares explicitly in *Le comique du discours* that such works of literature as *Tristram Shandy* and *Don Quixote* generate the ludic, which is prepared and evoked from their very first lines (35). Indeed, she sees such a comedic literature as *Don Quixote* as exemplifying the whole of the rhetoric of comedy: in a passage in which she explains how her conception of allegory as analogy differs from that of Arthur Schopenhauer's, she declares, "What makes us laugh, I think, is not allegory, even as Schopenhauer understands it. The comic aspect of *Don Quixote* is not that of analogy, or metaphor, or allegory. It is rather the comic of rhetoric in its entirety" (319).

Such literary monuments of the comic as *Tristram Shandy* and *Don Quixote*, whose brief appearances in the *Traité* are transformed and elaborated in *Le comique du discours*, function as important markers of Olbrechts-Tyteca's new rhetoric. Consider *Don Quixote*, which is quoted twice in the *Traité*. First, Perelman and Olbrechts-Tyteca refer to a speech from Sancho Panza in Cervantes's work as an example of how argumentation by causal link—where proof of an event is made by its cause, and vice versa—may be made ludicrous: "'Holy God!' shouted Sancho. 'Is it possible that there are in the world enchanters and enchantments so strong that they have turned my master's good sense into foolishness and madness?'" (Cervantes 112–13). Perelman and Olbrechts-Tyteca comment that the comic here arises from the antinomy between the interpretation of the event by its cause and the interpretation of the cause by the event (*Traité* 356–57; *New Rhetoric* 265). Similarly, they later quote *Don Quixote* as a comic example of the juxtaposition of *phoroi*: "For the knight errant without a lady is like a tree without leaves, a building without a foundation, a shadow without a body to cast it" (Cervantes 671; *Traité* 526; *New Rhetoric* 392).

Olbrechts-Tyteca, on the other hand, quotes (in Spanish) or cites *Don Quixote* some thirty times in *Le comique du discours*. Her use of *Don Quixote* provides nuance to the conclusions she and Perelman had reached earlier. For example, Olbrechts-Tyteca employs the above "knight errant" quotation and redefines it in her own work. Whereas in the *Traité*, this example from *Don Quixote* was proffered as an instance in which the juxtaposition of *phoroi* might become comical, with no further comment, Olbrechts-Tyteca notes that the comical here does not derive from the incompatibility of a juxtaposition but rather from redundancy: "The comic derives not so much from an incompatibility, for all these *phoroi* can exist perfectly well together, to [the point of] redundancy. We seem to forget that the analogy must be enlightening, persuasive; that is to say, that it must give us some knowledge of the theme, of its structure and its value" (*Comique* 299). What she develops here is the idea that it is precisely this redundancy that clarifies the structural use of *phoroi*, suggesting how the comic may play a role in persuasion.

Olbrechts-Tyteca's contribution to the new rhetoric project is exemplified, then, by her humanistic reading of comic literature. Olbrechts-Tyteca's description of *Don Quixote* as marked by a deep sense of humanity—"with all the richness that the profound humanity of the author and his characters gives to it" (*Comique* 319)—manifests her expansion of the universal audience; in other words, she develops from *Don Quixote* a keen sense of how humanity is a key feature of the universal audience. Olbrechts-Tyteca's use of the canon of comic literary works in the development of a theory of argumentation thus serves as an imprint of her contribution to the new rhetoric project.

Le comique du discours was translated into Italian in 1977 but has yet to find its way into English. The book has often been cited in journal articles and books dealing with laughter, humor, and rhetoric. Perelman, in his 1977 *L'Empire rhétorique: Rhétorique et argumentation*, cites Olbrechts-Tyteca's *Comique* ten times and, in the chapter on quasi-logical arguments, uses the book to help distinguish formal from rhetorical reasoning. Building in part from Olbrechts-Tyteca's ideas, Perelman maintains that ridicule and the comic expressed through rhetoric allows humans to remain free of the constraints imposed by apodictic logic. As Olbrechts-Tyteca noted in 1974, "Laughter furthers the theoretical realization of argumentation" (*Comique* 398).

Reflections on Rhetorical Collaborations

What, then, have we contributed to an understanding of the Perelman–Olbrechts-Tyteca collaboration and to collaborations more generally? We have identified three expressions of the new rhetoric project: Perelman's philosophically and legally oriented scheme; Olbrechts-Tyteca's literary and comedic rendition; and that of their collaboration, which is a blend of the two sets of impulses. In this essay, we have attempted to identify and describe the characteristics of Olbrechts-Tyteca's new rhetoric and the contribution she made to the *Traité*. To accomplish this objective, we argued that Olbrechts-Tyteca's trajectory to and beyond the *Traité* suggests that an understanding of her role in the new rhetoric project should be considered diachronically—that the pattern of her work between 1950 and 1983, not just the 1958 collaboration with Perelman, will best reveal her contributions. Perelman set the initial agenda for the new rhetoric project, promoted the project to domestic and foreign scholars and publishers, and coined the notion of the universal audience. A host of ideas developed in the *Traité* were initially introduced in Perelman's solitary work. Yet, Perelman may not have made his rhetorical turn without Olbrechts-Tyteca, as she was the one who had read literary theorist Jean Paulhan's *Les fleurs de Tarbes* and shared it with Perelman, who then experienced what he called a "revelation" when he read the appendix of Paulhan's book with Latini's summary of Cicero's rhetoric. The literary illustrations of the philosophical notions in the *Traité*, which give their collaboration "presence," were a result of Olbrechts-Tyteca's command of the canon of Western (and some Eastern) classics. When Perelman, in his letter to Dearin, noted that Olbrechts-Tyteca was "no philosopher" but "studied sociology and literature," he was accurately describing the strengths she brought to the collaboration. A more generous description might have placed their strengths in proportion: he could have represented himself as a philosopher who did not study literature and Olbrechts-Tyteca as a colleague with a command of the canon, which he lacked.

There is no evidence that Olbrechts-Tyteca felt mistreated or diminished, and there are no hints in her history of the new rhetoric project that Perelman purposefully or intentionally sought to exploit her work. At the same time, her reports may not provide sufficient evidence to assess how Perelman treated her. They appeared to be distinctly different personalities. From the existing reports, Olbrechts-Tyteca did not seek the limelight. Michel Meyer reports that he saw Olbrechts-Tyteca only once during his years as Perelman's student; and she did not found journals, organize conferences, travel, or attend scholarly conventions, nor was she active in the political sphere. Her first series of publications, beginning in 1950, were in collaboration with Perelman, and she joined him in 1947 to pursue the agenda he set in the wake of his conclusion in *De la justice*.

If we use the criteria set forth by scholars for the determination of the order of authorship, then Perelman deserved to be first author in their collaboration between 1947 and 1958. The first author is the "individual who often had the original idea" and "did the most work" or "who wrote the first draft of the paper" (Elliott and Stern 130); the "first author is usually the researcher who developed the idea and plan for the research" (Thomas, Nelson, and Silverman 81). Perelman seemed to have the original idea as he saw rhetoric as an answer to his dissatisfaction with logical positivism, set forth the plan for research based on Frege's analysis of mathematical proof, and wrote the first draft of the *Traité*. It is hard to assess who "did most of the work."

How, then, should scholars understand the contributions made by Lucie Olbrechts-Tyteca to the new rhetoric project? By considering the status of collaborative writing, placing Olbrechts-Tyteca and Perelman in their rhetorical situations, reading the project diachronically, expanding the frame beyond the *Traité*, and offering a close reading of *Le comique du discours* with evidence that it is a significant extension of the new rhetoric, we can better answer this question. She played second chair to Perelman between 1947 and 1958, making at the same time a substantial contribution to their collaboration.

Perelman and Olbrechts-Tyteca were, in the terminology of the new rhetoric project, a "philosophical pair." Pairs, they note, can be placed in value hierarchies, with one value serving as the criterion by which the other is judged. Olbrechts-Tyteca, in an extended and sophisticated analysis of philosophical pairs, describes how they are subject to reversal given the rhetorical situations in which they are nested—that the criterion and its subject of judgment can be reversed. Perelman and Olbrechts-Tyteca also acknowledge the role of compromise in constructing a new social reality out of conflicts arising out of antithetical pairs. When a philosophical pair is incompatible or requires compromise, it may invite a dissociation, which will create a new constellation of values.

The *Traité* might be seen as a dissociation of philosophical and literary impulses brought to bear on the problems of postwar Europe. The new rhetoric project might be seen as a series of dissociations. They begin with Perelman's dissociation of logical positivism with Latini's rehearsal of Cicero's rhetoric, his invention of the universal audience out of the ideas of Kant and the vocabulary of nonformal logic out of the language of formal logic, and the ten-year Perelman–Olbrechts-Tyteca collaboration, in which Perelman established the agenda for and wrote the first draft of the *Traité*. However, after 1958, Olbrechts-Tyteca offered a major extension of the new rhetoric project, effectively reversing with *Le comique du discours* her second chair status. Her *Le comique du discours*, according to Perelman and our reading, expands and refines notions that remained latent and underdeveloped in the *Traité* and in Perelman's work. Olbrechts-Tyteca thus emerged as an independent scholar of note by associating rhetoric with the comic. Even though Perelman and Olbrechts-Tyteca would come to develop different aspects of the new rhetoric project, they did agree from the beginning, and returned to this agreement in their final article, that argument is the alternative to violence.

When the new rhetoric project is read diachronically, Olbrechts-Tyteca's contribution comes into focus, both in collaboration with Perelman and on her own. Our study, the product of a collaboration, demonstrates that scholars writing together over time develop relationships that can defy rigid classifications and proscribed roles. The Perelman–Olbrechts-Tyteca collaboration achieved a rapprochement between the "human reasoning" and the "human laughing," the philosopher and the literary critic, which explains why *The New Rhetoric* is considered one of the landmark rhetorics of the twentieth century.

Notes

1. For reference, we provide the relevant pages from the 1969 translation by Wilkinson and Weaver, *The New Rhetoric* (whose translation merits some modification).

2. All translations, unless otherwise noted, are ours.

3. After the publication of the *Comique*, Olbrechts-Tyteca published one brief article, a collaboration with Perelman on the work of Vilfredo Pareto in 1983. Pareto's *Traité de sociologie générale* served as a major inspiration for Perelman and Olbrechts-Tyteca's theory of argumentation in the new rhetoric project. Their article, published on the sixtieth anniversary of Pareto's death, rehearses the importance of Pareto's work and concludes by celebrating argumentation as reason's alternative to violence. This final collaboration marks, if not a reconciliation, then a rapprochement of the various expressions of the new rhetoric project, rejoining Perelman the philosopher and Olbrechts-Tyteca the literary critic for an encomium to the prominent Italian economist.

4. We must pause here to give a definition of "*le comique*," since the French term has a slightly different meaning from the English, and our use of the English "the comic" here is informed by the former. In English, the comic deals with the matter of comedy (as opposed to tragedy); it is the mirth and laughter that arise from wit, burlesque, humor, exaggeration, or incongruity, intentional or not. In French, however, *le comique* is a more global term. While associated with comedy and the cause of laughter, *le comique* is also a generic term that encompasses tones, registers, and gestures (wit, burlesque, grotesque, farce, lyric) as well as genres (satire, parody). For example, Véronique Sternberg-Grenier's *Le comique* presents a veritable diversity of texts, as does Jean Emelina's *Le comique: Essai d'interprétation générale*. Humor and irony are not, however, always aspects of *le comique*, unlike the English use of the terms. See Moran and Gendrel, "Humour, comique, ironie."

Works Cited

Bergson, Henri. *Laughter: An Essay on the Meaning of the Comic*. London: Macmillan, 1911.

Cervantes, de Miguel. *Don Quixote*. Trans. Edith Grossman. Vol. 6. New York: HarperCollins, 2003.

Crossman, Richard. *Palestine Mission: A Personal Record, with Speech Delivered in the House of Commons, 1st July 1946*. London: Hamish Hamilton, 1947.

Dearin, Ray. Letter to Chaïm Perelman. 22 May 1969. Chaïm Perelman Archives. Université Libre de Bruxelles, Brussels, Belgium.

Ede, Lisa S., and Andrea A. Lunsford. *Singular Texts/Plural Authors: Perspectives on Collaborative Writing*. Carbondale: Southern Illinois UP, 1992.

Elliott, Deni, and Judy E. Stern, eds. *Research Ethics: A Reader*. Hanover, NH: UP of New England, 1997.

Emelina, Jean. *Le comique: Essai d'interprétation générale*. Paris: Sedes, 1991.

Frank, David A. "A Traumatic Reading of Twentieth-Century Rhetorical Theory: The Belgian Holocaust, Malines, Perelman, and de Man." *Quarterly Journal of Speech* 93.3 (2007): 308–43.

Gross, Alan G., and Ray D. Dearin. *Chaïm Perelman*. Albany: State U of New York P, 2003.

Maneli, Mieczyslaw. *Perelman's New Rhetoric as Philosophy and Methodology for the Next Century*. Boston: Kluwer, 1994.

Marchal, Joseph A. *Hierarchy, Unity, and Imitation: A Feminist Rhetorical Analysis of Power Dynamics in Paul's Letter to the Philippians*. Atlanta: Society of Biblical Literature, 2006.

Mattis, Noémi Perelman. Personal interview by David Frank. 16 May 2008.

Meyer, Michel. Personal interview by David Frank. 16 July 2004.

Moran, Patrick, and Bernard Gendrel. "Humour, comique, ironie." *Fabula: La recherche en littérature* (2005): n.pag. Web. 23 October 2007.

Olbrechts-Tyteca, Lucie. *Le comique du discours*. Brussels: Université de Bruxelles, 1974.

———. "Rencontre avec la rhétorique." *Logique et analyse* 3 (1963): 1–15.

Perelman, Chaïm. Letter to Letizia Gianformaggio. 1973. Chaïm Perelman Archives. Université Libre de Bruxelles, Brussels, Belgium.

———. *The New Rhetoric and the Humanities: Essays on Rhetoric and its Applications*. Dordrecht, Holland: D. Reidel, 1979.

———. "Raison éternelle, raison historique." *L'homme et l'histoire, Actes du 6e congrès des sociétés de Philosophie de Langue français* (1952): 346–54.

Perelman, Chaïm, and Lucie Olbrechts-Tyteca. *The New Rhetoric: A Treatise on Argumentation*. Trans. John Wilkinson and Purcell Weaver. Notre Dame: U of Notre Dame P, 1969.

———. *Traité de l'argumentation: La nouvelle rhétorique*. Paris: Presses Universitaires de France, 1958.

Scott, Robert. "Chaïm Perelman: Persona and Accommodation in the New Rhetoric." *Pre/Text* 5.2 (1984): 89–97.

Steinberg, Lucien. *Le Comité de défense des juifs en Belgique, 1942–1944*. Brussels: Université de Bruxelles, 1973.

Sternberg-Grenier, Véronique. *Le comique*. Paris: Flammarion, 2003.

Thomas, Jerry R., Jack K. Nelson, and Stephen J. Silverman. *Research Methods in Physical Activity*. 5th ed. Champaign, IL: Human Kinetics.

Warnick, Barbara. "Lucie Olbrechts-Tyteca's Contribution to The New Rhetoric." *Listening to Their Voices: The Rhetorical Activities of Historical Women*. Ed. Molly Meijer Wertheimer. Columbia: U of South Carolina P, 1998. 69–85.

SECTION TWO

Extensions of *The New Rhetoric*

The essays in this section share a concern with the question of whether the theory of argumentation in *The New Rhetoric* may be enriched by connecting it to theoretical perspectives beyond its specific range. This question is at issue whenever *The New Rhetoric* is compared to other texts or theories, even those that precede it, as for instance Jeanne Fahnestock does in her essay (in section 1) when she points out similarities and differences between *The New Rhetoric* and rhetoric manuals of the past. To a degree, this question is also behind the connections made by Linda Bensel-Meyers between Chaïm Perelman's and Richard McKeon's views of pluralism (in section 3) and Mark Hoffmann's use of Richard Weaver to extend *The New Rhetoric*'s description of "act-essence" arguments (in section 4).

Alan G. Gross demonstrates here that *The New Rhetoric*, with its emphasis on discursive argumentation, needs to be augmented with a theory of the visual image in order to acknowledge the argumentative function of information communicated graphically. He adopts concepts from Wolfgang Köhler and Charles S. Peirce to extend and redefine the concept of "presence" from *The New Rhetoric*, enabling it to stand for the "synergy" of all the means of persuasion, even those means not discussed by Perelman and Lucie Olbrechts-Tyteca. This clarifies the idea of "presence" by explaining how a perceptual phenomenon can have an argumentative effect. Gross's extensive analysis of a text by Charles Darwin also serves to reinforce the idea maintained in *The New Rhetoric* that scientific discourse makes use of numerous informal argumentative techniques, as does the essay by Maria Freddi (in section 4). As a demonstration of the application of concepts from *The New Rhetoric* to the analysis of specific texts, Gross's essay shares a central intention with those in section 4.

Richard Graff and Wendy Winn examine the connection between Kenneth Burke and Perelman–Olbrechts-Tyteca through the "convergence" of their respective terms for rhetorical engagement with an audience: "identification" and "communion." Despite their differences, Burke and Perelman–

Olbrechts-Tyteca are shown by this means to have taken similar theoretical paths, and consideration of this leads to the question of how *The New Rhetoric* may be conceived in terms of a broader attempt in the twentieth century to define a "new rhetoric." Graff and Winn show how the effect of identification and communion is especially seen by Burke and Perelman–Olbrechts-Tyteca as a consequence of linguistic and stylistic features of a text, thus further emphasizing Fahnestock's analysis of the way *The New Rhetoric* views style as essentially argumentative. Their specific analysis of the proverb as having this function also links this essay to the analysis of maxims by Paula Olmos (in section 4).

Roselyne Koren uses Perelman and Olbrechts-Tyteca's treatment of self-evidence to correct the inability of linguistic discourse analysis, especially as practiced in France, to deal with ethical statements asserted as facts in both science and journalism. Her idea of rational axiology corrects the privileging of discourse that purports to be but cannot be "objective." By putting *The New Rhetoric* into dialogue with contemporary linguistic methods of analysis, Koren argues that an ethics of discourse is needed to resolve the tension between the stance of objectivity and the utterance of value norms that characterizes the discourse of the press. The ethical dimensions of *The New Rhetoric* are explored further in the essays in section 3. The relation of discourse analysis to the methodology of *The New Rhetoric* is also discussed by Jeanne Fahnestock in her essay.

7

Solving the Mystery of Presence: Verbal/Visual Interaction in Darwin's *Structure and Distribution of Coral Reefs*

Alan G. Gross

In *Chaïm Perelman*, Ray D. Dearin and I contend that presence transcends the isolated effects that Perelman and Lucie Olbrechts-Tyteca catalog; we claim that there is a global form, a synergy of effects, in which "to be persuaded is to live in a world made significantly different by the persuader" (151). In "Presence as Argument in the Public Sphere," I extend this form of presence from the verbal to the visual. In this essay, I attempt to further the analysis of presence, to offer a systematic account of the verbal/visual interaction on which it depends, to offer, in effect, a genealogy of presence. Such an account is essential if we are to explain the mystery of verbal/visual presence, to explain what is, in fact, the central mystery of Perelmanian presence, the transformation of the perceptual into the argumentative. According to *The New Rhetoric*, presence is based on the fact that "the thing on which the eye dwells, that which is best or most often seen is, by that very circumstance, overestimated." Initially, then, presence is perceptual; its effect is "to [fill] the whole field of consciousness." But, according to Perelman and Olbrechts-Tyteca, such is the nature of presence that what is "at first a psychological phenomenon, becomes an essential element in argumentation" (116–18).

Although for Perelman and Olbrechts-Tyteca, presence is the product of verbal interaction alone, this cannot be true of a text in which information-bearing images contribute significantly to meaning. A genealogy of the presence that is a consequence of verbal/visual interaction requires recourse to theories that are broader in scope. Accordingly, I employ Wolfgang Köhler's Gestalt theory to account for our perceptions and Charles S. Peirce's semiotics to account for their interpretation. Both theories suffer from a visual bias. Gestalt categories that apply flawlessly to the visual apply only awkwardly to other modes of perception. Peirce himself acknowledges a visual bias in his thinking: "I do not think I ever reflect in words. I employ visual diagrams, firstly, because this way of thinking is my natural language of self-communion and secondly, I am convinced that it is the best system for the purpose" (qtd. in Leja 97). While such a bias leads to difficulties when we try to incorporate the other senses in a general hermeneutic of presence, it suits my present purposes exactly, the analysis of presence in Charles Darwin's first masterpiece, *The Structure and Distribution of Coral Reefs*.

The Genealogy of Presence

Presence has its beginnings in the patterns of perception our sensory systems produce, organized in accord with the "laws" of Gestalt psychology. Köhler and his followers were certainly mistaken when they hypothesized that perceptual processes were actually organized along Gestalt lines, hardwired into the brain (Köhler). Given the current state of our knowledge of such processes, it would probably be best to regard the Gestalt "laws of organization [as] opportunistic guides to the viewer as to what will afford desired visual information" and to support the view "that they probably vary widely in level, speed, and power" (Hochberg 291). In one plausible accounting, there are five Gestalt principles. According to *figure-ground*, we see objects automatically as shaped, framed against a shapeless background, one that may, in fact, also have a shape, though we do not perceive it as such. When this background actually does have a shape—as in the case of the cell structure of tables or the latitude-longitude coordinates of maps—we can direct our attention alternately to it and to the foreground of data elements. In the depictions of coastlines or letters of the alphabet, we see another Gestalt principle in operation, *good continuation*. Tables are characterized by the Gestalt principle of *enclosure*; on the other hand, relationships among their cells are highlighted by means of the fourth principle of *similarity and contrast*. A final principle, *proximity*, groups adjoining letters of the alphabet into words (Pinker, "Theory" 84; Hochberg 260–61; see also Pinker, *Pattern Perception*).

Gestalt patterns are meaningful only insofar as they participate in a system of value-laden differences. Ferdinand de Saussure articulates this principle for language:

In all these cases what we find, instead of *ideas* given in advance, are *values* emanating from a linguistic system. If we say that these values correspond to certain concepts, it must be understood that the concepts in question are purely differential. That is to say they are concepts defined not positively, in terms of their content, but negatively by contrast with other items in the same system. What characterizes each most exactly is being whatever the others are not. (115)

Saussure's principle applies generally to any semiotic system. For example, traffic signals and electrical wiring diagrams also rely for their interpretation on value-laden differences. To differentiate these systems from languages, let us call them codes.

Patterns of perception made potentially meaningful according to Saussure's principle are interpreted as Peircian symbols, icons, or indexes. Patterns recognized as verbal are understood as symbols, whose relation to their objects may be, but need not be, arbitrary. Alphabets are systems of wholly arbitrary signs; ideograms are symbols that are not wholly arbitrary. Patterns recognized as nonverbal are understood either as symbols, icons, or indices. An icon is a sign that depicts; a photograph or a drawing of a microbe is an icon. An index is a sign whose relation to its object is causal or indicative. Geiger counter readings are causally linked to the external world; in a photograph, an arrow pointing to a cell nucleus is merely indicative. To avoid ambiguity, let us call this latter category of signs deictic.

For the purposes of exegesis, Peirce's categories are insufficiently fine-grained to capture all meaningful transactions within a system of signs. Accordingly, to interpret the verbal, I borrow from linguistics, narrative theory, logic, and rhetorical theory, analytical perspectives that are, I judge, compatible with his semiotics. I single out as linguistic a semantic concern for the relationship between words and the world, a syntactic concern for the legitimate combinational possibilities of words in sentences, and a pragmatic concern for the effect of natural-language utterances on interlocutors.

Utterances also partake of larger systems of meaning, organized either in chronological sequences or according to logical operations. There are two types of chronological sequences: those that are repeated without change and those that are unique. The first we call processes; the second, narratives. I single out as logical the following operations: definition, classification, implication/inference, and generalization by induction. Definition operates by genus and differentia: a chair is an article of furniture designed for sitting; it has a back and four legs. The genus is furniture; the differentia, designed for sitting, having a back, having four legs. Classification operates by division; it creates hierarchies of categories, each level of which has the same cognitive status within the system specified: for example, the animal kingdom can be divided into creatures with and without backbones. Implication is a property of propositions whereby to commit to one is to commit to another. If all humans are mortal, then by implication, all Armenians are mortal. Inference is the psychological process by which this implication is realized. Induction is generalization from a necessarily limited set of instances: from the genetics of some peas to the genetics of all peas, from the genetics of all peas to all genetics.

I single out as rhetorical the three traditional canons that are the sources of persuasion in oral and written communication: the invention of arguments that, however persuasive, would not pass muster in formal logic; the arrangement or organization of discourses with persuasion in mind; and style, the systematic use of persuasively significant variations in the means of expression. Traditionally, invention is subdivided into three forms of appeal: to *logos*, appeals from reasoning; to *ethos*, appeals based on the trust that the author creates in the reader; and to *pathos*, appeals to the emotions of the auditor or reader.

I now move from the verbal to the visual. While we see images, we do not ordinarily see words; rather, we see through them to their underlying concepts. This is what reading means. The verbal and the visual also differ in the way they are organized. Words are ordered in sequential hierarchical structures composed of combinations of smaller units. A paragraph is composed of a sequence of sentences, composed of sequences of clauses and phrases, composed of sequences of words, composed of sequences of letters. Images, on the other hand, are ordered into synchronous hierarchies or nested sets. A face is composed of a nested set of eyes, eyebrows, nose, mouth, teeth, ears, brow, and cheeks. When organized into larger units, moreover, words never entirely lose their separate identities; the components of images, on the other hand, lose their separate identity as they become embedded or nested. We see a face, not its components; we see, not an intricate nesting of various Gestalts, but a single Gestalt. The verbal and the visual are also processed differently. Words are processed sequentially; in contrast, images can be processed not only sequentially but also in parallel and simultaneously.

Images differ from words in one other important respect: they are subject to semiotically relevant spatial transformations. They can be rotated on their axes: subjected to this transformation, topographical surfaces reveal geological depths. Three-dimensional objects may also be projected onto two-dimensional surfaces; we do so when we create a map. One image, moreover, may be superimposed on another, an effect achieved when lines of latitude or longitude are applied to maps. In addition, a sequence of visuals may be animated; this is how temporal progression is routinely represented in films.

Other transformations are possible. Some take place within a particular category of sign. For example, a photograph of an eye may be used to construct a drawing of the eye, a shift from one iconic mode to another. Some transformations involve a shift from one category of sign to another. The iconic may be transformed into symbolic: photographs of *an* eye may become a diagram of *the* eye. Finally, the iconic may be transformed into the indexical: a chest X-ray may reveal the cause of a persistent cough. Thomas A. Sebeok makes the essential point about the plasticity of the Peircian categories:

> In general, it is . . . inane to ask whether any given subject "is," or is represented by, an icon, an index, or a symbol, for all signs are situated in a complex network of syntagmatic and paradigmatic contrasts and oppositions, i.e., simultaneously participate in a text as well as a system; it is their position at a particular moment that will determine the predominance of the aspect in focus. (1433n)

As Gérard Deledalle points out:

> We must insist . . . on the functional character of these distinctions: what is an index in one semiosis may be a symbol in another. Take, for instance, the symptom of an illness. . . . If this symptom is referred to in a lecture on medicine as always characterizing a certain illness, the symptom is a symbol. If the doctor encounters it while he is examining a patient, the symptom is an index of an illness. (19–20)

The contention of Sebeok and Deledalle that context is central to semiotic interpretation is a generalization of Saussure's principle that meaning is constituted by difference.

This understanding of Peirce's taxonomy is consonant with the views of Nelson Goodman on meaning-making, a position worth quoting at length:

> Comparative judgments of similarity often require not merely selection of relevant properties but a weighing of their relative importance, and variation in both relevance and importance can be rapid and enormous. Consider the baggage at an airport check-in station. The spectator may notice shape, size, color, material, and even make of luggage; the pilot is more concerned with weight, and the passenger with destination and ownership. Which pieces of luggage are more alike than others depends not only upon what properties they share, but upon who makes the comparison, and when. Or suppose we have three glasses, the first two filled with colorless liquid, the third with

a bright red liquid. I might be likely to say the first two are more like each other than either is like the third. But it happens that the first glass is filled with water and the third with water colored by a drop of vegetable dye, while the second is filled with hydrochloric acid—and I am thirsty. Circumstances alter similarities. (445)

Texts that combine words and images constitute a wide-ranging category of communication, one that includes genres as different as comic strips and scientific monographs. These bear meaning as a consequence of the interaction of their verbal and visual components, interpreted in all cases as Peircian signs ever and exquisitely sensitive to the changes in context to which Sebeok, Deledalle, and Goodman refer.[1]

With the assistance of Gestalt psychology and Peirce's semiotics, I have outlined a process by which the interaction of the verbal and the visual leads from perception to meaning. In so doing, seemingly, I face a difficulty: surely, a theory of meaning and a theory of presence are not the same. This difficulty, however, is only apparent. In *Chaïm Perelman*, Dearin and I defined a "superordinate" form of presence as the "cumulative effect of interactions" among arrangement, style, and invention (135). But to say this, I think, is the equivalent of saying that while rhetoric's function is, in Aristotle's words, "to see the available means of persuasion in each case" (1355a), the function of superordinate presence is to synthesize these available means so as to create a unitary effect. In persuasive texts, therefore, to trace the genealogy of presence is no more and no less than to reveal it as the synergy of "all the available means of persuasion." In this essay, for example, I solve the mystery of presence in Darwin's *The Structure and Distribution of Coral Reefs* by showing that the synergy of all of the available verbal and visual means of persuasion creates a perceptual, an argumentative, and, eventually, a narrative presence. This last transformation is necessary because geology is a historical science that must explain a sequence of unique events, the history of the earth.

The Perceptual Base

Darwin begins his book with a description of Keeling Atoll, a description so detailed that readers are cast in the role of virtual witnesses who can attest to the congeries of facts soon destined to be transformed into evidence for Darwin's argument. Below is an example of this stylistic technique, this thick description that creates perceptual presence, a presence that is, at the same time, a testament to Darwin's meticulousness, a projection in every sentence of the ethos of the careful researcher who, literally, leaves no stone unturned:

On the outside of the reef much sediment must be formed by the action of the surf on the rolled fragments of coral; but, in the calm waters of the lagoon, this can take place only in a small degree. There are, however, other and unexpected agents at work here: large shoals of two species of Scarus, one inhabiting the surf outside the reef and the other the lagoon, subsist entirely, as I was assured by Mr. Liesk, the intelligent resident before referred to, by browsing on the living polypifers. I opened several of these fish, which are very numerous and of considerable size, and I found their intestines distended by small pieces of coral, and finely ground calcareous matter. This must daily pass from them as the finest sediment; much also must be produced by the infinitely numerous vermiform and molluscous animals, which make cavities in almost every block of coral. Dr. J. Allan, of Forres, who has enjoyed the best means of observation, informs me in a letter that the Holothuriæ (a family of Radiata) subsist on living coral; and the singular structure of bone within the anterior extremity of their bodies, certainly appears well adapted for this purpose. (14)

In his creation of perceptual presence, Darwin now shifts to the visual. He begins with a navigator's chart (figure 1), the basis for a diagram he will soon produce, a semiotic spatial transformation that will reveal aspects of the atoll's structure that will prove pertinent to the persuasive case he wishes to make.

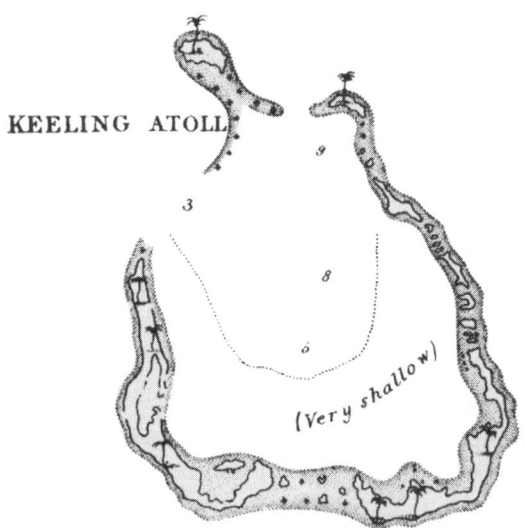

Figure 1. A navigator's chart of Keeling Atoll. From Darwin, *The Structure and Distribution of Coral Reefs*, plate I, fig. 10, n. pag.

In constructing his diagram from this chart (figure 2), Darwin rotates the chart 90 degrees on its axis to disclose it in vertical section. At the same time, he simplifies its contours to reveal its essential structural features. By means of considerable distortion, he also clarifies aspects of those features that would be masked by a rendering in true proportions.[2]

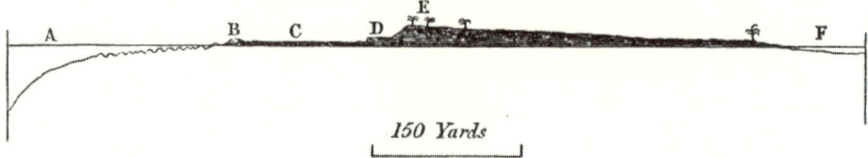

Figure 2. A diagram displaying the structural features of Keeling Atoll.
"*A*—Level of the sea at low water: where the letter *A* is placed, the depth is 25 fathoms, and the distance rather more than 150 yards from the edge of the reef.
B—Outer edge of that flat part of the reef, which dries at low water: the edge either consists of a convex mound, as represented, or of rugged points, like those a little farther seaward, beneath the water.
C—A flat of coral-rock, covered at high water.
D—A low projecting ledge of brecciated coral-rock, washed by the waves at high water.
E—A slope of loose fragments, reached by the sea only during gales: the upper part, which is from six to twelve feet high, is clothed with vegetation. The surface of the islet slopes to the lagoon.
F—Level of the lagoon at low-water."
From Darwin, *The Structure and Distribution of Coral Reefs*, p. 5.

The diagram permits us to see the island's structural features as a single Gestalt, a task no words could accomplish. But it is only words that can identify these *as* features; moreover, it is only words that can highlight the crucial role of one particular feature: "The wood-cut represents a section across one of the islets on the reef, but if all that part which is above the level of *C* were removed, the section would be that of the simple reef, as it occurs where no islet has been formed. It is this reef which essentially forms the atoll" (Darwin, *Structure* 10). Words and diagram are closely interwoven, a linkage marked by the letter *C*, not in this case primarily a symbol but a Peircian deixis.

The diagram has undergone another semiotically significant spatial transformation. In creating it, Darwin has displaced the atoll from its geographical context; he has recontextualized it geometrically by means of a superimposed grid that signals an epistemic shift: from an object in the world of nature to an object in the world of theory. The diagram's geometrical character is now at the center of our field of attention: the atoll has become its structure.

But it will be crucial to Darwin's argument to show that the structure of Keeling Atoll is, in all its essential aspects, typical. In pursuit of this goal, chapters 2 through 4 of *The Structure and Distribution of Coral Reefs* detail the similarities among the three classes of reef-island systems—atolls, barrier reefs, and fringing reefs. They do so by means of an extensive catalog of reef-island systems and a comprehensive anthology of charts whose comparison is made simpler by the adoption of a uniform visual code the chart of Keeling Atoll exemplifies.[3] This catalog and these charts demonstrate that reef-island systems share all of their essential structural features:

> The general resemblance between the reefs of the barrier and atoll classes may be seen in the small, but accurately reduced charts. . . . [T]his resemblance can be further shown to extend to every part of the structure. . . . If we look at a set of charts of barrier-reefs, and leave out in imagination the encircled land, we shall find that, besides the many points already noticed of resemblance, or rather of identity in structure with atolls, there is a close general agreement in form, average dimensions, and grouping. (41, 45)

By the end of the first part of Darwin's *Structure*, then, Keeling Atoll has come to stand for all reef-island systems. This is a transformation from the iconic to the symbolic, effected through verbal/visual interaction.

Darwin's initial structural model is static, a status emphasized by the assignment of agency to persons rather than to geological forces. Darwin and Robert Fitzroy observe and measure; Liesk and Allan observe and inform; the earth holds still for its portrait. Nevertheless, Darwin anticipates the dynamic theory he will soon disclose, a theory that accounts for the structural features he has just revealed. Twice in the first part of *Structure*, he suggests that these features are "the effect of uniform laws . . . that some renovating agency (namely subsidence) comes into play at intervals, and perpetuates their original structure" (24, 31). These hints foreshadow a transformation that will allow us to reread a passage like the one below as evidence in an argument for the theory of subsidence he will soon proffer:

> On the western side, also, of the atoll, where I have described a bed of sand and fragments with trees growing out of it, in front of an old beach, it struck both Lieutenant Sulivan and myself, from the manner in which the trees were being washed down, that the surf had lately recommenced an attack on this line of coast. Appearances indicating a slight encroachment of the water on the land, are plainer within the lagoon: I noticed in several places, both on its windward and leeward shores, old cocoa-nut trees falling with their roots undermined, and

the rotten stumps of others on the beach, where the inhabitants assured us the cocoa-nut could not now grow. Captain Fitzroy pointed out to me, near the settlement, the foundation posts of a shed, now washed by every tide, but which the inhabitants stated, had seven years before stood above high watermark. (17–18)

The Argumentative Superstructure

The same facts that were employed in the first part of *Structure* to build a static model of the reef-island system form in its second part the inductive basis of a causal argument for a dynamic theory based on the subsidence of large portions of the earth's crust. In this radical recontextualization, we move from description secured by facts to theory secured by evidence; we move from perceptual to argumentative presence. Despite his theory's actual origin—in a bold analogical leap, a heroic reenvisioning "in imagination"[4]—Darwin understood that it was only by means of accumulation of overwhelming evidence that he could convince his professional peers of its truth. He devoted five years to this tedious but necessary task: "It is very pleasant easy work putting together the frame of a geological theory," he wrote, "but it is just as tough a job collecting & comparing the hard unbending facts" (*Correspondence* 207).

If his argument was to be given a fair hearing and an opportunity to become fully present in the minds of readers, Darwin had to give a fair hearing to competing theories. It was his personal and professional misfortune, however, that his chief competitor was his mentor and friend Charles Lyell. "The circular or oval forms of the numerous coral isles of the Pacific with the lagoons at their centre," Lyell had asserted in his magisterial *Principles of Geology*, "naturally suggest the idea that they are nothing more than the crests of submarine volcanoes, having the rims and bottoms of their craters overgrown by corals" (290). In Darwin's view, Lyell's theory had to be abandoned because it could not explain the presence of fringing or of barrier reefs. Neither could it explain the fact that all reef-island systems were low-lying or that the coral of which they were mainly composed could live only in relatively shallow waters. In addition, the theory was undermined by the general distribution of reef-island systems far from volcanic areas.

Darwin solved his rhetorical problem—his need to dismiss Lyell's theory without criticizing Lyell—by an exercise in diplomacy. Lyell is treated as an authority and, in one particular case, as an authority on subsidence, the very mechanism behind Darwin's own theory: "It is very remarkable that Mr. Lyell, even in the first edition of his Principles of Geology, inferred that the amount of subsidence in the Pacific must have exceeded that of elevation, from the area of land being very small relatively to the agents there tending to form it, namely, the growth of coral and volcanic action" (*Structure* 95; see also 29, 71–72, 118, 137, 143, 175).

This strategy succeeded. When Darwin published his theory, Lyell's concurrence was virtually immediate and especially gratifying: "I must give up my volcanic theory for ever," Lyell wrote, "though it cost me a pang at first, for it accounted for so much, the annular [circular] form, the central lagoon, the sudden rising of an isolated mountain in a deep sea" (Darwin, *Life* 1:293). Vital to that acceptance was the fact that Darwin's rival theory is at bottom Lyellian, an application of Lyell's own central insight that the earth's current configuration is the result of gradual change over eons of geological time.

Having dealt with and dismissed rival theories, most especially that of his mentor, Darwin could now devote the penultimate chapter of *Structure* to an argument in favor of his own. According this theory, subsidence, the gradual descent of large portions of the earth's crust, when accompanied by slow coral growth, causes the transformation from fringing to barrier reefs and from barrier reefs to atolls. This is a *vera causa* argument with a tripartite structure: subsidence exists, is competent as a cause of the evolution of reef-island systems, and is in fact responsible for that evolution. This is also the structure of the central argument in *On the Origin of Species*.[5]

This causal claim is an inference from two sets of facts, introduced by Darwin in the form of a rhetorical question:

> What cause, then, has given to atolls and barrier-reefs their characteristic forms? Let us see whether an important deduction [that is, inference] will not follow from the consideration of these two circumstances, first, the reef-building corals flourishing only at limited depths; and secondly, the vastness of the areas interspersed with coral-reefs and coral-islets, none of which rise to a greater height above the level of the sea, than that attained by matter thrown up by the waves and winds. (*Structure* 90)

Bora Bora, characterized by these defining features, was the exemplar for Darwin's dynamic theory. An island surrounded by a barrier reef, it is in an intermediate stage between fringing reef and atoll.

Readers first meet Bora Bora in the form of a woodcut, seeing it as a traveler would (figure 3). Mt. Otemanu, dotted with coconut palms, dominates the scene. Behind the mountain is a placid lagoon. In the background is a barrier reef, surmounted by palm trees. But even in this realistic depiction, Bora Bora's recontextualization as a theoretical object has stealthily begun.

Darwin says that he has "taken the liberty of simplifying the foreground, and leaving out a mountainous island in the far distance" (*Structure* 2n). The woodcut has begun to reveal Bora Bora's essential structural features.

Figure 3. View of Bolabola [Bora Bora] featuring Mt. Otemanu, the island's highest point. From Darwin, *The Structure and Distribution of Coral Reefs*, p. 3.

The next step toward a dynamic theory is the transformation of Bora Bora into a chart, a semiotically significant 90-degree rotation of its eye-level depiction (figure 4). In this rendering, the illusion of depth in figure 3—the product of an artistic code composed of shading and perspective—has been replaced by the imposition of a scale: what was perceived is now measured.[6] In the interest of bringing the reef-island's structure unequivocally in the foreground, the actual has also been simplified: some lagoon islets have been omitted, and no attempt has been made to depict the distribution of the island's flora. In line with this purpose, the actual has also been enhanced: the depth of the lagoon in fathoms is variously indicated, and the lagoon is, as it were, drained in order to reveal the contours of its underlying reef. In this transformation, what is representational in the realistic rendering is symbolized in the chart so as not to distract from its essential purpose. In the realistic rendering, light and shade represent the mountain as a three-dimensional object; in the chart, the height of the mountain is symbolized by parallel lines, signaling a change from an artistic to a cartographic code. In the artistic rendering, the size and location of the coconut palms is reproduced; in the chart, the repeated coconut palms are transformed into symbols designed to help viewers differentiate the land from the reef below (Darwin, *Structure* 215). It is a uniformity of representation that facilitates structural comparisons among reef-island systems, a uniformity that in turn facilitates the transformation of facts on the ground into evidence for Darwin's argument.

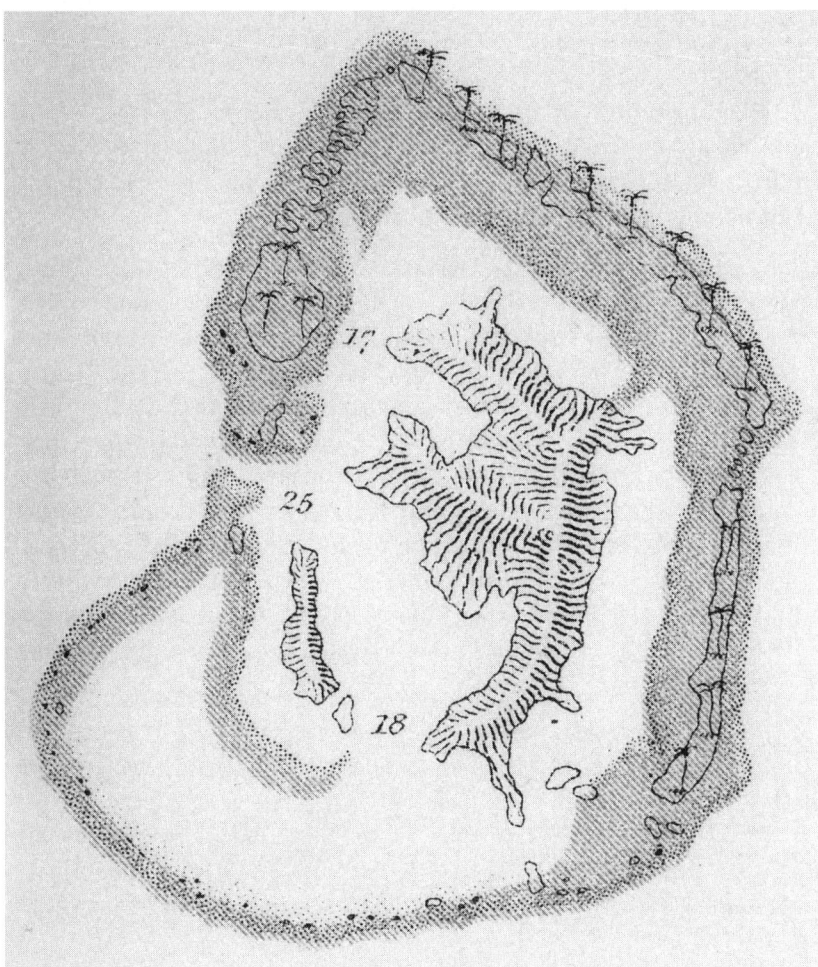

Figure 4. Chart of Bolabola [Bora Bora]. From the survey of Captain Duperrey in the *Coquille*. Scale: ¼ inch = 1 mile. The tinted area shows the extent of the reef. The area that encloses the coconut trees (exaggerated in scale) represents the coral islets. The numbers 17, 25, and 18 are the depth of the lagoon in fathoms of six English feet. From Darwin, *The Structure and Distribution of Coral Reefs*, plate I, fig. 5, n. pag.

In transforming the chart of Bora Bora into two companion diagrams (figures 5 and 6), Darwin advances further into the realm of theory. He now rotates the chart 90 degrees on its axis to disclose a vertical section, simplifying the atoll's contours to reveal its essential structural features; at the same time, by means of considerable vertical distortion, he clarifies aspects of those features that would be masked by a rendering in true proportions. Finally, he superimposes a grid so that the reader can view those features through a geometrical lens. So far, he is following the procedure he used in the case of Keeling Atoll.

In the case of these diagrams of Bora Bora, however, the static has been transformed into the dynamic. Figure 5 depicts evolutionary succession as a consequence of subsidence, a result Darwin asks the reader to reproduce by animating the diagram "in imagination":

> Let us in imagination place within one of the subsiding areas, an island surrounded by a "fringing reef,"—that kind, which alone offers no difficulty in the explanation of its origin. Let the unbroken lines and the oblique shading in the woodcut [figure 5] represent a vertical section through such an island; and the horizontal shading will represent the section of the reef. Now, as the island sinks down, either a few feet at a time or quite insensibly, we may safely infer from what we know of the conditions favourable to the growth of coral, that the living masses bathed by the surf on the margin of the reef, will soon regain the surface. The water, however, will encroach, little by little, on the shore, the island becoming lower and smaller, and the space between the edge of the reef and the beach proportionally broader. (*Structure* 98–99)

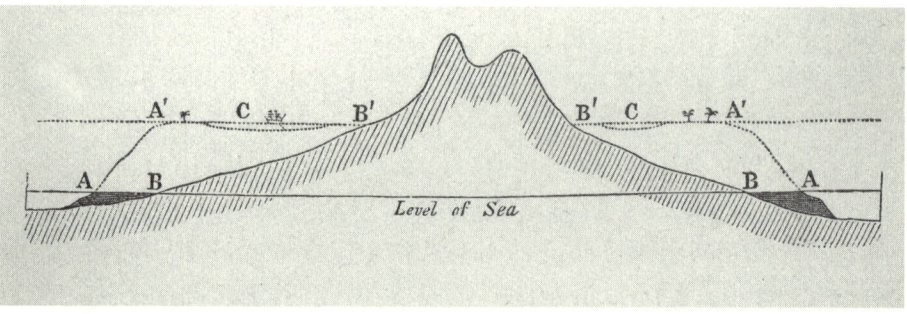

Figure 5. This figure stands for any reef-island system: the anchored boat stands for the depth of any lagoon; the palm trees, the existence of land on any coral reef; the differential hatchings, any reef and its island; the solid lines, the present shape of any reef-island system; the dotted lines, its future shape.

In figure 6, Bora Bora has subsided further still: the barrier reef has become an atoll. Now A'' designates the sea, C' the lagoon. The island has disappeared.

Solving the Mystery of Presence   97

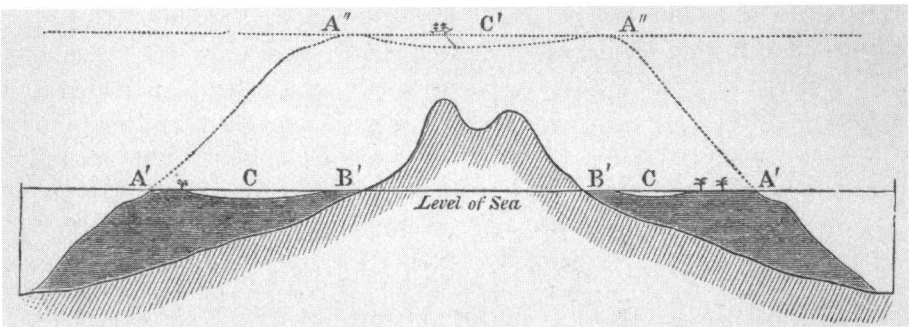

Figure 6. Vertical view of Bolabola [Bora Bora], showing the formation of an atoll. Note the ship anchored in the lagoon to the left of C'.
"$A'\ A'$—Outer edges of the barrier-reef at the level of the sea. The cocoa-nut trees represent coral-islets formed on the reef.
$C\ C$—The lagoon-channel.
$B'\ B'$—The shores of the island, generally formed of low alluvial land and of coral detritus from the lagoon-channel.
$A''\ A''$—The outer edges of the reef now forming an atoll.
C'—The lagoon of the newly-formed atoll. According to the scale, the depth of the lagoon and the lagoon channel is exaggerated."
From Darwin, *The Structure and Distribution of Coral Reefs*, p. 100.

In Figures 5 and 6, Darwin has shifted our attention from the appearance of Bora Bora at any one time to the evolution of any reef-island system over time. This is a transformation from the iconic to the indexical and, at the same time, from the indexical to the symbolic. Bora Bora has become a model for the dynamics of all reef-island systems: "We are now able to perceive that the close similarity in form, dimensions, structure and relative position . . . between fringing and encircling barrier-reefs, and between these latter and atolls, is the necessary result of the transformation, during subsidence, of the one class into the other. On this view the three classes of reefs ought to graduate into each other" (*Structure* 102).

As a consequence of this transformation, Darwin's initial classification of reef-island systems is revealed as a convenient fiction, a concession to the short lifespan of human beings, who, though they cannot see, can by means of argument bring to the forefront of their consciousness the evolution of these systems and the *vera causa* of that evolution.[7] Darwin's causal argument for the evolution of reef-island systems is now fully present.

The Narrative Superstructure

In *The Voyage of the Beagle*, published three years before *The Structure and Distribution of Coral Reefs*, Darwin had envisioned the unique history of the earth as the interplay of tectonic forces over geological time: "We may thus, like unto a geologist who had lived his ten thousand years," he said, "and kept a record of the passing changes, gain some insight into the great system by which the surface of this globe has been broken up, and land and water interchanged" (480). To realize this vision in fact, however, the master argument of *Structure* must be transformed into a master narrative: argumentative must be transformed into narrative presence. Geological theories cannot stop at process explanations because geology is a historical science.

It may seem illegitimate to extend Perelman and Olbrechts-Tyteca's theory of presence to narrative. Nevertheless, this application makes sense in this case. Unlike their fictional counterparts, scientific narratives are credible only so long as their underlying arguments hold true. In a historical science like geology, arguments and the narratives inferred from them are therefore epistemologically equivalent. By the time Darwin concludes his argument in favor of his theory of subsidence, Keeling Atoll and Bora Bora have been transformed into typical reef-island systems; at the same time, they have been turned from material into theoretical objects, defined by their geometry in relation to their surrounding seas, and characterized by subsidence, a fundamental force that alters that relationship. But they have not yet been transformed into historical objects.

To do so, what has been decontextualized in the interest of theory must be recontextualized as narrative under the dominance of theory: "the history of [a particular] atoll" can be reconstructed only if the general argument for subsidence is "modified by occasional accidents which might have been anticipated as probable" (Darwin, *Structure* 114). Only insofar as the geological features of a particular reef-island system are taken into consideration can we imagine what its past might have been and what its future is likely to be. The particular geological features of New Caledonia, for example, allow us to turn a general process into a specific narrative, to envision the story of a unique future that stems from a unique past:

> If, in imagination, we complete the subsidence of that great island, we might anticipate from the present broken condition of the northern portion of the reef, and from the almost entire absence of reefs on the eastern coast, that the barrier-reef after repeated subsidences, would become during its upward growth separated into distinct portions; and these portions would tend to assume an atoll-like structure, from the coral growing with vigour round their entire circumference, when freely exposed to an open sea. (110)

The final chapter of *Structure* demonstrates that what applies to New Caledonia applies to every reef-island system. In it, we are introduced to a map of the Pacific Ocean that indicates the location of every reef-island system and of the "Ring of Fire," the chain of volcanoes at the margins of the Pacific (figure 7). (On this map, Darwin uses color—not seen in the reproduction here—to designate those systems visually, blue for areas of general subsidence, light brown for areas that "have remained stationary or have been upraised" [124], vermilion for areas of volcanic activity.)

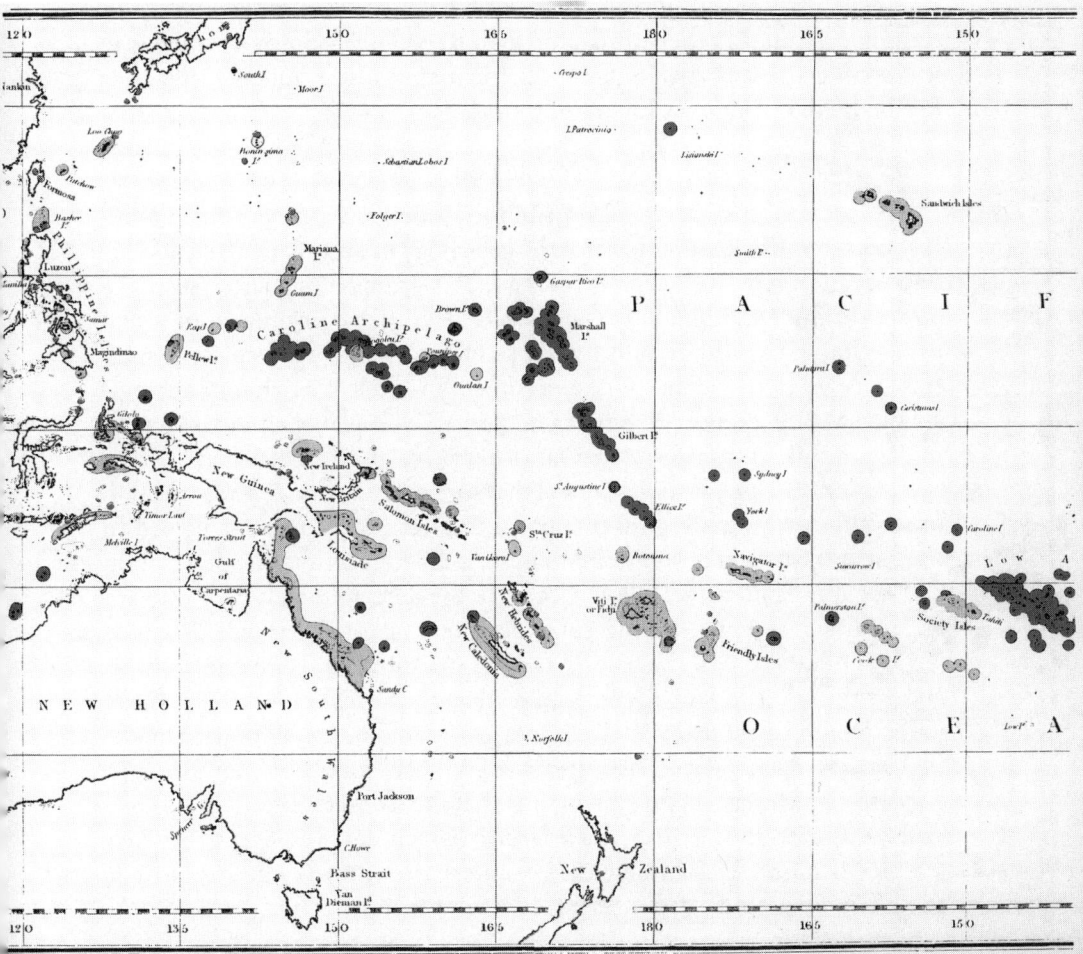

Figure 7. Atolls, barrier, and fringing reefs of the Pacific. The scale is such that each square contains 810,000 square miles. (The darker and lighter highlights seen here are the areas Darwin designated by using colors in the original.) From Darwin, *The Structure and Distribution of Coral Reefs*, plate III, n. pag. For an updated version of Darwin's map, see Schuhmacher, *Korallenriffe*, inside front and back covers and their flyleaves.

In this map, the reversion to description is only apparent; from the start we are asked to see the map "under the theoretical point of view of the last chapter" (*Structure* 123). Given this point of view, the map is, equally, a representation of the network of Pacific reef-island systems and a representation of a theory of their distribution in space and time: it is "corroborative of the truth of the theory" that reef-island systems are distributed according to whether the surrounding areas have subsided, been elevated, or remained stationary (124). In other words, the map is, equally, iconic and indexical: it is an effect that points to its cause. The map is also symbolic—it stands for the truth of Darwin's theory of subsidence.

Conclusion

I have explored the exegetical possibilities inherent in Gestalt theory and Peirce's semiotics in order to trace the genealogy of argumentative and narrative presence back to its perceptual base. In Darwin's first masterpiece, *The Structure and Distribution of Coral Reefs*, details that originated in visual perception, expressed initially by means of description and depiction, were transformed into evidence for an argument in favor of a dynamic geological theory. But because geology is a historical science, this argument had to undergo a further transformation into a narrative specific to science, one that compels only so long as the argument that supports it holds. The organization of *Structure* firmly undergirds this argumentative and narrative structure. In its first part, the text is organized to move deliberately from the description and depiction of one reef-island system to the description and depiction of all reef-island systems. It is this generalization that forms the inductive base of Darwin's theory. In the second part of *Structure*, in arguing for subsidence as the *vera causa* of all reef-island systems, the text moves by means of inductive argument from a static model to its dynamic counterpart, a model that, however general its constitutive forces, must produce a unique story in the case of each reef-island system, one that incorporates the accidents of a geological past. In the historical sciences, perceptual presence is regularly transformed into its argumentative counterpart; in turn, argumentative is transformed into narrative presence, a final transformation.

Notes

1. An effective illustration of verbal/visual interdependence is found in Eisner (110), where identical visual images are shown to be interpreted differently when different verbal cues are assigned to them.

2. "The section is true to the scale in a horizontal line, but it could not be made so in a vertical one, as the average greatest height of the land is only between six and twelve feet above high-water mark" (*Structure* 6).

3. "In the several original surveys, from which the small plans on this plate have been reduced, the coral-reefs are engraved in very different styles. For the sake of uniformity, I have adopted the style used in the charts of the Chagos Archipelago, published by the East Indian Company, from the survey by Captain Moresby and Lieutenant Powell" (*Structure* xvii).

4. Darwin did not arrive at his theory by an inductive route; far from it:

>No other work of mine was begun in so deductive a spirit as this, for the whole theory was thought out on the west coast of South America, before I had seen a true coral reef. I had therefore only to verify and extend my views by a careful examination of living reefs. But it should be observed that I had during the previous two years been incessantly attending to the effects on the shores of South America of the intermittent elevation of the land, together with denudation and the deposition of sediment. This necessarily led me to reflect much on the effects of subsidence, and it was easy to replace in imagination the continued deposition of sediment by the upward growth of corals. To do this was to form my theory of the formation of barrier reefs and atolls. (*Life* 1:58)

5. The argument in *Structure* is therefore a precursor to the central argument in *On the Origin of Species*, as analyzed by Hodge: natural selection exists, is competent to cause the evolution of species, and is in fact responsible for that evolution.

6. Darwin presents the scale separately on page 216.

7. Species will have a similar status in Darwin's *On the Origin of Species*.

Works Cited

Aristotle. *On Rhetoric: A Theory of Civic Discourse*. Trans. George A. Kennedy. New York: Oxford UP, 1991.

Darwin, Charles. *The Correspondence of Charles Darwin: Volume 2, 1837–1843*. Ed. Frederick Burkhardt, Sydney Smith, et al. Cambridge: Cambridge UP, 1986.

———. *The Life and Letters*. Ed. Francis Darwin. 2 vols. New York: Basic, 1959.

———. *The Structure and Distribution of Coral Reefs*. Tucson: U of Arizona P, 1984.

———. *The Voyage of the Beagle*. Ed. Leonard Engel. New York: Doubleday, 1962.

Deledalle, Gérard. *Charles S. Peirce's Philosophy of Signs: Essays in Comparative Semiotics*. Bloomington: Indiana UP, 2000.

Eisner, Will. *Comics and Sequential Art: Principles and Practice of the World's Most Popular Art Form*. Tamarac, FL: Poorhouse, 1985.

Goodman, Nelson. *Problems and Projects*. Indianapolis: Bobbs-Merrill, 1972.

Gross, Alan G. "Presence as Argument in the Public Sphere." *Rhetoric Society Quarterly* 35.2 (2005): 5–21.

Gross, Alan G., and Ray D. Dearin. *Chaïm Perelman*. Albany: State U of New York P, 2003.

Hochberg, Julian. "Gestalt Theory and Its Legacy: Organization in Eye and Brain, in Attention and Mental Representation." *Perception and Cognition at Century's End*. 2nd ed. Ed. J. Hochberg. San Diego: Academic, 1998. 253–306.

Hodge, M. J. S. "The Structure and Strategy of Darwin's 'Long Argument.'" *British Journal for the History of Science* 10.3 (1977): 237–46.

Köhler, Wolfgang. *Gestalt Psychology: An Introduction to New Concepts in Modern Psychology*. New York: Liveright, 1947.

Leja, Michael. "Peirce, Visuality, and Art." *Representations* 72 (2000): 97–122.
Lyell, Charles. *Principles of Geology*. Vol. 2. Chicago: U of Chicago P, 1991.
Perelman, Chaïm, and Lucie Olbrechts-Tyteca. *The New Rhetoric: A Treatise on Argumentation*. Trans. John Wilkinson and Purcell Weaver. Notre Dame: U of Notre Dame P, 1969.
Pinker, Steven. *Pattern Perception and the Comprehension of Graphs*. Cambridge, MA: Department of Psychology and Center for Cognitive Science, MIT, 1983.
———. "A Theory of Graph Comprehension." *Artificial Intelligence and the Future of Testing*. Ed. Roy Freedle. Hillsdale, NJ: Lawrence Erlbaum, 1990. 73–126.
Saussure, Ferdinand de. *Course in General Linguistics*. Ed. Charles Bally, Albert Sechehaye, and Albert Riedlinger. Trans. Roy Harris. Chicago: Open Court, 1986.
Schuhmacher, Helmut. *Korallenriffe: Verbreitung, Tierwelt, Ökologie*. Munich: BLV Verlagsgesellschaft, 1976.
Sebeok, Thomas A. "Iconicity." *MLN* 91.6 (1976): 1427–56.

8

Kenneth Burke's "Identification" and Chaïm Perelman and Lucie Olbrechts-Tyteca's "Communion": A Case of Convergent Evolution?

Richard Graff and Wendy Winn

Histories of rhetoric regularly emphasize the tension and interplay between preservation and innovation, between intellectual conservatism and originality or even iconoclasm. Contemporary rhetorical studies have been invigorated by reflection on this dialectic, with scholars frequently fixing their gaze on the problem of "rhetorical tradition." In one recent contribution to the discussion, Alan G. Gross proposes that the rhetorical tradition be conceived in terms of the development, refinement, and occasional contestation of key concepts, that is, of distinct idea-elements within larger theories ("Rhetorical Tradition"). Thus construed, the tradition emerges as a historical and intertextual process, as authors in different places and times engage—explicitly or possibly implicitly—with one another's ideas. Although the case Gross uses to illustrate this process (tracking from Aristotle's "bringing-before-the-eyes" to George Campbell's "vivacity" to Chaïm Perelman's "presence") stresses the development of concepts over a long period and across disparate cultural circumstances, we believe the idea can be usefully employed to investigate a concept's emergence and elaboration in shorter spans as well and to illuminate, by means of comparison, the work of roughly contemporary thinkers.

In this essay, we consider cognate concepts closely associated with two figures typically placed at the head of the canon of twentieth-century rhetorical thought, Kenneth Burke and Chaïm Perelman. Both saw their work as extending the classical tradition of rhetoric, but both recognized a need to supplement inherited classical lore. For Burke and Perelman, the impulse toward the development of "new" rhetorics does not entail a radical break with the "old" but gives prominence to certain ideas that were not or could not be clearly articulated in rhetorical theories of past ages. Burke's notion of Identification is a familiar and widely cited case in point. Though Burke's promotion of the concept has sometimes been interpreted as an effort to supplant rhetoric's traditional focus on persuasion, Burke himself characterized Identification as a supplement or "accessory" to classical theory.[1] Perelman and his collaborator Lucie Olbrechts-Tyteca's cognate concept, Communion, has drawn much less attention in the literature and is, consequently, less well understood. Yet, like Identification, it lies at the heart of, and thus is essential for a proper understanding of, an elaborate and powerful theory of rhetoric founded, in large part, on reinterpretation and refurbishment of classical ideas.

We have termed Identification and Communion "cognates," and in what follows we attempt to show in what ways and to what extent this label fits.[2] Because Burke's concept is much more familiar, our chief aim here is to elucidate Perelman and Olbrechts-Tyteca's Communion. But in juxtaposing Identification and Communion to locate areas of overlap and of difference, we find that the distinctive features of both concepts come into sharper focus. Identification and Communion are obviously similar but in ways that (to our knowledge) have not been carefully studied; these similarities make a case for what we would like to call the "convergent evolution" of concepts.[3] There are notable differences in emphasis, however, as well as occasional points of incongruity. Some of these, we suggest, may be attributed to the distinct origins and genealogies of the two concepts and the different intellectual traditions they reflect. Recognition of these differences will, we hope, contribute to a more general understanding of the thought of Perelman and of Burke.

Evolution of Concepts

The concepts of Identification and Communion did not emerge fully formed at a single point in their respective authors' work, nor did they develop in a vacuum. To lay foundations for comparing the two ideas, it will be helpful to track the development of each and point out some of the sources and forces that influenced the evolutionary process.

The case of Burke's Identification is rather complex. Fortunately, recent scholarship has done much to illuminate the sources for Burke's concept as well as the steps of its evolution over the course of Burke's career. Ross

Wolin has noted that Burke's fascination with Identification might be traced as far back as the 1920s, specifically to the term's usage by James Sibley Watson Jr., co-owner and editor of the *Dial*, who was a mentor to Burke and regularly published Burke's early essays and reviews (17, 228 nn. 27, 29). Burke's engagement with Freud's thought has been cited as another early and abiding influence (Wright; Davis); it has in fact been claimed that aspects of Burke's interpretation of Freudian identification can be discerned as early as *Counter-Statement* (Heath 31–32; Wright 302). Debra Hawhee has recently located another early influence in Sir Richard Paget's "gesture-speech theory" (341). Burke was also encouraged by the work of University of Chicago social psychologist George Herbert Mead. Collections of Mead's work, published posthumously beginning in 1934, were reviewed by Burke in 1939, and the review indicates that he was particularly impressed by the remarks on identification throughout Mead's texts (Burke, *Philosophy* 382). Mead raised the subject in his discussion of the individual's status vis-à-vis larger organizations; on this, he wrote:

> The principle which I have suggested as basic to human social organization is that of communication involving participation in the other. This requires the appearance of the other in the self, the identification of the other with the self, the reaching of self-consciousness through the other. . . . The very organization of the self-conscious community is dependent upon individuals taking the attitude of the other individuals. (253, 256)

If there is dispute about the closest antecedent to Burke's idea of Identification as it appears in its fullest form in his later works, a previously unpublished essay by Burke, "On Persuasion, Identification, and Dialectical Symmetry"—recently edited by James Zappen, who dates its composition to the mid-1940s—adds new evidence that Mead's work strongly influenced Burke's thinking in the years leading up to the publication of *A Rhetoric of Motives*.[4] One of the sources of appeal in Mead's formulation was in its dual emphasis on questions of individual identity or selfhood and its push beyond individual psychology to an explanation of modes of social existence. As we will see, the same themes and general trajectory are featured in Burke's work of the later 1930s and in his analysis of Identification-as-Consubstantiality in *A Rhetoric of Motives*.

Rather than reducing Burke's conception to a single source, however, we should understand his formulation of Identification as evolving over time, picking up elements from various quarters as he pursued his inquiry into symbolic action and human motives. For this reason, it has (rightly) been observed that a full understanding of Burkean Identification requires consideration of its appearances in works prior to its elevation to the status of "key term" in *A Rhetoric of Motives*. As several recent studies have done much of this work already, providing coordinates for tracking the concept's development over the course of Burke's career (Wolin; White; Jordan 265–69; George and Selzer), our summary will be brief.

References to (the idea of) Identification grew in frequency and prominence in the theory and criticism Burke produced over the course of the 1930s. In works of this period, Identification is sometimes conceived rather baldly in terms of rhetorical strategy or persuasive efficacy. One example of such usage comes in Burke's speech "Revolutionary Symbolism in America," delivered at the First American Writers Congress of 1935—a text thought to contain Burke's first (published) use of the term "identification" (Jordan 266; compare George and Selzer 26–29, 257–58 n. 4)—where he argues that communists' appeals would be more effective with the American middle classes if their call was to identify with "the people" rather than, as was the then-prevailing (but more exclusionary) practice, with "the worker." Another example comes from Burke's famous essay "The Rhetoric of Hitler's 'Battle,'" where Burke several times relates the Führer's powerful hold over the German populace to his insistence on the "total identification between leader and people" (Burke, *Philosophy* 195 n. 1, 198 n. 2, 207, 210). A more elaborate, theoretical treatment of Identification appears in *Attitudes Toward History*, where "Identity, Identification" is given its own entry in the concluding "Dictionary of Pivotal Terms" (263–73). There, Burke advances the thesis that individual identity, "the so-called 'I,'" is in fact "merely a unique combination of partially conflicting 'corporate we's'" (264). And against the view promulgated in psychoanalysis that "bad" or "faulty identification" is the source of malaise or maladjustment in the individual and thus a condition to be "cured," he reorients the perspective so as to emphasize the role of Identification as an essential condition of social existence: "One's participation in a collective, social role cannot be obtained in any other way [than through Identification]. *In fact, 'identification' is hardly other than a name for the function of sociality*" (266–67; our emphasis).[5] Further developments appear in Burke's next book, *The Philosophy of Literary Form*. There, as in *Attitudes Toward History*, he invokes Identification in the context of critiquing prevailing psychological conceptions of selfhood (or "*individualistic* concepts of identity") and in reasserting that, as a social actor, "the individual's identity is formed by reference to his membership in a group" (*Philosophy* 310–11, 306). Throughout, the concept is related specifically to *group* identification:

> By "identification" I have in mind this sort of thing: one's material and mental ways of placing oneself as a person in the groups and movements; one's ways of sharing vicariously in the role of leader or spokesman; formation and change of allegiance; the rituals of suicide, parricide, and prolicide, the vesting and divesting of insignia, the modes of initiation and purification, that are involved in the response to allegiance and change of allegiance; the part necessarily played by groups in the expectancies of the individual. (227)

While the works of the 1930s and early 1940s anticipate the concept's later development, in *A Rhetoric of Motives* Identification is raised to a new level of prominence and complexity (Wolin 178). In addition to explicitly marking Identification's status as a "key term" of his new rhetoric, in this work Burke introduces several new aspects and points of emphasis that would be further augmented and clarified in subsequent publications. For one, the notion of Identification is now elucidated by means of reference to ideas on substance and the "paradox of substance" presented in the preceding *Grammar of Motives*, leading Burke to recognize and utilize the alternative term, "Consubstantiality" (*Grammar of Motives* 31–58; *Rhetoric of Motives* 20–23). A second new element is a stress on Identification's corollary, Division, and Burke's clear recognition of the inseparability and simultaneity of the two conditions. These two aspects of Identification are highlighted in a famous passage from early in *A Rhetoric of Motives*:

> A is not identical with his colleague, B. But insofar as their interests are joined, A is *identified* with B. Or he may *identify himself* with B even when their interests are not joined, if he assumes that they are, or is persuaded to believe so. Here are ambiguities of substance. In being identified with B, A is "substantially one" with a person other than himself. Yet at the same time he remains unique, an individual locus of motives. Thus he is both joined and separate, at once a distinct substance and consubstantial with another. (20–21; see also 22, 45–46)

A third new element appearing in the evolved theory of Identification is a treatment of the concept at the level of formal technique and verbal style. In his analysis of "formal Identification," Burke reaches back to ideas on the "psychology of form" laid out in 1931's *Counter-Statement* and describes Identification as an effect of the speaker's or writer's use of certain rhetorical figures. This strategic understanding of Identification based on a functionalist interpretation of style is a factor largely neglected in the scholarship on Burke and, as it is a notion that calls for comparison with Perelman and

Olbrechts-Tyteca's account of Communion in *The New Rhetoric*, is a subject we consider in detail below.

Undergirding these elaborations of Identification in *A Rhetoric of Motives* and providing a basic rationale for the promotion of the concept to the status of "key term" in Burke's theory is Burke's engagement with the principles of traditional rhetoric. Although Burke took a "generally classical view of rhetoric" (Hochmuth 138), he explained that he developed the concept of Identification as a way to account for contexts not covered in the canonical texts of classical rhetoric focused on deliberate ("formally purposive") persuasion, usually as staged in conventional oratorical settings (Burke, *Philosophy* 268–69; compare "Rhetoric and Poetics" 301 and "On Persuasion" 336). The study of rhetoric, in Burke's view, should be able to account for more than an orator's overt or explicit aims and the effects wrought by deliberate design. Thus, he believed that a shift from persuasion, the key term of the "old" rhetoric, to Identification was needed to revive the study of rhetoric that, in the 1940s, he found exiled from humanistic inquiry (Burke, "Rhetoric—Old and New" 203; compare *Rhetoric of Motives* xiii). Burke noted that, unlike persuasion in the classical understanding, Identification could "include a partially 'unconscious' factor in appeal" ("Rhetoric—Old and New" 203). Hence, by centering itself on Identification, Burke's new rhetoric would be equipped to account for unintentional or unmotivated ("spontaneous," "unconscious," and the like) appeals, including those presented in communicative situations ignored by the classical rhetoricians. Burke's development of the idea of Identification, then, was in part motivated by his sense that the classical understanding of and focus on persuasion was unduly constraining.

Perelman came to the concept of Communion by a somewhat different path to and through classical rhetoric. In fact, Perelman did not set out to provide a theory of rhetoric at all. In the course of efforts to account for how people reason about values, Perelman and his collaborator Olbrechts-Tyteca sought a model of practical reasoning distinct from formal logic: the discovery of the classical tradition of rhetoric and of Aristotelian dialectic enabled Perelman and Olbrechts-Tyteca to approach the problem of values in ways demonstrative logic could not. Olbrechts-Tyteca later observed that it was their mentor and colleague Eugène Dupréel who encouraged them to consider classical rhetoric, of which they had previously been almost wholly ignorant (Olbrechts-Tyteca 3–6). Dupréel's work on the early Greek sophists—his book *Les sophistes* was published in 1948—illuminated the value of the ancient sources for emphasizing the centrality of common opinions, the reasonable, and the probable in rhetorical (nondemonstrative) argumentation (see also Dupréel, "Sur les origines de la dialectique").[6]

Dupréel's main body of work, in social philosophy, was an even more profound influence. Perelman had studied it carefully (see Perelman, "A Propos," "Fragments," and "Concerning Justice"), and it provided a rich source for the idea of Communion that would appear in publications he coauthored with Olbrechts-Tyteca beginning in 1950. Central to Dupréel's social theory was the idea of "rapports sociaux" (social rapports) (Dupréel, *Le rapport social*; *Traité de morale* 1:285–314; *Sociologie générale* 3–41). "A social *rapport* exists between two individuals when the existence and mode of behavior of the one has an influence upon the psychological states and acts of the other" (Tufts 221). Dupréel maintained that social groups form around and are held together by networks consisting of such "rapports." Chief among the sources of rapport undergirding large groups, Dupréel observed, are the values held in common by the group's members (*Sociologie générale* 179–95).

Dupréel's notion of social rapports explains the linkages of communities in terms of values shared by its members. For Perelman and Olbrechts-Tyteca, rhetorical argumentation requires just such a sense of community. This idea is most apparent in Perelman and Olbrechts-Tyteca's influential account of the function and effect of epideictic discourse. As was the case with Burke, Perelman and Olbrechts-Tyteca found the inherited lore of classical rhetoric wanting in certain respects, notably in its view of the epideictic genre. They claim that the classical authorities did not fully recognize the crucial social function of such discourse. Perelman and Olbrechts-Tyteca asserted that far from simply displaying a speaker's artistic talent, epideictic is argumentation aimed at reaffirming and strengthening the audience's adherence to the shared (communal) values lauded in the discourse.[7] The values promoted in any particular epideictic speech are presumed to command the assent of the audience addressed by the discourse, and as such, the discourse fosters a sense of solidarity or communal spirit among the members of the audience who share these values (*New Rhetoric* 48–53; compare Perelman and Olbrechts-Tyteca, "Logique et rhétorique" 13–14). "Communion" is the term Perelman and Olbrechts-Tyteca introduce to name this solidarity.[8] And with their assertion that *"values enter, at some stage or other, into every argument"* (*New Rhetoric* 75, our emphasis), epideictic and the idea of Communion thus prove to be crucial foundations for their entire theory of rhetorical argumentation.

Communion in this its primary sense is thus a sociological notion, one that carries forward Dupréel's ideas about shared values as a source of social rapport and cohesion into an understanding of the social function of rhetoric. One of the consequences of the reinterpretation of epideictic and positing of Communion as the aim of such discourse is a stretching of the classical paradigm of rhetorical action. Roughly parallel to Burke's shift of attention from persuasion to Identification, this aspect of Perelman and Olbrechts-Tyteca's "new rhetoric" works to free rhetorical theory from an exclusive focus on discrete instances of strategic communication in a bounded "rhetorical situation," a conception of rhetoric under which it is not surprising that epideictic would be neglected or misconstrued. This is so because, as Perelman and Olbrechts-Tyteca contend, epideictic, though celebrating values in the present, is oriented toward the future. The Communion it fosters is anticipatory and preparatory. Epideictic's principal effect is long-term and sets itself against *future* objections: "The argumentation in epidictic discourse sets out to increase the intensity of adherence to certain values, which might not be contested when considered on their own but may nevertheless not prevail against other values that might come into conflict with them" at some future date (*New Rhetoric* 51; compare "Logique et rhétorique" 14).

Perelman and Olbrechts-Tyteca first introduced their interpretation of epideictic and this idea of Communion—what we have elsewhere called its "strong" sense (Graff and Winn 64–65)—in a rather brief passage of an essay originally published in 1950 ("Logique et rhétorique" 13–14). As was the case with Burkean Identification, however, the concept of Communion was augmented in later work, assuming its greatest prominence in the *Traité de l'argumentation* (and its translation, *The New Rhetoric*), which features a more elaborate account of epideictic and the role of values in argumentation. An additional feature of *The New Rhetoric* is a discussion of Communion as an effect of verbal devices such as maxims, quotations, and certain rhetorical figures (163–79, discussed below). The notion of Communion emerging from the passages concerning verbal form—"a transient and localized effect of the individual discourse," or what we have termed the "weak" sense of Communion (Graff and Winn 64)—signals a development of the concept in Perelman and Olbrechts-Tyteca's thinking, but one that would not receive further elaboration in their subsequent publications.

In fact, the concept of Communion appears only infrequently following *The New Rhetoric*; explicit references to it are surprisingly rare, a problem compounded by the English translations of Perelman's work that tend to obscure his usage of the term.[9] (This reticence stands in marked contrast to Burke's forceful promotion of Identification in virtually all his work following *A Rhetoric of Motives*.) On the occasions when Communion does appear in his later work, however, Perelman places increased emphasis on the concept's importance for understanding the social and political functions of rhetoric. The culminating statement comes in one of Perelman's last essays,

"Rhétorique et politique," which appeared in French in 1982 and in English translation (as "Rhetoric and Politics") in 1984. There, Perelman returns to the issue of epideictic and the role of values in argumentation but states more directly and passionately his position on the centrality of Communion in the maintenance of political community. An epideictic speaker's goal, he writes,

> is to contribute to the enhancement of values, to create a spiritual communion around common values [*de créer une communion spirituelle autour des valeurs communes*]. . . . His role will be to exalt publicly the values around which the community is formed and through which it communes. *Without the common devotion to such values, there is no political or religious community.* ("Rhetoric and Politics" 131; our emphasis)

In addition to identifying Communion as a requirement for the existence of political communities generally, Perelman remarks on its specific function in the rhetoric that sustains democratic politics. Acknowledging that every political community will consist of individuals and groups with competing interests and values, Perelman points to the sense of Communion cultivated in epideictic discourses as the factor that enables the community to confront and transcend internal divisions that threaten to fracture it:

> It is this devotion [that is, Communion] which unites the members of [a political or religious] community, which permits it to surmount the passing crises, the discords over secondary problems, and the personal conflicts which never fail to surface in all human groups where members maintain between themselves multiple and durable relations. . . . In order for a democratic regime to function, that is, in order for a minority to accept the decision of the majority, after deliberation, the values common to all members of the community must be considered more fundamental than those which tend to separate it. Without these values, without the spiritual unity [*l'unité spirituelle*] which the epidictic discourse properly reinforces, there is neither a majority nor a minority, rather two antagonistic groups which clash, where the strongest group dominates the weakest and where nothing counts except the power struggle. Political life, when it is something other than oppression of the weakest by the strongest, presupposes support for the community values [*présuppose l'adhesion à des valeurs communes*], to common traditions and institutions, to common interests which will serve as the norms and the criteria for the solution of conflicts in both political and judiciary matters. ("Rhetoric and Politics" 131–32)

In Perelman's final analysis, then, Communion emerges as the crucial variable enabling the formation of consensus on questions of importance to the entire community through reasonable deliberation and argument and, thus, as a condition that must be cultivated in communities opposed to alternative arrangements under which the compliance of the weak is procured through the use of force.

Burke wrote that "if men were not apart from one another, there would be no need for the rhetorician to proclaim their unity" (*Rhetoric of Motives* 22). Perelman's account of epideictic discourse and the Communion it promotes comports well with this assessment. Epideictic proclamations of unity testify to the fact of separation. In stressing the importance of Communion, Perelman does not propose to eliminate or deny social or personal divisions or to render dissent impossible. In fact, in *The New Rhetoric*, Perelman and Olbrechts-Tyteca expressly oppose their conception of rhetorical argumentation to the model of analytical logic and demonstrative reasoning that requires the sublimation of such factors to the formal standards of an abstract rationality and aims at the production of incontrovertible proofs. Deliberation relating to human interests and values, they maintain, must honor the autonomy of individuals, and argumentation in such contexts is an act of "mental cooperation" rather than a formal calculation (*New Rhetoric* 16). But such cooperation is not guaranteed. Hence, the rhetor's first priority must be to secure the specific audience's willingness to be reasoned with, and all his or her arguments must be adapted to that audience, to its beliefs, values, and interests. These will be diverse and often competing within any sizable audience. Through the idea of Communion, Perelman and Olbrechts-Tyteca describe the minimal level of commonality (between a speaker and a particular audience and between disparate audience members) required for genuine deliberation in the face of social diversity and difference.

Our remarks here are sufficient to indicate that Identification and Communion developed from different intellectual contexts. Nevertheless, by the time the concepts had "evolved" into their fullest articulations, their convergence is apparent in several areas. As mentioned earlier, one point at which the two appear to move especially close is in their authors' treatments of linguistic techniques for achieving Communion and Identification. This impression can be confirmed, though, only by a detailed comparison of these techniques, to which we now turn.

Verbal Techniques and Stylistic Effects

In *The New Rhetoric*, Perelman and Olbrechts-Tyteca describe three groups of verbal techniques for establishing Communion.[10] Listed in the first group are modes of expression bound to a particular cultural milieu. Of these, maxims and proverbs receive special consideration for their role in circulating and promulgating the values that sustain social groups. Maxims express norms or value judgments by "condens[ing] the wisdom of the nations—they are also one of the most effective means of promoting this wisdom and causing it to develop" (165). Proverbs are a type of maxim, short, popularized statements that "illustrat[e] a standard." Perelman and Olbrechts-Tyteca observe that a proverb may be used as a premise (starting point) for argumentation provided that the audience accepts it as valid. Although agreement with a value judgment or standard expressed in a maxim or proverb is "never compulsory," the authors state that "so great is its force, so great the presumption of agreement attaching to it, that one must have weighty reasons for rejecting it" (166). Slogans and catchwords are also included in this initial grouping, though their argumentative force is reduced and depends entirely on the particular context:

> They are designed to secure attention through their rhythm and their concise and easily remembered form, but they are adapted to particular circumstances, require constant renewal, and are too recent to enjoy the wide traditional agreement accorded to proverbs. [Slogans and catchwords] may be able to stimulate action, but they are much less effective at inducing beliefs. (167)

Listed in the second group are devices that achieve Communion "through references to a common culture, tradition or past" (177). Perelman and Olbrechts-Tyteca single out allusion and quotation as devices that serve to bring to mind a culture's shared heritage or common knowledge. An allusion hints at a historical event or cultural fact for the audience to recall "without actually naming it" (177). Because the speaker can presume the audience's recognition of the allusion, as well as its agreement with and communion around the values it engenders, the device "will nearly always have argumentative value" (170). A quotation, stated without reference to author or source, can of course elicit a similar response. Devices of this sort can function argumentatively only where there is a community already in place; indeed, their effective usage at a given moment would seem to make this fact salient.[11]

It should be apparent that there is a degree of overlap between these first two classes of Communion-building devices. Especially significant for our purposes is the fact that both classes are "value-related" or even "value-centered." Both have to do, that is, with the reaffirmation of values presumed to be held by the audience addressed. This is naturally the case in a speaker's use of a proverb or maxim (provided it is used seriously, not in parody or the like) but is equally the case with allusions and quotations, assuming that the values of the source text (if it is one honored by the community addressed) are affirmed and not challenged or subjected to criticism or ridicule. Of course, the opposite would hold for allusions to or quotations of sources held in low esteem by the audience: Communion could be built by a speaker's rough or dismissive treatment of the values associated with such a source at the time it is alluded to or quoted. Perelman and Olbrechts-Tyteca's analysis of these particular techniques of Communion, then, is basically continuous and consistent with the earlier sections of *The New Rhetoric* in which Communion is associated with epideictic discourse, emerging as conceptual shorthand for the state of agreement on values shared by members of a community.

Perelman and Olbrechts-Tyteca's third group consists of Communion-establishing techniques of a different sort. They include "all those figures whereby a speaker endeavors to get his audience to participate actively in his exposition, by taking it into his confidence, inviting its help, or identifying himself with it" (178). Following this definition, Perelman and Olbrechts-Tyteca name these devices:

- use of the interrogative mood or oratorical question
- use of the vocative mood and figures of address such as apostrophe and imaginary direct address
- the shifting of grammatical categories, specifically pronouns, as in the traditional figure of enallage of person, "in which 'I' or 'he' is replaced by 'thou,'" or in a simple "*change in the number of persons,* in which 'I' or 'thou' is replaced by 'we'" (178)

It is immediately apparent that this third group of techniques for increasing Communion stands apart from the other two. While the devices in the first two groups—maxims, proverbs, allusions, quotations—could be considered "value-centered," the devices in the third group could be considered "value-neutral" because the techniques used to promote an audience's involvement do not function by evoking values presumed to be shared by its members. This group of devices seeks instead to "effect a merger" between the speaker and the audience or to invite an audience's participation in the discourse without the aim of "getting information" or "securing agreement" (178). As we have elsewhere observed, Perelman and Olbrechts-Tyteca's account of this third group of stylistic techniques thus has the effect of enlarging the concept of Communion beyond a community's active agreement on values, extending it to include "the audience's involvement in the discourse and its perception of a generic affiliation with the speaker" (Graff and Winn 61).

Comparison to Burke's remarks on the function of figurative language in relation to Identification will help to underscore and clarify the distinction we are making between "value-centered" and "value-neutral" techniques for establishing Communion. In the section of *A Rhetoric of Motives* devoted to the "Traditional Principles of Rhetoric," Burke includes a discussion of figures that is at least superficially similar to Perelman and Olbrechts-Tyteca's treatment. In a subsection devoted specifically to Identification (*Rhetoric of Motives* 55–59), Burke observes that "many purely formal patterns can readily awaken an attitude of collaborative expectancy in us" (58).[12] Here, Burke's account of Identification rests on the theory of form and formal appeal from his early book *Counter-Statement*, in which form is defined as the arousal of an appetite or expectation and its satisfaction (29–44, 123–212). Further amplifying ideas from *Counter-Statement*, Burke next identifies several patterning devices that have the effect of inviting the audience's "participation" and inducing its "collaboration" with the verbal form. He adds that rhetorical schemes such as "antithesis" or "gradatio" will elicit the hearer's or reader's participation "regardless of the subject matter." To thus collaborate with the form is to surrender or yield to it, and in this way the form of an utterance prepares the audience to accept the proposition it expresses:

> [A] yielding to the form prepares for assent to the matter identified with it. Thus, you are drawn to the form, not in your capacity as a partisan, but because of some "universal" appeal in it. And this attitude of assent may then be transferred to the matter which happens to be associated with the form. . . .
>
> [R]ecall a gradatio of political import, much in the news during the "Berlin crisis" of 1948: "Who controls Berlin, controls Germany; who controls Germany controls Europe; who controls Europe controls the world." As a proposition, it may or may not be true. . . . But regardless of these doubts about it as a proposition, by the time you arrive at the second of its three stages, you feel how it is destined to develop—and on the level of purely formal assent you would collaborate to round out its symmetry by spontaneously willing its completion and perfection as an utterance. Add, now, the psychosis of nationalism, and assent on the formal level invites assent to the proposition as doctrine. (Rhetoric of Motives 58–59)

Burke concludes with a summary of his view of the relationship between Identification and form: "The expressing of a proposition in one or another of these rhetorical forms [figures] would involve 'identification,' first by inducing the auditor to participate in the form, as a 'universal' locus of appeal, and next by trying to include a partisan statement within this same pale of assent" (59). In a later essay, Burke remarks:

> In my *Rhetoric of Motives*, I have suggested the possibility that the appeal in the sheer *forms* of expression—be they called poetic or rhetorical—is *universal*. Hence, an audience can readily yield to this aspect of an exhortation. And in thus responding to the *doctrinally neutral* aspects of the address, the audience is in more of a mood to accept by contagion the rest of the author's plea. ("Rhetoric and Poetics" 296).

It should be apparent that Burke's ideas on the universal appeal of form distinguish his account of the effects of figurative language from the "value-centered" techniques of Communion noted by Perelman and Olbrechts-Tyteca. In contrast to the use of proverbs, maxims, or even allusion, the figures of gradatio or antithesis will provoke Identification with the formal pattern independent of the "content" of the utterance. Burke's comments on certain figures' capacity to induce collaboration with the form, however, appear at first glance quite similar to Perelman and Olbrechts-Tyteca's remarks on the figures of Communion of the third type, those that elicit audience participation or involvement in the discourse. But again, there are crucial differences. First, very different figures are identified as producing these effects. Where Perelman and Olbrechts-Tyteca identify figures of address and pronoun shifts, Burke focuses exclusively on rhetorical schemes, that is, on figures featuring pronounced patterns of repetition and syntactic balance or symmetry, especially those that yoke ideas of complementary or opposing senses. This emphasis can be seen most clearly when the devices Burke mentions as especially potent in commanding "formal assent" are put in a list:[13]

- antithesis
- climax or gradatio
- epanaphora (the repetition of initial words in successive clauses)
- homoioteleuton (repetition of sounds at the end of successive clauses)
- asyndeton

All of these devices of stylistic Identification turn out to be traditional figures of diction or grammatical schemes and are to be distinguished from the rhetorical figures appearing in Perelman and Olbrechts-Tyteca's account. Indeed, *none* of the devices Burke singles out is mentioned by Perelman and Olbrechts-Tyteca as a means of establishing or enhancing Communion.

A second difference, following from the first, concerns the precise nature of the audience's "participation" or "collaboration" implied in each account. As discussed above, the argumentative effect of Perelman and Olbrechts-Tyteca's figures of Communion would be to bring audience members to a new perspective in which they would perceive a connection with the speaker and/or with one another, either in terms of shared standards or cultural horizons or more basically in terms of the discursive context in which the speaker's "we" might reasonably be presumed to include them. By contrast, in Burke's account, the audience's "collaboration" is with the form of the utterance itself. Further, Burke describes this effect as virtually irresistible, "a *yielding* to the formal development, *surrendering* to its symmetry as such" (*Rhetoric of Motives* 58; our emphasis). For Burke, then, the "collaboration" involved in formal Identification turns out to be submission to the (verbal) form *as form*; it does not appear to involve a feeling or perception of oneness or togetherness with others but is a more private (even solipsistic?) effect produced in the individual hearer or reader. Indeed, it is just possible that Perelman and Olbrechts-Tyteca would count the "purely formal assent" Burke describes as a psychological or aesthetic effect outside the purview of their theory of argumentation.[14]

Verbal techniques for achieving communion or identification

	Perelman and Olbrechts-Tyteca			Burke
	Devices of Communion 1	**Devices of Communion 2**	**Devices of Communion 3**	**Formal Identification**
Devices	Maxims, proverbs, slogans, value-terms	Allusions, quotations	Oratorical question, apostrophe, enallage of person	Antithesis, gradatio, anaphora, asyndeton
Functions or effects	Express communal values, often in concise and rhythmical form	Evoke or refer to a shared past or cultural tradition; may express communal values or standards	Involve the audience in the discourse, elicit audience's participation in the argumentation, effect the verbal merger of speaker and audience	Invite participation of the audience, "awaken attitude of collaborative expectancy," compel assent to the form, surrender to verbal pattern or symmetry

The distinctions we have observed here are presented in schematic form in the table, in which Burke's notion of formal Identification, being entirely disconnected from the concern with values shown in Perelman and Olbrechts-Tyteca's first two categories of Communion-building devices, is placed in a separate column to the far right. A practical illustration of the differences in conception and nuance can be produced by means of a reference to Martin Luther King Jr.'s celebrated "I Have a Dream" speech. Consider the manner in which Burke and Perelman and Olbrechts-Tyteca would assess the following passage:

> There are those who are asking the devotees of civil rights, "When will you be satisfied?"
> We can never be satisfied as long as the Negro is the victim of the unspeakable horrors of police brutality.
> We can never be satisfied as long as our bodies . . . cannot gain lodging in the motels of the highways and the hotels of the cities.
> We cannot be satisfied as long as the Negro's basic mobility is from a smaller ghetto to a larger one.
> We can never be satisfied as long as our children are stripped of their selfhood and robbed of their dignity by signs saying "For Whites Only."
> We cannot be satisfied as long as a Negro in Mississippi cannot vote and a Negro in New York believes he has nothing for which to vote.
> No, no, we are not satisfied, and we will not be satisfied until justice rolls down like waters and righteousness like a mighty stream. (King 781–82)

Burke would likely call attention to the insistent anaphoric variations on the phrase "we can never [cannot] be satisfied as long as . . ." These form a clear syntactic and sonic pattern but also generate a sense of tension that increases with each succeeding sentence, culminating in the antithesis (with homoioteleuton), "We cannot be satisfied as long as a Negro in Mississippi cannot vote and a Negro in New York believes he has nothing for which to vote." This tension is released only in the conclusion of the series—"No, no, we are not satisfied, and we will not be satisfied . . ."—with its breaking of the regular pattern of epanaphora and in the opening of the syntax and rhythm in the second half of the final sentence, "until justice rolls down like waters and righteousness like a mighty stream." Burke would undoubtedly describe how the audience is carried along by the insistently repeated lexical units and grammatical constructions, eventually yielding to the pattern. This "assent" or "acquiescence" to the form might then be attached to the content of King's statements: the reality of continuing racial injustice and the legitimacy of King's insistence that the situation is no longer tolerable and will no longer be tolerated.[15]

By contrast, Perelman and Olbrechts-Tyteca would presumably describe a different effect of the phrasal repetition—anaphora for them being the chief figure of "Presence," not of Communion (*New Rhetoric* 174–75). They would perceive an effort to forge Communion, instead, in King's deployment of the device of reported address or "oratorical communication" in which the "devotees of civil rights" (that is, King's immediate audience) are being asked by an unspecified "those" (presumably non-devotees), "When will *you* be satisfied?" Perelman and Olbrechts-Tyteca might then note how King immediately breaks away from this narrated hypothetical exchange, shifting the reference "you" (all) to "we" and thereby speaking "as one" with his audience: "'When will *you* be satisfied?' *We* can never be satisfied as long as the Negro is the victim of the unspeakable horrors of police brutality." The insistent repetition of the pronoun "we" in the remainder of the passage, they would observe, simultaneously increases the referent's (that is, "devotees of civil rights") Presence and reinforces its sense of solidarity. And Perelman and Olbrechts-Tyteca would observe a further reinforcement of Communion in the near-quotation of Amos 5:24 in the final sentence (a passage rendered in the King James Version as, "But let judgment run down as waters, and righteousness as a mighty stream"). These features exemplify two major aspects of Communion as an effect of the verbal form of discourse, both of them quite distinct from Burke's ideas on formal Identification: they seek to involve the audience in a sort of virtual dialogic interaction and to effect a merger with the speaker (in the pronoun "we"), and they evoke a shared tradition through the familiar (biblical) reference.

Points of Convergence/Divergence

While the previous section exposed differences between Perelman and Olbrechts-Tyteca's Communion and Burke's Identification in details related to style and verbal technique, our focus now shifts to broader similarities and differences between the two concepts and to some difficulties they raise.

We begin by recalling Burke's programmatic remarks on Identification from *A Rhetoric of Motives*:

> [W]e might well keep it in mind that a speaker persuades an audience by the use of stylistic identifications; his act of persuasion may be for the purpose of causing the audience to identify itself with the speaker's interests; and the speaker draws on identification of interests to establish rapport between himself and his audience. So, there is no chance of our keeping apart the meanings of persuasion, identification ("consubstantiality") and communication (the nature of rhetoric as "addressed"). (46)

Taken in combination with Burke's remarks on figures discussed above, this passage enables us to distinguish two aspects of Identification: (1) it is an effect of style, inasmuch as the form of expression (*how* an utterance is expressed) compels a "submission" to the form regardless of the content; and (2) it has a broader social sense, one not necessarily bound to form, involving a speaker's establishment of rapport with the audience by his or her calling to mind areas of shared interest or experience through *what* he or she says; Identification, or "consubstantiality," in this sense results from the content of the utterance, not its form.[16] As we have seen, there is a corresponding split in Perelman and Olbrechts-Tyteca's notion of Communion: (1) it is a local effect of style insofar as certain figures and other verbal devices express traditional value judgments, call up shared cultural knowledge, or elicit the participation of the audience in the discourse; (2) in its more prominent guise, Communion denotes a community's sense of solidarity, a solidarity reinforced in the periodic extolling of communal values through epideictic discourse.

The foregoing comparison indicates an overarching convergence in the evolution of Identification and Communion but at the same time suggests some differences in detail or nuance. The convergence of the two concepts is witnessed most basically in a progressive broadening of function and significance. As we have seen, both have a strategic dimension. As effects of verbal style, Identification and Communion can be understood and analyzed as factors contributing to the efficacy of a discourse. Secured through the strategic use of language, they are transitory states under which the audience becomes especially receptive to the rhetor's arguments or claims—or, in Burke's formulation, in submitting to the form of the discourse, the audience finds itself "in more of a mood to accept by contagion the rest of the author's plea" ("Rhetoric and Poetics" 296). In this aspect, Identification and Communion may be described as technical *means* of rhetorical discourse and appear to be placed chiefly in the service of a rather traditional conception of rhetoric-as-persuasion.

But Identification and Communion are also characterized as *ends*, as rhetorical objectives alternative or complementary to persuasion. This is clearly the case when each is described as a consequence of single or multiple related discourses that promote a feeling of solidarity among audience members, the perception of belonging to a community, or a sense of consubstantiality.[17] In many passages in Burke, Identification appears as the goal or culmination of symbolic action; and though Burke claims that a focus on Identification entails a new orientation for rhetorical theory, he also admits that "there is no chance of our keeping apart the meanings of persuasion, identification ('consubstantiality') and communication" (*Rhetoric of Motives* 46)—that is, in practice, Identification and persuasion commonly overlap. When described as a rhetorical objective, Communion is more closely circumscribed. It is genre-specific; Communion is the end of epideictic discourse, as epideictic's chief aim is to reinforce the audience's adherence to communal values and standards. Insofar as these values and standards enjoy a level of agreement prior to the discourse, the epideictic speaker is not engaged in persuasion of a conventional sort. Nevertheless, the speaker does utilize argumentation in seeking to increase the "intensity" of the audience's adherence to the by-and-large uncontroversial theses advanced in the discourse (Perelman and Olbrechts-Tyteca, *New Rhetoric* 48–53).

In both theories, how means and ends interact is not always clear. For Perelman and Olbrechts-Tyteca, the application of the "figures of Communion" is not restricted to any particular type or genre of discourse, epideictic or otherwise. Rather, these figures appear to be generally applicable in rhetorical argumentation, within which they would play an auxiliary or contributory role in the speaker's larger effort to secure the audience's adherence to a possibly controversial thesis. Their contribution to Communion in the sense sought by epideictic discourse seems clear in the case of the devices that function through the evocation of communal values (that is, the first two classes of devices identified above—proverb, allusion, and so on). However, other devices described as bringing about Communion do not have this direct link to the values or "rapports" that function over time to constitute and sustain a community: they are, rather, localized strategies that seek to create more transitory bonds between the participants involved in the rhetorical transaction. In Burke's account of the figures, the meaning of Identification is stretched beyond the typical understanding of the concept. According to Burke's analysis, figures like gradatio and climax do not function to merge the "substance" of author and audience (that is, to forge "consubstantiality"); rather, they bring about the reader's or hearer's "identification" with the verbal form of the discourse. If there is a connection between the latter effect and the former, it is indirect and somewhat tenuous. Identification with the form, Burke observes, reduces the audience's ability to resist the content or "matter" of the discourse—presumably, this content could sometimes include elements indicating zones of consubstantiality, but this possibility is not essential to Burke's account of the figures of Identification per se.

The recognition of Identification and Communion as discursive goals or ends implies a third dimension of both concepts, namely, a socially *constitutive* function. In both cases, this constitutive function can be understood to stand prior to individual efforts of persuasion and, in fact, to make such efforts possible. Maurice Charland has made this point well regarding Burkean Identification:

> [T]he very existence of social subjects (who would become audience members) is already a rhetorical effect.... [M]uch of what we as rhetorical critics consider to be a product or consequence of discourse, including social identity, religious faith, sexuality, and ideology is beyond the realm of rational or even free choice, beyond the realm of persuasion. As Burke notes, the identifications of social identity can occur "spontaneously, intuitively, even unconsciously." ... Such identifications are rhetorical, for they are discursive effects that induce human cooperation. They are also, however, logically prior to persuasion. Indeed, humans are constituted in these characteristics; they are essential to the "nature" of a subject and form the basis for persuasive appeals. (Charland 133–34)[18]

A similar picture emerges from Perelman's account of the Communion around shared values brought about and intensified through epideictic discourse. Especially in his later essays, Perelman is quick to emphasize that epideictic rhetoric is necessary for the initial establishment of Communion around values and, further, that community (political or religious) itself *requires* adherence to a set of concrete and abstract values (see, for example, "New Rhetoric" 116; "Rhetoric and Politics" 131). Such adherence "identifies" a community's members.

In the concept of Communion, then, Perelman and Olbrechts-Tyteca (no less than Burke) describe a constitutive function for rhetoric. Charland argues that Burke's concept of Identification, unlike traditional theories of "rhetoric as persuasion," provides a means of understanding how individuals become social subjects and rhetorical objects (that is, audiences that a rhetor aims to persuade). After observing—quite rightly, in our view—that such an understanding is "critical to the development of a theoretical understanding of the power of discourse," Charland remarks:

> If it is easier to praise Athens before Athenians than before Laecedemonians [sic], we should ask how those in Athens come to experience themselves as Athenians. Indeed, a rhetoric to Athenians in praise of Athens would be relatively insignificant compared to a rhetoric that constitutes Athenians as such. (134; our emphases; for the classical reference, compare Burke, *Rhetoric of Motives* 55)

Perelman and Olbrechts-Tyteca's ideas on epideictic and Communion indicate how a "rhetoric to Athenians in praise of Athens" is, precisely, a rhetoric "that constitutes Athenians as such."[19]

Perelman and Olbrechts-Tyteca's Communion is "prior" to persuasion in a narrower, more technical sense as well. The construction of public or political arguments relies on and makes use of certain fore-agreements of the audience. The values around which a community forms are a source of the sorts of agreement from which, Perelman and Olbrechts-Tyteca maintain, rhetorical argumentation must begin. They may be used as premises or "starting points" for argumentation but are especially important ones in that (to repeat an earlier reference to *The New Rhetoric*) "values enter, at some stage or other, *into every argument*" (75; our emphasis). Communion is, at once, a product of epideictic discourses and a necessary prerequisite to any rhetorical argumentation.

To crystallize the points of convergence and divergence between Perelman's Communion and Burke's Identification, we offer the following summary:

- Communion in its dominant sense relates to the values shared by members of a community, values that are a chief source of a community's cohesion. By contrast, Identification in its primary sense pertains to any conceivable zone of common interest or experience (any ground of "consubstantiality"), values constituting only one zone among many.
- Communion and Identification are both described as effects of verbal style. Different formal devices produce these effects, however. Where Perelman and Olbrechts-Tyteca emphasize style's capacity to evoke sources of a community's cohesion or to create liaisons between speaker and audience, Burke's account of the psychological appeal of form focuses on the audience or reader's "submission" to verbal patterns; this submission to form may in turn increase the likelihood of assent to the propositional content of the discourse. In both cases, there is not an exact correspondence between the stylistic and dominant social dimensions of the concepts.
- For Perelman and Olbrechts-Tyteca, Communion is the objective of epideictic argumentation but a precursor to or starting point for argumentation in all genres; shared values are necessary for the constitution of communities and, as potential premises of argumentation, represent a resource for rhetorical invention. Identification, too, is described in terms of both process and objective in symbolic action, and it too performs a constitutive function; Identification is not related to specific genres of discourse, however, or even to argumentation per se but rather expands so as to be implicated in all communication.

Final Thoughts

We have indicated that the concepts of Identification and Communion developed, in part, out of their respective authors' engagement with the principles of classical rhetoric—Burke sought to broaden the purview of rhetorical theory beyond its conventional focus on deliberate persuasion; Perelman and Olbrechts-Tyteca sought to highlight the social function of rhetoric they believed was obscured in the classical accounts of epideictic. In both cases, classical stylistic theory is refurbished by an emphasis on a functional rationale for figurative language. It is equally apparent that the concepts of Identification and Communion developed as parallel responses to the historical circumstances of the mid-twentieth century, including, most saliently, the trauma of World War II and its aftermath, although this is a topic we do not consider here.

We have suggested that some of the differences in emphasis or nuance in their theories may be attributed to the fact that they originated in different circumstances—the authors' initial and primary interests in rhetoric being quite distinct—and that they reflect different intellectual sources and influences. But because Perelman was familiar with Burke's work, we think it appropriate, by way of conclusion, to ask whether Burke's ideas on Identification, which appeared before Perelman and Olbrechts-Tyteca began their rhetorical investigations, might have had any direct influence on their conception of Communion.[20] Although any answer will be speculative, there is at least one passage that encourages us in the attempt. In the essay "The New Rhetoric: A Theory of Practical Reasoning," originally published one year after the English translation of *The New Rhetoric*, Perelman, in the course of summarizing his view of the significance of epideictic, makes reference to Burkean Identification, and his language hints at a correspondence to Communion:

> The orator's aim in the epideictic genre is not just to gain a passive adherence from his audience but to provoke the action wished for or, at least, to awaken a disposition so to act. This is achieved by forming a community of minds, which Kenneth Burke, who is well aware of the importance of this genre, calls *identification*. As he writes, rhetoric "is rooted in an essential function of language itself, a function that is wholly realistic and is continually born anew; the use of language as a symbolic means of inducing cooperation in beings that by nature respond to symbols." (Perelman, "New Rhetoric: A Theory" 7; compare Burke, *Rhetoric of Motives* 43)

The explicit reference to Identification here is in itself notable, for Perelman mentions Burke's key term surprisingly infrequently. On this point, the occasion of the essay may be significant. Although originally written in French, it was published in English translation in 1970 as part of the

University of Chicago's "Great Ideas" series. Perelman undoubtedly had an American readership in mind, and this fact might explain the unusually prominent mention of Burke, who was by that time well known to this audience.[21] However, it is not entirely clear from the context what Perelman has in mind in relating Identification to Burke's keen awareness of the importance of epideictic. Burke's most extensive discussion of the epideictic genre, found in *A Rhetoric of Motives* (69–73), a work with which Perelman was familiar, is actually quite conventional—quite close, in fact, to the classical, basically Aristotelian view that Perelman claims to oppose. Nor does Burke describe a specific connection between epideictic and Identification in that work.

In a later essay, however, in the context of defending his thesis on the interpenetration of rhetoric and poetics, Burke again remarks on epideictic and there reconsiders the genre's role and function ("Rhetoric and Poetics"). He observes that while epideictic discourse does often become art for art's sake, its literary character does not mean it is without social significance. To designate epideictic's social function, Burke refers to the concept of "phatic communion" borrowed from social anthropologist Bronislaw Malinowksi: "[D]oes not epideictic readily become transformed into a display art, pure and simple? Indeed, . . . there seem to have been times when, the less men had to say, the greater was their delight in the saying. The anthropologist Malinowski proposed the term 'phatic communion' to designate the social satisfaction of sheer chatter" (Burke, "Rhetoric and Poetics" 295–96).[22] While Burke's reference to "phatic communion"—specifically in relation to epideictic, no less—might suggest a case of terminological borrowing, the possibility can be discounted regarding *The New Rhetoric*: there is no indication that Perelman knew this essay, and its date (1966) means that it comes after the detailed account of epideictic and Communion in *The New Rhetoric*. Burke does make reference to the concept of phatic communion in earlier works, however, and he occasionally also uses the unqualified term "communion," usually in relation to the experience of mystical transcendence (for example, *Attitudes Toward History* 235; *Rhetoric of Motives* 269–70; *Grammar of Motives* 297–99). Though Perelman was familiar with some of these works, his own usage of the term has a very different primary meaning—that is, community members' devotion to shared values—and nowhere is it aligned with either "the social satisfaction of sheer chatter" or "the experience of mystic unity" (Burke, *Grammar of Motives* 297), as it is in Burke.[23]

Moreover, it is possible that the phrase "community of minds" in the English translation of the passage from "The New Rhetoric: A Theory of

Practical Reasoning" quoted above renders an original French "*communauté des esprits*"—with the same sense this phrase carries in the section of *The New Rhetoric* devoted to the "contact of minds" (14–17)—rather than such plausible alternatives as "*communion des esprits*" or "*communion des consciences.*"[24] Though it remains beyond confirmation, the reading "*communauté des esprits*" would point to the base-level "intellectual contact" Perelman considers a requirement for any argumentation (*New Rhetoric* 14; see Graff and Winn 50–51), without necessarily implying the sharing of values that defines Communion in its primary sense in *The New Rhetoric*. From this, it stands to reason that by his reference to Burke's Identification, Perelman may mean to call up the notion of a preliminary contact and of an "effective community of minds" that joins divided interlocutors, at least temporarily, in order for argumentation to proceed. A similar dialectic of connection and division is of course central to Burke's conception of Identification,[25] and Perelman's quotation of Burke's statement on language as "a symbolic means of inducing cooperation" resonates strongly with the principle that rhetorical argumentation seeks the audience's "adherence," "assent," and "mental cooperation" (*New Rhetoric* 16)

Obviously, beneath the layer of speculative correspondences we have just sketched, there is a bedrock of agreement on matters of considerable theoretical significance. In his reference to Burkean Identification in the passage of "The New Rhetoric: A Theory of Practical Reasoning" quoted above, Perelman is clearly *interpreting* Burke to mean what he himself asserts concerning the role and significance of epideictic. And indeed, Perelman's "community of minds" (whatever French expression this approximates) emerges as interchangeable with Burke's Identification. But in this substitution there is also loss. We sense that Perelman here defers to Burke: Identification, a concept presumably familiar to many (American) readers of Perelman's essay, is invoked as shorthand for a complex of interrelated notions—the community of minds, the Communion of auditors and speaker—elaborated in irregular fashion but in considerable detail in *The New Rhetoric* and elsewhere. The effect of Perelman's summary in the "Theory of Practical Reasoning" essay—admittedly, only a digest of the complex theory presented in *The New Rhetoric*—is thus a fairly drastic simplification, a flattening of distinctions between these notions, and, consequently, an understatement of the distinctiveness of his own conceptual innovation relative to Burke's. In attempting to foreground this distinctiveness, we hope this essay has put these powerful thinkers of twentieth-century rhetoric into productive dialogue.

Notes

1. Although at times one senses that Burke intends Identification to displace, if not replace, persuasion as the focus of rhetoricians' attention, his explicit statements on the matter suggest otherwise: "Traditionally, the key term for rhetoric is not 'identification,' but 'persuasion.'... *Our treatment, in terms of identification, is decidedly not meant as a substitute* for the sound traditional approach. Rather, as we try to show, *it is but an accessory* to the standard lore" (Burke, *Rhetoric of Motives* xiv; our emphasis). Admittedly, though, Burke can be slippery on this point; see Jasinski 307 n. 1.

2. Throughout, we will indicate the central concepts—Identification and Communion—with the initial capital.

3. In an unpublished article, Jim Hanson provides a first step in this direction by considering the "convergence" between Burke and Perelman with respect to the social dimensions of their respective theories (cf. also Kremer-Marietti 82–85). Hanson's discussion of Identification and Communion, however, is brief and not entirely satisfactory.

4. For Mead's influence on Burke's notion of Identification, see Zappen's commentary on Burke, "On Persuasion" 338 n. 10; cf. Heath 31. On Burke and Mead generally, see George and Selzer 183, 188, 241 n. 57, 242 n. 59, 271 n. 11. Allusions to or discussions of Mead can be found throughout Burke's work of the 1940s; see, e.g., Burke, *Philosophy* 111–12, 282, 444; *Grammar of Motives* 236–38; *Rhetoric of Motives* 193; and especially "On Persuasion."

5. For helpful discussion of the social aspect and emphasis of Burkean Identification, with specific reference to *A Rhetoric of Motives*, see Duncan 143–76 and Biesecker 40–51.

6. For a study of Perelman's complex engagement with classical rhetoric and dialectic, see Tordesillas. For more on Dupréel's influence on Perelman and Olbrechts-Tyteca's new rhetoric, see Frank and Bolduc, "From Vita Contemplativa" 73–75; cf. Gross and Dearin 1, 17; Eubanks 76–78, 82 n. 18; and Frank and Bolduc, "Chaïm Perelman" 185–86.

7. On Perelman and Olbrechts-Tyteca's (in some respects problematic) interpretation of the classical theory of epideictic discourse, see Graff and Winn 47–48.

8. The term "communion" may itself have been suggested to Perelman and Olbrechts-Tyteca by the work of Dupréel (see *New Rhetoric* 55, with Perelman, "Fragments" 76), although Dupréel himself used it infrequently; see, e.g., Dupréel, *Traité de morale* 2:447–48, 648; and *Sociologie générale* 92, 228.

9. Notably, in *The Realm of Rhetoric*, Communion has vanished from the sections on epideictic where it was most prominent in the corresponding, more elaborate presentation in *The New Rhetoric*. The term "communion" *does* appear in the account of epideictic in the French original of the book, but its presence is obscured in Kluback's English translation, where it is rendered by the terms "unity" and "consensus"; compare Perelman, *L'Empire rhétorique* 33, and *Realm of Rhetoric* 20.

10. For additional details on the matter discussed here, see Graff and Winn 51–61.

11. For further discussion of Perelman and Olbrechts-Tyteca's ideas on allusion and quotation, see Gross and Dearin 129–30; Tindale 68–69; and Graff and Winn 55–57.

12. In *The Philosophy of Literary Form*, Burke had commented on what he there terms "stylistic identification":

> Even a materially dispossessed individual may "own" privilege vicariously by adopting the "style" (or "insignia") of some privileged class. Thus did typical poets of the age of Pope vicariously own the privileges of the squirearchy, by embodying in style the ideals that the squirearchy approved of.... We see a petty clerk ... who can "identify" himself either by "owning the style" of the

workers or by "owning the style" of his boss. The *boss*'s style often appeals the more strongly, because it symbolically promises him advancement. . . . One may note another variant of "stylistic" identification when the immigrant, rich in gesture speech, seeks to "possess" the insignia of middle-class status in the most paradoxical way imaginable: by learning deliberately to *cramp* the expressiveness of the body, suppressing marked gesticulation and range of voice. . . . So the insignia here acquired "stylistically" are hardly more than the laborious attainment of zero. (309–10)

It is clear, however, that Burke's ideas here do not truly anticipate those found in *A Rhetoric of Motives*—which have to do with specific linguistic forms (figures)—that we discuss presently. Rather, the discussion describes what Duncan terms "style as social identification" (112, 273–75) and is more akin to the notion expressed in Burke's famous statement that "you persuade a man only insofar as you can talk his language by speech, gesture, tonality, order, image, attitude, idea, *identifying* your ways with his" (*Rhetoric of Motives* 55); cf. also the reference to "stylistic identifications" at *Rhetoric of Motives* 46.

13. Burke acknowledges that the list can be extended and also that "the invitation to purely formal assent (regardless of content) is much greater [in some figures] than others" (*Rhetoric of Motives* 59). See Carpenter for the argument that the effects of "expectancy" and "participation" Burke describes derive from an underlying redundancy in the grammatical schemes and figures of repetition.

14. Perelman and Olbrechts-Tyteca insist on distinguishing between aspects of style that make a demonstrable contribution to argumentation and those that do not. They observe that there are certain "forms of expression capable of producing an aesthetic effect, connected with harmony, rhythm, and other purely formal qualities," but that "such forms of expression can be of influence through the admiration, delight, relaxation, excitement, and the rise and fall of attention that they provoke without its being possible to analyze them directly in terms of the argumentation." In contrast to Burke, they proclaim that such "purely formal qualities" fall outside the parameters of their theory (*New Rhetoric* 142–43; see also 167–72).

15. Richard Lischer gives an excellent account of the various "strategies of style" utilized in Reverend King's entire oratorical oeuvre, as well as of the many strategies King employed to create Identification with multiple audiences (119–62). Yet, we note that of the devices Lischer describes specifically as contributing to Identification, by far the most salient are of the kind discussed by Perelman and Olbrechts-Tyteca as means of establishing Communion (maxim, allusion, and the like). Lischer's analysis of features like alliteration, anaphora, antithesis, climax, parallelism, repetition, and rhythm does not connect them directly to Identification.

16. We would add that this second, "social" sense is clearly the one most commonly stressed in the scholarly literature. Only a few scholars attend to Burke's ideas on Identification as an effect of style or figurative language. Ronald Carpenter's study is to our knowledge the only one to consider the stylistic aspect of Burkean Identification in depth and is helpful in distinguishing the formal and nonformal or ideational dimensions of Burke's key concept. Jeanne Fahnestock's summary of Burke's account of figuration and Identification is also on point and is followed by a useful account of Perelman and Olbrechts-Tyteca's innovative account of figures' argumentative functions (Fahnestock 34–36; see also 94–95).

17. For alternative statements on Burkean Identification as means and ends, see Hochmuth 136, and Carpenter 19; cf. Jasinski 306. For an account of Perelman's Communion as means and ends that differs slightly from the one presented here, see Graff and Winn 50–51.

18. Drawing on Charland, Robert Wess has stated that "in [*A Rhetoric of Motives*], identification is the condition of persuasion.... By constituting subjects as participants in a distinctive culture, identifications on a sub- or unconscious level make possible the activity of persuasion on a conscious level" (Wess 200; cf. Jasinski 307).

19. For a study of Athenian epideictic oratory—specifically, the *epitaphios*—that proceeds along this "Perelmanian" line, see Loraux.

20. *The New Rhetoric* cites Burke's *Grammar of Motives* or *Rhetoric of Motives* on pages 78, 124 n. 26, 135, 294, and 413. The last of these instances speaks to our interests here, at least obliquely, in that it shows that Perelman and Olbrechts-Tyteca gave Burke's notion of Identification careful consideration. However, the passage occurs in Perelman and Olbrechts-Tyteca's chapter on the "dissociation of concepts" and in a context that does not enable us to draw any conclusions about their view of the relationship between Communion and Identification:

> What Remy de Gourmont terms phenomena of association and dissociation ... and Kenneth Burke [at *Rhetoric of Motives* 150] terms identifications are, in our view, simply connections and rejections of connections, for the associated and dissociated concepts appear, after the operation, to remain as they were in their original state, like bricks saved intact from a building that has been pulled down. The dissociation of concepts, as we understand it, involves a more profound change that is always prompted by the desire to remove an incompatibility arising out of the confrontation of one proposition with others, whether one is dealing with norms, facts, or truths. (*New Rhetoric* 413)

21. This idea was suggested to us by David Frank (email to Richard Graff, 28 July 2004), who also noted that Perelman's essay was composed in response to an invitation from Otto Bird; Bird and E. Griffin-Collart were responsible for the English translation. We are unaware whether the French original was ever published or exists in manuscript.

22. Burke refers to Malinowski. In a useful study of current understandings of phatic communion, Meltzer and Musolf note that "numerous depictions of phatic utterances are available: Such expressions are typically formulistic or stereotyped, composed of clichés and platitudes, non-committal or perfunctory, minimally self-involved, avoidant of comments that are too personal, given to saying what one is expected to say, and marked by subordination of literal or 'real' meaning." The authors reiterate Malinowski's stress on the fact that "phatic communion functions to affirm and reaffirm social bonds" (98, 97).

23. For the sake of fairness and completeness, we should pause to consider Burke's reflections on a somewhat broader idea of "communion" found in *Attitudes Toward History*. Included in that work's "Dictionary of Pivotal Terms" is an entire, if short, entry entitled "Communion" (234–36). The entry might be said to resonate with aspects of the concept that emerge in *The New Rhetoric*. It reads, in part:

> In society, as a going concern, the network of co-operative practices is matched by a network of communicative symbols. "Communion" involves the interdependence of people through their common stake in both co-operative and symbolic networks.

> The artist specializes in the manipulation of the symbolic structure. He tends generally to communicate by reaffirming the norms of the co-operative structure. (And when discrediting one of the norms, he usually does so by affirming another of the norms: he pits one of his society's values against another of its values, so that even in an attitude of "rejection," he is not wholly "outside" the values of his society . . .)
>
> Malinowski has a term, "phatic communion," to designate the exchange of words not for explicit informative purposes, but as an easy way of establishing a bond. Stereotyped greetings, comments on the weather, polite inquiries about health, are examples. A subtler variant would be gossip, where people malign an absent friend, not so much because of a vindictive attitude towards the absent, but as an easy way of making allies for the moment. By setting up a "common enemy," they establish a temporary league. (234–35)

Burke's account of "communion" here suggests affinities with his own notion of Identification, as well. He nowhere troubles to elaborate on the relationship, however; note, too, that the "Dictionary" in *Attitudes Toward History* has a separate entry for "Identity, Identification" (on which, see above).

24. As it appears that the essay "The New Rhetoric: A Theory of Practical Reasoning" was never published in its original French, these points on the phrase translated "community of minds" are purely conjectural. We suggest that it might stand for "*communauté des esprits*" (cf., e.g., *New Rhetoric* 14, 55), but it is still possible that it renders an original "*communion des esprits*" or "*communion des consciences*"; there are precedents for such expressions elsewhere, but they prove inconclusive (see, e.g., *New Rhetoric* 55, 56). We must admit that Perelman's use of several closely related or possibly exactly synonymous terms or expressions around ideas of "communion," "community," and the like can be a source of confusion, a difficulty that is often exacerbated in the translation to English.

25. See the especially trenchant remarks to this effect at *Rhetoric of Motives*, a passage that incidentally contains Burke's only use of the term "communion" in any significant connection to Identification:

> [T]o begin with "identification" is . . . to confront the implications of *division*. And so, in the end, men are brought to that most tragically ironic of all divisions, or conflicts, wherein millions of cooperative acts go into the preparation for one single destructive act. We refer to that ultimate *disease* of cooperation: *war*. (You will understand war much better if you think of it, not simply as strife come to a head, but rather as a disease, or perversion of communion. Modern war characteristically requires a myriad of constructive acts for each destructive one; before each culminating blast there must be a vast network of interlocking operations, directed communally.) (*Rhetoric of Motives* 22)

Works Cited

Biesecker, Barbara. *Addressing Postmodernity: Kenneth Burke, Rhetoric, and a Theory of Social Change*. Tuscaloosa: U of Alabama P, 1997.

Burke, Kenneth. *Attitudes Toward History*. 1937. 3rd ed. Berkeley: U of California P, 1984.

———. *Counter-Statement*. 1931. 2nd ed. Berkeley: U of California P, 1953.

———. *A Grammar of Motives*. 1945. Berkeley: U of California P, 1969.
———. "On Persuasion, Identification, and Dialectical Symmetry." Ed. James Zappen. *Philosophy and Rhetoric* 39.4 (2006): 333–39.
———. *The Philosophy of Literary Form: Studies in Symbolic Action*. 1941. 3rd ed. Berkeley: U of California P, 1973.
———. "Revolutionary Symbolism in America." 1935. *The Legacy of Kenneth Burke*. Ed. Herbert W. Simons and Trevor Melia. Madison: U of Wisconsin Press, 1989. 267–73.
———. "Rhetoric and Poetics." *Language as Symbolic Action*. Berkeley: U of California P, 1966. 295–307.
———. *A Rhetoric of Motives*. 1950. Berkeley: U of California P, 1969.
———. "Rhetoric—Old and New." *Journal of General Education* 5 (1951): 202–9.
Carpenter, Ronald H. "A Stylistic Basis of Burkeian Identification." *Today's Speech* 20.1 (1972): 19–24.
Charland, Maurice. "Constitutive Rhetoric: The Case of the 'Peuple Québécois.'" *Quarterly Journal of Speech* 73.2 (1987): 133–50.
Davis, Diane. "Identification: Burke and Freud on Who You Are." *Rhetoric Society Quarterly* 38.2 (2008): 123–47.
Duncan, Hugh Dalziel. *Communication and Social Order*. London: Oxford UP, 1962.
Dupréel, Eugène. *Le rapport social: Essai sur l'objet et la méthode de la sociologie*. Paris: Alcan, 1912.
———. *Sociologie générale*. Paris: Presses Universitaires de France, 1948.
———. *Les sophistes: Protagoras, Gorgias, Prodicus, Hippias*. Neuchatel: Éditions du Griffon, 1948.
———. "Sur les origines de la dialectique." *Dialectica* 1 (1947): 367–70.
———. *Traité de morale*. 2 vols. Brussels: Presses Universitaires de Bruxelles, 1932.
Eubanks, Ralph T. "An Axiological Analysis of Chaïm Perelman's Theory of Practical Reasoning." *Practical Reasoning in Human Affairs: Studies in Honor of Chaïm Perelman*. Ed. James L. Golden and Joseph J. Pilotta. Dordrecht: D. Reidel, 1986. 69–84.
Fahnestock, Jeanne. *Rhetorical Figures in Science*. New York: Oxford UP, 1999.
Frank, David A., and Michelle K. Bolduc. "Chaïm Perelman's 'First Philosophies and Regressive Philosophy': Commentary and Translation." *Philosophy and Rhetoric* 36.3 (2003): 177–88.
———. "From Vita Contemplativa to Vita Activa: Chaïm Perelman and Lucie Olbrechts-Tyteca's Rhetorical Turn." *Advances in the History of Rhetoric* 7 (2004): 65–86.
George, Ann, and Jack Selzer. *Kenneth Burke in the 1930s*. Columbia: U of South Carolina P, 2007.
Graff, Richard, and Wendy Winn. "Presencing 'Communion' in Chaïm Perelman's New Rhetoric." *Philosophy and Rhetoric* 39.1 (2006): 45–71.
Gross, Alan G. "The Rhetorical Tradition." *The Viability of the Rhetorical Tradition*. Ed. Richard Graff, Arthur E. Walzer, and Janet M. Atwill. Albany: State U of New York P, 2005. 31–45.
Gross, Alan G., and Ray D. Dearin. *Chaïm Perelman*. Albany: State U of New York P, 2003.
Hanson, Jim. "Sociality in the Rhetorics of Kenneth Burke and Chaïm Perelman: Toward a Convergence of Their Theories." The National Communication Association Conference. Chicago, IL. November 1997. College of Liberal Arts and Department of English, Purdue University, 1999. Web. 10 July 2010.

Hawhee, Debra. "Language as Sensuous Action: Sir Richard Paget, Kenneth Burke, and Gesture-Speech Theory." *Quarterly Journal of Speech* 92.4 (2006): 331–54.
Heath, Robert L. *Realism and Relativism: A Perspective on Kenneth Burke*. Macon, GA: Mercer UP, 1986.
Hochmuth, Marie. "Kenneth Burke and the 'New Rhetoric.'" *Quarterly Journal of Speech* 38.2 (1952): 133–44.
Jasinski, James. "Identification." *Sourcebook on Rhetoric: Key Concepts in Rhetorical Studies*. Thousand Oaks, CA: Sage, 2001. 305–8.
Jordan, Jay. "Dell Hymes, Kenneth Burke's 'Identification,' and the Birth of Sociolinguistics." *Rhetoric Review* 24.3 (2005): 264–79.
King, Martin Luther, Jr. "I Have a Dream." 1963. *American Rhetorical Discourse*. 2nd ed. Ed. Ronald F. Reid. Prospect Heights, IL: Waveland, 1995. 777–83.
Kremer-Marietti, Angèle. "Perelman et Lacan: Enjeu social et jeux de la métaphore." *Perelman: Le renouveau de la rhétorique*. Ed. Michel Meyer. Paris: Presses Universitaires de France, 2004. 81–101.
Lischer, Richard. *The Preacher King: Martin Luther King, Jr. and the Word that Moved America*. Oxford: Oxford UP, 1995.
Loraux, Nicole. *The Invention of Athens: The Funeral Oration in the Classical City*. Trans. Alan Sheridan. Cambridge, MA: Harvard UP, 1986.
Malinowski, Bronislaw. "The Problem of Meaning in Primitive Languages." *The Meaning of Meaning: A Study of the Influence of Language upon Thought and the Science of Symbolism*. Ed. C. K. Ogden and I. A. Richards. London: Routledge and Kegan Paul, 1923. 451–510.
Mead, George Herbert. *Mind, Self, and Society: From the Standpoint of a Social Behaviorist*. Ed. Charles W. Morris. Chicago: U of Chicago P, 1934.
Meltzer, Bernard N., and Gil Richard Musolf. "'Have a Nice Day!' Phatic Communion and Everyday Life." *Studies in Symbolic Interaction* 23 (2000): 95–111.
Olbrechts-Tyteca, Lucie. "Rencontre avec la rhétorique." *Logique et analyse* 3 (1963): 3–18.
Perelman, Chaïm. "A Propos de la philosophie de M. Dupréel." *Revue de l'Université de Bruxelles* (1932): 385–99.
———. "Concerning Justice." 1945. *The Idea of Justice and the Problem of Argument*. Trans. John Petrie. New York: Humanities Press, 1963. 1–60.
———. *L'Empire rhétorique: Rhétorique et argumentation*. Paris: J. Vrin, 1977.
———. "Fragments pour la théorie de la connaissance de M. E. Dupréel." *Dialectica* 1 (1947): 354–66; 2 (1948): 63–77.
———. "The New Rhetoric." Trans. E. Griffin-Collart. *The Prospect of Rhetoric: Report of the National Development Project*. Ed. Lloyd F. Bitzer and Edwin Black. Englewood Cliffs, NJ: Prentice-Hall, 1971. 115–22.
———. "The New Rhetoric: A Theory of Practical Reasoning." Trans. E. Griffin-Collart and O. Bird. *The New Rhetoric and the Humanities: Essays on Rhetoric and Its Applications*. Boston: D. Reidel, 1979. 1–42.
———. *The Realm of Rhetoric*. Trans. William Kluback. Notre Dame: U of Notre Dame P, 1982.
———. "Rhetoric and Politics." Trans. James Winchester and Molly B. Verene. *Philosophy and Rhetoric* 17.3 (1984): 129–34.
———. "Rhétorique et politique." *Langage et Politique/Language and Politics*. Ed. Maurice Cranston and Peter Mair. Brussels: Bruylant, 1982. 5–10.

Perelman, Chaïm, and Lucie Olbrechts-Tyteca. "Logique et rhétorique." 1950. *Rhétorique et philosophie: Pour une théorie de l'argumentation en philosophie*. Paris: Presses Universitaires de France, 1952. 1–43.

———. *The New Rhetoric: A Treatise on Argumentation*. Trans. John Wilkinson and Purcell Weaver. Notre Dame: U of Notre Dame P, 1969.

———. *Traité de l'argumentation: La nouvelle rhétorique*. 3rd ed. Brussels: Université de Bruxelles, 1970.

Tindale, Christopher. *Rhetorical Argumentation: Principles of Theory and Practice*. Thousand Oaks, CA: Sage, 2004.

Tordesillas, Alonso. "Chaïm Perelman: Justice, Argumentation and Ancient Rhetoric." Trans. Serge Nicholas and Hugh Barton-Smith. *Argumentation* 4.1 (1990): 109–24.

Tufts, J. H. Rev. of *Le rapport social: Essai sur l'objet et la méthode de la sociologie*, by Eugène Dupréel. *Philosophical Review* 23.2 (1914): 221–22.

Wess, Robert. *Kenneth Burke: Rhetoric, Subjectivity, Postmodernism*. Cambridge: Cambridge UP, 1996.

White, Zachary M. "Re-examining Kenneth Burke on 'Identification' in the 'New' Rhetoric." Diss. Purdue U, 2003.

Wolin, Ross. *The Rhetorical Imagination of Kenneth Burke*. Columbia: U of South Carolina P, 2001.

Wright, Mark H. "Burkeian and Freudian Theories of Identification." *Communication Quarterly* 42.3 (1994): 301–10.

9

Language and Axiological Rationality: The "Non-thought" of French Linguistics in the Mirror of *The New Rhetoric*

Roselyne Koren

Language philosophers, linguists, and discourse analysts are essentially interested, when dealing with ethical dilemmas, in the question of the utterer's commitment to referential truth. However, the issue of discursive responsibility is not limited to this type of commitment. We need also to take account of the ethical rectitude of value judgments and of the unavoidable interactions of vericonditional and axiological dimensions of language. American argumentation theories as well as the Amsterdam school of argumentation accord the subject of argumentative fallacies foremost importance, but this does not allow us to solve all the questions raised by the ethical constituents inherent in language and discourse. Almost all value issues are met with silence or marginalized in French language theories, which are still anchored in a narrow Cartesian conception of rationality. Ethics, moralization, and normative objectives are intermingled in these theories. Researchers who risk venturing into the dangerous territory of value judgments and exploring the axiological dimension of discourse become at once suspect of being incapable of dissociating scientific description from subjective position taking, as if the axiological subject may infect the rationalist researcher.

This is where the ideas in *The New Rhetoric* take on an essential role. Indeed, this work is frequently cited nowadays in France in linguistic publications, placing Chaïm Perelman side by side, for example, with Ferdinand de Saussure, Roman Jakobson, Louis Hjelmslev, and Noam Chomsky.[1] However, this is not to indicate that *The New Rhetoric* is a logic of values or to suggest that it could serve as a model for the conceptualization of an ethics of discourse. This essay will therefore attempt to demonstrate that Perelman and Lucie Olbrechts-Tyteca's theory of argumentation permits an understanding of the roots of this epistemological lacuna and also to propose answers to the following questions:

- Why does the question of referential truth still occupy a leading place although most linguists no longer share the belief in an ontological objectivist conception of meaning nor in the ability of language to "tell" the truth?
- Why do discursive effects of objectivity still play a primary role in most social discourses, even when the rules of the genres permit subjective position taking?
- Why are the merits of freedom of thought, communication, verbal interactions, and consensus-seeking negotiations highly praised while at the same time they employ verbal strategies intended to forcibly impose ideological positions disguised as rationalistic judgments of fact?

Neither Perelman nor Olbrechts-Tyteca was a discourse analyst or specialist in linguistics. Current language theories in France permit us to consider linguistic subjectivity and intersubjectivity, the integration of a rhetorical component into the deep structure of a language and the necessity to think of language in the pragmatic terms of action and interaction. As for the passage from a single decontextualized utterance to discourse in interaction with its sociohistorical context, the linguist has recourse to discourse analysis. Why then would a discourse analyst, who is able to draw on complex language theories, need for her demonstrations to resort to *The New Rhetoric*? The nature of the deficiency that *The New Rhetoric* allows me to overcome is the conceptualization of an ethics of discourse and the scientific justification of the notion of axiological rationality. The authors of *The New Rhetoric* stress repeatedly that a logic of values and of the preferable is deeply embedded in the argumentative dimension of discourse and is as crucial as the connection to referential truth and veridiction. They therefore suggest widening the "narrow" Cartesian conception of rationality to include the implications of an axiological rationality. I will apply the conclusions of this set of arguments to some illustrations concerning the rhetoric of press writing that Perelman and Olbrechts-Tyteca viewed as a favored area of research.[2]

Preliminary Theoretical Remarks

The rationalist dissociation of reality judgments from value judgments and its disastrous consequences play a central role in *The New Rhetoric* (see especially

66, 75, 510). The authors believe that there is a direct link between this dissociation and the rationalist thesis that assigns the monopoly of validity to a vericonditional, "constricted," and "absolutist" conception of Reason. They wish, therefore, to "combat uncompromising and irreducible philosophical oppositions" (510). To them, it is a matter of proposing a "broadened" and "enriched" conception of rationality that integrates a logic of values and of the preferable. From their epistemological point of view, it is unacceptable to dissociate within discourse these two crucial aspects of "human activity" (512). Perelman and Olbrechts-Tyteca question whether "those who recognize that scientific investigation enjoys a special, preeminent status" can "save the norms of human action from arbitrariness and irrationality" (512).

My hypothesis is that the marginal or nonexistent place of the axiological dimension of discourse in the majority of language theories is linked with this dissociation. Linguists today no longer believe in the myth of a strictly informational language, a faithful mirror of preestablished ontological truths, but their nearly complete silence on everything that in discourse touches on the verbalization of values and an ethics of language is an eloquent silence. The perfect match of words and things is no longer believed, but, paradoxically, the dissociation evoked above is still deeply embedded in linguistic thought. The after-effects can be discerned in the preservation of the "dualism" of reason and passion, in the valorization of objectivity and neutrality, and in the devalorization of axiological stances considered suspect.[3] The staying power of this dissociation can be measured by the fact that essentially what counts is still the discursive assumption of responsibility for referential truth; what touches on values is ignored or marginalized. Another symptom allowing us to observe that the consequences of this dissociation have survived is the overriding interest in objectivity in the erasing from utterances of any linguistic subjective trace of the utterer's presence. What stands out from the multiple strategies indexed by Perelman and Olbrechts-Tyteca that attempt to pass off a value judgment as a judgment of fact and hence an opinion as an indisputable fact is the intention to secure the adherence of an audience by displaying the ethos of an "objective" rationalist utterer, thus making him or her trustworthy and credible.[4]

Perelman in the body of his work has no hesitation in recognizing that in representations and constructions of extralinguistic realities, value systems are as important as verbalizations of truths presented as rational evidence. He is not the only one to stress the heterogeneity of language. Pragmatic linguistic theories thus stress the fact that to speak is not only to inform and to vouch for the truth of representations of the extralinguistic real but also to make speech acts and to try to exert influence on the point of view of others. The concept of heterogeneity of language is shared by pragmatic linguistics and by Perelman. However, he does not dissociate between saying and doing but between *ontology* and *axiology*. He distinguishes between "what is" and "what has worth" (*De la justice* 73), between "the reflection of an objective reality" (Perelman and Olbrechts-Tyteca, *New Rhetoric* 513) and ethical evaluation, not in order to rank but in order to prove that these two constituents of language are interdependent. For Perelman, language thus has a crucial role to play in procedures attempting to compensate for the arbitrary character of the choice of values. The justification of values is clearly destined to remain imperfect, since where there is subjective choice, there cannot be absolute rationality. Discursive argumentation where the utterer attempts to construct norms and rules capable of justifying initial arbitrary choices thus contributes, nevertheless, to rationalizing them. The judgment of others, their resistance, their potential refutations, and their requests for readjustments do the rest. Perelman maintains that "value may be distinguished from reality" through its intrinsically "precarious" nature (*De la justice* 73), but the obligation to justify our choices and to take into account the objections of the audience perfect the discursive exercise of a logic of values. The work of rationalizing value judgments is never definitive since everything is argued and arguable, as Perelman never tires of repeating, but the refusal of linguists or of French discourse analysts to see and to know the logic of values resolves nothing; essentially it contributes to the anchoring of an epistemological non-thought.

Perelman does not perceive value systems or processes of verbal valorization or devalorization as mechanisms that utterers would be satisfied to activate more or less consciously. Contrary to a good number of language theoreticians, he believes in the autonomy of the utterer. This autonomy is partial, since the rationalization of the words of the Self depends on the Other's acceptance of the position upheld, but discursive practices can be founded on this autonomy. For example, when transferring values from the *theme* to the *phoros*, and vice versa, in the case of analogy (*De la justice* 382–83) or in appeals to vague notions such as Good, Just, or Equitable, the plasticity of discourse allows autonomous utterers to exploit the polysemic, semantic vagueness of these notions and to develop the meanings necessary for contemporary social life while simultaneously leaving them "open to the future" (*Rhétoriques* 135, 141) and to the ethical dilemmas left unresolved.

Case Study One: On the "Neutral Involvement" of Press Writing

The following three excerpts from an article by Pierre Georges in *Le Monde* (19 April 2003) titled "Self-Evident Facts" (in French, "Évidences") illustrate how the concept of "neutral involvement"[5] allows us to clarify and formulate a problem. "Neutral involvement" refers to the paradoxical tension between two contradictory deontological axioms presented by journalists as compatible by separating "facts" from "commentaries." The tension results from the dissociation between the "categorical imperative" of discursive objectivity and the well-known "duty to disrespect" in regard to executive political power. (The article was published at the end of the war led by the United States against Iraq. In each excerpt below, the English translation is mine.)

1. "In the tumult, the confusion, the anarchy, the insecurity, the penury, in a word, in everything that makes up the daily life of a country, and especially of cities devastated by war, at least one truth comes to light day after day, from the discoveries and the eye-witness accounts. It was already patently obvious, now it is an established fact: Saddam Hussein's regime was indeed an abominable dictatorship, enforcing through terror, repression, torture and executions, his own power and his own longevity."

"Dans le tumulte, le désordre, l'anarchie, l'insécurité, la pénurie, bref, dans tout ce qui fait le quotidien d'un pays, et surtout de ses villes dévastées par la guerre, au moins une vérité apparaît, jour après jour, au travers des découvertes et des témoignages. C'était une évidence déjà, c'est un fait établi désormais: le régime de Saddam Hussein fut bien cette abominable dictature, imposant par la terreur, la répression, la torture et les exécutions son propre pouvoir et sa propre longévité."

2. "So it would need quite appalling bad faith not to recognize that out of evil, war, came good, doubtless very fragile and precarious, the end of a heinous oppression."

"Il faudrait donc être d'une assez détestable mauvaise foi pour ne pas reconnaître que d'un mal, la guerre, est sorti un bien, sans aucun doute très fragile et précaire, la fin d'une oppression abominable."

3. "Hence, perhaps, the necessity, by way of an alibi for compromises of their own making with a situation that was well-known and deliberately concealed for interests of greater importance, to find a pretext for action after decades of inaction. This time it was the search for weapons of mass destruction. Will any be found? Or not? The question remains open. As for the answer, it was closed and definitive."

"D'où peut-être la nécessité, en guise d'alibi à ses propres accommodements avec une situation connue et délibérément occultée pour des intérêts supérieurs, de trouver un prétexte à l'action après des décennies d'inaction. Ce fut, cette fois, la recherche d'armes de destruction massive. En trouverat-on? Ou pas? La question reste ouverte. La réponse, elle, fut fermée et définitive."

The title of this article, "Self-Evident Facts," is significant. What immediately comes to mind is the criticism that *The New Rhetoric* makes of the rationalist concept of self-evidence.[6] The article presents itself as objective and indisputable; the peremptory tone and the authoritarian ethos of the mediator give the outward appearance of a direct ontological connection with facts purporting to have been acknowledged as such. One might, then, expect the entire article to play the card of the "objective" news report or statement of facts, but it does not at all: we find numerous axiological or emotional terms such as "confusion," "penury," "devastated," "abominable dictatorship," "repression," "heinous oppression," "decades of inaction," and so on. So there are simultaneously the outward appearance of objectivity and stands taken on the basis of value judgments. The ethos of the spokesman, as mirror of preestablished self-evidence, and the ethos of the critical analyst seem neither mutually complementary nor legitimating but to be striving side-by-side to seize discursive power. The neutrality of the transparent locutor seems to "redeem" the axiological stands taken. These positions reflect opinions validated by the rhetoric of fact. The objective of such rhetoric would be to intimate to the audience that the point of view upheld by the journalist is absolute truth and that the content of the article is above any discussion. Instead of explicitly assuming responsibility for the stands he has taken—which would be entirely legitimate in an editorial, the kind of article that implies and entitles subjective, reasoned, and justified stands—the journalist accumulates discursive objectivity effects. He thus seems to be seeking to impose what he might have chosen to justify by arguing his point of view. Two of the utterances where these discursive practices occur are "at least one truth comes to light" and "It was already patently obvious, now it is an established fact." Such statements use "truth" strategically as independent of human interpretation. The impersonal "objective" idiom "it is" and appeals to "obviousness" and "established fact" presuppose the existence a priori of such notions in international political space that the spokesman can reflect, as a mirror, just as they are. The stands taken are affirmed through subjective qualifications, but responsibility for them is not explicitly assumed. The role of journalist seems to be limited to giving anonymous media coverage to "truths" that surface on their own. As for criticism directed against international political authorities, criticism that implies a second antithetical ethos (see the axiological and/or affective qualifications cited above), the writer checks off responsibilities and imputes offenses (see example 3: false political "alibis" masquerading as justifications, refusal to see and be aware of what is contrary to the interests of the State, "inaction," and so on) but without attributing them to anyone, seeming to neutralize a priori any inclination of the reader to refute.

The Perelmanian approach allows one to perceive the modalities of the act of judging, the author's reticence to take explicit responsibility for his axiological stands, and the recourse to numerous effects of objectivity, including the erasing of the utterer's identity. These passages display discursive strategies that consist of saying and promptly masking what has just been said. They presume direct access to preestablished ontological "self-evidence." The implicit or euphemized character of value judgments constitutes an obstacle for the transition from reflection to action. The debate on the responsibility of the states involved in the Iraq conflict is replaced by the moralizing censure of those states. As Perelman has many times underscored, moralizing is not to be confused with practicing ethical questioning. The purpose of a logic of values is not to impose absolute answers but to search for sharable solutions to common problems. Where the question of the collective responsibility and the consequences of the war should have been formulated as a problem through the prism of a "practical reason," that is to say, discussing the future,[7] the journalist is satisfied to pose as an "imprecator" who resorts to intimidation to gain an advantage over those who would maybe dare to uphold a different point of view.

The second quotation clearly illustrates these points: "it would need quite appalling bad faith not to recognize that . . ." The categorical tone of the impersonal turn of phrase—an effect of objectivity—is relativized here by the modal value of the potential conditional "would," but the accusation of "appalling bad faith" constitutes a double threat: the audience's right to disagree is not recognized. The audience has only two options: to identify with or to be excluded from the group of those who hold the monopoly on the rationalist definition of "self-evident."

Case Study Two: The Binary Oscillation of Press Writing

One of the fundamental rhythms of press writing is surely the "static"[8] oscillation between two opposite poles—for and against. *The New Rhetoric* allows a link to be established between this primary cadency and an "egalitarian," rationalist conception of mediation (Perelman, *Rhétoriques* 202). A rationalist mediator is under the obligation—if he or she has any integrity—to treat in the same way all those who defend opposing positions (see *The New Rhetoric*'s "rule of justice"). The mediator has to restrict himself or herself to the neutral and "static" presentation of divergent points of view and refuse to move from the role of impartial observer to that of a participant who takes a stand, valorizing or devalorizing the respective arguments. The authors of *The New Rhetoric* recognize, in "Argumentation and Commitment" (59–62), the importance and the necessity for impartiality at the heuristic stage of the analysis of points of view, but they dissociate such impartiality from objectivity, deemed to be incompatible with the necessities of action, at all stages of argumentative procedures where a final decision is the point at issue. A third party cannot "adopt the viewpoint of someone on Sirius" (60) in the frame of argumentation. That person has to take a stand, because he or she belongs to the group as a whole or at least is "at one" with its value systems. The systematic "static" oscillation between antithetical options cannot be an end in itself in the case of civil truths that journalists have to construct together with the public at large. "Where an opinion influences action, objectivity is no longer sufficient" (60). The skepticism that leads to the decision not to decide is, in the eyes of the authors of *The New Rhetoric*, as dangerous as fanaticism. The skeptic "refuses" "commitment" because he or she equates "adherence to a thesis" with the adherence to a "demonstrative proof of compelling force" (62). But, if argumentation "aims at justifying choices, it cannot provide justifications that would tend to show that there is no choice, but that only one solution is open to those examining the problem" (62). In short, the skeptic's "idea of adherence is similar to that of the fanatic: both fail to appreciate that argumentation aims at a choice among possible theses" (62). The rationality of the choice is not guaranteed in *The New Rhetoric* by "the absolute truth of the thesis" but by the explicit justification of establishing a hierarchy of points of view and by a decision linked to an explicit and considered "commitment."

"Egalitarian" rationalism, then, runs the risk of striving to maintain the status quo but also of constituting the possibility of "quasi-logical" reasonings where truth and falsehood, established historic truths and their denial, the concomitant criminalizing and idealizing of the same individual, would be presented as equivalent theses or transformed into matters of taste. What is problematic in such a case is the "objective" attitude that absolves itself of the responsibility to decide, defined in these terms by French philosopher Vincent Descombes in *Philosophie par gros temps*:

> The event, more often that not, is given a moral identity ... in words that ... prepare the community for the decisions that this event calls for. Only an event that does not require any personal and collective decision can be reduced to a physical identity and to a description rendered in a neutral vocabulary. But if the group to which we belong has to react, it has to have been informed of the recent or imminent change in the current state of affairs in a language that clearly lays down the responsibilities and the advantages, the obligations and the rights: what is happening signifies a threat or help, victory or defeat, crime or punishment. (77; my translation)

> [L]'événement consiste le plus souvent à donner une identité morale à ce qui vient d'arriver... dans des mots qui... préparent la communauté aux décisions qu'appelle cet événement. Seul un événement qui ne requiert aucune décision personnelle et collective peut se contenter d'une identité physique, d'une description donnée dans un vocabulaire neutre. Mais si le groupe auquel nous appartenons doit réagir, il faut que le changement récent ou imminent de l'état des choses lui soit annoncé dans une langue qui fixe clairement les responsabilités et les mérites, les tâches et les droits: ce qui arrive veut dire menace ou secours, victoire ou défaite, crime ou châtiment.

Conclusion

A common denominator exists between the discursive journalistic practices analyzed here and those of scientific discourse: the rationalist axiom that places primary importance on "objective," "neutral" descriptions and thus essentially on the commitment toward referential truth. Rationalist, "egalitarian" impartiality would be the ethical option par excellence: position taking, value judgment, and subjective decision are what ought to be justified and made acceptable. My intention here is not to argue against this axiom nor to defend an absolute subjectivism (no researcher can uphold such an absolute subjectivism) but to show that *The New Rhetoric* permits one to demarcate the axiom's limits if one wishes to be a "whole" person and not to dissociate or to rank judgments of reality and value. The "rationalist axiom" presents a partial conception of rationality.

Every rationalist utterer, as in the case of the *Le Monde* journalist, who assumes that he or she has a monopoly on Truth will consequently be intolerant and authoritarian to his or her audience. When a researcher, or any utterer, deals with critical interpretation and conveys it to an audience, his or her words cannot neutralize the inherent axiological subjectivity of language. It is here that *The New Rhetoric* possesses the considerable advantage of admitting that scientists judge, evaluate, and may even take subjective ethical stands without compromising the rules of the scientific game, since they must, like all utterers, explicitly justify their subjective decisions. An argumentative type of rationalism is thus advocated and defined in these terms at the end of *The New Rhetoric*: argumentative rationalism "transcends the duality 'judgments of reality—value judgments,' and makes both judgments of reality and value judgments dependent on the personality of the scientist or philosopher, who is responsible for his decisions in the field of knowledge as well as in the field of action" (514). This assertion could be, for example, the ground for the decision to cross the artificial demarcation line between judgments of reality, scientific descriptions, and value judgments and not to neutralize their correlations whenever the authors of a text attempt to pass off intransigent, biased opinions as indisputable judgments of fact. We saw above that one of the means used for the discursive circulation of values is argumentation by analogy. This implies, for example, that in the case of the polemical equating of a contemporary army with the Wehrmacht of the Nazi regime, the scientific description of the argumentative procedures at work in the analogy allows us to delimit the places where the partial similitude has been implicitly transformed into total assimilation and where the discourse analyst can therefore legitimately decide to cross the line beyond which it becomes possible to deal with the notion of fallacy and of "ethical" discursive "rectitude."

Notes

1. See "Les courants de la linguistique au XXe siècle" (30–31) and Koren, "La Nouvelle Rhétorique" about the reception of *The New Rhetoric* in France in linguistics, discourse analysis, rhetoric, argumentation theories, and semiotics.

2. "We seek to construct it [the theory of argumentation] by analyzing the methods of proof used in the human sciences, law, and philosophy. We shall examine arguments put forward by advertisers in newspapers, politicians in speeches, lawyers in pleadings, judges in decisions, and philosophers in treatises" (Perelman and Olbrechts-Tyteca, *New Rhetoric* 10).

3. *The New Rhetoric*: "We combat uncompromising and irreducible philosophical oppositions presented by all kinds of absolutism: dualisms of reason and imagination, of knowledge and opinion, of irrefutable self-evidence and deceptive will, of an universally accepted objectivity and an incommunicable subjectivity, of a reality binding on everybody and values that are purely individual" (510).

4. See Koren, "Perelman et l'objectivité discursive."

5. See Koren, "Argumentation, enjeux et pratique de l' 'engagement neutre.'" The notion of "neutral involvement" is borrowed from Charaudeau (262).

6. For example: "Where rational self-evidence comes into play, the adherence of the mind seems to be suspended to a compelling truth, and no role is played by the processes of argumentation. The individual, with his freedom of deliberation and of choice, defers to the constraining force of reason, which takes from him all possibility of doubt" (Perelman and Olbrechts-Tyteca, *New Rhetoric* 32). And: "An established fact, a self-evident truth, an absolute rule, carry in themselves the affirmation of their unquestionable character, excluding the possibility of pro and con argumentation" (57). See also Perelman, *Rhétoriques*, "Opinions et vérités" ("Opinions and truths"): "*L'évident est indubitable; il s'impose à nous quels que soient nos efforts pour lui résister ou pour l'ébranler: c'est la plus solide de nos certitudes*" (426–27). My translation: "The self-evident is undoubtable; it imposes itself on us no matter how much we try to resist and undermine it: this is the firmest of certitudes."

7. Regarding the ties that link the concept of argumentation to that of the future, see Perelman and Olbrechts-Tyteca, *New Rhetoric*, "Abstract Values and Concrete Values" (79).

8. See Perelman and Olbrechts-Tyteca, *New Rhetoric*, on the subject of the "static manner" through which, outside of the field of argumentation, the essentially ontological "descriptive" significance of notions is approached (140).

Works Cited

Charaudeau, Patrick. *Le discours d'information médiatique: La construction du miroir social.* Paris: Nathan, 1997.

Descombes, Vincent. *Philosophie par gros temps.* Paris: Editions de Minuit, 1989.

Georges, Pierre. "Évidences." *Le Monde* 19 April 2003.

Koren, Roselyne. "Argumentation, enjeux et pratique de l' 'engagement neutre': Le cas de l'écriture de presse." *Semen* 17 (2004): 19–40. Web. 6 July 2010.

———. "La Nouvelle Rhétorique, 'technique' et/ou 'éthique du discours': Le cas de l'engagement du chercheur." *Après Perelman: Quelles politiques pour les nouvelles rhétoriques? L'argumentation dans les sciences du langage.* Ed. Roselyne Koren and Ruth Amossy. Paris: L'Harmattan, 2002. 197–228.

———. "Perelman et l'objectivité discursive: Le cas de l'écriture de presse en France." *Chaïm Perelman et la pensée contemporaine.* Ed. Guy Haarscher. Brussels: Bruylant, 1993. 469–82.

"Les courants de la linguistique au XXe siècle." *Sciences Humaines* 27 (December 1999–January 2000). Web. 6 July 2010.

Perelman, Chaïm. *De la justice.* Brussels: Institut de Sociologie Solvay, Actualités Sociales, Office de Publicité, 1945.

———. *Rhétoriques.* Brussels: Université de Bruxelles, 1989.

Perelman, Chaïm, and Lucie Olbrechts-Tyteca. *The New Rhetoric: A Treatise on Argumentation.* Trans. John Wilkinson and Purcell Weaver. Notre Dame: U of Notre Dame P, 1969.

———. *Traité de l'argumentation: La nouvelle rhétorique.* 1958. 2nd ed. Brussels: Université de Bruxelles, 1970.

SECTION THREE

The Ethical Turn in Perelman and *The New Rhetoric*

The essays in this section deal explicitly with the ethical dimension of the new rhetoric project, examining its ideas of responsible and open argument and what they tell us about rhetoric's commitments. Such concerns are present in other essays, as well, mostly notably in Noémi Perelman Mattis's opening memoir that explicitly discusses the values inherent in Perelman's life's work. The ethical dimensions of *The New Rhetoric* are also present in Barbara Warnick's sense of *The New Rhetoric*'s "integrity" (in section 1) and Roselyne Koren's analysis of "axiological rationality" (in section 2). James Crosswhite's view of *The New Rhetoric* as "developing an identity between freedom and reason" certainly connects his pedagogical application of *The New Rhetoric* (in section 4) to the ethical concerns of this section.

Ray D. Dearin's historical essay here demonstrates that the ethical precondition underlying the new rhetoric project of "equal rights of speech" derives from Perelman's philosophical interest in "confused notions," carried out in his study of "justice" during World War II and his work on the UNESCO "democracy" project following the war. The difference between the two projects, carried forward into *The New Rhetoric*, is that in the UNESCO discussions, Perelman distances himself from the positivist assumptions of his earlier work. Perelman's ideological commitment as a philosopher is not to any particular idea of democracy but to the study of uses of the term in argumentation. The political situation within which Perelman formulated his ideas is also discussed by David A. Frank and Michelle K. Bolduc in their essay (in section 1).

Linda Bensel-Meyers here also uses the postwar UNESCO project, in which Perelman and Richard McKeon both participated, as a starting point to compare their respective philosophies of pluralism. In their different but complementary senses of rhetoric as the negotiation of value, Bensel-Meyers finds a justification for thinking of the Aristotelian enthymeme as a basis for exploring the universal/particular dynamic and from there appeals to the need for a specifically rhetorical education to make the ethical entailments of argumentation central. The potential practical uses of *The New Rhetoric* in teaching ethical argument are also developed in Crosswhite's later essay.

Jean Nienkamp here uses *The New Rhetoric* to represent how rhetoric necessarily entails ethical considerations and references the work of Stephen Toulmin (and others) on ethics to show that ethics necessarily entails rhetorical considerations. Thus, she makes a case for the fundamental mutuality of ethics and rhetoric, or in her terms for the merging of these practices, "the rhetoricality of ethics" and "the ethicality of rhetoric." Nienkamp's discussion of arguments from value intersects productively with Koren's earlier essay. A different use is made by Crosswhite of contrasts between Toulmin and Perelman.

10

Perelman on Democracy as a Confused Notion
Ray D. Dearin

On a cold winter evening, 27 January 1978, Chaïm Perelman lectured at the Iowa Colloquium on Rhetoric and Public Policy in Iowa City. He began his talk with a personal recollection:

> In 1962, before receiving the Prix Francqui from the King of Belgium for my work on argumentation and rhetoric, I delivered a short speech in which I expressed my gratitude to those who had contributed to my intellectual formation. On this occasion, I thanked my mentor Eugène Dupréel for having made me understand the importance of confused notions. This statement so intrigued the King that, at the reception following the ceremony, the first thing he asked me was to explain the importance of confused ideas. After hearing my explanation, he told me that he was going to recommend to all his ministers that they read my "new rhetoric." (*Justice* 95)[1]

As the Belgian visitor went on to explain, Western thought since the seventeenth century "has been profoundly influenced by the development of mathematical physics and the natural sciences, both based on experimentation, measurement, weight, and calculation. Everything that was not reducible to a quantifiable value was, by that very fact, considered to be vague and confused, something foreign to clear and distinct knowledge." He then reiterated a claim he had made more than thirty years before the Iowa lecture, namely, that "the specific task of philosophy is the systematic study of confused notions" (95).[2]

Perelman's first study of a "confused notion" began in 1944, while he was still in hiding from the Nazis, when he undertook an extensive analysis of the idea of "justice." This study resulted in an eighty-four-page treatise entitled *De la justice* (1945), in which he sought to empty the concept of its emotive aspects, a process that resulted in a residual structure he called "formal justice," according to which beings or situations that are essentially the same should be treated alike. From this finding, Perelman postulated the "rule of justice," a principle he believed to be the underlying basis of all rational activity. Students of Perelman's philosophical and rhetorical ideas would come to see a direct evolution from this early study of justice to the appearance of *Traité de l'argumentation*, which he jointly authored with Lucie Olbrechts-Tyteca in 1958 (Golden and Pilotta 155–85). It is understandable, therefore, that the Belgian king, after his conversation with Perelman, would advise his ministers to read that book.

What is not so well known by students of *The New Rhetoric*, however, is the part played by the Belgian philosopher in an extensive research project conducted under the aegis of the United Nations Educational, Scientific and Cultural Organization (UNESCO) a few years after World War II. Beginning in 1948, this initiative involved the collaboration of scores of individuals—including political theorists, philosophers, semanticists, linguists, and other specialists—in a massive effort to clarify the meanings attached to the term "democracy." As Richard McKeon, who edited the volume that resulted from this study, explained: "The inquiry was not conceived either as a 'scientific' investigation of the nature of democracy or as an 'opinion' poll concerning differences in conceptions of democracy; it was an effort, rather, to uncover the traditions of thought and the basic assumptions of theory which influence discussions and negotiations in which 'democracy' is involved" (vii).

From its outset, the UNESCO project was conceived of as the kind of analytical enterprise Perelman had engaged in with the idea of justice a few years earlier. It involved a philosophical analysis of "meanings, conceptual differentiations, theoretical implications, and normative foundations." The stakes were higher, however, as Cold War strife between the East and West grew hotter with each passing day. As Arne Naess and Stein Rokkan explain in their "Analytical Survey of Agreements and Disagreements," "the preparation of the inquiry was guided by the idea that considerable progress toward the clarification of the grounds of current conflicts could be made through the initiation and organization of philosophically detached debates across national and ideological frontiers" (McKeon 447).

No single individual was more heavily involved in the UNESCO project than Chaïm Perelman. He served on both the six-person Committee

Concerning the Importance of the Problem (the so-called Committee of Experts) and the Committee on the Philosophical Analysis of Fundamental Concepts, also a six-person group, of which he was the vice chairman. These small working teams furnished the intellectual fiber of the enterprise and produced the elaborate questionnaire sent out to nearly six hundred persons around the world. The questionnaire, which was intended to elicit a common body of analysis, context, and association, was returned by more than one hundred respondents. Thirty-four contributions, including Perelman's own, were published under Richard McKeon's editorship in 1951. The material collected was "said to make up a significant cross-section of enlightened opinion on the foundations of current conflicts concerning democracy" (McKeon 450).

The purpose of this essay is to examine Perelman's reflections upon the confusions surrounding the concept of democracy. With his contributions to the UNESCO project as anchor point and by examining scattered references in his prolific writings as well as in the less formal observations of persons who spoke with him about his views on government, it is possible to gain insights into his personal political and ideological views. My goal here, it should be noted, is not simply to satisfy an idle curiosity. Rather, because the "democracy" project coincided with the incipient stages of the "new rhetoric" enterprise, it would seem fruitful to look for intellectual crosscurrents between the two undertakings. Indeed, it will become clear, as I hope to show, that while Perelman's idea of democracy did not result from the kind of rigorous cerebration that had characterized his analysis of justice, it nevertheless corresponds closely to the philosophy of openness and pluralism that underlies the new rhetoric project.

1

The UNESCO Committee of Experts established as its first postulate that democracy had emerged as an uncontested value following the defeat of fascism in the just-completed war: "For the first time in the history of the world, no doctrines are advanced as antidemocratic.... The acceptance of democracy as the highest form of political or social organization is the sign of a basic agreement in the ultimate aims of modern social and political institutions" (McKeon 522–23). Respondent John Dewey noted, "One of the most significant findings of the discussion of democracy is its conclusion that every nation now claims to be a democracy" (63). Karl Marx and Frederick Engels had used the word "democracy" only once in *The Communist Manifesto*, in a vaguely positive sense: "The first step in the revolution by the working class, is to raise the proletariat to the position of ruling class, to establish democracy" (30). And Paul M. Sweezy, whose forceful advocacy of the Soviet system provoked the only extended rebuttals among the UNESCO participants, wrote: "It should be particularly noted that neither Lenin nor Stalin deny the right of capitalist countries to use the term 'democracy.' What they claim is that democracy as practiced in capitalist countries is democracy for the few, while democracy for the many can be realized only under socialism" (McKeon 401).

It is instructive to notice that even in 1948, as Perelman pondered the status of democracy as a "positive value, for which men will fight," he realized that the problem was not purely semantic but involved the manipulation of meanings for ideological purposes: "By giving 'democracy' a certain definition, this positive value is transferred to the meaning just defined, so that the discussion on the meaning of 'democracy' centers, not on the question of language, but on the ideal political régime." He recognized democracy as a *"confused* concept" and believed it would "probably be mistaken to try to put it forward as a *clear* concept" (McKeon 296). The "consoling thought" that "all political philosophers proclaim the same ultimate goal" should not obscure the fact that the "ideological differences relate to real societies and not to utopia" and that ideologues would continue to exploit the emotional element in words like "democracy" and "freedom" to win support for their particular views (301).[3] From such remarks, we can see that a decidedly rhetorical perspective was already coming into focus, even as the new rhetoric project was still in an embryonic stage.

The question as to whether a common or essential meaning of democracy exists was addressed by several of the UNESCO participants. C. J. Ducasse, who gave a spirited defense of Western-style democracy in contrast to Sweezy's Marxist interpretation, might almost be assumed to have read Perelman's essay "On Justice" when he wrote:

> I believe there is probably some core of meaning of all the different kinds of "democracy." It seems to be that *all* the people should, for such purpose as one has in view, be taken into account, rather than only some privileged category of them. This is connected with the idea of "justice" of treatment. But justice cannot plausibly be taken to mean that everyone should be treated alike; but only that everyone *that is alike* should be treated alike. And since it is impracticable to take into consideration *all* respects of likeness and of difference, the question then arises as to *which* respects of likeness between persons shall be made the basis of rules of equal treatment and which respects of difference shall be ignored. (McKeon 70)

Another respondent, G. A. Borgese, asserted that democracy exists "wherever and whenever the source of sovereignty is laid in the people," rather that in divine right, or inherited caste privilege, or sheer force, although he conceded that there are "cross-breeds, such as constitutional monarchies where certain remainders of the dynastic and caste principle are preserved while the popular will plays a preponderant role" (32). For G. C. Field, a state could be called "democratic" not *if* but "*insofar as* the whole body of citizens, or the great majority of them, exercise an effective influence on the decisions of government" (80). Richard McKeon held that "very few discussions of democracy, adverse or favorable, would be distorted by interpreting 'democracy' as 'the rule of the people in their own interest'" (195). Jørgen Jørgensen had no compunction about calling some definitions of democracy misuses—Hitler's, for example, in *Mein Kampf*, who defined "the true Germanic democracy" as "the free election of a Fuehrer," who would then dispense with any further consultation of the electorate. "I have no hesitation in calling this a case of misuse," said Jørgensen, "because it is used in a sense essentially divergent from the ones it has otherwise commonly been used in" (106). Likewise, C. I. Lewis opined that although no perfect manifestation of a democracy existed in history, even as no circle ever satisfied the requirements of perfect circularity, there can still be a single clear meaning of "democracy." He analogized that the word "triangle" has a clear meaning, even if there are a wide variety of big or little triangles, right triangles, acute-angled triangles, and so forth (165–66).

A careful reading of Perelman's response to the UNESCO inquiry shows clearly that the positivistic assumptions that had undergirded his analysis of the idea of justice a few years earlier no longer dominated his thought. Whereas several other respondents, including the ones just quoted, believed that an inner core of meaning could be found in the term "democracy," Perelman did not seek to locate such a meaning. No *formal* definition analogous to the "rule of justice" could be advanced. Because of the emotive overtones democracy as a "ideal form of government" had taken on in the mid-twentieth century, it could no longer be simply contrasted, as the Greeks did, with tyranny, autocracy, oligarchy, or demagogy, or with the monarchical systems of the eighteenth century, or even with the fascist governments of the twentieth century. (To do so would simply transfer the problem of identifying the "essence of true democracy" to the problem of defining "fascism.") Perelman mused about the possibility of arriving at a synthetic definition of democracy:

> An attempt might be made to determine empirically the elements common to the various known historical uses of the word "democracy." We should then arrive at a formula containing at least one variable (which would take the form of a propositional function fx) and it might be possible to agree on this formula by centering the discussion on the different values to be assigned to the variable. We should thus obtain a quite general definition of democracy as a political régime the purpose of which could be described as the well-being, equality or freedom of its citizens. (McKeon 297)

But, as can be seen, the discussion would simply shift to the meaning given to words such as "well-being," "equality," "freedom," and so on. In the absence of a generally accepted usage, a "correct sense," Perelman, McKeon, and many other respondents to the UNESCO survey concluded that no charge of "misuse" could be brought against anyone who uses the term "democracy" in any sense, "normal" or otherwise. Thirty years after the democracy project was finished, Perelman said in his Iowa lecture:

> The passage from use to abuse, from permitted usage to the condemned use of a notion, as with everything else, supposes the existence of a separation between the two, a border which one cannot cross without giving rise to opposition. If one is not in agreement with the line of this border, to designate a usage as an abuse can also constitute a "petitio principii" hidden in a single word. In effect, the act of recognizing the existence of an accepted distinction between use and abuse does not mean that in any particular case one finds oneself in the presence of a marked abuse. (*Justice* 103)

The members of the Committee on the Philosophical Analysis of Fundamental Concepts, with Perelman as vice chair, had recognized that "the use and abuse of the term is conceived as a mode of argumentation in supporting or depreciating particular forms of democracy," but they chose to put an optimistic spin on their findings: "In one sense, the agreement on a single term with at least some nucleus of common meaning holds forth some hope for some resolution of the ideological conflict" (McKeon 527).

2

One of the most intriguing clusters of responses to any of the items in the UNESCO questionnaire was prompted by a seemingly off-handed reference to Abraham Lincoln's well-known Gettysburg phrase "government of the people, by the people, for the people." Respondents were asked whether the prepositions in the "Lincoln formula" could clarify the "essential criteria of 'democracy'; the preposition *of* indicating the obedience of the people to the government, the preposition *by* indicating the active participation of the people in the formation of the decisions taken by the government, and the preposition *for* indicating the value of these decisions for the general welfare of the people" (McKeon 516). Some writers found the Lincoln formulation to be highly illuminative. "The use of the words *of*, *by*, and *for* in Lincoln's famous Gettysburg Address were not coincidental," said James Marshall. "Without benefit of modern psychology he understood the importance of popular participation if government was to be *for* the people" (214). Other respondents found little definitional value in Lincoln's words. G. C. Field considered them vague and hackneyed: "Every government must necessarily be *of* the people. Almost any form of government can, theoretically at any rate, be *for* the people. The crucial question is what meaning we can attach to the phrase 'government *by* the people,' which is the distinguishing mark of a democracy" (79). In a similar vein, C. I. Lewis chose to interpret the Gettysburg Address "as a tribute to the dead, and not as a political document," adding that "in any language, prepositions are among the most ambiguous of all words" (166). Barna Horvath noted that since methods of decision-making are easier to identify than the contents of the decision made, "it is easier to check whether a government is directed *by* the people than to determine whether it is conducted *for* the people" (101). Alf Ross believed that, at best, the Lincoln phrase was "a vague and sloganized approximation to possible definitions":

> The preposition *of* would not seem to indicate anything beyond the bare fact that a government exists: any government is a government of the people. Who else should it govern?
>
> The preposition *by* indicates in the briefest possible way the essence of democracy: the form of government that gives to the whole people the ultimate and decisive control of the will of the state and the execution of public authority.
>
> The preposition *for* does not indicate any element of relevance to the concept of democracy as defined the way I think it should be defined. No consideration should be given, in defining the term, to the social conditions that are aimed at by the government or regularly related to it. (367)

McKeon weighed in with the view that all three prepositions are essential to the concept of democracy. All government is *of* the people in a variety of possible senses, he maintained, but a government *by* the people "cannot long endure unless it succeeds to some extent in achieving the common good *for* the people" (200).

Perelman did not offer a detailed critique of the Lincoln formula. Its success among political philosophers, he thought, resulted from its malleability when separated from its context; it could "always be given an interpretation to fit in with opposed political ideals." The closest he comes to revealing a personal interpretive preference occurs when he remarks:

> I was rather surprised at the interpretation of the expression "government of the people" suggested in the basic document of the UNESCO inquiry: the preposition "of" is there taken to indicate the *obedience* of the people to the government. Personally, I interpret this expression to indicate that the people is the *source* of power in a democracy, for I fail to see how the obedience of the people to the government is more characteristic of democracy than of any other system. (McKeon 297)

Perelman completes his discussion of the Lincoln formulation by noting that its lack of precision allows it to be used by governments that "many would be loath to regard as democratic" (298). His point is astute, for indeed the most ardent champion of the Lincoln formula among the UNESCO respondents was Paul M. Sweezy, who offers the most penetrating analysis of that formula from an avowedly socialist perspective. Like Perelman, Sweezy thought the interpretation of the preposition "of" in the questionnaire was "a complete misreading of Lincoln's thought." Lincoln meant that the government *belongs* to the people, not simply that they are bound to obey it, Sweezy wrote, adding that Lincoln voiced the revolutionary view that the people must staff and run their own government when he used the expression "*by* the people" (393–94). Whether the Gettysburg pronouncement was intended by the drafters of the questionnaire to expose an ideological fissure or not—and there is reason to believe its use was intentionally provocative[4]—it served to highlight the growing rift between Western-style democracy and the "people's democracies" that were emerging in the East.

It was precisely to avoid the narrowing of all of the different political systems in the world to an opposition between two ideologies that the UNESCO study had been devised. "Clarification of issues," it was hoped, "should show that there may be ideological opposition without bad faith" (McKeon 525). While Perelman and the other steering committee members were under no illusion that mere clarification of differences would be sufficient to ensure world peace, they believed that an important first step toward that end would be the recognition that "words, facts, intentions, and theories are all involved in uncertainty and confusion" and that "discussion and clarification of ideas is an important means for promoting co-operation and common action" (523–24).

In spite of the earnest wishes of the project organizers, the responses to the meaning of democracy inquiry became polarized into two camps: the Marxist or socialist versus the liberal or Western conceptions of democracy. To the communist or socialist theorists, including Charles Bettelheim, Ladislaus Rieger, and Henri Lefebvre, the idea of democracy as a political category had little interest. After the dictatorship of the proletariat had been achieved and capitalism had disappeared, the state would wither away, social antagonisms among classes would disappear, political parties would be unnecessary, and the questions raised by the UNESCO committee concerning the limits of toleration of dissent would be rendered meaningless. Bettelheim argued that a socialist society in a postcapitalist era would be "the only really democratic form of society" (McKeon 17). "We are . . . convinced that the future belongs to socialism as the higher form of civilization," echoed Rieger. "The capitalist and socialist civilizations are facing each other in a great struggle. The development of history will prove which of the two—imperialistic capitalism or democratic socialism—is capable of insuring a higher degree of civilization for the people, a better life for all, the progress of the whole of mankind" (354–55). And, paraphrasing Marx and Engels, Lefebvre exclaimed: "The 'specter' is becoming flesh and living reason. All roads lead to communism!" (160)

For the most part, the proponents of a Western-style or "political" interpretation of democracy did not confront the socialists head-on in the UNESCO project. They did not deny that inequality existed in the social life of Western countries, as represented by lingering forms of racism and colonialism and vestiges of hereditary aristocracy. Rather, these writers simply rejected the "political-social" dichotomy and strove to transcend the economic determinism inherent in the socialist critique of society. Aimé Patri wrote that, "without political democracy, there can be no question of 'democracy' at all" (McKeon 283). Horace M. Kallen said, "It is a matter of record that where 'political democracy' obtains people are disposed to employ their political power in order to extend the democratic relation to other fields. As to priorities, there is no evidence yet of 'social democracy' leading to 'political democracy' while there is evidence of 'political democracy' finding extension to 'social democracy'" (133). Ricardo R. Pascual thought that "social life cannot be split up into exclusive airtight compartments labeled political, economic, or social. Therefore there is no 'democracy' unless it is taken in its broad sense" (276). Similar positions were taken, with variations, by Petrov Plamentz, Lord Lindsay of Birker, Jørgen Jørgensen, and Stanislaus Ossowski (342, 103, 302, 176, 112, 251).

At this point, we might ask how Perelman responded to the deep ideological cleavages that were revealed in the UNESCO study. The answer lies in his philosophical commitment to reason (or the "promise of reason") rather than to political expedients as the solution to human dilemmas. Both sides of the Cold War dispute would doubtless find elements of agreement with Perelman when he wrote:

> The mere fact of voting for a given form of government can by no means be considered democratic unless all the citizens are sufficiently well informed to grasp the significance of their vote and provision is made to insure for the citizens the choice between several possibilities. We all know that in a Western democracy, the government in power can seldom claim to represent as large a proportion of citizens as voted for the National Socialists in Germany at all elections after 1933. (McKeon 298)

In his response, Perelman seemed consciously to avoid taking sides in ideological disputes. Concerning the term "right to work," for example, he pointed out that the phrase could be interpreted as meaning no one should be prevented from working (a liberal view) or that everyone should be able to demand work (a socialist tenet). The Belgian professor was content to state the diverging claims: "For the liberals, the independence and dignity of the individual must be safeguarded against interference by the public authorities; for the Marxist, this independence and dignity would be no more than a sham without the intervention of the authorities" (298).

Perelman's apparently even-handed analysis of the two competing views of government should not be taken as mere intellectual detachment from—much less indifference toward—the momentous issues at stake. He maintained that "in a utopian society, neither the liberals nor Marxists desire the interference of the public authorities; ultimately both views are reconciled in their support of an anarchical form of society. The present conflict between them is due to the fact that we are not living in utopia and account has to be taken of the real inequalities found to exist between citizens" (McKeon 299). Perelman believed that the disagreements between ideologists who stress either "political" or "social" democracy over the other were more than a wrangle over terminology. Even though he eschewed political polemics in his own writings, he recognized that "philosophical debate is a permanent struggle between ideologies attempting, in the name of truth, to dominate each other." This he affirmed in "Authority, Ideology, and Violence," an essay written decades after the completion of the democracy project: "It is only through an ideology that recourse to force can be denied; if we reject all ideologies as being baseless rationalizations, if all political life is a balance of forces, then not only the right or the stronger is always the best but even the idea of right disappears and there is only place for violence" (*New Rhetoric and the Humanities* 144).

Before leaving Perelman's contributions to the UNESCO project entirely, it is worth noting that he evinced a wariness, if not outright antipathy, toward any single-party system of government. "Reasons could certainly be found for regarding a one-party system as democratic, but any government which history has recognized as fascist might make the same claim without attributing any absurd meaning to the word 'democratic'" (McKeon 300). Even when making such observations, however, Perelman remained a philosopher rather than a political scientist or polemicist—a stance he steadfastly maintained in his scholarly writings for the rest of his life.

3

With the benefits afforded by hindsight, however, as we have access to materials after 1948, it is possible to gain a deeper understanding of Perelman's conception of democracy. Certainly this view entailed a commitment to openness of dialogue and toleration of pluralism, both tenets that have become hallmarks of democracy in the Western tradition. This attachment became clearer as the new rhetoric project unfolded, and it was amplified both in his writings and in comments to interlocutors who quizzed him concerning his political beliefs.

In an essay titled "Liberty, Equality and Public Interest," Perelman asserted the primacy of "political" democracy over the doctrinaire claims of Marxists who argued for a more thoroughgoing "social" democracy. Wrote Perelman: "Liberal ideology succeeded in the name of the rights of man and of the citizens to reorganize the structures of the State by setting up the principles of a liberal democracy which gradually became social democracy by setting real against formal liberty and equality" (6). In contrast to "philosophical monism characteristic of Nazi totalitarianism," as David A. Frank has written, Perelman derived "a dialectic based on a metaphysics of pluralism, freedom, and justice" (Frank 113). Both social and political life, Perelman believed, depend upon a democratic society in which freedoms of thought, of the press, and of association are protected, in an environment he called "sociological pluralism" ("La philosophie" 11). The kind of "democratic ideology" espoused by Perelman "is opposed to the idea that objectively valid rules exist in matters of conduct, because the majority cannot decide what is true or false" (*New Rhetoric and the Humanities* 142). This being the case, a "democratic regime of free expression of opinions" is indispensable to the promotion of "practical reason," the philosophical underpinning of the new rhetoric (132). Perelman believed that the norms and values of a society are changeable through dialogue and consensus, but such changes have to be agreed upon and justified. After an extensive analysis of his views on individual autonomy as a precondition for such changes, Algis Mickunas concluded that "Perelman is a monumental representative of political enlightenment and resultantly of democratic institutions" (Golden and Pilotta 328).

Attempts to deduce the Belgian philosopher's own political opinions from his formal writings have been frustratingly inconclusive. Mieczyslaw Maneli, who knew Perelman quite well, claims that he was more forthcoming about his social and political ideas "in private conversations with friends," although Maneli offers few personal recollections concerning the content of those beliefs. Maneli points to Perelman's "respect for and friendship with Professor Tadeusz Kotarbinski, the symbol of Polish open-mindedness, secular thought, and tolerance," as worthy of notice (357). And, in an article based on an interview Perelman gave to Polish journalist Wiktor Osiatynski in the summer of 1973, Maneli makes several pertinent observations. First,

> the interlocutor, Dr. Osiatynski[,] remarked that Dr. Perelman at times speaks as if he were a socialist and at other times as if he were a conservative; does he intend to remain a "pure" philosopher with "clean hands"? Perelman characteristically gave no straight answer to any of these inquiries, but in subsequent argumentation he presented enough material to outline his political philosophy and his real reply to the bluntly posed questions. (352)

Second, Perelman's theory of argumentation was developed as both a theory and a methodology, without recourse to any form of teleology. He did not "accept uncritically the existing situation in western countries," but neither did he embrace socialism and communism as "the only alternatives to parliamentary democracy." Maneli's paraphrase of one answer in the 1973 interview reminds us of Perelman's own response to the UNESCO questionnaire twenty-five years earlier: "[Perelman] does not believe in utopias. He does not believe in any kingdom of complete equality and happiness, he rejects any ideas of sacrifices for unattainable ends, for unreasonable dreams. He insists that methods which can humanize existing situations in our world are most important without specifying what the goals or results should be" (354). A third point extrapolated by Maneli from the Osiatynski interview gives heart to the champions of a free market economy:

> The minimum degree of equality a society requires is that the least favored people not be so desperate as to rebel; on the other hand there

should be at least enough inequality so that those who are more competent, more industrious, and gifted should not feel exploited. We know from historical experience that when everyone is always treated equally, the society starts to degenerate. Those who are more intelligent and active prefer to join societies were [sic] they will be better rewarded. (353)

Rather than attempt to label Perelman as a socialist or conservative, Maneli regards Perelman's theory of argumentation as "a critical instrument of social reform," as "a way to find reasonable solutions in the period of decline and transformation of all existing social and political systems and institutions in the West and in the East" (355).[5]

Even though efforts to identify Perelman's ideological leanings have been inconclusive, the new rhetoric that he put forth in collaboration with Lucie Olbrechts-Tyteca carries implications for the modern political state. In such a state, each individual or group must be free to posit norms and values to be countered by those of other persons or groups. "Implicit in Perelman's new rhetoric," as Mickunas has written, "are political institutions of democracy guaranteeing equal rights of speech and opinion and their public expression" (Golden and Pilotta 335). With this conclusion, no serious student of Perelman's philosophical or rhetorical ideas can take issue.

Conclusion

In a 2007 article in *Time* magazine, Nathan Thornburgh probes deeply into the collective psyche of contemporary Russia. "Do Russians really want to be free?" he asks. "Russians are, after all, the people who actually begged Ivan the Terrible to return to rule them after he threatened to abdicate. . . . The Kremlin and its backers use new catchphrases like *sovereign democracy* to intone that they have their unique form of freedom" (72). Had they lived to hear this phrase, the world's leading authorities commissioned by the UN more than sixty years ago to study the elusive concept of democracy would not be surprised to find that term still being used as a shibboleth. In his Iowa lecture on "confused notions," Chaïm Perelman says: "Insofar as we consider justice, liberty and democracy to be positive values, it will suffice for us to furnish our own definition of these notions and attempt to obtain the agreement of our listener to the content which we give to these uncontested values" (*Justice* 102). You will notice that I use the present tense in introducing this quotation: Perelman *continues* to say this. The participants in the UNESCO conference are all dead now, but the dialogue is not over. To a group of seminar students at Ohio State in 1982, Perelman says: "In philosophy you would like to have universal agreement, and that's why philosophers continue to discuss even after they are dead. The only people who discuss after they are dead are philosophers" (Golden and Pilotta 17).

It is fitting that the dialogue on the meaning of democracy should continue over sixty years after the UNESCO project was undertaken—and over fifty years after *The New Rhetoric* was published—among scholars interested in the promise of reason. When it is a question of the application of a confused notion, as Perelman says, "there exists no unanimously accepted procedure concerning its handling, which is not to say that its handling is entirely arbitrary. Even then there is a limit not to be transgressed, that of *unreasonable* usage" (*Justice* 103). In the work of Chaïm Perelman, "The power of reason had found a vehicle of expression," writes William Kluback, and "in the limits of reason Perelman found the reasonable, the force of the '*confused* idea' that continuously seeks clarification through communication" (315–16).

Notes

1. Perelman's essay was first published in *ETC: A Review of General Semantics* 36 (1979): 313–24.

2. This idea was enunciated in Perelman's "De la méthode analytique en philosophie."

3. Another respondent, D. van Dantzig, also viewed the term "democracy" as "an emotive and a volitive" term, not one of a descriptive nature. In fact, he claimed that "*any effort to give a synthetic definition of 'democracy'* is an effort of a *political*, not of a *philosophical* nature, and therefore does not fulfill the requirements of UNESCO's Philosophical Analysis" (McKeon 52).

4. In their "Analytical Survey of Agreements and Disagreements," Arne Naess and Stein Rokkan say, "The *of* relation was provocatively interpreted to indicate the *obedience* of the people to the government." They were surprised that the majority of respondents accepted this interpretation (McKeon 474).

5. Malcolm O. Sillars, who met Perelman in Salt Lake City, commented that "Professor Perelman is quite different from Richard Weaver in his politics," presumably meaning that Perelman was a liberal. However, Sillars says that both Perelman and Weaver tried "to link the political stance of a person to argument choice" (11). Sillars also notes support for "Perelman's contention that liberals argue more from abstract, and conservatives from concrete, values." This conclusion was reported in a paper applying Perelman's system of values to political rhetoric by William Benoit and Pamela Benoit at the SCA convention in 1982.

Works Cited

Frank, David A. "Dialectical Rapprochement in the New Rhetoric." *Argumentation and Advocacy* 34.3 (1998): 111–26.

Golden, James L., and Joseph J. Pilotta, eds. *Practical Reasoning in Human Affairs: Studies in Honor of Chaïm Perelman*. Dordrecht, Holland: D. Reidel, 1986.

Kluback, William. "The Implications of Rhetorical Philosophy." *Law and Philosophy* 5.3 (1986): 315–29.

Maneli, Mieczyslaw. "Perelman's Achievement beyond Traditional Philosophy and Politics." *Law and Philosophy* 5.3 (1986): 351–67.

Marx, Karl, and Frederick Engels. *The Communist Manifesto*. New York: International Publishers, 1948.

McKeon, Richard. *Democracy in a World of Tensions*. Chicago: U of Chicago P, 1951.

Perelman, Chaïm. "De la méthode analytique en philosophie." *Revue philosophique* 138 (1947): 40.

———. *Justice, Law, and Argument: Essays on Moral and Legal Reasoning*. Dordrecht, Holland: D. Reidel, 1980.

———. "La philosophie du pluralisme et la Nouvelle Rhétorique." *Revue Internationale de Philosophie* 33.127–28 (1979): 5–17.

———. "Liberty, Equality and Public Interest." *Equality and Freedom, Past, Present, and Future*. Wiesbaden: Steiner, 1977. 1–7.

———. *The New Rhetoric and the Humanities*. Dordrecht, Holland: D. Reidel, 1979.

Sillars, Malcolm. "Chaïm Perelman, Rhetoric and Values." Speech Communication Association Annual Convention. Denver, CO. 10 November 1985. Presentation.

Thornburgh, Nathan. "Person of the Year 2007: In Search of Russia's Big Idea." *Time* 19 December 2007: 64–76.

11

Philosophical Art or Rhetorical Skill: How Perelman's Ethical Pluralism Makes McKeon's Analytical Pluralism Ethically Conscientious

Linda Bensel-Meyers

> I have been concerned successively . . . with three problems which are problems of our times: . . . problems of philosophic scholarship, of educational practice and administration, and of international and intercultural relations. Viewed in retrospect, these three problems seem so closely interrelated and interdependent that they may be described more nearly accurately as three approaches to the same problem.
> —Richard McKeon, "Spiritual Autobiography" (1953)

> All language is the language of a community, be this a community bound by biological ties, or by the practice of a common discipline or technique. The terms used, their meaning, their definition, can only be understood in the context of the habits, ways of thought, methods, external circumstances, and traditions known to the users of those terms. . . . Only the existence of an argumentation that is neither compelling nor arbitrary can give meaning to human freedom, a state in which a reasonable choice can be exercised.
> —Chaïm Perelman and Lucie Olbrechts-Tyteca, *The New Rhetoric: A Treatise on Argumentation* (1969)

The outbreak of World War II in the twentieth century instigated a new purpose for philosophers of rhetoric, an inquiry that would have implications both for international relations and for the way higher education could prepare global citizens for tomorrow. Early on, I. A. Richards responded to the charge by seeking in rhetoric a means by which we could study global misunderstandings and their remedies, only to be countered by the more conservative work of Richard Weaver as he explored how to foreground ethical consequences in a rhetorical theory. As these and other scholars sought a theory to address how international communication could resolve the value conflicts that erupted in worldwide conflict, the United Nations, in 1945, created UNESCO—the United Nations Educational, Scientific and Cultural Organization—to address specifically international cooperation in educational, scientific, and cultural objectives, citing these as "the means to a far more ambitious goal: to build peace in the minds of men" (*UNESCO.org*). This mission also brought together Richard McKeon and Chaïm Perelman as members of the Committee of Experts on the Philosophical Principles of the Rights of Man convened by UNESCO (Paris, 1947). The experience set them forth on similar paths of inquiry to explore how rhetorical analysis might enable the global community to work together productively when the cultural values governing the behavior of player states appeared so incommensurate. As stated in UNESCO's preamble, the issue confronting them then was (and still is for us today) how to achieve "a moral solidarity" in a global community defined by its intercultural clash of values and opposing statements about them and how to prepare tomorrow's citizens to maintain that solidarity.

Both McKeon and Perelman were in agreement that the international conflicts they were addressing were paralleled within the interdisciplinary battles that crippled the goals of a truly liberal (and liberating) education. They saw the problems in intercultural negotiation grounded in a citizenry educated in the hierarchy of values maintained by disciplinary specialization, where the tyranny of scientific method privileged the demonstrable certainty of facts over the apparently irrational and intuitive value judgments of humanistic disciplines. If the world were to achieve the coexistence of a diversity of values in international communication, it would, simultaneously, need to achieve the coexistence of a diversity of methods of inquiry in its educational system, a careful orchestration of all disciplinary methods of inquiry within an environment of value pluralism that could nurture and sustain the education of a humane citizenry. Their individual perspectives on how to reform both international negotiation and higher education, though, have not been recognized as systematically compatible. McKeon's schema of philosophical semantics is often seen as too analytical and static for rhetorical use, whereas Perelman's foregrounding of the rhetorical exigencies that circumscribe a logic of value judgments is seen as too ephemeral. In this essay, I attempt to reconcile the two rhetorical approaches as similar philosophies of negotiating value judgments that can present us with a programmatic approach to higher education with implications for the role of rhetoric and writing across the curriculum in the formation of tomorrow's global citizens. These two different methods of describing a rhetorical art that foregrounds value within the principles and methods of rhetorical argumentation have much to teach us about how to construct rhetorical programs that are themselves rhetorical arguments for preserving the "presence" of values and their ethical entailments in all learning.

UNESCO and the Mission of New Rhetoric

Perelman and McKeon uncovered the problem at the heart of transglobal communication as one of constructing a logic of values through their work with UNESCO. The committee began its work with the belief that "philosophic issues were involved in the so-called 'ideological conflict' which affects the discussion of diplomats, the reports and editorials of newspapers, and the ideas and formulations of men everywhere" (McKeon, "Spiritual Autobiography" 31). The first step was to identify the fundamental terms: "human rights," "democracy," and "freedom." The committee's first report, published in 1947, led to the formal Declaration of Human Rights as a point of consensus in international affairs, although there were concerns about how the various definitions that different cultures brought to the term "human rights" led, at times, to opposing ends. These concerns next led the committee to explore the term "democracy," specifically by canvassing the different national representatives about the ambiguities that surrounded the term itself. The resulting 1951 report has become infamous for its despairing claim that "the answers . . . brought to light a basic ambiguity in the word 'ambiguity'" (McKeon, *Democracy* 526). As McKeon relates the response of the committee at the time, it was recommended "that a second project be set up to treat the hierarchies of values characteristic of cultures and expressed in artistic and intellectual productions as they bear on the relations of peoples and the problems which peoples face in common" ("Spiritual Autobiography" 31). At this point, Perelman and McKeon went their separate ways to uncover just how humans reason about value terms and how those different methods of reasoning could be articulated as not irrational but as identifiable modes of linguistic inquiry. Although their philosophical approaches differed, the issues they engaged with were the same.

Kalon, Eudaimonia, and the Adjudication of Competing "Goods"

To fully understand how McKeon's and Perelman's rhetorical theories are comparable, we might best put their efforts in the context of the historical debate over the rational judgment of values. Although this has been traced in different ways by both Perelman and McKeon (and others), I propose to cast the classical inquiry in the humanistic perspective of the goals of liberal education, particularly as the issue was discussed in relation to moral action. The battle between notions of the "good" was sown as a contrast between Protagorean relativism (where "man is the measure of all things" that entailed value) and Platonic idealism (where there is an immutable and transcendent summum bonum against which all values can be rationally adjudicated into a hierarchy of goods). Both extremes are insufficient for a workable logic of values. A relativistic view of value leads only to pragmatic arguments, where, as Ralph T. Eubanks summarizes Perelman's argument, "'any action, or any event, or a rule, or whatever it may be' is judged 'in terms of its favorable or unfavorable consequences....' Its basic rhetorical maneuver is to transfer 'all or part of the value of the consequences... to whatever is regarded as causing or preventing them'" (233). In Perelman's view, this was "taking a pharisaical view of morality" ("Pragmatic Arguments" 25). On the other hand, the Platonic alternative, where dialectic leads to an absolute ideal standard of the good represented by the concept of *kalon*, leads only to a Weaverian ethical rhetoric that does not reason about values but sermonizes, importing values onto an instrumental rhetoric. Instead of opening up an inquiry of contesting values that can initiate understanding and peaceful coexistence, sermonic reasoning only perpetuates propagandistic warfare.

This classic debate is contextualized as a humanistic one when initiated in Plato's *Protagoras* as a problem of *akrasia*, the Greek term for when humans choose to act contrary to what they know or believe is best, a choice that is defined as "irrational" in terms of logical judgment. As Martha C. Nussbaum describes it, this subject of the *Protagoras* leads to "the establishment of a *techne* of practical reasoning" (108)—although a form of "practical reasoning" quite different from Perelman's later conception—and Plato explores the question of just what this *techne* would look like. While Protagoras argues for a plurality of incommensurable values, Socrates is uncomfortable without a rational science for measuring values against one another. He explores the logical rule of quantitative and qualitative measurement systems for adjudicating value—one can see the source for *The New Rhetoric*'s *loci* of the "preferable" here (66, 84). The quantitative measurement (for example, "If one dollar is 'good,' then ten dollars is better") suffices only if we don't have competing qualities of the "good" (for example, to parody a current commercial, "Two trips to Bermuda: $8,000.00; one trip to heaven, priceless!"). Plato's argument for the latter depends on the problem of *akrasia*, or the potential of acting contrary to what one believes is the "good," for it is only within an incommensurable value system, where one has no way to measure competing "goods," that acts of *akrasia* can happen (for example, "I'll take the tickets to Bermuda . . ."). Plato demonstrates that only a commensurate understanding of all values adjudicated as a species of *kalon*, the morally beautiful, can enable all "goods" to coexist, albeit as a value hierarchy.

For Plato, the problem of *akrasia* is not a problem at all within a proper educational system where "scientific knowledge of the good is sufficient for correct choice" (Nussbaum 108). He effectively argues that a change in belief about what is ultimately valuable will transform emotions—such as love, grief, and fear—that are deeply entwined with our beliefs. And even though later in the *Republic* he acknowledges that this will not eradicate all conflict, since these emotions are not all that accounts for our baser "appetites," the principle of "commensurability makes the problem [of our baser desires] far less disturbing and hardly grave at all" (Nussbaum 120).

However well Plato rationalized away the problem of *akrasia*, his idealism and the educational system he proposed did not allow for how *humans* reason from a complex of values and desires—looking at all values as species of *kalon* actually excluded some primary values that shape human reasoning and choice. This is what Nussbaum identifies as the residual problem in Plato's argument: even if commensurability is possible as a way to eradicate some irrational choices, it does not account for the apparently absurd human choice to act "in a perverse and irrational way" (121). The Platonic system fails at controlling practical reasoning when the consequence of norming values in an educational system erases the notion of free will, where the value of the individual is subordinated to a social, collective good. Nussbaum cites as an example a passage from Dostoyevsky's *Notes from the Underground*, where he argues that the tyranny of commensurability incites the individual's desire for the human freedom to act completely contrary to expectations. However unsatisfying Plato's position, though, he did recognize the urgency this issue had for the polity: as Nussbaum puts it, "What he told us, and Protagoras agreed, is that only an ethical science of measurement will *save our lives*" (110).

Aristotle agreed that the issue of the weakness of human will to choose what people know to be right was an important issue; however, he also observed that "[t]his account of Socrates' conflicts plainly with what seems to be the case and what people say" (*NE* 1145b21, qtd. in Wiggins 247). His resolution was to make the practical deliberation of values more humanistic, based on contingent, probable goods rather than on universal ideals. Whereas Plato posited *kalon* as a universal good against which lesser values are adjudicated, Aristotle posited the more human but ephemeral concept of *eudaimonia*—"happiness"—as the end against which humans adjudicate their decisions about values. This allows for what Perelman and Lucie Olbrechts-Tyteca later articulate as the roles of universal and particular audiences in *The New Rhetoric*. Note how David Wiggins's translation of the following passage from the *Nicomachean Ethics* emphasizes how Aristotle's practical syllogism—the enthymeme—unites a universal probable value with a particular species of that value for pragmatic deliberation about values, choice, and action:

> The one premise [the major] is universal, the other premise is concerned with the particular facts, which are the kind of thing to fall within the province of perception. When a single proposition results from the two premises, then . . . the soul must of necessity affirm the conclusion; while in the practical sphere it must of necessity act. . . . So it turns out that a man behaves incontinently under the influence (in some sense) of reason and belief. For he has argued himself to his practical conclusion from true beliefs, and these beliefs are not in themselves inconsistent with reason. It is the appetite itself that opposes reason, not the premises of the appetite's syllogism. . . . And so, because the second premise is not universal (still less an object of scientific knowledge) in the way the major premise may be universal, the point that Socrates most insisted upon turns out to be correct. . . . For it is not demonstrable knowledge that is manhandled like [passion's] slave. What passion overwhelms is a man's perception or appreciation of a particular situation. (1147a24, qtd. in Wiggins 248–49)

As a logic of value judgment, Aristotle's enthymeme becomes a means of identifying a universal good in the major premise that would vary with rhetorical context and logically legitimate the minor premise as a species of that contingent good. This method of practical reasoning unites the major premise as a representation of a universal, field-invariant commonplace with the minor premise as a representation of a field-variant particular topic, giving value both to *The New Rhetoric*'s conception of the role of universal and particular audiences in rhetorical negotiation and to the role of universal educational values with disciplinary preferences as a species of that universal goal in an integrated, liberal education.

Uniting McKeon's Schema with the Logic of Value Judgments

In *The Realm of Rhetoric*, Perelman contextualizes the process by justifying the endeavor to connect specific values with universals as a particularly humanistic one:

> Universal values play an important role in argumentation because they allow us to present specific values, those upon which specific groups reach agreement, as more determined aspects of these universal values. This insertion of specific values into a framework which goes beyond them shows that we wish to move beyond specific agreements by recognizing both the importance of the universalization of values and also the importance that we attach to the agreement of the universal audience. (27)

Harold Zyskind has argued that Perelman's new rhetoric was opposed to Aristotle in that it "rather merges the *Rhetoric*'s relativity to the audience and focus on action with dialectic's universal opinions" (xi); however, when one looks at Aristotle's enthymeme as a logic of value judgments, that method of reasoning justifies Perelman's concept of the universal audience as the locus of the contingent concept of *eudaimonia*. As Eubanks has argued, the distinction Perelman makes between the universal audience and the particular audience is really in the realm of values: the "objects of agreement" that command adherence of the universal audience are in the realm of the "real," whereas the adherence of particular groups is in the realm of the "preferable," the realm that is to be "seen as the final arbiter of agreement with regard to the premises of rhetorical argumentation" (228).

The adherence of particular groups—or for McKeon, for national cultures—locates the site of contestation within the minor premise, or particular audience. McKeon's schema of philosophic semantics uses this point as the place of entry in his analytical system for distinguishing what he sees as the *mode* of reasoning from the contesting *conclusions* advanced in the apparent incompatibility of nations on the world stage. To do so, he catalogs the differentiating components of modes of reasoning into four: Selections, Principles, Methods, and Interpretations. His end is "to relate the stages of different solutions based on different interpretations of common problems," foregrounding within them the different values that need to be allowed a place in the discussion ("Philosophic Semantics" 244). Perelman's *loci* of the "preferable" as the basis of audience adherence is parallel to McKeon's placement of philosophic semantics, where he analyzes the constituent parts of philosophic methods "to make unambiguously clear the meanings that are attributed in a proposed interpretation to statements made in any philosophy" ("Philosophic Semantics" 243). In doing so, he is demystifying the ambiguities that had plagued UNESCO's work, for as McKeon puts it, "The ambiguities arise in part because each of the methods assumes the functions of the others" (244). As with *loci* of the "preferable," the point is not to oppose different methods but to identify how each is related to others, all as a kind of species of a universal ideal, a kind of *kalon* of problem resolution. In fact, we can locate within the realm of McKeon's Selections the various *loci* of quantity and quality that Perelman and Olbrechts-Tyteca attribute to classicism and romanticism, respectively, extrapolated into a variety of "philosophical pairs" constructed to allow the coexistence of contesting perspectives. Both are systems by which one can navigate the realm of competing values, for as McKeon summarizes the end of his schema, "the differentiation of methods, and the relations of the methods to principles, interpretations, and selections can be rendered precise only by reference to common problems and to the modes of philosophic inquiry" (244).

Perelman's concept of the universal audience as the location of a general value by which particular interests can be given voice actually humanizes McKeon's more analytical project. However, their ends are the same, and as if recalling Plato's call for education as the answer to the problem of mistaken belief in all values as irrational and relative, McKeon too calls upon educational reform of a system where "it is only by accident that the student . . . acquires the arts by which to perceive and appreciate the values achieved in the natural sciences, the social sciences, and the humanities or the arts by which to relate them to each other" ("Character" 112). His schema of philosophic semantics, when applied as the means to analyze the constituent parts of *The New Rhetoric*'s approach to pragmatic reasoning, can give us a method of interdisciplinary pedagogy, where we teach not just "the language and customs of a particular culture . . . [but] the arts by which different cultures approach common problems" (112).

Works Cited and Consulted

Dearin, Ray D. "The Philosophical Basis of Chaïm Perelman's Theory of Rhetoric." *The New Rhetoric of Chaïm Perelman: Statement and Response*. Ed. Ray D. Dearin. Lanham, MD: UP of America, 1989. 17–36.

Eubanks, Ralph T. "An Axiological Analysis of Chaïm Perelman's Theory of Practical Reasoning." *The New Rhetoric of Chaïm Perelman: Statement and Response*. Ed. Ray D. Dearin. Lanham, MD: UP of America, 1989. 221–38.

McKeon, Richard. "Character and the Arts and Disciplines." *Ethics* 78.2 (1968): 109–23.

———, ed. *Democracy in a World of Tensions: A Symposium Prepared by UNESCO*. Chicago: U of Chicago P, 1951.

———. *Freedom and History and Other Essays: An Introduction to the Thought of Richard McKeon*. Ed. Zahava K. McKeon. Chicago: U of Chicago P, 1990.

———. "Philosophic Semantics and Philosophic Inquiry." *Freedom and History and Other Essays: An Introduction to the Thought of Richard McKeon*. Ed. Zahava K. McKeon. Chicago: U of Chicago P, 1990. 242–56.

———. "Spiritual Autobiography." 1953. *Freedom and History and Other Essays: An Introduction to the Thought of Richard McKeon*. Ed. Zahava K. McKeon. Chicago: U of Chicago P, 1990. 3–36.

Nussbaum, Martha C. "Plato on Commensurability and Desire." *Love's Knowledge: Essays on Philosophy and Literature*. New York: Oxford UP, 1990. 106–24.

Perelman, Chaïm. "Pragmatic Arguments." *Philosophy* 34.128 (1959): 18–27.

———. *The Realm of Rhetoric*. Trans. William Kluback. Notre Dame: U of Notre Dame P, 1982.

———. "Value Judgments, Justifications and Argumentation." *The New Rhetoric of Chaïm Perelman: Statement and Response*. Ed. Ray D. Dearin. Lanham, MD: UP of America, 1989. 91–98.

Perelman, Chaïm, and Lucie Olbrechts-Tyteca. "Classicism and Romanticism in Argumentation." 1958. *The New Rhetoric and the Humanities: Essays on Rhetoric and Its Applications*. Dordrecht, Holland: D. Reidel, 1979. 159–67.

———. *The New Rhetoric: A Treatise on Argumentation*. Trans. John Wilkinson and Purcell Weaver. Notre Dame: U of Notre Dame P, 1969.

UNESCO.org. UNESCO. 1995–2010. Web. 10 July 2010.

Wiggins, David. "Weakness of Will, Commensurability, and the Objects of Deliberation and Desire." *Essays on Aristotle's Ethics*. Ed. Amélie Oksenberg Rorty. Berkeley: U of California P, 1981. 241–65.

Zyskind, Harold. Introduction. *The New Rhetoric and the Humanities: Essays on Rhetoric and Its Applications*. Dordrecht, Holland: D. Reidel, 1979. ix–xxii.

12

RhETHorICS

Jean Nienkamp

I am coining the portmanteau word "rhethorics" to explore the implications of the claim that rhetoric and ethics are two "terministic screens" (Burke 44) for the same characteristically human activity: value-based action in the social world. From the perspective of rhetoric, language that has persuasive function and accomplishes action in the human world is, at bottom, ethical. From an ethical perspective, acting on ethical principles requires deliberating on how those principles—and which principles—apply to situations we face on a daily basis: a classically rhetorical act. To make the ethical argument, I rely on characterizations of practical ethics from Peter Singer and Stephen E. Toulmin and of case ethics or casuistry from Albert R. Jonsen and Stephen Toulmin. To make the rhetorical argument, I use Chaïm Perelman and Lucie Olbrechts-Tyteca's *The New Rhetoric*.

In arguing that rhetoric is inevitably bound up with ethics, I am making a different argument from Quintilian's definition of an orator as a *vir bonus dicendi peritus*, because I do not assume that rhetors and rhetoricians will necessarily speak or act from agreed-upon values or standards of the "Good." Rather, I claim that rhetoric is inescapably based on values or value hierarchies of some sort, just as ethics is inescapably based on rhetorical deliberation about ends and actions. For this reason, rhetoric and ethics are two mutually enabling and effecting aspects of the same critical enterprise. I will proceed, in making this argument, first to discuss the rhetoricality of ethics and then the ethicality of rhetoric and will sum up by indicating some of the implications of this union.

rhETHorICS

I will start with the rhetoricality of ethics, since that is probably a less familiar notion to rhetoricians than the ethicality of rhetoric. As an area of inquiry, ethics is even more contentious and varied than rhetoric, encompassing as it does a long and worldwide history not only in philosophy but also in religious and folk traditions. For this reason, my purpose is not to unify every aspect of rhetoric with every manifestation of ethics but to point out critical areas in which ethics—the inquiry into "the question of how [people] ought to live," according to Singer (Afterword 544)—is a rhetorical enterprise. Ethics, like rhetoric, is an integral part of our daily lives: "Ethics deals with values, with good and bad, with right and wrong. We cannot avoid involvement with ethics, for what we do—and what we don't do—is always a possible subject of ethical evaluation. Anyone who thinks about what he or she ought to do is, consciously or unconsciously, involved in ethics" (Singer, *Companion to Ethics* v).

Ethics is both theoretical and practical, just as rhetoric is. The theories are many. Singer's *Companion to Ethics* includes three essays on the "roots" of ethics, six on the "great ethical traditions," three on a "short history" of Western philosophical ethics, ten on various ethical theories, eight on metaethics, five on critiques of ethical theories, and twelve on "applications."[1] From Classical Chinese ethics to "The Significance of Evolution," from "Politics and the Problem of Dirty Hands" to "Universal Prescriptivism," the theories of ethics presented by these essays are so divergent that one would be hard-pressed to generalize a central description of ethics from the evidence in Singer's collection. But this very diversity of views is what makes ethics rhetorical: ethics consists of contested and contestable theories and thus proceeds by deliberation and argumentation. Singer, in his afterword to the *Companion to Ethics*, notes that in the contentious discussions in his "Applied Ethics" section, "they share an implicit assumption: that even the most difficult practical ethical issues are amenable to discussion and argument" (544).

It is not just the theories of ethics that proceed argumentatively; it is also the *practice* of ethics that has a rhetorical basis. In his book *Practical Ethics*, Singer argues that "the notion of living according to ethical standards is tied up with the notion of defending the way one is living, of giving a reason for it, of justifying it" (10). He continues:

> If we are to accept that a person is living according to ethical standards, the justification must be of a certain kind. For instance, a justification in terms of self-interest alone will not do. . . . The notion of ethics carries with it the idea of something bigger than the individual. If I am

to defend my conduct on ethical grounds, I cannot point only to the benefits it brings me. I must address myself to a larger audience. (10)

Singer is making a very interesting turn here, from noting the kind of warrant that is applicable in an ethical argument—one that goes something like "give the same weight to the interests of others as one gives to one's own interests" (11)—to arguing subsequently that ethical arguments are made to what Perelman and Olbrechts-Tyteca call the universal audience.[2] This very interesting conflation of audience with warrant leads us to a philosopher who has written at length about both ethics and rhetoric, Stephen Toulmin. He and Singer turn out to have much in common in their views of the importance of argumentation to ethics, although Toulmin distances himself from Singer's use of the term "applied ethics" in the *Companion* volume. I will first explain Toulmin's rejection of that term and describe Jonsen and Toulmin's argumentative formulation of casuistic reasoning.

In his 2001 book *Return to Reason*, Toulmin eschews the term "applied ethics" because he rejects the idea that "our experience and practice in the moral realm" (121) are applications of any "universal moral principles" or theories to the circumstances of daily life (131). Toulmin argues that "assuming that ethical theory and moral practice alike must be grounded in principles whose relevance is timeless and universal" is "the error of all rationalist philosophy" (134). Instead, he argues that "Theory (so to speak) is not a foundation on which we can safely construct Practice; rather, it is a way of bringing our external commitments into line with our experience as practitioners" (133). In other words, ethical theory grows out of ethical practice, rather than the other way around. As Toulmin sees the working out of ethical practice in our daily lives, it closely resembles his own layout of arguments, as presented in Jonsen and Toulmin's *The Abuse of Casuistry*. Jonsen and Toulmin's description of the relation of theoretical to practical ethics recalls Toulmin's earlier description of the relation of theoretical logic to practical argumentation:[3]

> The heart of moral experience does not lie in a mastery of general rules and theoretical principles, however sound and well reasoned those principles may appear. It is located, rather, in the wisdom that comes from seeing how the ideas behind those rules work out in the course of people's lives: in particular, seeing more exactly what is involved in insisting on (or waiving) this or that rule in one or another set of circumstances. Only experience of this kind will give individual agents the practical priorities that they need in weighing moral considerations of different kinds and resolving conflicts between those different considerations. (Jonsen and Toulmin 314)

Jonsen and Toulmin call this a modern casuistry or case ethics, which is, in Aristotelian terms, an example of paradigmatic reasoning: comparing a current situation to past, paradigmatic cases in order to create presumptions for what to do in morally charged situations. This reasoning requires wisdom and prudence (*phronesis*) when the paradigms apply ambiguously or when two or more paradigms seem to apply in conflicting ways (307). Jonsen and Toulmin also argue that "the social and cultural history of moral practice reveals" both "a progressive clarification of the 'exceptions' admitted as rebutting the initial moral presumptions" and "a progressive elucidation of the recognized type cases themselves" (307).

The language that Jonsen and Toulmin use to describe such moral reasoning reflects Toulmin's layout of arguments at work (as developed in *The Uses of Argument*)—in fact, they use Toulmin diagrams to illustrate their analyses of moral reasoning (see, for example, *Abuse of Casuistry* 35, 321, 323, 324). The "exceptions" would be the *rebuttal conditions*; the "type cases" are *warrants* or *backing* for the argument. One example that Jonsen and Toulmin cite is the case of what an obstetrician should do when he diagnoses an ectopic pregnancy—a fetus developing within the fallopian tube: "He knows that this condition could be fatal to the mother and so operates to remove that portion of the fallopian tube in which the fetus is growing. He saves the mother's life and allows the fetus to die" (312).[4] Jonsen and Toulmin note that even in the eyes of the stringently anti-abortion Catholic church, "this kind of 'indirect killing' of the fetus does not . . . constitute a prohibited abortion" (312). So, in a layout of the latter, ethical argument, the *data* would be that the mother has an ectopic pregnancy, a fatal condition; the *warrant* would be that in situations in which neither mother nor fetus can survive, a physician may take the necessary measures to ensure the mother's life (or it might be a more specific warrant: in the situation of an ectopic pregnancy, treatment causing the death of the fetus is called for); and the *backing* for that warrant (if the mother is a strict Catholic) would be the established teachings of the Catholic church.[5] Depending on the warrant chosen, we might have no qualifier for the specific warrant or a qualifier and a rebuttal condition such as "depending on the viability of the fetus outside the uterus," and the *claim* would be that therefore the obstetrician should perform the surgery necessary to save the mother's life.

Jonsen and Toulmin present this as an argument from paradigms: case ethics consists of making moral decisions based on comparing the current situation to paradigmatic cases. Singer describes his "practical ethics" as being "broadly utilitarian," that is, premised on the belief that people should act so as to "[further] the interests of those affected" by their actions (*Practical*

Ethics 14). I have previously argued that *any* ethics, when it is applied in daily life, must go through this rhetorical transformation, because its adherents must deliberate on how to apply their principles to the situations they encounter (see *Internal Rhetorics*). This, then, is my case that ethics is inevitably a rhetorical enterprise: when we act as moral agents, when we make ethical decisions, we necessarily act and deliberate within a social sphere, in response to ethical and rhetorical exigencies, offering reasons and evidence to an audience sometimes internal, sometimes external.

RHEThORICs

At the same time, rhetoric is inevitably an ethical enterprise, bound up with values. Perhaps the most important impetus for the writing of *The New Rhetoric* was the inability of analytic philosophy to reason about values, an inability that Perelman illustrated in his 1945 monograph *De la justice* (republished in *The Idea of Justice and the Problem of Argument* as "Concerning Justice"). In it, he analyses several different conceptions of justice into one formal proposition—"a principle of action in accordance with which beings of one and the same essential category must be treated in the same way" (16)—with several concrete manifestations based on the different values held by a society. Writing from a Fregian perspective (Conley 296), Perelman must admit, "If we regard a rule as unjust because it accords pre-eminence to a different value, we can only note the disagreement. No reasoning will be able to show that either one of the opponents is in the wrong" ("Concerning Justice" 53). Considering that Perelman wrote this during the German occupation of Belgium (Conley 296) when clashes of values were not only salient but also life-threatening, it is clear that the analytic limitations on the field of reasoning could not be allowed to stand. There is, then, in the English edition of *De la justice* a footnote that reads, "Since these lines were written, the author has tried to present, through his theory of argumentation, a way of reasoning about values" ("Concerning Justice" 57).

Perelman and Olbrechts-Tyteca began their exploration of "a way of reasoning about values" in a series of essays published as *Rhétorique et philosophie: Pour une théorie de l'argumentation en philosophie* in 1952 (Gross and Dearin 8). Their most complete exposition of this "new" rhetoric—new to modern philosophy, that is, as it had abandoned rhetoric for dialectic and Cartesian certainty since the seventeenth century[6]—was in *Traité de l'argumentation: La nouvelle rhétorique* in 1958 (translated as *The New Rhetoric: A Treatise on Argumentation* in 1969).

Perelman and Olbrechts-Tyteca's explicit discussion of values forms the most fully developed of their sections on the "premises of argumentation."

They classify values among the "objects of agreement" concerning the "preferable," those adhered to by a particular rather than a claimed universal audience (66). Although they modify this claim of particularity later, they reiterate it in the section on values: "Agreement with regard to a value means an admission that an object, a being, or an ideal must have a specific influence on action and on disposition toward action and that one can make use of this influence in an argument, although the point of view represented is not regarded as binding on everybody" (74). This connection to action is important as well, because it is precisely the aspect of argumentation missing in analytic philosophy: its concern with practical effects in society. In section 10, "The Effects of Argumentation," Perelman and Olbrechts-Tyteca discuss the philosophical split between action on the mind and action on the will, which they attribute to the "error" of "conceiving man as made up of a set of completely independent faculties. The impasse consists in removing all rational justification from action based on choice, and thus making the exercise of human freedom absurd" (47). It is clear from many comments such as these in *The New Rhetoric* that the authors see their treatise as not just a technical exposition of argumentation about values but as a vitally important argument about the value of rhetorical (that is, nonanalytical) argumentation.

Perelman and Olbrechts-Tyteca argue that values play a ubiquitous role in everyday argumentation: "Values enter, at some stage or other, into every argument.... One appeals to values in order to induce the hearer to make certain choices rather than others and, most of all, to justify those choices so that they may be accepted and approved by others" (75). Values are among the "premises" of argumentation, because they constitute "the unfolding as well as the starting point" of argumentation (65). Moreover, values are discussed implicitly and explicitly in many of the sections in part 3, "The Techniques of Argumentation," such as "Ends and Means," "The Argument of Waste," "The Argument of Direction," "Unlimited Development," and "The Person and His Acts." In an unfootnoted, devastating example in section 65, "The Argument of Waste," Perelman and Olbrechts-Tyteca write, "It was by an analogous process that certain Nazi torturers tried to explain how they reached the point of treating their prisoners with bestiality: the first pain inflicted on a man makes the perpetrator a sadist unless torture is continued up to the point when the victim talks" (280–81). This is, clearly, an ethical argument, using an explicit value (though hardly universally held) as a premise.

Not only are values ubiquitous in argumentation, they seem to creep outside of their designated area of demarcation in Perelman and Olbrechts-Tyteca's taxonomy of premises of argumentation. The initial division seems simple enough: three premises concerning the real, "characterized by a claim to validity vis-à-vis the universal audience" (facts, truths, and presumptions, occupying different levels of adherence) and three premises concerning the preferable, "connected with a specific viewpoint" (values, hierarchies, and *loci* of the preferable) (66). However, Perelman and Olbrechts-Tyteca are then forced to admit that some values, such as "the *True*, the *Good*, the *Beautiful*" (76), are claimed to have universal adherence, while others are treated as facts or truths by their adherents (as is the value of getting a victim to talk, in the example above). In the former situation, Perelman and Olbrechts-Tyteca argue that "the claim to universal agreement, as far as they are concerned, seems to us to be due solely to their generality. They can be regarded as valid for a universal audience only on condition that their content not be specified; as soon as we try to go into details, we meet only the adherence of particular audiences" (76). So take, for example, "family values" on the American political scene: no one can afford to be against them, but with what policies and values does a particular politician fill that "universal value"? Anti-gay marriage? Living wages? Anti-abortion? Pro-childcare? Universal health care? Any specific policy that reflects a particular value and ethic that one puts under the rubric of "family values" immediately targets the "universal value" to a particular audience.

Similarly, in a deeply divided society, we see values being treated as facts and truths—and vice versa, reflecting the malleability of the universal audience and how far people will go to "disqualify the recalcitrant" (Perelman and Olbrechts-Tyteca, *New Rhetoric* 33). For all those who accept homosexuality as a fact, there are others who dismiss it as a (bad) "value," a "lifestyle choice." Likewise, regardless of the acceptance by the scientific community of the theory of evolution as factual, there are those (creationists) who would either disqualify it as a mistaken value contrary to a literal reading of the Bible or those who would consider it an alternate value to their own preferred value of the intelligent design of the universe.

Another way that we see values slipping into other kinds of premises is in the *loci* of quantity, in the discussion of the normal: "That which occurs most often, the usual, the normal, is the subject of one of the most commonly used *loci*, so much so that for many people the step from what is done to what should be done, from the normal to the norm, is taken for granted" (Perelman and Olbrechts-Tyteca, *New Rhetoric* 88). Hence, "what everybody does" becomes a justifying reason for behavior for everyone, from teens drinking alcohol to drivers exceeding the speed limit on the highways. It is perhaps a low form of the high invocation of democratic values. In fact, all of the *loci*, being lines of argument about the preferable, are based on values of some sort, so for example the *loci* of quantity and quality are strongly related to the discussions of concrete and abstract values, respectively.

What is interesting for my argument about the ethical nature of rhetoric is how closely Perelman and Olbrechts-Tyteca's discussion of reasoning about values tracks the rhetoric of ethics I outlined earlier. For example, Perelman and Olbrechts-Tyteca claim that "in a discussion, it is not possible to escape from a value simply by denying it" (*New Rhetoric* 75). They go on to explain that "when a value is in question, a person may disqualify it, subordinate it to others, or interpret it but may not reject all values as a whole: this would amount to leaving the realm of discussion to enter that of force" (75). Compare that to some of Jonsen and Toulmin's casuistic steps: where Perelman and Olbrechts-Tyteca mention disqualifying a value with regard to a particular argument, Jonsen and Toulmin write that one can challenge a paradigm when it fits a case ambiguously (307). When the former mention subordinating a value to other values, the latter suggest mediating among paradigms when two or more apply in conflicting ways (Jonsen and Toulmin 307). Finally, where Perelman and Olbrechts-Tyteca mention interpreting a value, Jonsen and Toulmin not only argue that case ethics is a matter of "moral debate" resolved by "paradigm and analogy" but also say that there has been a progressive clarification of exceptions and elucidation of type cases (306, 307).

Another instructive example is to be found in Perelman and Olbrechts-Tyteca's section 13, "Argumentation and Violence," where they discuss the provisions that communities make to resolve differences peacefully. They point to critical philosopher Guido Calogero, who sees "in the willingness to understand others, in the very principle of dialogue, the absolute basis for a liberal ethic" (56). They use Calogero as a starting point to begin a highly ethical discussion of the situations in which dialogue and discussion must be—or can be, or are—curtailed by societies. In this section, ethics becomes a crucial part of the "Framework for Argumentation"—the metarhetoric that determines what can and cannot be done rhetorically.

Finally, Perelman and Olbrechts-Tyteca's conclusion becomes a manifesto of the ethics and value of *The New Rhetoric*. They say that they will provide us with an architectonics or "framework that emphasizes its [argumentation's] philosophical significance" (510). The conclusion collects in one place the ethical and epistemological arguments they have been making throughout *The New Rhetoric* and makes clear what the implications of those arguments are. What could be stronger statements of ethical principle than "We combat uncompromising and irreducible philosophical oppositions presented by all kinds of absolutism" or "We do not believe in definitive, unalterable revelations, whatever their nature or their origin" (510)? What could be a stronger explication of ethical reasoning than their claim that "only the existence of an argumentation that is neither compelling nor arbitrary can give meaning to human freedom, a state in which a reasonable choice can be exercised" (514)? *The New Rhetoric* thus provides what Perelman was seeking when he was writing *De la justice*: "The theory of argumentation will help to develop what a logic of value judgments has tried in vain to provide, namely the justification of the possibility of a human community in the sphere of action when this justification cannot be based on a reality or objective truth" (514). Between their statements of principle in the conclusion and this claim, Perelman and Olbrechts-Tyteca provide a carefully reasoned argument of values in support of their position on argumentation, stating that "if essential problems involving questions of a moral, social, political, philosophical, or religious order by their very nature elude the methods of the mathematical and natural sciences, it does not seem reasonable to scorn and reject all the techniques of reasoning characteristic of deliberation and discussion—in a word, of argumentation" (512). Their conclusion, then, embodies in a condensed way the kind of argumentation about values that Perelman had been seeking.

I have argued that ethics is necessarily rhetorical and that rhetoric is necessarily ethical. But what is the point of saying that rhetoric is *the same thing as* ethics, as is implied by my invented portmanteau word "rhethorics"? When Perelman and Olbrechts-Tyteca say that the existence of reasonable argumentation gives meaning to human freedom, they are arguing that reasonable *discursive* action forms the basis for all other meaningful human action. Similarly, when I equate rhetoric with ethics, I am arguing that both are value-based action in the social world, whether that action be discursive or more broadly symbolic or meaningful. Without the language and argument to provide justification, there is no ethics; without the values, there is no rhetoric.

We must realize the import of what we do as rhetors, rhetoricians, and moral agents, because our rhetorical/ethical acts are necessarily value-laden: they affect others as well as ourselves. So perhaps I *am* coming the long way around to Quintilian's "good person speaking well," although I acknowledge that what "good" means to me might not be what "good" means to you (in a way that Quintilian never acknowledged—nor did he say "person"). What is important for Perelman and Olbrechts-Tyteca, and I would hope for the community of rhetoricians, is that we continue to have reasonable deliberations about what our values are and what they mean for the larger communities we inhabit.

Notes

1. Although Singer's book contains essays on Indian, Buddhist, Classical Chinese, Jewish, and Islamic ethical traditions and one on "the ethical systems of contemporary small-scale societies such as the Bushmen of the Kalahari Desert" (xi), the remainder of it concentrates on Western ethical bodies of thought, so even the variety indicated here is fairly narrowly conceived.

2. My argument that Singer's audience here is Perelman and Olbrechts-Tyteca's universal audience follows from Singer's subsequent discussion where he discusses several philosophical positions that take "universalizability" as a basic ethical concept. He concludes:

> They agree that an ethical principle cannot be justified in relation to any partial or sectional group. Ethics takes a universal point of view. This does not mean that a particular ethical judgment must be universally applicable. Circumstances alter causes, as we have seen. What it does mean is that in making ethical judgments we go beyond our own likes and dislikes. From an ethical point of view, the fact that it is I who benefit from, say, a more equal distribution of income and you who lose by it, is irrelevant. (*Practical Ethics* 11–12)

So Singer's "universal point of view" seems to be just as imaginary, and necessary, as Perelman and Olbrechts-Tyteca's "universal audience."

3. Essay 4, "Working Logic and Idealised Logic," in Toulmin's *The Uses of Argument* is particularly devoted to this question; one succinct statement of Toulmin's argument in that essay that pertains particularly to my argument is, "In logic as in morals, the real problem of rational assessment—telling sound arguments from untrustworthy ones, rather than consistent from inconsistent ones—requires experience, insight, and judgement, and mathematical calculations (in the form of statistics and the like) can never be more than one tool among others of use in this task" (173).

4. For the medical community, the question of what to do in the case of an ectopic pregnancy, the second leading cause of maternal mortality during pregnancy in the United States, is not an ethical one but a medical question of not only how to save the mother's life but how to do so in such a way as to preserve her future fertility and best prevent future ectopic pregnancies. See Cunningham et al. 705.

5. James F. Keenan provides a summary of a number of arguments held by Catholic theologians over the case of ectopic pregnancies in his article "The Function of the Principle of Double Effect" and in fact disagrees with Jonsen and Toulmin's assessment that ending an ectopic pregnancy would be an "indirect killing" of the fetus, even while using *The Abuse of Casuistry* to argue for case ethics over "geometrical" applications of ethical principles to ethical practice.

6. Toulmin presents a similar analysis in *Cosmopolis* in 1990. Strikingly, he had come to a similar rejection of the limits of analytic philosophy in *The Uses of Argument*, published the same year as *Traité de l'argumentation: La nouvelle rhétorique*.

Works Cited

Burke, Kenneth. "Terministic Screens." *Language as Symbolic Action: Essays on Life, Literature, and Method*. Berkeley: U of California P, 1966. 44–62.

Conley, Thomas M. *Rhetoric in the European Tradition*. Chicago: U of Chicago P, 1990.

Cunningham, F. Gary, et al. *Williams Obstetrics.* 19th ed. Norwalk, CT: Appleton and Lange, 1993.
Gross, Alan G., and Ray D. Dearin. *Chaïm Perelman.* Albany: State U of New York P, 2003.
Jonsen, Albert R., and Stephen Toulmin. *The Abuse of Casuistry: A History of Moral Reasoning.* Berkeley: U of California P, 1988.
Keenan, James F. "The Function of the Principle of Double Effect." *Theological Studies* 54.2 (1993): 294–315.
Nienkamp, Jean. *Internal Rhetorics: Toward a History and Theory of Self-Persuasion.* Carbondale: Southern Illinois UP, 2001.
Perelman, Chaïm. "Concerning Justice." *The Idea of Justice and the Problem of Argument.* Trans. John Petrie. New York: Routledge and Kegan Paul, 1963. 1–60.
Perelman, Chaïm, and Lucie Olbrechts-Tyteca. *The New Rhetoric.* Trans. John Wilkinson and Purcell Weaver. Notre Dame: U of Notre Dame P, 1969.
———. *Traité de l'argumentation: La nouvelle rhétorique.* Paris: Presses Universitaires de France, 1958.
Singer, Peter. Afterword. *A Companion to Ethics.* Ed. Peter Singer. Oxford: Blackwell, 1997. 543–45.
———, ed. *A Companion to Ethics.* Oxford: Blackwell, 1997.
———. *Practical Ethics.* 2nd ed. Cambridge: Cambridge UP, 1993.
Toulmin, Stephen E. *Cosmopolis: The Hidden Agenda of Modernity.* New York: Free Press, 1990.
———. *Return to Reason.* Cambridge, MA: Harvard UP, 2001.
———. *The Uses of Argument.* 1958. Cambridge: Cambridge UP, 2003.

SECTION FOUR

Uses of *The New Rhetoric*

How might concepts from *The New Rhetoric* be applied? The essays in this section address this question in two related ways: first, by showing how the descriptive theory of argumentation it sets forth might become a prescriptive source for invention by students of written reasoning and how the pedagogy of science makes use of argumentative devices, and second, by using specific ideas from *The New Rhetoric* as tools to analyze discourse of various kinds. The pedagogical implications of Perelman and Olbrechts-Tyteca's ideas are also discussed by Linda Bensel-Meyers in her essay (in section 3). Other essays in this volume include analysis of texts in making their cases, notably Alan Gross's analysis of Darwin, Richard Graff and Wendy Winn's brief analysis of a speech by Martin Luther King Jr., Roselyne Koren's analysis of argument in the press (all in section 2), and Jeanne Fahnestock's analysis of newspaper headlines (in section 1).

James Crosswhite here investigates the pedagogical potentialities of *The New Rhetoric* by looking for sources of invention in its treatment of *topoi*, arguing that it provides a better model for moving from the analysis of arguments to invention than do more reductive analytical models, such as Stephen Toulmin's. The very richness of *The New Rhetoric*'s model, however, though more adequate to real-world argumentation, raises questions of its teachability. Crosswhite delineates these questions not only in the context of the treatise's philosophical depth but also in relation to the exigencies of higher education. Thus, Crosswhite gives a detailed account of the possibilities and problems of the kind of rhetorically based education called for by Bensel-Meyers in her essay. *Topoi* in *The New Rhetoric* are also treated by Barbara Warnick in her essay (in section 1). Crosswhite's discussion of the relationship between audience and rhetor as dialogic, though brief, connects this essay with the treatment of dialogue in Loïc Nicolas's essay (in section 1).

Maria Freddi here examines the technique of reasoning by analogy as used in the pedagogy of science, analyzing passages from physicist Richard Feynman's lectures as representative. Her study connects Perelman and Olbrechts-Tyteca's ideas with those of philosopher of science Thomas Kuhn. By combining linguistic and rhetorical approaches to analysis, Freddi makes good on Fahnestock's claim in her essay that "*The New Rhetoric*'s treatment of style can accommodate the quantitative methods of the discourse analysts to yield a much fuller rhetorical stylistics than one will find in the older manuals." This takes us back to issues of objectivity discussed by Koren in her essay.

Paula Olmos here studies the way Perelman and Olbrechts-Tyteca treat a particular figure, *paroemiai* or traditional sayings, emphasizing how their treatment makes use of but differs from the classical tradition, as reflected in her composite "optimal model." Given the possibility of less homogeneous cultural knowledge in our time, this figure might seem less useful, but Olmos proposes the continuing social functions of proverb-like expressions in new communications media and illustrates this with quotations from popular film. This essay links productively to others in this collection: Olmos's discussion of the argumentative force of this figure further illustrates Fahnestock's general view of style as argumentative; her discussion of the "comical play" of maxims exemplifies Olbrechts-Tyteca's theory of *le comique* discussed by David Frank and Michelle Bolduc in their essay (section 1), and her comments on audiences recalls the discussion by Nicolas. Olmos also makes use of *The New Rhetoric*'s idea of communion, which is discussed in more depth by Graff and Winn.

Mark Hoffmann here applies *The New Rhetoric*'s "act-essence" technique, together with Richard Weaver's "argument from definition," to describe the function of "arguments from definitional essence." This technique enables the arguer to appeal directly to a universal audience. The concept is illustrated in the argumentative strategies Leo Tolstoy used to argue the essential corruption of religion and government, thus giving his book *The Kingdom of God Is Within You* the ability to transcend its particular audience. Hoffmann's analysis thus returns us to the issue of the meaning of the universal audience and how it is addressed, discussed for instance by Nicolas in his essay. It is also an example of the way a concept from *The New Rhetoric* may be usefully augmented by reference to other theories (as done in the essays in section 2).

13

Awakening the *Topoi*: Sources of Invention in *The New Rhetoric*'s Argument Model

James Crosswhite

Models are simplified representations of complex phenomena that—we hope—will allow us to understand and interact with those phenomena better than we ordinarily do. "Better" in this case means in such a way that we can more consistently predict and control the outcomes of the processes in which we are interested. In the very event of modeling, then, we can already see the hermeneutical erosion of the reality of argumentation. Naturally, we want to control the outcomes of argumentative processes, and we want a model that will help us to do this effectively. However, one of the realities of argumentation is that we ourselves, our desires and goals, are implicated and at risk in the process. Argumentation presents the opening to follow an argument wherever it leads, to change one's mind about what outcomes are desirable. So just following the reductionist road of constructing a model already pares off some very interesting features of the phenomenon of argumentation.

So, more specifically, what is it that we want from such a model? It could be any of many things. Models are pursued mostly because they promise to aid us in our efforts to predict and control the outcomes of argumentative processes but also because they aid us in our attempts simply to understand the causes and effects in and of argumentation processes, to discover the measurable empirical features of these processes, to be able to build machines (which are themselves also models) that can produce these processes, and for other reasons as well—many of which are probably linked to Aristotle's still pertinent observation that we imitate simply because it delights us to do so and because it is the primary way we learn (1448b). However, we should note—sharply—at the outset that it is one thing to imitate models of what other people are doing and another thing to imitate those people and those actions themselves. This natural distancing of invention from the primary phenomenon is a recurring feature of attempts to use theories and models.

One of the primary results we want from a model of argumentation is a reliable method of inventing and teaching the invention of arguments. Of all the parts of rhetoric, invention is the most valuable, the one that historically dignifies rhetoric and lifts it from the occasional declines to which it has been subject. However, invention has also proven itself resistant to modeling. Take the case of the most widely used argument model of our time, the Toulmin model (*Uses of Argument*). Its features are well known. Essentially, there is a claim, there are data supporting that claim, and there is a warrant that justifies moving from the data to the claim. There is backing for the warrant, ultimately in the form of a rational enterprise that helps to constitute a field or domain of argument. Arguments also have qualifiers and conditions of rebuttal. All of this can be graphically exhibited in boxes and lines that resemble a flow chart. It appears to be a model of how to generate arguments and set them into motion so that one can move reasonably from data to a conclusion.

However, it is almost anything but. Its creator, Stephen Toulmin, never intended to write a book on rhetoric or invention (Olson 284). However, this fact is also evident on simple examination. There are no actions specified by the model. First of all, there is no context or motivation for argument in the model itself. To be fair, Toulmin explores argumentative contexts in detail in his writings (*An Introduction to Reasoning* [with Rieke and Janik], *Human Understanding*) but this is not evident in the model, in which the context begins slowly to emerge only when one questions the backing for warrants. There are no exigencies, no rhetorical situation. Further, there are no procedures for generating arguments. Just how one gets a claim and data to show up in the boxes is a mystery. There is a mostly suppressed dialogue hovering in a ghostly way around the model. Consider the model's first appearance in *The Uses of Argument*. *Someone* asks whether Harry is a citizen. We do not know why, or whether the question is appropriate, but we do know that, for some reason, someone (else?) answers, "Yes, presumably." But we are not at all sure how this happens, or who knows where Harry was born, or who knows about the citizenship laws and offers this knowledge to justify the answer. The truth is that it is only when we already have an argument, or something like an argument, that we can use the model to represent it and then analyze it and, some say, better evaluate it. But where do arguments come from? The Toulmin model may be a reasonably good way of diagramming an isolated argument for purposes of analysis and evaluation, but it does not provide an answer to that question.

The New Rhetoric describes argumentation in a way that provides more satisfactory answers, but it too leaves us with some problems when it comes to invention. *The New Rhetoric* does not intend to offer a model, and the complexity of what it does offer raises doubts about whether it can even be referred to as a model. The aim of the treatise is "the justification of the possibility of a human community in the sphere of action when this justification cannot be based on a reality or objective truth" (Perelman and Olbrechts-Tyteca, *New Rhetoric* 514). This is a philosophical aim. To determine the conditions for the possibility of something sounds like a Kantian project. And there is also a Kantian aura here around establishing what we may hope—whether we may hope—for reasoned accord in the sphere of action. The project also involves developing an identity between freedom and reason, another Kantian theme. There is in fact a consistent philosophical project going on throughout *The New Rhetoric* and Perelman's other writings. However, it is *not* a project of transcendental reflection or transcendental philosophy. Within the philosophical clearing the treatise creates, the main argument is an argument by example, showing that that there are forms of reasoning in conditions of uncertainty that have been successfully used across a broad range of cultures and times and occasions. Yet these forms of reasoning have been neglected in modernity, a period during which certainty and self-evidence came to be taken as essential marks of the rational and logic became essentially connected with necessity. In the course of this philosophical effort, the new rhetoric project had to say a great deal about what argument is and how it works. Accidentally, but inevitably, the project expressed something like a model of argument.

However, it is nowhere near as simple as the Toulmin model, with its six elements and its resemblance to a flow chart in which reasonable warrantability runs from data through warrant and backing and back down, with qualifications, to claim, though a claim still subject to rebuttal. Toulmin's model has no agents and no social relations, aside from the ghosts who prompt with questions and activate the model. It has no account of what arguers must know or what deep skills or virtues they must have. There is no sense of a historical or ethical framework. Its marketability as a model is due to its simplicity. The new rhetoric project has never been as marketable.

If there is something like a model of argumentation in *The New Rhetoric*, it is set forth in the division of the treatise into its parts and perhaps some of their sub-subsections. The first part of such a model would delineate the framework of argumentation, "*les cadres de l'argumentation*" (Perelman and Olbrechts-Tyteca, *Traité*, sections 11–62), which could also be translated "the bounds of argumentation." Identifying the bounds helps to distinguish between what is argumentation and what is not, first and essentially by distinguishing between demonstration and argumentation (*New Rhetoric* 13–14), but then by setting forth the necessary conditions for argumentation to occur. The first condition is that there must be a meeting of minds (14–17), and in fact all of argumentation is a continuous and specific kind of "*contact des esprits*" (*Traité* 19). This meeting of minds is made possible and sustained by having a common language (hardly a simple matter); a reason to argue, and so a goal that has a plausible chance of being achieved by argument; a situation or conflict about which the parties are willing to change their minds—that is, conditions in which people are receptive to arguments; rules that govern the beginning, the conduct, and the ending of arguments, including rules for turn-taking, the length of the arguments allowed, and so on; interlocutors who are willing and able to argue with one another, who respect each other enough to change their minds because of what the other says; and interlocutors with knowledge of the other party sufficient and accurate enough to permit appeals to what is held in common and of the use of appropriate argumentative forms. Further, there must be no violence or bribery or any other form of coercion (*New Rhetoric* 54–59). The reasons for being convinced must be discursive.

There must also be the equivalent of a speaker and an audience, the *esprits* who will modify their ordinary non-argumentative ways and will both restrain themselves and assert themselves in the ways that will allow them to fulfill their argumentative roles in conformity with the bounds of argumentation (17–23). Ultimately, it will be the role of the audience to judge the arguments that are offered. In this model, all evaluations of arguments are ultimately supported by an audience.

If one were beginning a diagram of this, one might imagine moving from a box marked "pre-argumentative conditions" along an arrow to another box marked "argumentative conditions." However, the border between these two sets of conditions is anything but simple. The accomplishment of any of the many conditions I have listed is a matter of degree, and the judges of whether the conditions actually achieved are good enough are first the interlocutors (who may not participate if the conditions are judged wanting) and then the audience (which may fail to be convinced because the conditions are not sufficiently realized).

That is the first part of the model, if there is a model. It marks off what can be argumentation from what cannot. It defines the boundaries within which argumentation is possible. However, in doing so, it also assigns some significant dimensions of invention to these conditions. Certain conditions produce argumentation, without which one cannot produce arguments. To teach invention as the generation of arguments outside of these conditions is not to teach the invention of arguments at all. And ignoring these conditions as a source of arguments is to ignore a significant source. There is quite a difference between "thinking up arguments about some subject" and looking for the arguments that are taking shape—or might possibly take shape—in an actual situation that is defined by the bounds of argumentation. I will soon argue that teaching invention formally is possible, but such teaching will not be effective without a pedagogy that also takes the framework of argumentation seriously as a source of arguments. If one fills in the blanks of *The New Rhetoric*'s account of the framework—fills in the speaker and audience, the reason to argue, the common language, the level of trust among the parties, the extent to which they are willing to change their minds, the rules of the forum in which the arguments will take place, and so on—one cannot help but begin to think of the arguments that would or would not be convincing in that situation. When one looks at the empty boxes or spaces of the Toulmin model, one has very little guidance about how to fill them in. Where do claims come from? Those ghostly voices are emanating from where? *The New Rhetoric*'s model lacks the simplicity of the Toulmin model, but even the first part of this model provides more concrete sources of invention.

It is one thing for the minimal conditions of argumentation to be in place; it is another to have a shared world of *logoi* on the basis of which one can actually begin to speak and argue. Part 2 of *The New Rhetoric* is titled "The Starting Point of Argument," and it describes the worlds in terms of which *esprits* exist and which they carry with them into argumentation. These worlds are largely shared; otherwise, argumentation would not be possible. Seen from the point of view of argumentation, a world and its order are made up of all those features of language and its use that fall within the bounds of argumentation, including potential premises and forms of appeal, but the treatise does not at all neglect other verbal persuasives. Although it is not evident in the model, Toulmin's data, warrants, and backing come from out of such an ordered world.

The first chapter of part 2 is titled "Agreement" and runs through some of the constituents of a shared world: facts organized by theories and other systems of beliefs that are generally held in accord (67–70), values ordered in hierarchies that are held in accord only by particular groups (74–83), presumptions that are generally held in accord but not in all cases (70–74), and general forms of argument acknowledged to carry varying degrees of weight in different times and places and circumstances (83–110). This overall accord varies relative to special audiences and occasions. It is significant here that this general agreement is ordered into what I am calling a world. Invention from isolated facts or values is misconceived. Certain facts are held in accord because of their relation to other facts in a "theory" (or a "truth" in *The New Rhetoric*'s terms), although these "truths" may sometimes be micro theories compared to what we usually think of as theories. Facts held in accord in one context may not be held in the same accord in a different context. For example, something may count as a fact in a psychotherapeutical setting that would not count as a fact in a courtroom. Similarly, a value may be held in accord, but it will not carry the same force in all argumentative situations because different hierarchies may be at play. A person may have a strong adherence to truth-telling, and it may overrule most other considerations, but it might also fail on an occasion when saving a life seems to require a lie. Invention on the basis of such accords is complex, but this is the only world in town.

One cannot simply load isolated fact and value propositions into a database and expect a machine to apply argumentative schemes and then come up with anthropomorphic results. Because we are human beings, the facts and values to which we adhere are what they are only in relation to the wholes to which they belong—the theories and systems of belief and organized forms of life that give coherence to our experience and action. These forms of coherence do not always cohere well with each other, and this creates interesting effects in the ways we try to reason with ourselves and others. Modeling this is not an easy task. The project of engineering artificial intelligences that are anthropomorphic enough to be helpful to human beings has evolved into work on multi-agent systems, in which machines that are programmed differently are taught to "argue" with one another (Norman et al.). This is at once a dramatic and unsurprising outcome because in manifesting our ability to reason by constructing a mimesis in machine form, and so creating a mirror in which to understand ourselves, we are simply rediscovering what we have long known: inward reasoning has the form of outward social dialogue. In its Isocratean form, it is put this way: "The same arguments which we use in persuading others when we speak in public, we employ also when we deliberate in our own thoughts; and, while we call eloquent those who are able to speak before a crowd, we regard as sage those who most skillfully debate their problems in their own minds" (Isocrates 15.257). And, as L. S. Vygotsky insisted millennia later, we learn to think by internalizing the multiple voices we have witnessed in conversation with each other (51). We reason from out of a world in which we have achieved whatever coherence or integrity we have. Any model that does not acknowledge this will take us off the path, although it may do so in an impressively elegant and efficient and focused and teachable way.

Out of a world, when rhetorical exigencies press, invention happens. Something is given for argumentation. However, once again, this invention is not simply a deliberate act. Situations invent arguments. Worlds are not inert systems. They are active and historical. They exist in time, and they change. They are not isolated from the situations through which they act and change. Invention happens when worlds move into new situations, and much of what rhetorical invention is about is watching what is happening in the particular situation—which constituents of the world are coming into question and being put to action at this time and in this place. Invention happens without any practice or teaching or theory of invention. It happens "by nature," as people used to say. And part of invention therefore requires being attuned to what is already happening, the forces already at play that are producing arguments.

Training for becoming aware of what invention is already happening thus requires a fairly serious set of background abilities. First, one must be acquainted with the world in play and with its constituents. As the tradition would put it, one must have "common sense." This requires a coherent and fairly comprehensive formation through a broad education. Second, one must have a sense for what is happening in a situation. It is one thing to know that there are hierarchies of values; it is another to be able to sense or recognize a hierarchy as it actually comes into play in a situation. Third, one must have both good judgment, to organize everything one is sensing in a situation into a form that will guide discursive action, and practical judgment, to decide which among the available discursive actions is the most appropriate one. Again, these are capabilities that are acquired in a broad education that involves both knowledge of the world and repeated practical experience with arguments that arise in real situations.

There is another side of invention from the world here, and it is covered in chapter 2 of part 2 of *The New Rhetoric*. Out of a world, the arguer retrieves and adapts what is to function as given in a particular situation. Much is given in a world, but relatively little is actually received into argumentation, and what reception there is requires rhetorical invention, deliberate or not. In *The New Rhetoric*, this involves selecting, bringing to presence, interpreting, qualifying, and categorizing (115–21). So here is another point at which *The New Rhetoric*'s model opens up the possibility of teaching and learning to invent. One has a world (as the way one is), but one can, so to speak, turn around and observe it as an object. There is a kind of world box in a graphical representation of a model. Then there are actions taken by a rhetorical agent, actions that can be studied and taught and made to be more deliberate and mindful. *The New Rhetoric* says a great deal about these actions. For categorizing alone, there are many ways we can stretch and contract categories and many ways we can clarify and obscure by means of them. These actions are taken in order to adapt what is given to the particular challenges of the argumentative situation. So these inventional actions make sense only in relation to the coherent world that gives the given, the audience that will receive the given as given, and the situation as a whole. The interaction and overlapping of these different agencies would be difficult, if not impossible, to diagram, and the resulting model would be complicated.

The final part of *The New Rhetoric*'s model of argumentation (part 3) consists of argumentative forms themselves—the *techniques* of argumentation. They are not necessarily truth-preserving, like the formed proofs of logical systems, but they are supposed to preserve adherence as the argument moves from the starting points to the claim. In *The New Rhetoric*'s terminology, they are something like presumptions that are generally effective, but not universally so, and whose effectiveness is variable from situation to situation. Every argument requires speaker and audience, operating within the bounds that define argumentation, drawing on a shared world, shaping starting points into discourse, and then moving toward a claim in a way that has an identifiable form associated with an argumentative technique. The form is not the only persuasive in the system, but it is the most prominent part of the model. In the conclusion of *The New Rhetoric*, after explaining the philosophical purpose of the treatise, in the very last sentence, Perelman and Olbrechts-Tyteca write about the new theory of argumentation they have elaborated: "And its starting point . . . is an analysis of those forms [*formes*] of reasoning which, though they are indispensable in practice, have from the time of Descartes been neglected by logicians and theoreticians of knowledge" (514). End of treatise. Before the end, the authors analyze over fifty different argumentative forms, frequently with a counterform that leads reasoning in an opposite direction. They have certainly realized the virtue of copiousness. And this is in the reduced version of a manuscript that was several times its published size.

However, they have also accurately described their rhetoric as an *analysis* of argumentative forms. In the entire treatise, there is nothing directly focused on invention, on a process or procedure for *using* these forms to discover and invent arguments. And yet, these "techniques" resemble nothing more than the *topoi* of the rhetorical tradition, which were essentially tools of invention, general headings under which arguments could be discovered in particular situations. There is a tension in the treatise's use of the word "technique." A technique is a way of doing something, but the way is not random or accidental. It has a form. A technique is a proceduralized form. It is not a pure form one simply sees in a text but a form that is embodied in an action. *The New Rhetoric* refers to both forms and informed actions as "techniques" because it has not thematized the distinction between form and technique, between analysis and invention. Such a distinction is not directly relevant to its aim of establishing the possibility of what it calls argumentation. Establishing its possibility does not depend on teaching people how to do it skillfully. Nevertheless, the treatise has, in its attempt to bring the rhetorical tradition back to life, brought the *topoi* back along with everything else, only as undifferentiated form/techniques. In reality, the techniques are sleeping *topoi*, waiting for someone to breathe into and through them again.

What we can only haltingly call "*The New Rhetoric*'s argument model" is nonetheless a richer and truer account of argument than the simpler models that can fit on a board or a screen and be explained in a fifty-minute hour. Its inventional potential has not even begun to be explored, but it will take some serious mining to haul out its treasures and some labor-intensive processing to make them useful for the teaching and learning of invention. However, in relation to invention, even Perelman's account suffers from the general weakness of almost all models and accounts of argument. This weakness is a drift in intellectual work and in teaching that has taken shape and consolidated over a long period of time, and it is one expression of a drift that philosophers and writers and religious thinkers have identified with being human itself. We gravitate "naturally" toward sinking ourselves into what is already before us rather than toward seeking out and imagining and creating what is not yet before us. Resisting the inertia of this drift is unnatural and takes effort. Models of argumentation and most theories of argument are focused on the description, analysis, or evaluation of arguments, not their discovery and invention. Discovery and invention not only struggle against all the forces that naturally infuse and command our experience but also are inherently difficult. The prevailing idea of "critical thinking" is far more broadly valued and much more influential in education and in research than discovery and invention, and critical thinking as generally thought is focused on analysis and evaluation and not on the creation of arguments. This gravitational bent toward focusing on analyzing and evaluating existing arguments is also warranted by a reigning dissociation of discovery from justification in disciplinary and scientific work. There are, this view goes, established and reliable procedures for justifying ideas, but there are no established procedures for coming up with ideas in the first place. The critical evaluation of arguments has in fact come to be equivalent to argumentative reason itself. Strengthening this inertial drift is the fact that analysis and interpretation do seem to be necessary parts of any pedagogical process that includes invention. One comprehends patterns and strategies by learning to see them in examples. One studies how others have invented skillfully as a way of learning to invent for oneself. Principles and processes make sense and are reinforced in this turning toward analysis and interpretation and evaluation, toward reading rather than inventing. That comes later, when there will be less time left.

Giambattista Vico long ago exposed the inertia and narrowness in the modern critical enterprise (while at the same time acknowledging its many capabilities). "In our days . . . philosophical criticism alone is honored. The art of 'topics' . . . is utterly disregarded. . . . This is harmful, since the invention of arguments is by nature prior to the judgment of their validity. . . . [S]o in teaching, invention should be given priority over philosophical criticism" (14). However, in many textbooks from the fields of critical thinking, speech communication, and rhetoric and composition, criticism and analysis are often treated as nearly the whole of invention, or at least as prior to invention. Although there are exceptions and counter-tendencies, invention is rarely explored as being in some way prior to analysis and criticism.

Vico has something in mind here that is profoundly transformative, and there is an interesting logic to it. His premise is unassailable: the invention of arguments is by nature prior to the judgment of their validity. Without someone's having invented some arguments, there would be no arguments to criticize. However, Vico notices what is most significant about this obvious logical necessity. Criticism not only is made possible by invention but also is limited by invention. Criticism can make judgments only about arguments that have been invented by other means. Criticism might judge an argument to be better or worse, but it does not know if there are still other arguments to be discovered, and it does not know how to discover them. Criticism is limited by the work that has been accomplished through invention. The quality of criticism's results will be a function of the quality of the arguments with which invention has provided it. Rational criticism and analysis can never exceed the excessive gifts of invention.

Therefore, says Vico, invention should be given priority over criticism in teaching. He means not only priority in the sense of its being cultivated before criticism is taught but also priority of importance in the rational enterprise itself and in the amount of attention directed toward it in education. From its logical priority to criticism, he derives priorities of invention in the process of formation and in its status in relation to the different aspects of reasoning itself. Note that he does *not* here assume that there is one psychologically preferable composing process that speakers and writers should be taught to follow in all cases and which has invention as its starting point.

In this context, invention requires another supporting idea for its significance to become clear: copiousness. If invention invents prior to criticism, then it invents in some respects independently of criticism, outside of the limits it would impose. And if the value of critical results is dependent on the comprehensiveness of the set of arguments placed before them, then this is exactly what is required: as many arguments from as many sides as possible. Thus we have also activated that other idea: that it is a virtue to be able to argue from each side. The more arguments we have from more perspectives, the better chance criticism has of producing valuable results. Of course, this is part of what the *topoi* were for: copious invention.

In its model of argumentation, *The New Rhetoric* has retrieved the *topoi* as its major contribution to the project of a new rhetoric of argumentation but as undifferentiated forms/techniques that are themselves simply objects of analysis. They have been rescued, but they have not yet been awakened for the purpose of invention. Is it possible to reawaken them?

Practice, Application, Experience

One teaching opportunity in particular allowed me to begin to test the possibility. I had been carrying on conversations with Mark Johnson, my colleague at the University of Oregon, in which I would press him to speak about the inventional potential of work he had been doing in cognitive science. I explained to him what I had been thinking about *The New Rhetoric*'s techniques. He finally developed a response to my urgings: let's teach a course together. With support from the University of Oregon's Tom and Carol Williams Fund for Undergraduate Education, we developed a junior-level course that we would come to call Inventing Arguments. We took turns teaching two-week segments. Johnson taught on prototypes, basic-level categories, idealized cognitive models, metonymic models and radial categories, conceptual metaphor, primary metaphor, novel metaphor, and the creation of meaning. I taught a "Person-Act Techniques" section and a section I called "Binaries, Polarities, Dualities, Dissociations: Reasoning in Twos." Both of my sections were based directly on *The New Rhetoric*'s accounts of person-act arguments (293–331) and dissociation (411–59). Johnson's lectures were of course brilliant, and I have a yellow pad full of notes and reactions. Every day I listened, I thought, Let's turn this into an inventional procedure. Easier said than done.

Johnson's project is philosophical and involves overturning an old way of thinking about reason and reality that is based on a rational intelligence in the mind that corresponds to the intelligible categorical structure of the world. He wants to replace that with an account of how concepts and models of the world are generated from bodily experiences that can be remembered, modified, and extended to new applications by different kinds of cognitive operations. The universality and necessity and objectivity involved in the old way of thinking are replaced by a view of human cognition and reason as a function of the human body. He explained his project to students as a kind of thinking about thinking, becoming aware of how we think. He drew cognitive models on the board, diagrammed the radial structure of categories, and so on, and he led us through thought-provoking and illuminating examples. He had the students draw up a map of a category, identifying central members and novel extensions. However, by far, he devoted the most time and effort to explaining the competing theories and details of the new model and to teaching students to understand and identify the forms and structure of thinking according to the new account. As we were going through this, I kept thinking that, from the students' side, the challenge lay in something like pattern recognition. If they could spot the cognitive patterns that Johnson was explaining, then they could excel on the assignments he gave them. Some students seemed to be naturals; some just couldn't see the figure in the rug and struggled. Most learned the way most students do and accomplished what Johnson had hoped: they became more aware of how they themselves thought. The course ended with an assignment in which we asked them to analyze a controversy about some question regarding freedom (we had introduced some) by identifying some of the cognitive structures and argumentative techniques we had explored and explaining how they were functioning in the controversy. They were asked to follow this analysis with their own attempt to answer the question, based on what the analysis had achieved.

In the end, the students had taken a pretty rich course, and some of them had learned a great deal. However, I had two concerns afterward. First, about 20 percent of the students had great natural abilities for recognizing verbal-cognitive forms and structures, and about 20 percent seem to have great difficulty with it. The rest were spread over the middle. They struggled and learned. However, the difficulty of grasping the theories and understanding the abstract representations of the forms and techniques, even with models and examples, required lots of time and teaching. Second, the gravitational pull of analysis dragged us out of the orbit I was trying to achieve: to circle around the idea of invention and have students invent arguments copiously. My own efforts in teaching the techniques showed these same tendencies.

My teaching of the person-act techniques began with a reading—the story of Exodus—that would yield interpretations only on the basis of developing person-act arguments. One needs those arguments to come to any conclusions about Yahweh, or Moses, or the Israelites, or the wilderness or to understand their acts. But the effort remained predominantly analytical and interpretive. The students found person-act issues, but they did not see the point in inventing copiously. Things were a little better with dissociation. I used Emerson's "Self-Reliance" and its brilliant and bewildering dissociations to get the students familiar with the techniques. However, it was one thing to teach students to understand the techniques and to recognize them in a text. That took time and work enough. It was another to help them learn to generate arguments using the techniques. We did not fail at that, but once again gravity seemed to be pulling us toward analysis and interpretation. It's just easier to sight these forms when they are sleeping than it is to mount and ride them when they are awake—at least when one is also awake and riding them deliberately.[1]

I have taught a version of the course two more times since then, and I have made some qualified progress. Central to that progress was translating the techniques into *actions* described as clearly and simply as possible. I still explain the technique, with examples, as before; however, the weight of the teaching and learning is on direct invention, on generating lots of arguments. Here is the substance of a handout I give students with the procedures for inventing person-act arguments. It would be embarrassing to report how long it took me to simplify it to this degree.

How to Create Person-Act Arguments

The idea we have of a person and the ideas we have of a person's acts interact and have effects on each other. We make judgments about persons based on their acts, and we make judgments about their acts based on what we know of the persons.

General Principle: On the basis of what is more clearly known, make inferences about what is less clearly known.

Person: The stabilized character traits that make up a person's identity.

Act: Anything that can be considered an expression of the person—action, style, dress, judgment, speech, manners, emotion, appearance. Acts are more transitory while persons are more stable.

1. Reason from act to person. Draw conclusions about a person based on what is known about that person's acts. From acts we might draw conclusions about someone's personality, character, virtue, interests, basic goals and beliefs, etc.

1A. Counter this reasoning: separate the person from the act, and amplify the characteristics of the person that conflict with the act—for example, through narration, description, lists, presence, and opposing act-to-person arguments. This will support reinterpreting the act in light of the person, disqualifying the act as an anomaly, or shifting the discussion from the rightness or wrongness of the act to the responsibility and merit of the person.

1B. Counter this reasoning: reduce the importance of the act by assigning it to a sphere of less importance. For example, if one is arguing about politics, argue that acts concerning marital fidelity or religion are not relevant.

1C. Counter this reasoning: show that the act was a mistake, a result of clumsiness, an exception.

1D. Counter this reasoning: show that the action was caused by circumstances or something in the environment and is not an indicator of an agent's character.

2. Reason from person to act. Draw conclusions about the meaning or value of acts based on what is known about the person. Use elements most central to the person that will give meaning to the acts—intention, for example. Amplify the characteristics of the person that support the interpretation of the act—through narration, description, lists, presence, and supporting act-to-person arguments.

2A. Counter this reasoning: separate the act from the person and give it an independent description. Stress its independent status as an incontrovertible fact. Show that the act is well-known and is an important sign of character. Show that it is especially important in the circumstances in question. Use language that reveals the relevant features of the act. Give presence to the act.

3. Reason from act to person to act. Draw conclusions about lesser-known acts from better-known acts—for example, from past acts to future acts—but be sure to go through the person. This will combine each of the other two structures and their dynamics.

So, after we read sections 68–73 of *The New Rhetoric* and worked with examples and exercises for three days in class, I gave the following assignment:

Find a story/article/essay/book/web page/video/film or *something* of *some kind* that seems rich with person-act issues. Find a central question at issue (more than one if you need more than one). State the question(s) as clearly as possible. Then (1) generate as many arguments as you can, on all sides of the issue, using person-act techniques

(400–600 words), and (2) explain what person-act techniques you used to generate the arguments (400–600 words).

I was very specific about not being concerned with the strength of the arguments but only with the quantity. We were separating invention from criticism, and we were training in only one part of arguing well, inventing copiously. The results this time were more impressive. One student chose to invent arguments about the film *V for Vendetta*, in which V, a masked man who kidnaps Evey, a young woman, engages in acts of violence against a repressive regime led by Chancellor Sutler. The question was, "Who is the real terrorist?" The student invented thirty-two arguments: five act-to-person arguments that Sutler was a terrorist and one person-to-act argument that he was not; twelve act-to-person arguments that V was a terrorist and two person-to-act arguments that he was not; nine act-to-person arguments that V was not a terrorist and three person-to-act arguments that he was a terrorist. All this was accompanied by sound explanations of the techniques that were working in the arguments. Several other papers produced similar numbers and similarly sound analyses, and the students who performed well also succeeded with the other techniques in their final papers, in which they first invented copiously and then on the basis of that copious invention provided an answer to a question at issue, developed arguments that supported it, and wrote a paper that was appropriate for a particular situation.

Still, there were many students who struggled and simply did not gain much inventional power from learning these techniques in even the minimally abstract and formal way in which I wrote the procedures, even with examples and practice in class. The course evaluations spanned an unusually broad range, and the comments on the class reflected the range. I have taught no other course in which students split so decisively about the difficulty of the course. Several insisted that the material was "abstract," "dense," "difficult," and, for one, even "incomprehensible." One student said that the course was too much just studying "arguing for arguing's sake." Yet several others said it was "too easy" and "simplistic" and that it "could have been more demanding." Student course evaluations are often difficult to interpret and difficult to take, for all the familiar reasons. However, in this case, after some consideration, I believe that they show what *The New Rhetoric*'s model of argumentation might well lead us to expect.

Theory, Practice, Experience, Reflection

Invention has many sources. It arises first from one's being attuned to what is happening within a situation in which arguments are evolving. This requires perceptiveness and a familiarity with argumentative situations and what happens in them. As I mentioned above, if one can identify a speaker and an audience, the reasons they have for engaging in argumentation, and the purposes they hope to accomplish, then one is already almost involuntarily imagining the arguments they are likely to use. If one pays attention to the language people have already used in the situation and accurately estimates the level of trust among the parties and the extent to which they are willing to change their minds, then one is already imagining what kinds of arguments might be available. If one is also familiar with the rules of the forum or the usual ways arguments are conducted in the particular situation, then one has also received guidance in imagining appropriate arguments. This kind of perceptiveness and familiarity with situations requires experience and knowledge that are usually gained over time. Situations invent arguments in partnership with someone who has this perceptiveness and familiarity. Such capabilities are much more important than having an abstract knowledge of argumentative forms and being able to invent from *topoi*. Further, particular situations produce motivations for being interested in arguing. We undergo emotional and intellectual involvement when we become immersed in a particular situation and in the arguments occurring in it. Few of us undergo the same involvement and motivation when we back off to see all the arguments from all sides. To teach invention with this in mind is to teach real cases and to give the students guidance in perceiving the sources of invention in the particular cases.

The New Rhetoric's model would also lead us to expect that invention comes from common sense; from having a rich and ordered world from which to draw material for arguments; from perception that recognizes what hierarchies and systems are organizing people's adherence to certain facts and values in some situation; and from practical judgment, judgment that can organize and apply what one knows and perceives in relation to inventing arguments in the situation. These capabilities require a broad education and repeated and guided experience in judging and arguing in real situations. When one has these capabilities, the situation becomes one's partner in invention, and arguments begin to emerge without one's ever thinking about their form. Much the same is true of presentation and style. A significant field for invention is identified, but invention is actualized and learned only in connection with the specific situation, partly because *invention is ultimately adaptation to a particular situation*. One can help to cultivate attunement, perceptiveness, familiarity, common sense, and judgment and to inspire motivation, but one cannot provide abstract procedures for students to run through to acquire these qualities. They all lie more on the side of what takes time, repetition, experience, and immersion in particular cases—that is, on the side of virtues, habits, and dispositions.

According to *The New Rhetoric*'s model, this kind of invention involving common sense and an immersion in particular kinds of knowledge has a priority. It occurs in connection with establishing the framework and starting points of argumentation. The *topoi* or techniques cannot be activated unless these conditions are in place. Although *The New Rhetoric* does not speak about a pedagogical process, it is notable that Vico sets forth something like the same priorities that *The New Rhetoric* does, and Vico makes them emphatically pedagogical (13–14). However, he includes the *topoi* in his discussion in a way that makes the learning of them seem continuous with the acquisition of common sense. This is perhaps because he also or primarily has in mind, as David Fleming suggests, the material *topoi*, or commonplaces, rather than the more general formal *topoi* that are argumentative techniques ("Becoming Rhetorical" 100).

In contrast, learning formal *topoi* is more like learning procedures for generating arguments on all sides of an issue in *any* situation. Formal *topoi* are not as closely tied to specific situations as the other kinds of invention. At least as *The New Rhetoric* offers them in its techniques, and as I have developed them in my procedures, they are more abstract and distant. Inventing copiously requires in part not paying too much attention to the constraints of the situation. Adopting the big perspective and taking the time to methodically invent arguments on all sides of an issue also tend to dampen the positive motivation that many people have for engaging with arguments. There are ways to address this with carefully crafted exercises and assignments or with the design of competitive debate, but the fact is there nonetheless.

So, would awakening the *topoi* in *The New Rhetoric* really be pedagogically relevant? Are the techniques learnable and usable as sources of invention? There are many ways of answering. However, what is learnable is a function of the conditions in which learning takes place. In preparation for developing an undergraduate minor in Writing, Speaking, and Critical Reasoning, my rhetoric colleagues and I held a faculty seminar in which we read, among other influential works, David Fleming's "Rhetoric as a Course of Study." Fleming notes that training in rhetoric usually has three definitive features. First, it requires lots of time, with years of sequenced courses, at least, and with lots of preparation before students enter. Second, it is multiform, a "total experience" that demands broad learning and experience in different situations. Its success depends on the repetition, practice, discipline, and devotion required of any athlete. Third, its goal is the formation of a certain kind of person—in part, one with all the capabilities to speak or write well in any situation, but also one who would do so for a common and not simply a private aim. The training is especially focused on forming and developing a good citizen.

In a university, given the length of any term and the demands of undergraduate students' degree programs, there is very little time for a limited number of courses to devote to intense rhetorical training. This immediately affects the possibility of multiform training, too. How many different approaches can one take in ten or fifteen weeks without fragmenting and diffusing what is being learned? Further, it is very difficult to control the sequencing of courses. One can try to do this with prerequisites. According to the design of our minor, the students should have had two courses in written reasoning, a course in public speaking focused on argument, and a philosophy course on critical reasoning by the time they reach the third-year course, Inventing Arguments. They should also be enrolled in a major. The realities are different. We can control only what goes on in our own courses. Our writing courses are based on John T. Gage's *The Shape of Reason*, and so our students have used the enthymeme and the *stases* as part of the inventional process. But they have had only two courses in which to absorb, practice, and consolidate what they have learned. David Frank, a Perelman scholar, teaches and supervises the speech courses, and so the students have solid preparation there. However, the University of Oregon is part of a state system of higher education, which is part of a larger national system of mass higher education. Its leaders pursue the laudable (in principle) if fantastic goal of seamless integration among its parts. So our students may have completed the prerequisites not at our university but in specially designated high school courses, in community colleges, or in other four-year state schools, or they may have transferred credits from out of state and satisfied the prerequisites according to transfer articulation policies. They also may have taken our own writing courses two or three years previously, with almost no focused practice, repetition, or reinforcement since. Some students may not yet have declared a major and may still be wandering in the wilderness of the second year of "general education," with its vast lecture halls and vague intellectual anomie. They may have no focused experience in a subject. On the other hand, if they are in the minor, and they have a major, and they have had reasonably good luck in their education and experience, they are in a rich and coherent sequence of courses.

However, the truth is that we have a very brief amount of time with all of our students, many of whom have not had the preparation they need to take on a formal study of argumentative techniques. The preparation needed here is lots of time and instruction and immersion in argumentative practice in particular situations. Until they have acquired the understanding and competencies that come from this practice, they do not have the needs that training in formal techniques addresses. They have different needs, needs with more priority. They need more guided immersion in specific situations, more training in perceptiveness, more coaching in the development of judgment, more common sense and more experience in activating it for argument, and more knowledge and more experience in adapting it to argumentative situations.

The question of invention is not just a theoretical question or a question of the best model. Whether an account of invention and its learnability is supportable depends on what conditions are available for learning. *The New Rhetoric*'s model of argument, if it is a model, is powerfully illuminating of the complexity and richness of argumentative situations and the sources of invention that are hiding in them. The treatise also offers immense gifts to anyone interested in topical invention by describing in detail a large number of formal *techniques* of argumentation. However, the techniques are simply identified and analyzed and explained in existing texts; the treatise says nothing about how to teach people to *use* these techniques. And the model also suggests that, as sources of deliberate invention, the techniques are secondary to the more primary skills of invention developed through the less formal practices connected with the conditions and starting points of arguments. And, though the model says a great deal about the conditions necessary for argumentation to take place, it says nothing about the conditions necessary for learning to argue well or for teaching the sources of invention that the treatise uncovers.

Against these obstacles, I have tried to awaken the sleeping *topoi*, translate them into inventional actions, and teach them to students in an upper-division course. The difficulties I have encountered have forced me to rethink the approach, especially given the fact that *The New Rhetoric* itself explains the endemic nature of the difficulties. However, the successes I have had with students who had sufficient preparation prevent me from abandoning the task altogether. The awakened *topoi* can be powerful tools of copious invention for students who are ready. However, the general conditions available for teaching them are not optimal, and the conditions cannot be changed easily or in the near term. Given the conditions, I will build into the course a richer primary context of invention, and I will give more attention to the fundamental skills that belong to it. There will be a more consistent connection with particular cases. I will introduce fewer formal techniques, more slowly, in that richer context and provide more repetition and practice. The course will resemble the lower-level courses more than it does now. It will be a better and more effective course that will do more good for a larger number of students.

A simple, six-part model of argumentation can be mastered and taught and learned, in one way or another. It focuses attention and provides efficiencies that cannot be denied. It is elegant and, for its purposes, powerful enough. However, it does not give us as much help or as much trouble or as much truth as *The New Rhetoric*'s model of argument. It does not shed light on vast sources of invention the way *The New Rhetoric* does. Yet awakening the slumbering *topoi* in that treatise, and activating those sources, and translating *The New Rhetoric* into terms that could inform the teaching of invention, and then applying all that knowledge in the development of actual courses and the teaching of actual students in the actual conditions we have available to us, is a very difficult and challenging task, pretty much still before us.

Note

1. Although I am drawing a contrast here between invention and interpretation, I am not at all denying that interpretation and invention can be two sides of the same coin, especially when we take "interpretation" in Gadamer's sense, in which interpretation is a way we are. Even when we take "interpretation" to mean a way of resolving the conflict among different readings of a text, or of making an obscure text clear, there is certainly a process of invention included in those activities. Likewise, to construct and adapt to an audience requires interpretation, or else the activity would be arbitrary. And there is no inventing arguments without retrieving and adapting agreements from a background world, and that too is an act of interpretation. However, there is an important difference between recognizing the forms in a text or a speech, or recognizing where they could fit into the gaps of a text or speech to explain it, and using them in an argument of one's own invention.

Works Cited

Aristotle. *Poetics*. Ed. and trans. Stephen Halliwell. *Aristotle: Poetics; Longinus: On the Sublime; Demetrius: On Style*. Cambridge, MA: Harvard UP, 1995. 27–142.

Fleming David. "Becoming Rhetorical: An Education in the Topics." *The Realms of Rhetoric: The Prospects for Rhetoric Education*. Ed. Joseph Petraglia and Deepika Bahri. Albany: State U of New York P, 2003. 93–116.

———. "Rhetoric as a Course of Study." *College English* 61.2 (1998): 169–91.

Gadamer, Hans-Georg. *Truth and Method*. 1960. Trans. Joel Weinsheimer. New York: Continuum, 2006.

Gage, John T. *The Shape of Reason: Argumentative Writing in College*. 4th ed. New York: Macmillan, 2006.

Isocrates. *Antidosis*. *Isocrates: Vol. II*. Trans. George Norlin. Cambridge, MA: Harvard UP, 1929. 179–366.

Norman, Timothy, et al. "Argument and Multi-agent Systems." *Argumentation Machines: New Frontiers in Argument and Computation*. Ed. Chris Reed and Timothy J. Norman. Dordrecht, the Netherlands: Kluwer Academic Publishers, 2004. 15–54.

Olson, Gary A. "Literary Theory, Philosophy of Science, and Persuasive Discourse: Thoughts from a Neo-postmodernist." *Journal of Advanced Composition* 13.2 (1993): 283–309.

Perelman, Chaïm, and Lucie Olbrechts-Tyteca. *The New Rhetoric: A Treatise on Argumentation*. Trans. John Wilkinson and Purcell Weaver. Notre Dame: U of Notre Dame P, 1969.

———. *Traité de l'argumentation: La nouvelle rhétorique*. Paris: Presses Universitaires de France, 1958.

Toulmin, Stephen. *Human Understanding: The Collective Use and Evolution of Concepts*. Princeton, NJ: Princeton UP, 1972.

———. *The Uses of Argument*. Cambridge: Cambridge UP, 1958.

Toulmin, Stephen, Richard Rieke, and Allan Janik. *An Introduction to Reasoning*. New York: Macmillan, 1979.

Vico, Giambattista. *On the Study Methods of Our Time*. Trans. Elio Gianturco. Ithaca: Cornell UP, 1990.

Vygotsky, L. S. *Thought and Language*. Ed. and trans. Eugenia Hanfmann and Gertrude Vakar. Cambridge, MA: MIT P, 1962.

14

Analogical Reasoning in the Teaching of Science: The Case of Richard Feynman's Physics

Maria Freddi

The use of analogy in the history of science—from Newton's color spectrum as the diatonic scale to Niels Bohr's internal structure of atoms as the solar system,[1] from the electric circuit as a hydrodynamic system to light as waves and/or particles—has variedly served the purpose of advancing the understanding of natural phenomena and sometimes been the object of impassioned controversies among groups of scientists.

Richard Feynman exemplifies this widespread practice, having also made extensive use of analogies in his arguments about physics. This essay is an attempt to isolate some fundamental analogies in his pedagogic writings in order to investigate their role as the locus of negotiation of scientific contents and controversy resolution, or, in Kuhnian terms, incommensurability. The examples discussed are drawn from the collection of lectures published as *Six Easy Pieces: Essentials of Physics Explained by Its Most Brilliant Teacher*. Winner of the Nobel Prize in physics in 1965, Feynman represents one of the most interesting and distinctive personalities in science over the last fifty years. He was not only a theoretical physicist par excellence but also a great teacher and keen popularizer of physics, both in his academic and public lectures and in his books. Through his work and unconventional methods of teaching science, he became one of the world's most publicly known scientists.

The theoretical background to this study is offered by Chaïm Perelman and Lucie Olbrechts-Tyteca's pages on reasoning by analogy in *The New*

Rhetoric, together with Thomas Kuhn's *Structure of Scientific Revolutions*. The analysis of Feynman's style is also related to work on the rhetoric of science, specifically by Alan G. Gross in *The Rhetoric of Science* and Jeanne Fahnestock in *Rhetorical Figures in Science*. In passing, I make use of the treatment of analogical reasoning as creative problem-solving by a philosopher of science (Meheus), as well as of a linguistic model of argumentation structure (Stati).

Analogical Reasoning in *The New Rhetoric*

In *The New Rhetoric*, analogy is said to be an essential factor of invention as well as a means of proof, thus having an argumentative function (see especially sections 82–86). According to Perelman and Olbrechts-Tyteca, an apt analogy can make the audience prefer one hypothesis to another, and it should therefore be included in any complete account of argumentation. In the authors' view, the argumentative role of analogy is best understood as structural similarity between two terms, which they call the *theme* and the *phoros*. The *theme* is the focal point of the line of reasoning, the term to which the conclusion relates, while the *phoros* is the linchpin of the argument; the *phoros* is usually more familiar to the audience than the *theme* and thus links to the latter, whose sense it helps clarify. In virtue of the resemblance between *phoros* and *theme* and of the comparison established, the *theme* becomes clearer. Consequently, the *theme* and the *phoros* must come from different knowledge fields. Whenever there is a sense of "separate spheres" or incommensurate arenas, or different orders of existence, reasoning by analogy becomes particularly useful.[2] The example given is drawn from Aristotle: intellect is to evidence (A is to B) as the bat's eyes are to light (C is to D), where the first term is the *theme* (intellect) followed by the comparative element "as" introducing a comparison with the *phoros* (bat's eyes) in virtue of the resemblance relation between the two spheres. That is, intellect cannot see evidence as much as bats cannot see the light.

Later on, Perelman and Olbrechts-Tyteca observe that by virtue of the analogy, A gets closer to C and B to D, thus leading to a reciprocal action between *theme* and *phoros*, a value transfer such that the *theme* acquires a new sense. Moreover, the comparison can occasion developments of concepts that might extend the scope of the original analogy. The authors here give a classic example taken from science, namely the comparison of electrical and hydraulic phenomena occasioning developments in the history of science, which completes the original analogy.

In stressing that *theme* and *phoros* must belong to separate knowledge spheres, Perelman and Olbrechts-Tyteca ask themselves whether it is possible to have true analogies within a single discipline. There is indeed a kind of reasoning by analogy in which the two terms of the comparison come from the same knowledge field. These are example and illustration, whereby the two terms of the analogy are different instances of the same generalization.[3] Reasoning both by example and by illustration is said to be typical of the sciences: "If the analogy is a fruitful one, *theme* and *phoros* are transformed into examples or illustrations of a more general law, and by their relation to this law there is a unification of the fields of the *theme* and the *phoros*" (Perelman and Olbrechts-Tyteca 396).

Perelman and Olbrechts-Tyteca offer the caveat that analogy is an unstable means of argument since it can be used by the audience or interlocutor to refute the argument it was meant to support. It works better as a heuristic, especially in science, where, the authors state, as a link in the chain of inductive reasoning, it serves as a means of invention rather than as a means of proof.[4]

Kuhn on Incommensurability between Scientific Paradigms

In Kuhn's 1962 book, *The Structure of Scientific Revolutions*, and in the 1969 postscript containing his reply to criticism of the book, the analogies preferred by a community of scientists together with the shared exemplars are perhaps the most original aspect of Kuhn's paradigms. Indeed, transmission of scientific knowledge among peers and to young adepts is in Kuhn's own judgment the most innovative aspect of his paradigms: "The paradigm as shared example is the central element of what I now take to be the most novel and least understood aspect of this book" (*Structure* 187). His stress on the inextricable relation between science and the community of people who engage in its practice—"by studying them [the community's paradigms] and by practicing with them, the members of the corresponding community learn their trade" (43)—makes of Kuhn's account a sociology of science.[5]

The content of the paradigms of science is articulated in the postscript to *The Structure of Scientific Revolutions* as the elements of the "disciplinary matrix," that is, an orderly complex of elements, which need further specification, shared by a community of practitioners. The contents of the disciplinary matrix can be said to consist of four main types: symbolic generalizations, heuristic and ontological models, values and beliefs, and exemplars. The second and fourth contents, namely heuristic and ontological models together with exemplars, are the most relevant to an analysis of analogical reasoning in Feynman's lectures. In fact, heuristic and ontological models consist of analogies and metaphors common to a scientific community, while exemplars comprise a set of cases, problems, and shared examples that the novice needs to recognize in order to be able to understand science. In his postscript, we read: "The student discovers, with or without the assistance of his instructor, a way to see his problem as like a problem he has already encountered. Having seen the resemblance, grasped the analogy between two or more distinct problems, he can interrelate symbols and attach them to nature in the ways that have proved effective before" (*Structure* 189). This latter content leads to Kuhn's notion of incommensurability between paradigms, a view that was accused of being relativistic by many, including Karl Popper. Both in the 1969 postscript and in his last published lecture ("Remarks on Incommensurability and Translation"), Kuhn puts forward the idea that paradigms in science are incommensurable. Scientists within one paradigm see examples of situations differently from practitioners of another paradigm, and therefore they cannot communicate with each other. As I will contend, in Feynman's argument the role of analogies is particularly crucial to controversy resolution, or, in Kuhnian terms, incommensurability.

Rhetorical and Epistemological Approaches to Science

Analogical reasoning in the hard sciences is the object of study of rhetorician of science Alan G. Gross in his book *Starring the Text: The Place of Rhetoric in Science Studies*. Although Gross no longer views rhetoric as constitutive of science, as in his earlier more radical and provocative view, science certainly shapes its discourse in a way that might bring about audience persuasion, whether for peers or new adepts. Such an approach to the study of scientific discourse is particularly relevant here, in that one can see a didactic genre, such as the series of lectures I will be discussing, as having some of the features of persuasive discourse. Argumentation in general, and argument by analogy in particular, are especially relevant when communicating an understanding of science—here, physics—to neophytes.

In the chapters devoted to analogy, Gross distinguishes between a probative and heuristic function and shows a difference in the role analogies play in science as opposed to other disciplines. While in political discourse, analogy has a probative and thus argumentative role only, in scholarly argument regarding philosophy, it is both heuristic and probative in function (Gross, *Rhetoric of Science* and *Starring the Text*). Things are different in science, where analogy serves a heuristic function. Moreover, Gross argues, it is only in science that analogy combined with quantitative methods has the power to settle controversies and reach a level of significant agreement (*Starring the Text* 37).

Gross gives two examples, the first of which, from mathematics, is Bernoulli's series. Daniel Bernoulli was unable to find the sum of the infinite series of squares, while a century later by means of an analogy, Swiss mathematician Leonhard Euler solved Bernoulli's series. The analogy consisted in extending algebra designed for finite mathematics to an unalgebraic equation (*Starring the Text* 37). However, solution by analogy was not a demonstration, which was only later achieved through mathematical verification. Therefore, analogy worked as a heuristic but was not probative.

The second example is taken from the realm of genetics and concerns the discovery of the helical structure of DNA. Gross again illustrates the heuristic as separate from the probative use of analogies in the sciences, in that James D. Watson and Francis Crick were led to the correct interpretation of the structure of DNA by developing Erwin Schrödinger's analogy but by the same means were led to an incorrect formulation of the way the genetic code was read. He also notices how as a result of the same analogy, Marshall W. Nirenberg and Heinrich J. Matthaei got to the correct formulation (*Starring the Text* 39).

In sum, Gross's argument shows that while analogy can indeed facilitate invention, it cannot be used to verify a scientific statement without observational and experimental evidence and quantitative methodologies.

For a logico-philosophical perspective on the functions of analogical reasoning, particularly related to creative problem-solving processes, I will refer to the contribution by Joke Meheus in Fernand Hallyn's 2000 collection of essays on metaphors and analogies in the sciences. The author is interested in those novel analogies developed to generate a solution to a problem, that is, analogies that have a heuristic function. Analogical reasoning is defined by Meheus as "any process in which inferences are made on the basis of certain similarities between two domains (this is, two objects, two classes of objects, two systems . . .)," a "source domain" chosen as showing relevant similarities and a "target domain" where a problem has to be solved (24–25). The example is given of the structure of atoms: in order to solve the problem of the internal structure of atoms, one can select the solar system as a source domain on the assumption that the relation between the sun and the planets (the *phoros*, in Perelmanian terms) is similar to the relation between the nucleus and the electrons (the *theme*, in Perelmanian terms). On the basis of such resemblance, the relevant items of the original context can be extended from one domain (the *phoros*) to the other (the *theme*), so that inferences can be made on the basis of the analogy. The reasoning process thus developed can lead to the solution of the target problem.

Meheus makes a further distinction between the heuristic function of "weak" and "strong" analogies. She gives two examples as cases in point: Bohr's analogy of the solar system to understand the internal structure of atoms and Newton's use of the diatonic scale in designing a color wheel. According to the author, this latter type of analogy is strong in that Newton reconsidered his observational findings in light of the analogy. In a sense, the analogy was a sufficient reason for reconsidering the observational findings, so it had a strong heuristic function, or one could say (after Gross) it was to some degree probative. On the contrary, in the Bohr example, the hypothesis that electrons move around the nucleus in the same way that planets move around the sun was not accepted until it proved successful in explaining a set of phenomena (for example, in chemistry). In this respect, the distinction between weak and strong analogies seems to overlap with Gross's heuristic and probative functions.

Meheus also notices how analogical reasoning allows for "ampliative" and deductive inferences to be made, the former being extensions of the source domain to the target domain and the latter drawn exclusively from observational information pertaining to the target domain but not related to the analogical process. For example, it follows from Bohr's analogy that electrons cannot jump from one orbit to another, but the conclusion is rejected if it is possible to establish deductively that electrons do jump. From the point of view of logic, this entails a dynamic relation between ampliative and deductive inferences.

To show how this dynamic reasoning process works, a last example is given by Meheus concerning the Carnot cycle and how the analogy with water mills led Sadi Carnot to the solution of the problem, moving from more specific claims (like water in water mills, heat *falls* from a higher point to a lower point) to more generic formulations (heat *moves* from one point to another) and to the specialized conclusion that in steam engines, heat moves from a reservoir at a higher temperature to a reservoir at a lower temperature (31).

Although Jeanne Fahnestock devotes her 1999 study to rhetorical figures in science other than metaphor and analogy, the argument running throughout her book—that rhetorical figures (including metaphor and analogy) are epitomes of lines of reasoning—is extremely useful and suggestive of a potential linguistic analysis of scientific texts. She shows how figures of speech (among others, gradatio, that is, climax; polyptoton, that is, a figure of variation within lexical repetition; chiasmus and antimetabole, that is, a subtype of antithesis) play a powerful conceptual role in scientific arguments because of the connection between patterns of language and patterns of reasoning.[6] Fahnestock thus paves the way for a rhetorical approach to scientific texts that combines linguistic analysis. The analysis of Feynman's prose I propose in the next section acknowledges her call for a combination of the two.

Analogy in *Six Easy Pieces*: A Linguistic and Rhetorical Approach

In the early 1960s, Feynman was asked to teach an introductory physics course to Caltech freshmen and sophomores. This course became so popular not only with the students it was intended for but also with Feynman's colleagues and the general public that it was later published as *Six Easy Pieces: Essentials of Physics Explained by Its Most Brilliant Teacher.*

For a linguistic reading of argumentation, I will refer to the model proposed by Sorin Stati in 2002, in which argumentation is considered as part of the pragmatic potential of a text identified by certain argumentative "moves" in discourse.[7] As a linguist, Stati identifies ways of expressing argument by segmenting argumentative text into smaller, more manageable units signaled by linguistic manifestations. His "auxiliary lexicon of argumentation" (my translation)[8] consists of a wide array of resources pertaining to different levels of discourse, both the lexico-grammatical and the textual, including names of argumentative roles (for example, reasons, statements, axioms, deductions, objections); verbs of arguing, or *verba dicendi* (for example, argue, claim, maintain, suppose, object, show); connectives (for example, first, second, therefore, but, however) and particles (for example, Yes/No); complex phrases or clauses corresponding to whole moves (for example, "You might ask why . . ." anticipating an objection); modulators expressing epistemic stance (for example, certainly, probably, clearly, obviously, of course); and textual cohesion realized by means of anaphoric and cataphoric chains establishing argumentative relations (straight lexical repetition, co-reference, substitution, and ellipsis). All of these mark the units of the argumentative structure of a text, which acquire an argumentative force and thus function as moves.[9] Although it is clear from Stati's analysis that total convergence between lexico-grammar and argumentation is not possible (argumentation pertaining to the pragmatic level of discourse), an attempt is made to map the lines of argument onto the levels of lexico-grammar and text. For example, the author shows how a clause signaled by a causal connective may function as Justification or Argument in an argumentative sequence made up of a Claim + Argument but does not inherently do so.

The structure of argumentative discourse thus described is of help in this study of Feynman's use of analogies. By using concordancing software, I could search for occurrences of the imperative form of such lexemes as "imagine," "suppose," and "consider," which may be expected to trigger the chunks containing reasoning by analogy, together with the lemma "analogy" (with its inflectional variants "analogous" and "analogue"). Also, another linguistic feature typical of analogical reasoning was searched for, namely the comparative prepositions "like" and "as." Five analogical chunks were thus retrieved, namely the analogy of "Dennis the Menace,"[10] one analogy used to explain the electromagnetic field,[11] the analogy of the "chess game,"[12] the analogy used to elucidate gas behavior,[13] and, finally, one concerning activation energy.[14] I will discuss the first three of these.

Having identified the analogical excerpts but before dealing with them, Feynman's preface is worth considering. Several key principles contained therein are developed throughout his lectures and give us a flavor of their argumentative style. His pedagogical tenets have direct implications for his rhetoric and for the kind of strategies he uses to teach physics to novices and to make new acolytes, as will become apparent in the cases discussed below. Feynman's aim is to maintain the interest and enthusiasm of the better and more motivated student. In order to do so, he asserts that he will apply concepts in directions that go beyond mainstream argumentation (in a programmatic manner that recalls Galileo Galilei's pedagogy of digressions) and that he will report as accurately as possible all the statements of physics by showing those ideas and equations that belong to the accepted corpus of physical knowledge and how they are changed by more advanced understanding. He also suggests that he will alternate the deductive and inductive approach to show when something new cannot be deduced from previous knowledge.

On the other hand, he says he does not want to leave behind the less smart students for whom a core of topics (he calls it the "backbone" of physics) should be accessible, and he stresses the importance of developing a corpus of problems and examples to illustrate the ideas in the lectures "to make more realistic, more complete and more settled in the mind the ideas that have been exposed" (*Six Easy Pieces* xxvii). His principle of reducing deep ideas to simple, understandable terms is evident throughout the lectures. Reasoning by example and illustration thus constitutes a founding strategy of his didactics, as does the less orthodox pedagogic principle of presenting the most difficult theories first, in reverse fashion, in order to maintain the enthusiasm and excitement of the smartest students in the class.

Analogies in *Six Easy Pieces*

Chapter 4 on conservation of energy contains one of the most brilliant analogies of the whole course. To illustrate the kind of reasoning that is used in theoretical physics, Feynman examines one of the basic laws of physics, namely the law of the conservation of energy, and to explain the meaning of this abstract concept, he uses an extended analogy. Here is a long extract from that chapter (bold has been added to all the excerpts that follow to highlight those expressions of the auxiliary lexicon of argumentation):

Since it is an abstract idea, **we shall illustrate the meaning of it by an analogy. Imagine** a child, perhaps "Dennis the Menace," who has blocks which are absolutely indestructible, and cannot be divided into pieces. Each is the same as the other. **Let us suppose** that he has 28 blocks. His mother puts him with his 28 blocks into a room at the beginning of the day. At the end of the day, being curious, she counts the blocks very carefully, and discovers a phenomenal law—no matter what he does with the blocks, there are always 28 remaining! This continues for a number of days, until one day there are only 27 blocks, but a little investigating shows that there is one under the rug—she must look everywhere to be sure that the number of blocks has not changed. One day, however, the number appears to change—there are only 26 blocks. Careful investigation indicates that the window was open, and upon looking outside, the other two blocks are found. Another day, careful count indicates that there are 30 blocks! This causes considerable consternation, until it is realized that Bruce came to visit, bringing his blocks with him, and he left a few at Dennis' house. After she has disposed of the extra blocks, she closes the window, does not let Bruce in, and then everything is going along all right, until one time she counts and finds only 25 blocks. However, there is a box in the room, a toy box, and the mother goes to open the toy box, but the boy says "No, do not open my toy box," and screams. Mother is not allowed to open the toy box. Being extremely curious, and somewhat ingenious, she **invents a scheme**! She knows that a block weighs three ounces, so she weighs the box at a time when she sees 28 blocks, and it weighs 16 ounces. The next time she wishes to check, she weighs the box again, subtracts sixteen ounces and divides by three. She discovers the following:

(number of blocks seen) + [(weight of box) − 16 ounces] / 3 ounces = constant. (4.1)

There then appear to be **some new deviations**, but careful study indicates that the dirty water in the bathtub is changing its level. The child is throwing blocks into the water, and she cannot see them because it is so dirty, but she can find out how many blocks are in the water by adding another term to her formula. Since the original height of the water was 6 inches and each block raises the water a quarter of an inch, **this new formula** would be:

(number of blocks seen) + [(weight of box) − 16 ounces] / 3 ounces + (height of water) − 6 inches / ¼ inch = constant. (4.2)

In the gradual increase in the complexity of her world, she finds a whole series of terms **representing** ways of calculating how many blocks are in places where she is not allowed to look. As a result, she finds **a complex formula, a quantity which has to be computed, which always stays** the same in her situation. (*Six Easy Pieces* 70–71)

This extended analogy is opened by discursive strings typical of analogical reasoning, namely "Imagine" and "Let us suppose." The hortatory "imagine" points forward to the fictitious scenario of the child playing with his building blocks and hiding them from his mother. The mother in the analogy acts as careful investigator, possibly a metaphorical representation of the researcher[15] who, during the course of her inquiry, is sometimes hit by *new deviations*, an expression that has an interesting precedent in the usage made by Galileo in *Dialogues Concerning Two New Sciences*.[16]

Reading on, the *scheme* the mother invents appears to be in a lexical and co-referential relation with "this new formula" later on and with the "whole series of terms representing ways of calculating," as well as "a complex formula, a quantity which has to be computed." These elements form the lexical chain corresponding to the quantitative apparatus of the verification procedures. There thus seems to be a smooth transition from the *phoros* of the analogy to the *theme* with its quantitative features, ultimately condensed in the two formulas in (4.1) and (4.2) and in the main Claim that we do not know what energy is and yet we can calculate it, made in the next excerpt where the terms of the analogy are spelled out explicitly:

> **What is the analogy of this to** the conservation of energy? The most remarkable aspect that must be abstracted from this picture is that there are no blocks. Take away the first terms in (4.1) and (4.2) and we find ourselves calculating more or less abstract things. **The analogy has the following points. First**, when we are calculating the energy, sometimes some of it leaves the system and goes away, or sometimes some comes in. In order to verify the conservation of energy, we must be careful that we have not put any in or taken any out. **Second**, the energy has a large number of different forms, and there is a formula for each one. These are: gravitational energy, kinetic energy, heat energy, elastic energy, electrical energy, chemical energy, radiant energy, nuclear energy, mass energy. If we total up the formulas for each of these contributions, it will not change except for energy going in and out. **It is important to realize that** in physics today, we have no knowledge of what energy is. We do not have a picture that energy comes in little blobs of a definite amount. **It is not that way. However,** there are

formulas for calculating some numerical quantity, and when we add it all together it gives "28"—always the same number. It is an abstract thing in that it does not tell us the mechanism or the reasons for the various formulas. (*Six Easy Pieces* 71–72)

At the linguistic level, we can observe how discourse is paced by explicit markers of the flow of argument. The argumentative climax is reached by the statement "in physics today, we have no knowledge of what energy is." (Notice incidentally that an expression of positive evaluation or stance is associated to it, namely "It is important to realize that"). The Claim is made that although we do not know what energy is, we can calculate it (see the contrastive connective "However" introducing the Counter-Claim "there are formulas for calculating some numerical quantity"). At least in this context, the Claim is particularly forceful as it appears to say that we will not know what energy is, no matter how far knowledge advances ("We do not have a picture that energy comes in little blobs of a definite amount. It is not that way"), and yet in its varied forms—gravitational, kinetic, electrical, nuclear, and so on—we can calculate a numerical quantity that always stays the same and that we call energy.

Thus, at a macro level, it seems possible to say that the analogy plays a probative role to the extent that it functions as Argument to Feynman's Claim that energy is an abstract concept. The analogy also serves a crucial didactic function, in that it helps students understand the principle of the conservation of energy while also teaching that when we experiment, we sometimes forget we might have introduced some external elements or dissipated part of the initial quantities we are experimenting with (for example, Bruce's blocks or the block hiding under the rug).

A different example of analogical reasoning is offered in chapter 2 on basic physics: the idea of an electromagnetic field, a difficult physical concept, is explained through an analogy between electromagnetic waves and the waves in a pool of water. The fact that a parallel is established with a more concrete field, or, to use Perelman and Olbrechts-Tyteca's terminology, a more familiar sphere, namely the mechanical one, makes the problem easier to grasp:

Here is an analogy: If we are in a pool of water and there is a floating cork very close by, we can move it "directly" by pushing the water with another cork. **If** you looked only at the two corks, all you would see would be that one moved immediately in response to the motion of the other—there is some kind of "interaction" between them. **Of course**, what we **really** do is to disturb the water; the water then disturbs the other cork. We could make up a "law" that if you pushed

the water a little bit, an object close by in the water would move. **If it
were farther away, of course**, the second cork would scarcely move,
for we move the water locally. **On the other hand, if** we jiggle the cork
a new phenomenon is involved, in which the motion of the water
moves the water there, etc., and waves travel away, so that by jiggling,
there is an influence very much farther out, an oscillatory influence,
that cannot be understood from the direct interaction. **Therefore** the
idea of direct interaction must be replaced . . . with what we call the
electromagnetic field. (*Six Easy Pieces* 31)

On the micro-argumentative level, the analogy is marked by a sequence
of "if" clauses setting the hypothetical yet observable situation of the corks
in the water. Among the moves that can be identified, Conclusion 1 ("We
could make up a 'law' that . . .") ends the first part of the analogy. The connective "On the other hand" signals the second part where Conclusion 2
replaces the previous one ("Therefore the idea of a direct interaction must
be replaced . . . with what we call the electromagnetic field").

The argumentative rhythm is intense and the structure of the analogy
complex, as a relation is established between the jiggling of the water on
the one hand and the generation of the electromagnetic waves on the other.
The corks are compared to the electric charges, and the direct interaction
between them caused by the pushing is the electric (or magnetic) field. The
analogy draws together two diverse spheres: the *phoros* of the analogy is
the more concrete and observable sphere of the water, where the effects of
both the pushing and the jiggling can be experimented; the *theme* is the
more abstract concept of the electromagnetic field.

Moreover, in marking the passage from an old concept, the electric (and
magnetic) field considered separately (the pushing and the direct interaction), to the new concept of the electromagnetic field (the jiggling and the
oscillatory influence), the analogy overrules, in Kuhn's terms, the paradigm's
incommensurability. To this extent, it is a real analogy more than an example or illustration and can be said to have a heuristic function.

In the same chapter, in adumbrating the reductionism hypothesis, Feynman uses another analogy to explain how science proceeds by cumulative
knowledge in the "hope that we may be able to reduce the number of different things and thereby understand them better" (*Six Easy Pieces* 24). In
an attempt to explain what "understand them better" means, he uses the
analogy of a chess game:

We can imagine that this complicated array of moving things which
constitutes "the world" is something like a great chess game being

> played by the gods, and we are observers of the game. We do not know what the rules of the game are; all we are allowed to do is to watch the playing. Of course, if we watch long enough, we may eventually catch on to a few of the rules. The rules of the game are what we mean by fundamental physics. Even if we knew every rule, however, we might not be able to understand why a particular move is made in the game, merely because it is too complicated and our minds are limited. If you play chess you must know that it is easy to learn all the rules, and yet it is often very hard to select the best move or to understand why a player moves as he does. (*Six Easy Pieces* 24)

The analogy offers a clear representation of what understanding science really means by establishing a similarity relationship between the *phoros*, the chess game, and the *theme*, the laws of nature, with the inferences that the *phoros* brings about. Playing chess implies learning the rules while not necessarily being able to play well or not knowing what the best move is. If you know the rules of the game, it does not mean that you know how to use them to win the game. Analogously, although we might understand all rules by which nature behaves, this is not enough to be able to tame nature. In fact, the way we apply the rules might lead to aberrant results. Rarely has such a clear vision outlined the limitations of science by means of an analogy.

> **So** it is in nature, **only much more so**; but we may be able at least to find all the rules. Actually, we do not have all the rules now. (Every once in a while **something like** castling is going on that we still do not understand.) (*Six Easy Pieces* 24)

In anticipating a potential objection (that is, how can we know that the rules we guess at are correct?), Feynman offers three criteria by which one can verify the validity of a scientific theory. The first of them is the simplification principle: scientists isolate the phenomenon under examination to be able to predict what will happen (in one corner of the board there may be only a few chess pieces at work, and that we can figure out exactly). In other words, observation and experiment require a certain degree of abstraction to get to the general law.

The second criterion consists in the intellectual honesty that should characterize scientific progress: it is the law that does not work that opens up situations for the scientist to pursue. In the following passage, Feynman's language resonates with Kuhn's alternation of normal and revolutionary science; notice "For a long time we will have a rule" as opposed to "some time we may discover a new rule":

A second good way to check rules is in terms of less specific rules derived from them. For example, the rule on the move of a bishop on a chessboard is that it moves only on the diagonal. One can deduce, no matter how many moves may be made, that a certain bishop will always be on a red square. So, without being able to follow the details, we can always check our idea about the bishop's motion by finding out whether it is always on a red square. Of course it will be, for a long time, until all of a sudden we find that it is on a black square (what happened of course, is that in the meantime it was captured, another pawn crossed for queening, and it turned into a bishop on a black square). **That is the way it is in physics.** For a long time we will have a rule that works excellently in an overall way, even when we cannot follow the details, and then some time we may discover a new rule. From the point of view of basic physics, the most interesting phenomena are of course in the new places, the places where the rules do not work—not the places where they do work! That is the way in which we discover new rules. (*Six Easy Pieces* 25)

Finally, in introducing the third criterion of accuracy (or approximation), perhaps taking us back to the community's shared values (see Kuhn's third content of the disciplinary matrix), the analogy of the chess game is returned to (the *phoros* and *theme* are linked by the connective in bold):

The third way to tell whether our ideas are right is relatively crude but probably the most powerful of them all. That is, by rough approximation. While we may not be able to tell why Alekhine moves this particular piece, perhaps we can roughly understand that he is gathering his pieces around the king to protect it, more or less, since that is the sensible thing to do in the circumstances. **In the same way**, we can often understand nature, more or less, without being able to see what every little piece is doing, in terms of our understanding of the game. (*Six Easy Pieces* 25)

In setting up the argument on verification criteria, the analogy reflects Feynman's reductionist view that when we try to understand nature, we discover one law and then later something happens we did not expect ("something like castling") that leads to a deeper understanding. This is how physics proceeds, through gradual integrations of older laws into new laws, which, he says elsewhere, turn out to be simpler and more beautiful than they looked before. Because of the unification procedure it depicts, it seems possible to read the chess game analogy as serving the purpose of overriding incommensurability between scientific paradigms.

These, and other extended analogies in *Six Easy Pieces*, reflect Feynman's effort to help students visualize abstract concepts. By means of analogical reasoning, the topic is made more accessible and the fundamental laws of physics are explained from a unified perspective—indeed, the scientist's perspective—which ultimately aims at controversy resolution and the advancement of knowledge. The analogical reasoning, in turn, is made more understandable by the strategic use of linguistic or stylistic devices to mark the argumentative moves.

Conclusion

Combining rhetorical approaches to science discourse with linguistic tools for the analysis of argumentation in the wake of Fahnestock's invitation has proved useful on two counts. On one hand, rhetorical approaches such as those by Alan G. Gross have been shown to be a valid model of interpretation of reasoning by analogy in scientific argument. On the other hand, linguistic approaches, by permitting close reading of the argumentative structure of discourse, allow for the interpretation of passages where analogical reasoning is the strategy used to explain key scientific contents.

A more general observation and one specific to Feynman's prose can be made by way of conclusion. First, analogy gives some visual quality to reasoning as an aid to understanding and learning science. Analogies represent the shared ability on the part of the teacher and the student to create and see resemblances, respectively. With regard to this, Kuhn's statement that the student "has meanwhile assimilated a time-tested and group-licensed way of seeing" (*Structure* 189) is particularly pertinent. Second, analogical reasoning as used by Feynman may function to undo incommensurability between paradigms by aiding the conceptualization of physical law as a gradual, deeper understanding of nature: "We keep trying to put the jigsaw puzzle together" (*Six Easy Pieces* 26–27).

The use Feynman makes of analogies in physics appears to go beyond Perelman and Olbrechts-Tyteca's theoretical distinctions between reasoning by analogy on the one hand and argument by example and illustration on the other. In his analogies, a variety of functions are at work: the illustrative-didactic, in strengthening visual presence and thus increasing adherence on the part of the students; the heuristic, by facilitating experimental procedures and invention and overriding incommensurability between paradigms in an attempt to unify the fundamentals laws of physics; the probative-argumentative, in making the law of conservation of energy crystal clear; and the pedagogic, in involving the interlocutor as part of a dialogic community of practice in a fresh and dynamic way.

Feynman's argument not only has a logical and deductive function but also heuristic and inductive functions. It is aimed at developing imagination and emotion in the audience, dimensions that are indeed indispensable for understanding science. Thus it is an instance of how rhetoric may achieve a fundamental aim of *The New Rhetoric*, "to combat dualisms of reason and imagination" (Perelman and Olbrechts-Tyteca 510).

Notes

1. See Meheus.

2. This is why Perelman and Olbrechts-Tyteca can claim that the mathematical proportion is only a schematized version of analogy, having the structure of A : B = C : D, where the similarity of relationship is at its clearest. However, they say that the mathematical proportion does not display the feature peculiar to analogy, namely that the terms compared, the A and B of the *theme* and C and D of the *phoros*, must belong to separate spheres. I will add that, while such an abstracted structure of analogy can be easily exemplified in philosophical argument, it is not very typical of analogies in science.

3. See also sections 78, "Argumentation by Example," and 79, "Illustration."

4. A concise reading of Perelman and Olbrechts-Tyteca's pages on analogical reasoning and its role in argumentation is also offered by Italian scholar Bice Mortara Garavelli in her handbook of rhetoric (100–102).

5. In linguistics, this sociological view of science has been taken up by, among others, Gunther Kress and his colleagues in their analysis of science as situated activity and of the language of science as inextricably linked to the activity of the science classroom.

6. See also her contribution to this volume, "'No Neutral Choices': The Art of Style in *The New Rhetoric*" (section 1), where she emphasizes that one cannot isolate argumentative content from its form and should pay attention to argument as actually expressed.

7. Stati's account partly draws from the pragma-dialectal school of argumentation developed in Amsterdam by Frans H. van Eemeren and Rob Grootendorst in the 1980s. For a recent update of their theory and practice of argumentation, see van Eemeren and Houtlosser.

8. The expression translates the Italian "*lessico ausiliario dell'argomentazione*" as formulated in the latest 2002 version of the model, while in 1998 it was simply phrased as "*lessico dell'argomentazione*." I interpret the addition of "auxiliary" as stressing the role of language in assisting the reasoning process.

9. For the complete list of argumentative roles, see Stati (64–65). Stati frequently quotes Perelman and Olbrechts-Tyteca's *The New Rhetoric*, particularly in trying to define the object of his investigation, namely argumentation, and in drawing the boundaries between formal and informal logic, rhetoric and argumentation.

10. See chapter 4, "Conservation of Energy," the lecture entitled "What Is Energy?"

11. See chapter 2, "Basic Physics," ending the lecture "Physics before 1920."

12. Also in chapter 2, "Basic Physics," "Introduction."

13. See chapter 1, "Atoms in Motion," particularly the lecture "Matter Is Made of Atoms."

14. See chapter 3, "The Relation of Physics to Other Sciences," under "Biology."

15. I would like to thank James Wynn, who pointed out to me this interpretation of the mother as researcher.

16. The term is used both in the original seventeenth-century Italian and in the later English translation when, at the end of the first day, Salviati adjourns the discussion to the following day (see the lemma in bold in both versions): "*Siamo giunti a sera e della proposta materia abbiamo trattato pochissimo o niente; anzi ce ne siamo in modo* disviati*, che a pena mi sovviene della prima introduzione e di quel poco ingresso che facemmo come ipotesi e principio delle future dimostrazioni*" (Galilei, *Discorsi* 118). In English: "The day is already ended and we have scarcely touched the subject proposed for discussion. Indeed, we have *deviated* so far that I remember only with difficulty our early introduction and the little progress made in the way of hypotheses and principles for use in later demonstrations" (*Dialogues* 108).

Works Cited

Fahnestock, Jeanne. *Rhetorical Figures in Science*. New York: Oxford UP, 1999.

Feynman, Richard. *Six Easy Pieces: Essentials of Physics Explained by Its Most Brilliant Teacher*. Cambridge, MA: Perseus, 1998.

Galilei, Galileo. *Dialogues Concerning Two New Sciences*. Trans. Henry Crew and Alfonso de Salvio. London: Dover, 1954.

———. *Discorsi e dimostrazioni matematiche intorno a due nuove scienze attinenti alla macanica ed i movimenti locali*. 1638. Torino: Einaudi, 1990.

Gross, Alan G. *The Rhetoric of Science*. Cambridge, MA: Harvard UP, 1990.

———. *Starring the Text: The Place of Rhetoric in Science Studies*. Carbondale: Southern Illinois UP, 2006.

Hallyn, Fernand. *Metaphor and Analogy in the Sciences*. Dordrecht, the Netherlands: Kluwer, 2000.

Kress, Gunther, et al. *Multimodal Teaching and Learning: The Rhetorics of the Science Classroom*. London: Continuum, 2006.

Kuhn, Thomas. "Remarks on Incommensurability and Translation." *Incommensurability and Translation: Kuhnian Perspectives on Scientific Communication and Theory Change*. Ed. Rema Rossini Favretti, Giorgio Sandri, and Roberto Scazzieri. Cheltenham, UK: Elgar, 1999. 33–37.

———. *The Structure of Scientific Revolutions*. 1962. Chicago: U of Chicago P, 1996.

Meheus, Joke. "Analogical Reasoning in Creative Problem Solving Processes: Logico-Philosophical Perspectives." *Metaphor and Analogy in the Sciences*. Ed. Fernand Hallyn. Dordrecht, the Netherlands: Kluwer, 2000. 17–34.

Mortara Garavelli, Bice. *Manuale di retorica*. Milano: Bompiani, 2002.

Perelman, Chaïm, and Lucie Olbrechts-Tyteca. *The New Rhetoric: A Treatise on Argumentation*. Trans. John Wilkinson and Purcell Weaver. Notre Dame: U of Notre Dame P, 1969.

Popper, Karl. "Normal Science and Its Dangers." *Criticism and the Growth of Knowledge*. Ed. Imre Lakatos and Alan Musgrave. Cambridge: Cambridge UP, 1999. 51–58.

Stati, Sorin. *Principi di analisi argomentativa: Retorica, logica, linguistica*. Bologna: Pàtron, 2002.

van Eemeren, Frans H., and Peter Houtlosser. *Argumentation in Practice*. Amsterdam: Benjamins, 2005.

15

From Laconic Apothegms to Film Quotations: Rhetorical Advantages of Shared *Paroemiai*

Paula Olmos

In this essay, I will review some classical and not-so-classical ideas about the argumentative and rhetorical possibilities of certain kinds of shared expressions such as maxims, proverbs, sayings, and *sententiae* or apothegms, which we can group together under the common denomination of *paroemiai*. These were studied and transmitted under different kinds of theoretical frameworks during the prolonged dominion of classical and humanist education. Apart from their uninterrupted presence in discourse and their analytical uses in cultural studies, anthropological and literary, they regained their status as argumentative with the renovation of rhetorical studies initiated by Chaïm Perelman and Lucie Olbrechts-Tyteca's *Traité de l'argumentation*. In their text, maxims are mentioned in several passages, always in relation to the key concept of "communion with the audience" and thus as "particular modes of expressing social communion" (163, 164) which may be used or perceived, in certain cases, as "figures of communion," functioning as "a sign of how rooted they are in a culture," or in the original French, "*l'enracinement dans une culture*" (*New Rhetoric* 171, 177; *Traité* 240).

I will argue, though, that Perelman and Olbrechts-Tyteca's study, and other more recent studies (for example, Yáñez) within the contemporary field of argumentation theory, might be taking for granted an already decaying—though still resisting and rather extended— practice based on the effective collective knowledge and recognition of these traditional standards of a shared culture. New and somewhat differently working sources of discursive communion may have become more relevant in today's usage. Consequently, in addition to the already heterogeneous traditional repertoire of paroemiai, I will look at certain related uses of other types of common expressions whose source is no longer popular wisdom but the immensely powerful and much more globalized realm of audio-visual arts and media. These new sources, however influential, provide us with paroemiai that have a much shorter life than traditional sayings; an ancient apothegm might still be widely used—at least in certain contexts—but last year's successful TV series cliché could have completely lost its appeal.

In order to examine the rhetorical value of the different types of common expressions, I offer in the first part of this essay what could be seen as an "optimal model" for a fully successful and efficient use of *paroemiai* based on the characteristics studied and fostered by classical rhetoricians and their contemporary successors. Then I take into account several traditional variations and ad hoc cases that fall short of the model, and finally I look at the particular traits of clichés taken from audio-visual sources and consider their possibilities in relation with the optimal model.

The Classical Rhetorical "Theory of Maxims" as an Optimal Model

There is no single rhetorical work or treatise—ancient, early modern, or contemporary—that contains or advances the whole theoretical model I am going to sketch here. It is based on certain traits that appear in various texts belonging to the classical tradition. Its main support and structure is taken from Aristotle's division of *entechnoi pisteis* (technical means of proof) into "pathetical," "ethical," and "logical" (1356a), but it does not try to convey an exact interpretation of Aristotle's viewpoints regarding maxims. Other sources such as the *Rhetorica ad Alexandrum*, Cicero's works, and texts belonging to Renaissance humanist rhetoric have inspired my model as well (see Olmos, "Las 'sentencias'").

The starting point of defining an optimal model is the widespread consciousness among the first Greek theoreticians of rhetoric—those probably not only already working on a systematic *technē rhētorikē* but even within previous reflections on still unspecific *logōn technē* (Schiappa)—of the communicative and persuasive force of well-known maxims and also the recognition of the ambition, among public speakers and literary authors, to create and provide society with sententious expressions to be subsequently used by others. To praise, in such a discursive context, the use of recognizable sayings appears thus as the counterpart of the aspiration to create—to be the acknowledged author of—quotable *paroemiai*.

Both Aristotle's *Art of Rhetoric* and the *Rhetorica ad Alexandrum* consider *gnomai* (that is, "maxims") among the acknowledged persuasive means. The fact that Aristotle, probably against a more standard doctrine such as the one presented in *Rhetorica ad Alexandrum*, argues that they are not in most cases real proofs (*pisteis* and, in this case, enthymemes) but generally just part of them (*meros enthymēmatos*) derives, in my opinion, from his own efforts to normalize a syllogistic theory in order to view enthymemes and other discursive argumentative means as progressively defective. This idea becomes very useful for his subsequent classification of *gnomai*, but it does not imply a very different estimation of the argumentative use of maxims in speech.

Neither the *Art of Rhetoric* nor the *Rhetorica ad Alexandrum* insists much on the previously shared and fixed character of *gnomai*, although Aristotle mentions the utility of the well-known Laconic apothegms (1394b, 35), repertoires of which seem to have circulated already in the fourth century B.C.E. In fact, the *Rhetorica ad Alexandrum* defines the maxim as a general opinion expressed by the orator as his or her own and usually starting with a clause like "It is my opinion" or "Methinks" ([Anaximenes] 1430b). For these sources, it is not, therefore, a necessary trait of such expressions that they be already fixed in speech, as it usually is for our contemporary consideration of *paroemiai*, but that they be recognizable as a condensed way of making explicit general standpoints on which, in principle, both the orator and his or her audience agree. As Aristotle remarks, "The hearers . . . are pleased if an orator, speaking generally, hits upon the opinions which they specially hold" (1395b, 1–4). In any case, the most efficient way to do this would be either to use an already well-known and sanctioned expression or to invent one upon such models (by imitation of form or content), a possibility clearly mentioned by Perelman and Olbrechts-Tyteca: "Although proverbs record traditional agreement, new ones can still come into being. But they immediately derive their status *qua* proverbs from existing proverbs, either by virtue of purely formal imitation or because the new proverb is simply a new illustration of a standard already illustrated by an earlier proverb" (*New Rhetoric* 166). Although a discourse must have originality and fluency, and an excessive use of borrowed and sententious material could become blameworthy, the classical approach presents *paroemiai* as bringing multiple rhetorical advantages, which can be described as related to the pathetical, ethical, and logical resources for persuasion contemplated in the Aristotelian *Rhetoric*.

I have already alluded to what might be called pathetical advantages of the use of maxims, as particularly represented by the concepts of "communion with," "invitation to," and, in general, "participation of" the audience in the discursive practices contemplated by rhetorical theory. Thus, Christopher W. Tindale, in discussing the related figure of allusion, claims: "A central characteristic of rhetorical argumentation is the way in which it anticipates the responses of the audience in the structure of the argument, inviting a co-development through expressed and implicit commonalities. Strategies of invitation include ways to capture the audience's prior beliefs and understandings" (1359). In this sense, maxims are also "strategies of invitation" that exploit the realm of prior agreement between the orator and the audience. This prior agreement is, according to Alessandro Grilli, "the most important theoretical element" of Perelman and Olbrechts-Tyteca's *Traité de l'argumentation*: "As the *Traité* repeatedly emphasizes, no argumentation is possible unless the speaker be able to rely on some shared foundation on which he can build his relationship with the audience" (529). Aristotle mentions, in this sense, a typical instance of the successful use of a maxim that gets the audience's consent based on a prior agreement: "For instance, a man who happened to have bad neighbors or children would welcome any one's statement that nothing is more troublesome than neighbors or more stupid than to beget children" (1359b, 10–12).

Regarding the ethical advantages of maxims, it is a classical rhetorical contention that they help to build the image of the orator as an honest person. Thus, Aristotle claims that the use of maxims "makes speeches bear a moral character" (*ēthikous gar poiei tous logous*), mainly because of the simple fact that they usually address virtuous and blameworthy behavior. He also points out that "he who employs them in a general manner declares his moral preferences; if then the maxims are good they show the speaker also to be a man of good character" (1395b). This was one of the most persistent ideas in the tradition of classical rhetoric and determined Cicero's advice that these kind of *sententiae* be extensively used within the *exordium*, the proper place for the *captatio benevolentiae*: "The *exordium* ought to be *sententious* to a marked degree and of a high seriousness, and, to put it generally, should contain everything which contributes to dignity, because the best thing to do is that which especially commends the speaker to his audience" (*De inventione* 1.25).

This classical idea continues to be present in the collective imagery of traditional lore and popular culture. A good example occurs in the French film *Amelie Poulain* (2001). In one scene, the character Gina questions the man with whom her friend Amelie is in love to see whether he is suitable to be her boyfriend. Gina recites the first part of a series of proverbs and makes him finish the sentences to see whether he knows them. She then explains, "They say in my family that he who knows well his proverbs cannot be a bad person" ("*Dans ma famille on dit que celui qui connaît bien ses proverbes ne peut pas être mauvais*"). The charm of *Amelie Poulain* is precisely how the old-fashioned is extensively exploited, but it is nevertheless remarkable that this ancient ethical view should have survived more or less intact. It seems that the use of maxims and proverbs reflects on a person's character, regardless of his or her own behavior, insofar as that person knows and shares the common, traditional values embedded in those expressions. They contribute to the making of a certain type of effective *ethos*.

Finally, the logical advantages of maxims in argumentative discourse are explored by Aristotle in his *Rhetoric* and attributed to two of their typical characteristics. The first is their usual form as assertions. In fact, Aristotle's definition of *gnomai* includes their assertive quality: "A maxim [*gnōmē*] is an assertion [*apofansis*], not however concerning particulars [*kath' hekaston*] ... but general [*katholou*]; it does not even deal with all general things ... but with the objects of human actions [*peri hosōn ai praxeis*] and with what should be chosen or avoided with reference to them [*pros to prattein*]" (1394a, 22–26). The second is their acceptability as highly probable, resembling truths either because of "(a) their being 'true for the most part' [*eikos*], or (b) their being agreed upon by everyone, or the wisest and most reputable among them [*endoxon*]" (*Topica ad Trebantium* 100b, 21–23).[1] These two conditions taken together (their assertive and their plausible character) make maxims the ideal source of premises for rhetorical reasoning, that is, extremely useful parts of enthymemes (*meros enthymēmatos*).

Regarding the logical structure of maxims, both Aristotle's *Art of Rhetoric* and the *Rhetorica ad Alexandrum* insist, however, on the fact that many of them do not express an idea that is easily acceptable but play with the paradoxical by means of opposition of concepts, antithetical statements, and the like. This further complicating consideration has to do with the rhetorical value attributed in the classical world to discursive forms in which the element of surprise reveals a special ingenuity, up to the point where the most appreciated and typical enthymemes—from a stylistic point of view (Vega and Olmos)—were precisely those "based on opposites."[2]

According to this idea, the *Rhetorica ad Alexandrum* (1430b) distinguishes two kinds of maxims: the *endoxon* (those that are reputed, recognized, and accepted) and the *paradoxon* (those that are perplexing, surprising, and even contrary to common opinion). The text says that these latter would need some justification. Aristotle, for his part, makes a more complete classification of *gnomai*, taking into account all these possibilities and his own idea of their being "parts of enthymemes." Thus, he advances the following taxonomy (1394b, 7–25):

1. Maxims that are not *paradoxon* and do not need explanation (*epilogos*) because they express either something already known (*to proegnōsthai*) and agreed upon by most people (for example, 1.1 in the list below) or something clear and evident once uttered (for example, 1.2).³
2. Maxims that are *paradoxon* and need an *epilogos*, of which some can be used to build enthymemes by adding such an epilogue or explanation (for example, 2.1). Others already have the explanation or epilogue within them and are true enthymemes all by themselves (for example, 2.2).

Those mentioned in first place could of course be part of enthymematic or probable (defeasible) reasoning, as any plausible premise, because of either their already fixed acceptability (for example, 1.1) or their immediate evidence (for example, 1.2). In the second case, we already start with something that asks for an explanation, and in this sense, such maxims become the "seed of enthymemes." Many of them might require the orator to provide explanation (for example, 2.1), although there is always the possibility of counting on audience discretion, encouraging a "strategy of invitation." Some maxims would have attained a highly commendable stylistic accomplishment by containing an *epilogos*, thus becoming "complete" enthymemes, while keeping the concision and the unitary expression of a single recognizable maxim. Aristotle offers the following examples of these four categories:

(1.1) "Health is a most excellent thing for a man."
(1.2) "He is no lover who does not love always." (from Euripides, *Troades*)
(2.1) "No man who is sensible ought to have his children taught to be excessively clever." (from Euripides, *Medea*)
(2.2) "Being a mortal, do not nourish immortal wrath."

These Greek sources have not insisted on differentiating newly coined maxims from known expressions. But nowadays, a basic assumption about *paroemiai* is precisely their fixed, formal character. My contention is that, regarding the optimal model I am here sketching, the fixed character of maxims might give them further advantages over those mentioned so far. Thus, in relation to the pathetical advantages, it is easy to understand that the communion is closer if what is shared and agreed upon is not only the content but the explicit form of expressing it. In this sense, we can infer the necessity to know the maxims and proverbs common within a certain society in Antonius's remark in Cicero's *De oratore*: "For bring me a man as accomplished, as clear and acute in thinking, and as ready in delivery as you please; if, for all that, he is a stranger to social intercourse, precedent, tradition and the manners and disposition of his fellow-countrymen, those commonplaces from which proofs are derived will avail him but little" (2.131). As for the ethical advantages, to be equipped with a ready and useful repertoire of traditional sayings implies a good education and even erudition, as when Aristotle says that the use of maxims is more appropriate for men of years and experience than for younger ones (1395a, 2–7). In any case, the classical humanist education encouraged the learning, recognition, and personal scavenging of literature for traditional sayings and smart *sententiae*, not only by means of accumulating repertoires but also by having students read the classics and take notes in a structured, "topically oriented" way (Declercq).

Regarding the logical advantages of fixed *paroemiai*, either when they derive from acknowledged authors or when they belong to traditional wisdom, maxims are invested with the authority of the "already sanctioned" in such a way that their use in reasoning implies an argument from authority. *Sententiae* were thus, in many cases, understood in classical rhetorical textbooks as one of the possibilities included in the topic of *testimonia*, that is, as means of persuasion not invented by the orator himself or herself but taken from what was already made available by the society, the kind of argumentative resources that Aristotle called nontechnical proofs (*atechnoi pisteis*, 1355b). Although Aristotle does not consider the maxims with which he deals in chapter 2, section 21, to be *atechnoi pisteis*, because he is at this point talking about the characteristics of their use in discourse and recommending their original creation, he mentions in chapter 1, section 15 (dedicated to nontechnical proofs), the poets and sages as suitable "witnesses" providing ready-made material for the orator: "Witnesses are of two kinds, ancient and recent.... By ancient I mean poets and men of repute whose judgments are known to all.... Further, proverbs are evidence; for instance if one man advises another not to make a friend of an old man, he can appeal to the proverb: Never do good to an old man" (1375b–1376a). Cicero likewise considers "poets" and "philosophers" as suitable providers of *testimonia* in the form of fixed sayings: "Nor do they hold such an opinion only about those who have been honoured by the people with public office and are busy with matters of state, but also about orators, philosophers, poets, and historians. Their sayings and writings are often used as authority to win conviction" (*Topica ad Trebantium* §78).

All the advantages mentioned would make of maxims and proverbs, either already fixed or built upon the model of the fixed ones, a kind of rhetorical panacea, and their learning, exploring, and scavenging were, consequently, highly encouraged by humanist promoters of classical eloquence, especially during the sixteenth and seventeenth centuries. Thus, in the sixteenth century there was a publishing boom of collections of traditional—

particularly ancient and classical—sayings, verses, and expressions. Erasmus of Rotterdam's *Adagiorum chiliades* (1500) was among the best known of these collections and served as a kind of model for the whole period. The seventeenth century saw the explosion of "aphoristic literature," especially in the fields of politics and ethics (Blanco), and original *sententiae* were devised, many of which became part of the available repository, for example, La Rochefoucauld's *Réflexions ou sentences et maximes morales* (1665).

Traditional Variants

Not all of the expressions we find in such traditional repertoires could, by means of their own particular form, comply with all the requirements of this optimal model, nor could all the situations in which they might be used allow for all such possible advantages to be effectively achieved. Many proverbs are not assertive but imperative, and some take the form of a question (usually a rhetorical question) or even an exclamation. This might complicate, in principle, their being directly used as premises for an argument without the aid of some circumlocution. Argumentative efficiency could be diminished in such cases. However, sometimes a less formalized allusion or evocation of a possible argument that is not explicitly developed works rather well, although in such cases the orator should count on the audience recognizing both the expression (even in a broken presentation) and the intention in using it.

On the other hand, the correspondence, more than tension, between the discursive predominance of the fixed and the original maxims is also something we must take into account. Paradoxically, it seems that newly devised maxims might be more effective within a cultural context in which the already fixed ones are widely known and appreciated. We are not nowadays precisely in a homogeneous cultural context of traditionally shared beliefs, and that means both that we use relatively fewer *paroemiai* in our speech and that, in general terms, we are not much engaged in devising new ones. This phenomenon would correspond to a cultural situation in which—according to Perelman and Olbrechts-Tyteca—the *esprit romantique* predominates over the *esprit classique*: a certain type of originality, not precisely based on aphoristic imitation, is appreciated over compliance with the tradition, and this implies that the kind of expressions we are dealing with are very easily perceived by audiences as uninteresting and affected clichés. In the words of Perelman and Olbrechts-Tyteca: "It is sufficient that the formulas be no longer compulsory, that one no longer listens to them in the same spirit of communion, for them to become stereotyped.... [S]ince the time of Romanticism, the cliché has been run to ground in our culture bent on originality at any price" (*New Rhetoric* 165). This perception is in part responsible for the fact that, even while the writing of new serious maxims is not a very extended literary practice, comical play, by means of humorous variations of well-known *sententiae*, is very effective with modern audiences. Consider, for example, the rather sophisticated way of using *paroemiai* to make jokes known as "wellerisms," made popular by Charles Dickens's *Pickwick Papers* and its character Sam Weller (Olmos, "La eficacia."). In the "wellerism," a proverb, maxim, or other idiomatic expression is first advanced and then attributed to a speaker and a situation in which its meaning is either directly inadequate or must be reversed in order to be understood, for comic effect. Two examples: "Business first, pleasure arterwards, as King Richard the Third said ven he stabbed the t'other king in the Tower, afore he smothered the babbies," and "Sorry to do any thin' as may cause an interruption to such wery pleasant proceedin's, as the king said ven he dissolved the parliament" (see Orero). Laughing at maxims and formulaic means of expression seems to be part of our *esprit romantique* ever since the nineteenth century.

Both playing with the maxims and rejecting them as clichés imply their recognition as such. *Paroemiai* have little rhetorical ability to create communion in a situation in which the speaker tries to use them in the traditional way and finds that the audience is unaware of the sense and intention of such expressions. Within a cultural context like that of the present day, in which traditional *paroemiai* as such are no longer part of the collective basic education, it seems unlikely that their use could easily have the ethical and pathetical advantages I have described in the "optimal model." Communion with the audience is an improbable result if traditional sayings are no longer recognized as such. To try to get the expected effect, we commonly have to resort to discursive and rather inelegant props like "There is a proverb that says . . ."

New Audio-Visual Sources of Commonalities

While the use, learning, and recognition of traditional *paroemiai* seem to be decaying, at the same time we are witnessing the expansion of widely shared quotations deriving from TV (at a local level) and film (at a more international level). Movie quotations especially are shared by a wide international community, perhaps in some cases because of the advertising advantages that derive from implanting memorable lines in film scripts.

To celebrate the hundredth anniversary of cinema, the American Film Institute (AFI) published a list of the 100 most famous quotations from American films and released a TV documentary (2005), hosted by Pierce Brosnan, to present them. Jurors were asked to consider the following criteria in making their selections, the first of which is merely intended as a length limitation:

1. movie quotation: a statement, phrase, or brief exchange of dialogue
2. cultural impact: movie quotations that viewers use in their own lives and situations; circulating through popular culture, they become part of the national lexicon
3. legacy: movie quotations that viewers use to evoke the memory of a treasured film, thus ensuring and enlivening historical legacy

It is the second criterion that is of primary interest in relation to the previous discussion of maxims in rhetoric. It assumes that there are, in fact, movie quotations that become idiomatic expressions and are incorporated into everyday speech in situations where no allusion to their origin is needed—the possible strict use of such an allusion being, in fact, the third criterion. Many expressions of this kind are found in the list. (I bear witness that a number of them have become as natural in their Spanish version as they are in their original English.)

Regarding their possible resemblance to traditional *paroemiai*, we must appreciate that most widely known film quotations come from dialogue in which the characters are not making general statements or engaged in persuasive speech. We see, thus, how film situations partake of the generalized *esprit romantique*, perhaps at the loss of the prestige of sententiousness. There are, nevertheless, some proverb-like expressions:

#13. Love means never having to say you're sorry. (*Love Story*)
#23. There's no place like home. (*The Wizard of Oz*)
#48. Well, nobody's perfect. (*Some Like It Hot*)
#58. Keep your friends close, but your enemies closer. (*The Godfather: Part II*)

Certainly, #23 and especially #58 have the flavor of classical "paradoxical" maxims in their use of opposite terms and their statement of unexpected claims (in these cases, without *epilogos*—but perhaps supplied by the narrative of the film). Moreover, #58, the only one among these that is not an assertion, relates nevertheless to human behavior and thus belongs within the characteristic subject area of traditional proverbs, adopting the imperative form of advice.

Some of the film quotations are assertive in form but, as deictic expressions, make particular rather than general statements. Nevertheless they are, in many occasions, employed to bear a universal meaning, usually by establishing an analogy between the real situation of their utterance and the one that is portrayed in the film—of course, a great deal of *successful* allusion is needed for this kind of use to be rhetorically effective. It seems, thus, that the following quotes are good examples of this possibility:

#31. After all, tomorrow is another day! (*Gone with the Wind*)
#43. We'll always have Paris. (*Casablanca*)

Among the most celebrated quotes, the ones that occupy the top ten positions (although this happens as well throughout the whole list), we mainly find expressions of character:

#1. Frankly, my dear, I don't give a damn. (*Gone with the Wind*)
2. I'm going to make him an offer he can't refuse. (*The Godfather*)
#6. Go ahead, make my day. (*Sudden Impact*)
#10. You talkin' to me? (*Taxi Driver*)

Of course, the *ethos* represented by this kind of expression is usually very different from the wise, educated, and virtuous model of the perfect orator and citizen that is the supposed reference point of classical rhetorical theory, but the way these quotations are repeated in certain contexts can be described in terms of strategies of communion (see Perelman and Olbrechts-Tyteca, *New Rhetoric* 163–67) and *captatio benevolentiae*. When speakers utter one of these, thus impersonating a well-known (either lovable or despicable) character from a film, they acquire that character's personality, making their speech bear a *moral* (even if blameworthy) character. In addition, they might be showing their knowledge of contemporary culture and exploiting a kind of repertoire that presents them positively as a film connoisseur, thus creating communion with those in the know.

In any case, as it happens with traditional *paroemiai*, the rhetorical advantages of such expressions depend, to a large extent, on the widely shared cultural background of the discursive agents. Thus, we might also wish to consider that, besides having peculiarities that might distinguish them from the characteristics required by the "optimal model," such quotations and their relatively ephemeral nature—in contrast with the longevity of maxims in the classical world—might result in their rhetorical failure because they are not recognized by the audience.

Conclusions

As we have seen, classical rhetoric provides us with enough material to reconstruct an interesting "optimal model" of the use of maxims and *paroemiai* in terms of their pathetical, ethical, and logical advantages that are associated with the social conditions of the "esprit classic." But if we want to take advantage currently of this model and its suggestions—even as a comparative standard—we have to be careful to take into account that our own discursive and cultural context might be different, in significant aspects, from the one that witnessed the dominion of classical eloquence. Some modern rhetoricians, though, seem to have incorporated at least parts of this model in a way that takes little note of these differences. In Perelman and Olbrechts-Tyteca's treatise, we find echoes of classical theory in discussions of the potential of proverbs to achieve a desired "communion with the audience" but also several warnings about their possible loss of efficiency and even acceptability within a social context dominated by an "*esprit romantique*" (see *New Rhetoric* 98–99). In more generalized terms, we have to agree with Perelman and Olbrechts-Tyteca's hypothesis that "to each social structure there correspond particular modes of expressing social communion" (*New Rhetoric* 164). That is why certain borrowed expressions coming from such sources as TV and film provide a good basis for examining the rhetorical potential of *paroemiai* for today's audiences. The optimal character of the classical model makes it useful, nevertheless, as a consistent point of comparison, even when we accept that it belongs within a very particular social context that is no longer the norm.

Notes

1. A subsequent tradition made of these concepts, mentioned by Aristotle in different texts, two sources of the "probable" to which a third one was added as representing the probability involved in the use of examples and analogies: "That is probable which for the most part usually comes to pass [*id quod fere solet fieri*], or which is a part of the ordinary beliefs of mankind [*id quod in opinione positum*], or which contains in itself some resemblance to these qualities [*quod habet in se ad haec quandam similitudinem*]" (Cicero, *De inventione* 1.46).

2. For the *Rhetorica ad Alexandrum*, *enthymemata* are

> facts that run counter to the speech or action in question, and also ... those that run counter to anything else. You will obtain a good supply of them by pursuing the method described under the investigatory species of oratory, and by considering whether the speech contradicts itself in any way, or the actions committed run counter to the principles of justice, law, expediency, honour, feasibility, facility or probability, or to the character of the speaker or the usual course of events. ([Anaximenes] 1430a)

3. The first category would include things generally considered *eikos* or *endoxon*, while the second has to do with what becomes evident in the discursive context of enunciation. This opposition could be related to the two types of enthymemes mentioned by Aristotle in both the *Art of Rhetoric* (1.2.6, 1357a31s) and the *Prior Analytics* (2.27, 70a2–3): "enthymemes from likelihoods" (*ex eikotōn*) and "enthymemes from signs" (*ex sēmeiōn*). For a discussion of these two types of enthymemes, see Allen (13–86).

Works Cited

"AFI's 100 Years . . . 100 Movie Quotes." *AFI.com*. 26 June 2010. Web. 1 July 2010.

Allen, James. *Inference from Signs: Ancient Debates about the Nature of Evidence*. Oxford: Clarendon, 2001.

[Aniximenes]. *Rhetorica ad Alexandrum*. Trans. H. Rackham. Cambridge, MA: Harvard UP, 1936–37.

Aristotle. *Art of Rhetoric*. Ed. and trans. J. H. Freese. Cambridge, MA: Harvard UP, 1982.

———. *Prior Analytics*. New York: Oxford UP, 2009.

Blanco, Emilio. "Aforismos políticos contra sentencias morales: El caso del siglo XVII." *Res Publica Litterarum: Documentos de trabajo del grupo de investión "nomos."* Ed. Francisco Lisi Bereterbide. Madrid: Instituto Lucio Anneo Séneca, 2006.

Cicero, Marcus Tullius. *De inventione, Topica ad Trebantium, De optimo genere oratorum*. Ed. and trans. H. M. Hubbell. Cambridge, MA: Harvard UP, 1976.

———. *De oratore I, II*. Ed. and trans. E. W. Sutton and H. Rackham. Cambridge, MA: Harvard UP, 1979.

Declercq, Gilles. "Schèmes argumentatifs et culture oratoire: L'example de Jean Racine." *L'argumentation aujourd'hui: Positions théoriques confrontations*. Ed. Marianne Doury and Sophie Moirand. Paris: Presses Sorbonne Nouvelle, 2004. 125–57.

Grilli, Alessandro. "Argumentation, Keywords and Worldviews." *Proceedings of the Sixth Conference of the International Society for the Study of Argumentation* (June 2006, Amsterdam). Ed. Frans van Eemeren et al. Amsterdam: SicSat, 2007. 529–33.

Olmos, Paula Gómez. "La eficacia argumentativa de la reversion de paremias: El caso de los 'wellerismos.'" *Actas del VI Congreso de la SLMFCE*. Valencia: Universidad de Valencia, 2009. 629–33.

———. "Las 'sentencias de un renglón' (1586) de Pedro Simón Abril: Un repertorio al servicio de la gramática, la retórica y la dialéctica . . . sin faltar a la moral." *Pandora: Revue d'études hispaniques* 7 (2007): 142–62. Web. 10 July 2010.

Orero, Pilar. "La traducción de wellerismos." *Quaderns: Revista de traducciò* 5 (2000): 123–33. Web. 10 July 2010.

Perelman, Chaïm, and Lucie Olbrechts-Tyteca. *The New Rhetoric: A Treatise on Argumentation*. Trans. John Wilkinson and Purcell Weaver. Notre Dame: U of Notre Dame P, 1969.

———. *Traité de l'argumentation: La nouvelle rhétorique*. 1958. Brussels: Université de Bruxelles, 1988.

Schiappa, Edward. *The Beginnings of Rhetorical Theory in Classical Greece*. New Haven, CT: Yale UP, 1999.

Tindale, Christopher W. "Textual Allusion as Rhetorical Argumentation: Gorgias, Plato and Isocrates." *Proceedings of the Sixth Conference of the International Society for the Study of Argumentation* (June 2006, Amsterdam). Ed. Frans van Eemeren et al. Amsterdam: SicSat, 2007. 1359–63.

Vega, Luis and Paula Olmos. "Enthymemes: The Starting of a New Life." *Proceedings of the Sixth Conference of the International Society for the Study of Argumentation* (June 2006, Amsterdam). Ed. Frans van Eemeren et al. Amsterdam: SicSat, 2007. 1411–17.

Yáñez, Cristián Santibáñez. "Sayings in Political Discourse: Argumentative and Rhetorical Uses." *Proceedings of the Sixth Conference of the International Society for the Study of Argumentation* (June 2006, Amsterdam). Ed. Frans van Eemeren et al. Amsterdam: SicSat, 2007. 1227–32.

16

A Timeless Attack: Essence and Definition Arguments in Leo Tolstoy's *The Kingdom of God Is Within You*

Mark Hoffmann

Late in Leo Tolstoy's life, years after he had written *War and Peace* (1865–69) and *Anna Karenina* (1878), he experienced an intense religious revival. He stopped writing secular fiction and started composing religious stories and essays. Of these writings, many consider the most fully developed to be *The Kingdom of God Is Within You* (1893)—a relentless, devastating polemic that fills five hundred pages. In this text, Tolstoy's argument is uncompromising; it refuses to bend or to allow for exceptions to its claims. At its crux, the text argues that governments—all governments—bind and oppress. It contends that churches—as churches—act contrary to Christian principles. And all military service, by definition, enslaves in the name of tradition. Tolstoy's argument allows no room for circumstances that might excuse or make exceptions for specific states or churches. In *The Kingdom of God Is Within You*, he argues that all churches, all governments, and all militaries prevent one from living in peace and in accord with the Bible. Therefore, according to Tolstoy, these institutions need to be abolished through peaceful nonparticipation.

In this essay, I contend that the core arguments in *The Kingdom of God Is Within You* are rooted in essences. I argue that Tolstoy's rhetoric turns the audience away from evaluating circumstances and toward the definitional and the essential. Tolstoy does not argue that his Russian government oppresses or that his Orthodox church perverts the teachings of Christ. Instead, he contends that all governments and all churches—in essence and by definition—can only oppress and pervert. More specifically, Tolstoy describes how churches, governments, and militaries must behave in order to be churches, governments, and militaries; then he argues that it is this behavior that creates the institutions' essence. This argumentative method, I contend, has important rhetorical consequences. For when Tolstoy turns to the essential and definitional in place of the circumstantial, he endows his argument with broader persuasive potential. By arguing that the behavior of an institution creates its essence, and by positing these essences as definitional, Tolstoy's argument can travel. It contains a rhetorical logic that can reach audiences outside his specific rhetorical situation—audiences in different countries and in different times. In this essay, I will analyze the rhetorical structure of a few key passages within the text to show how Tolstoy's argument works. To discuss the rhetorical methods, I will rely on the theories and vocabularies of Richard Weaver's *The Ethics of Rhetoric* and Chaïm Perelman and Lucie Olbrechts-Tyteca's *The New Rhetoric*. More specifically, I will fuse Weaver's "argument from definition" and *The New Rhetoric*'s "act-essence" theory into a rhetorical strategy I call an "argument from definitional essence."

Tolstoy lived his late life under police surveillance. The Russian authorities were not pleased with his religious and political defiance, and his religious writings were often banned. *The Kingdom of God Is Within You*, predictably, was no exception. Tolstoy could certainly have predicted as much. In the text, he condemns churches as "anti-Christian institutions" (75) and governments as "organization[s] of violence based on nothing but the grossest tyranny" (211). In late-nineteenth-century Russia, it was inevitable that a text filled with attacks on these established institutions would be instantly banned and burned. Tolstoy's text was notable even among banned materials; one censor declared it to be "the most harmful of all books that he had ever had an occasion to ban" (Simmons 191). *The Kingdom of God Is Within You*, however, took Tolstoy a frustrating four years to write. As Tolstoy himself reportedly said, "No book has ever given me so much trouble" (qtd. in Troyat 525). Why, then, would he struggle to compose an argument in the Russian language that he knew no Russian could legally read or publish? By examining the biographical history of Tolstoy's late life, we can begin to answer this question. After *What I Believe* was published abroad—his first text that preached nonresistance to evil and condemned churches as anti-Christian institutions—Tolstoy started receiving letters from Americans who had read translations. These letters commended Tolstoy on his interpretations of Christ's teachings, and they assured him that groups of Americans were living by these principles. Some scholars argue that Tolstoy felt motivated by these letters. They contend that, having discovered that other Christians read his religious writings and held similar beliefs on nonresistance and nonparticipation in state affairs, Tolstoy decided to write a more elaborate and explicit religious text professing his beliefs and interpretations of the teachings of Christ (Whittaker).

Biography alone, however, cannot answer the question sufficiently. We need to look inside the text to learn why Tolstoy labored for years to write an essay that his compatriots could read only clandestinely. If we analyze the text rhetorically, and if we think about his arguments and his anticipated audiences, Tolstoy's four-year struggle begins to make more sense. Because *What I Believe* had made its way around the world, and because Tolstoy could assume that *The Kingdom of God Is Within You* would be banned in Russia, he wrote the text anticipating that it would be smuggled abroad, translated, and published for audiences in foreign countries. If we keep this biographical information in mind as we turn to the "argument from definitional essence" within the text, three transnational audiences emerge. First, Tolstoy wrote to all Christians who were abstaining from state affairs and practicing nonresistance to violence. To this audience, *The Kingdom of God Is Within You* affirms and celebrates their lifestyles and beliefs. To borrow key terms from *The New Rhetoric*'s theory of argumentation, Tolstoy's text further "induces and increases" their "adherence" to the thesis of nonparticipation and nonresistance. Second, *The Kingdom of God Is Within You* addresses Christians who were being "hypnotized" by the church and the state. For this audience, the text presents the church and state in a new, disturbing light and is meant to decrease adherence to the idea of church and state infallibility and to increase adherence to nonresistance and nonparticipation. Finally, if we consider the rhetorical consequences of Tolstoy's arguments from definitional essences—arguments against all churches, all governments, and all militaries—we can see a third audience emerge that exists in neither a specific time nor a specific place. Because the argument is based upon definitional essences, it holds persuasive potential for any people, in any place, in any time, and of any religion.

While it may seem that I overstretch my argument by identifying non-Christians as one of the text's audiences, the following example should suggest the validity of their inclusion. As Mohandas Gandhi notes in his autobiography, he was deeply influenced by Tolstoy's pacifist arguments in *The Kingdom of God Is Within You*. According to Gandhi, he was "overwhelmed" when he read it while working as a lawyer in South Africa (137). Though Gandhi was not Christian, Tolstoy's book maintained its rhetorical appeal, I contend, because of its rhetorical method—a method that uses acts to define essences and posits that these essences are definitional. Though Gandhi lived under a very different form of oppression and read the text in an English translation six thousand miles away from Tolstoy, the argument had the power to "overwhelm" him. Because Tolstoy's argument posits that actions reveal definitional essences, *The Kingdom of God Is Within You* is more than a history lesson on the tyranny and brutality of the Russian Empire. It is a text that maintains rhetorical appeal across borders and through time. For the rest of this essay, I will focus on how Tolstoy's arguments function rhetorically. A close analysis, I believe, can help us work toward an understanding of how arguments can become "timeless" and "global."

From the early pages of *The Kingdom of God Is Within You*, Tolstoy's argument directs the reader's attention away from circumstances and toward essences. To analyze how he does this, it will be helpful to turn to *The New Rhetoric*'s discussion of "act-essence" arguments. As Perelman and Olbrechts-Tyteca contend, act-essence arguments "try to connect and explain particular, concrete, individual phenomena by treating them as manifestations of an essence" (327). In *The Kingdom of God Is Within You*, Tolstoy does exactly this: he identifies particular actions of the church, the government, and the military to argue that these actions reveal the institution's essence. For example, he contends that the church's act of ignoring the Sermon on the Mount is a manifestation of its essence. According to Tolstoy, the church's "omission to acknowledge the law of non-resistance to evil by violence . . . indicates how the Church doctrine perverts the teaching of Christ" (1). Thus, it is the church's selective disregard for the Bible's inconvenient passages that define the church's perverted essence. Similarly, Tolstoy constructs an act-essence argument to contend that churches are essentially anti-Christian institutions:

> The Churches as Churches have always been and cannot fail to be institutions not only alien to, but directly hostile towards, Christ's teaching. . . . The Churches, as Churches—as institutions affirming their own infallibility—are anti-Christian institutions. Between the Churches as such and Christianity, not only is there nothing in common except the name, but they are two quite opposite and opposing principles. The one represents pride, violence, self-assertion, immobility and death: the other humility, penitence, meekness, progress, and life. (75–76)

In this passage, the church's action of "affirming" its own "infallibility" defines its essence—prideful, violent, self-asserting, immobile, dead. And the repetition of "Churches as Churches" works to universalize this essence as inherent to all churches.[1]

Though *The New Rhetoric*'s discussion of act-essence arguments can help us unpack and analyze Tolstoy's arguments, there is additional work to do if we want to understand how the text's arguments can cross borders of time and place. Indeed, though *The New Rhetoric* provides a vocabulary for close analysis, Perelman and Olbrechts-Tyteca do not discuss how essences can become definitional. That is, they do not discuss how arguments can contend for the essence of a thing and then universalize that purported essence. In *The Kingdom of God Is Within You*, it is imperative that essences become universalized and definitional. When they do, the argument's appeal reaches audiences outside of Tolstoy's rhetorical situation. The most insightful treatment of this type of argumentation is to be found in Richard Weaver's *The Ethics of Rhetoric*. According to Weaver, an argument from definition is an "argument from the nature of the thing." An argument from definition contends that "[w]hatever is a member of the class will accordingly have the class attributes" (86). In other words, Weaver contends that essence is located in the "class" or the "genus" of the thing, not in the individual manifestation. To apply this analysis to Tolstoy's "Churches as Churches" argument above, one church is the same as any other church because, by definition, all churches share the same essential class or genus attributes—pride, violence, self-assertion, immobility, and death. And all churches, because they are churches, are "anti-Christian institutions." Because this passage argues "from definition," it does not allow circumstance to alter the church's opposition to true Christianity. While Weaver's theory of "argument from definition" helps us analyze this aspect of Tolstoy's argument, Weaver's discussion in *The Ethics of Rhetoric* is more philosophical than linguistic. He does not analyze how linguistic and grammatical choices can create arguments from definition, as does *The New Rhetoric*. Therefore, because neither Weaver's *The Ethics of Rhetoric* nor *The New Rhetoric*'s "act-essence" theory can fully account for Tolstoy's argumentative method, I wish to suggest a new term that can: "argument from definitional essence." This term combines "argument from definition" and "act-essence" to describe a specific kind of argument that first makes claims about an institution's essence and then posits that essence as a definitional, genus-level quality. The "Churches as Churches" passage above, I contend, is an argument from definitional essence. Furthermore, this passage shows us a unique characteristic of arguments of definitional essence. Because they build essences from actions and because these essences become genus-level, they deny exception, and they contain persuasive potential for audiences outside of the rhetor's specific rhetorical situation.

Arguments of definitional essence form the rhetorical nucleus of *The Kingdom of God Is Within You*, though there are, of course, other methods of argumentation in the text. I will focus on three additional passages that feature arguments of definitional essence. After the "Churches as Churches" passage above, Tolstoy continues his argument against the church, contending that it must and can only contaminate "true Christianity." He states:

> Above all, a man who believes in salvation through faith in the redemption or the sacraments, cannot employ all his strength in applying Christ's moral teaching in his life. A man who has been taught by the Church the blasphemous doctrine that he cannot be saved by his own efforts but that there is another means, will inevitably have recourse to that means rather than to his own efforts, on which he is assured it is a sin to depend. The teaching of any Church with its redemption and its sacraments excludes Christ's teaching, and the Orthodox doctrine with its idolatry does so most of all. (84–85)

In this passage, Tolstoy constructs essence through action. The verb phrases —to believe in salvation through sacraments, to teach blasphemous doctrine, to exclude Christ's teaching—are manifestations of the church's essentially "anti-Christian" nature. As Tolstoy frames it, there is an incompatibility between the "Christianity of the church" and the "Christianity of Christ." And this incompatibility, by definition, cannot be overcome. No circumstances can undo the incompatibility because it arises from the essential, definitional acts of the church. Additionally, this argument from definitional essences serves another interesting rhetorical function: it transitions the reader into the text's most radical, unorthodox claims. In the passage above, the argument from definitional essence walks the reader into heretical incompatibility. Because the act-essence argument comes first and because it is followed by an argument that makes essence definitional, the incompatibility of the church and "true Christianity" logically follows. If readers adhere to the "Churches as Churches" passages, they will be in the right frame of mind to understand Tolstoy's claim for incompatibility. Though it is beyond the scope of this essay to contend whether or not arguments from definitional essences generally work to moderate and/or transition the reader into heretical or radical claims, it is worth noting that in this text, these arguments do serve this function.

Similar to his attack on "Churches as Churches," Tolstoy argues against governments as governments. He argues that governments are violent, exacting, and unjust by their definitional essence. Like the argument against the church, this argument has important rhetorical consequences. Because it avoids circumstances that would pin the argument down to a specific rhetorical situation, the argument has "global" appeal. It is an attack not against Tsarist Russia but against all governments anywhere in the world. As Tolstoy maintains, one government is the same as any other government because they all belong to the same genus. He states:

> To suggest to governments not to have recourse to violence but to decide their differences in accord with equity, is a proposal to abolish themselves as governments, and no government can agree to that. . . . [I]t is the nature of a government not to submit to others but to exact submission from them, and a government is a government only insofar as it is able to exact submission and not itself to submit, and so it always strives to that end and will never voluntarily abandon its power. . . . [G]overnment has always in its essence been a force that infringes justice. (161–62)

Tolstoy's argumentative method here runs parallel to his argument against churches: first, he discusses the institution's actions; second, he uses these actions to posit its essence; third, he makes that essence definitional to all members of the genus. As we can see, this argument does not criticize the specific. It is not just Tolstoy's book-burning, police-monitoring Russia that is essentially violent and power-hungry but all governments—as governments. For governments, like churches, have essences that are not altered by time or place.

Later, Tolstoy deepens his argument about the inherent corruption of government. Through another argument of definitional essence, Tolstoy condemns the very act of ruling. He defines "ruling as ruling" at its most fundamental level, as he withholds any detail that could specify a single government rather than the genus of governments. The reference of his language broadens significantly, and it is impossible to locate his argument as relative to a single regime or a single country. While the preceding arguments attempt to make "timeless" or "global" claims, Tolstoy's argument here pushes even further. Tolstoy now argues that it is not governments but instead the essential act of ruling that is unjust:

> To seize power and retain it, it is necessary to love power. But love of power goes not with goodness but with the opposite qualities—pride, cunning and cruelty. Without self-aggrandizement and the abasement of others, without hypocrisy, deceit, prisons, fortresses, executions and murders, no power can arise or maintain itself. . . . [R]uling means using force, and using force means doing what the man subjected to violence does not wish done, and to which the perpetrator would

certainly object if the violence were applied to himself. Therefore to rule means to do to others what we would not have done to ourselves—that is, doing wrong. (264–65)

As Tolstoy contends, in order to rule, a person or an institution must act with pride, cunning, cruelty, violence, and selfishness. Ruling, therefore, is essentially cruel and violent because one must act in cruel and violent ways in order to rule. Lacking any specifying detail, these attributes apply to all ruling as ruling. It is not a specific government that has perverted ruling and made it tyrannical. As Tolstoy argues, ruling is, by its definitional essence, cruel, violent, deceitful and wrong. In the United States, South Africa, Germany, or Russia, ruling is and can only be an act that is essentially wrong. No circumstances can change this, and no reader can find room in the argument that allows any government to be different. Across borders and through eras, the argument refuses exception.

In *The Ethics of Rhetoric*, Richard Weaver states that Abraham Lincoln had the "habit of viewing things from an Olympian height . . . looking at the little act from some ultimate point in space and time" (109). Weaver uses this metaphor to illustrate the nature of both "the argument from definition" and the rhetor who makes it. The metaphor is as applicable to Leo Tolstoy's *The Kingdom of God Is Within You* and to the arguments of definitional essence that fill it. From an Olympian height, national borders disappear and all governments look the same. From some ultimate point in space and time, all churches become indistinguishable. From far enough away, and from outside of the "hypnotized" state in which we live, the essence of an institution emerges not from the power it holds but from the way it acts. As Gandhi learned in South Africa when he first read Tolstoy's text, neither time nor space can alter right from wrong. And as we learn from *The Kingdom of God Is Within You*, not all arguments are limited to their rhetorical situations.

Note

1. At this point in this essay, it would be reasonable for readers to question whether this close rhetorical analysis can really tell us anything when the text under consideration is translated. I argue that it can. Tolstoy, we must remember, lived under police surveillance in a tightly censored Russia when he wrote *The Kingdom of God Is Within You*. He knew that his text would be banned locally. Also, during the four years he spent writing the text, he was involved in active epistolary correspondences with people in Europe and North America. *The Kingdom of God Is Within You*, then, from its beginning, was meant for translation. Also, Tolstoy, who was a fluent multilingual, is reported to have read and approved of the English translation by Aylmer Maude that I am here citing.

Works Cited

Gandhi, Mohandas K. *An Autobiography: The Story of My Experiments with Truth.* Trans. Mahadev Desai. Boston: Beacon, 1957.

Perelman, Chaïm, and Lucie Olbrechts-Tyteca. *The New Rhetoric.* Trans. John Wilkinson and Purcell Weaver. Notre Dame: U of Notre Dame P, 1969.

Simmons, Ernest J. *Leo Tolstoy: The Years of Maturity.* Vol. 2. New York: Vintage, 1960.

Tolstoy, Leo. *The Kingdom of God and Peace Essays.* Trans. Aylmer Maude. New Delhi: Rupa, 2002.

Troyat, Henri. *Tolstoy.* Trans. Nancy Amphoux. New York: Doubleday, 1967.

Weaver, Richard. *The Ethics of Rhetoric.* Davis, CA: Hermagoras, 1985.

Whittaker, Robert. "Tolstoy's American Preachers: Letters on Religion and Ethics, 1886–1908." *TriQuarterly* 107/108 (2000): 561–629.

Contributors
Index

Contributors

Linda Bensel-Meyers is associate professor of English at the University of Denver, where she is director of undergraduate studies. Her primary areas of research are Renaissance literature and the history and theory of rhetoric. She has published *Rhetoric for Academic Reasoning, Literary Culture: Reading and Writing Literary Arguments,* and articles on rhetorical poetics and Renaissance emblem theory. She was formerly director of writing programs at the University of Tennessee.

Michelle K. Bolduc is associate professor in French, Italian, and comparative literature at the University of Wisconsin–Milwaukee. She has come to the field of modern rhetoric by way of the study of medieval rhetoric and the practice and theories of translation. In addition to her work on Chaïm Perelman and Lucie Olbrechts-Tyteca, she has written *The Medieval Poetics of Contraries* and has published articles on medieval French and Occitan literature and rhetoric. Her current book project examines medieval translation as a poetics of memory.

James Crosswhite is associate professor of English at the University of Oregon. His research focuses on the philosophy of rhetoric and theories of argumentation. He is author of *The Rhetoric of Reason*, which was awarded the MLA's Mina Shaughnessy Prize, and his recent articles include studies of Plato's *Gorgias* and the friendship of Emerson and Thoreau. He is currently completing a book titled *Deep Rhetoric: Philosophy, Reason, Violence, Justice, Wisdom*. Crosswhite has directed writing programs at the University of California, San Diego, and at the University of Oregon.

Ray D. Dearin is emeritus professor of English and political science at Iowa State University, where he was chair of speech communication and taught courses in rhetoric, public address, and political communication. Dearin wrote the first dissertation on *The New Rhetoric* in 1970, following his widely anthologized article on Perelman in the *Quarterly Journal of Speech*. Dearin translated Perelman's posthumously published memoir, "The New Rhetoric and the Rhetoricians," for the *QJS* and edited a special issue of the *Journal of the American Forensic Association* devoted to Perelman. His other writings on Perelman include numerous essays and two books, including *Chaïm Perelman*, coauthored with Alan G. Gross.

Jeanne Fahnestock is professor of English at the University of Maryland. She is author of *Rhetorical Figures in Science* and *Rhetorical Stylistics* and coauthor with Marie Secor of *A Rhetoric of Argument*. She has published articles and contributed chapters on rhetorical theory, argument, language analysis, and the rhetoric of science and has served on the board of directors of the Rhetoric Society of America and on the Council of the International Society for the History of Rhetoric. Fahnestock has directed the Professional Writing Program and the combined University Writing Programs at the University of Maryland.

David A. Frank is professor of rhetoric and dean of the Robert D. Clark Honors College at the University of Oregon. He has published, both alone and in collaboration with Michelle K. Bolduc, thirteen essays on the new rhetoric project. He is coauthor with Robert C. Rowland of *Shared Land / Conflicting Identity: Trajectories of Israeli and Palestinian Symbol Use* and has written articles on the Israeli-Palestinian conflict, the rhetoric of Barack Obama, and the theory and practice of intercollegiate debate and speaking.

Maria Freddi is assistant professor of English language and linguistics at the University of Pavia, Italy, where she currently teaches courses on English grammar and corpus linguistics. Her research interests include corpus linguistics applied to the study of translation, English for specific and academic purposes, and the discourse of science and technology, areas in which she has published articles and contributed to national and international conferences. She is author of *Functional Grammar: An Introduction for the EFL Student*.

John T. Gage is professor and former head of English at the University of Oregon, where he teaches rhetorical theory and poetics. His books include *In the Arresting Eye: The Rhetoric of Imagism* and *The Shape of Reason: Argumentative Writing in College*. His articles on teaching argumentation have appeared in numerous books and journals. He has been Distinguished Visiting Professor of Rhetoric and Writing Studies at San Diego State University and currently directs the Center for Teaching Writing at the University of Oregon.

Richard Graff is associate professor of rhetoric in the Department of Writing Studies at the University of Minnesota. He teaches and conducts research in classical rhetoric, modern rhetorical theory, and stylistic theory. His scholarship on ancient theories of prose style, evolving historiographies of rhetoric, and the rhetorical theory of Chaïm Perelman has appeared in numerous journals, and he is coeditor with Janet Atwill and Arthur E. Walzer of *The Viability of the Rhetorical Tradition*. Graff is past president of the American Society for the History of Rhetoric.

Alan G. Gross is professor of communication studies at the University of Minnesota–Twin Cities, specializing in rhetorical theory and scientific communication. He is author of *The Rhetoric of Science* and *Starring the Text: The Place of Rhetoric in Science Studies*. He is coauthor with Joseph E. Harmon of *Communicating Science: The Scientific Article from the 17th Century to the Present*, *The Scientific Literature: A Guided Tour*, and *The Craft of Scientific Communication*, and they are completing a book on verbal-visual interaction in the creation and communication of scientific meaning. Gross is coeditor with Arthur E. Walzer of *Rereading Aristotle's Rhetoric*.

Mark Hoffmann is a doctoral candidate in rhetoric and composition at the University of Maryland. His dissertation analyzes the rhetorical techniques of texts written to reach global audiences and applies that analysis to the teaching of composition to work toward a rhetorical pedagogy that can help both L1 and L2 students write and read in the globalized twenty-first century.

Roselyne Koren is professor of French at Bar-Ilan University in Israel and co-coordinator of ADARR Groupe de Recherche (Analyse du discourse, argumentation, et rhétorique) Tel-Aviv. Her research fields are the rhetoric of the written press, Perelman's contributions to linguistic theories, and the conceptualization and linguistic definition of an ethics of discourse. She is coeditor with Ruth Amossy of *Après Perelman: Quelles politiques pour les nouvelles rhétoriques? L'argumentation dans les sciences du langage* and author of *Les enjeux éthiques de l'écriture de presse et la mise en mots du terrorisme* and of various publications on discursive and argumentative responsibility in the media.

Noémi Perelman Mattis is the daughter of Chaïm and Fela Perelman. She is a practicing psychologist and social worker and serves as a participant on the faculty of the School of Medicine at the University of Utah in Salt Lake City.

Loïc Nicolas is at Université Libre de Bruxelles–EHESS (Ecole des Hautes Etudes en Sciences Sociales) / GRAL-GSPM (Groupe de Recherche en Rhétorique et en Argumentation Linguistique–Groupe de Sociologie Politique et Morale) and is research fellow of the FNRS (Fonds National de la Recherche Scientifique), where he holds a Lavoisier scholarship and is researching rhetoric in the nineteenth century. He has written *La force de la doxa: Rhétorique de le décision et la délibération* on the role of common opinion in the political and social process of constructing meaning. He has coedited with Luce Albert *Polémique et rhétorique de l'antiquité à nos jours* and coedited with Emmanuelle Danblon, Emmanuel De Jonge, and Ekaterina Kissina *Argumentation et narration*.

Jean Nienkamp is associate professor of English at Indiana University of Pennsylvania. Her research fields include rhetorical theory, history of rhetoric, argumentation, composition, and literacy studies. Her most recent book is *Internal Rhetorics: Toward a History and Theory of Self-Persuasion*. Her other writing includes work on Richard Whately and Plato, and she is currently researching internal rhetorics, ethics and rhetoric, Stephen Toulmin, and Isocrates.

Paula Olmos is postdoctoral researcher in the Lucio Anneo Séneca Institute of Classical Studies on Society and Politics at the University Carlos III of Madrid in Spain. Her research includes historical studies on the tradition and reception of the classical arts and sciences (especially dialectic and rhetoric) as well as studies in contemporary theory of argumentation. She has written *Los negocios y las ciencias: Lógica, argumentación y metodología en la obra filosófica de Pedro Simón Abril (ca. 1540–1595)* and was co-recipient, in 2007, of the J. Anthony Blair Prize at the Seventh Ontario Society for the Study of Argumentation Conference. She has published articles in *Informal Logic*, *Theoria*, and *Renaissance Studies* and has contributed chapters to *Methods and Methodologies* (edited by M. Cameron and J. Marembon) and *Meaning, Content, and Argument* (edited by J. M. Larrazabal and L. Zubeldia).

Barbara Warnick is professor and chair of the Department of Communication at the University of Pittsburgh. Her research interests include rhetoric and argument in online communication, theories of argumentation and their application, and rhetorical theory in general. She is a former editor of *Quarterly Journal of Speech* and currently serves on the editorial boards of *Rhetoric Review, Argumentation and Advocacy*, and *Rhetoric Society Quarterly*. Her publications include *The Sixth Canon: Belletristic Rhetorical Theory* *and Its French Antecedents, Critical Literacy in a Digital Era: Technology, Rhetoric, and the Public Interest,* and *Rhetoric Online: Persuasion and Politics on the World Wide Web.*

Wendy Winn is assistant professor at Appalachian State University. Her research interests include visual communication, the rhetoric of science, and rhetorical theory. Her publications include articles in *Journal of Technical Writing and Communication* and, with Richard Graff, in *Philosophy and Rhetoric.*

Index

Abuse of Casuistry, The. See under Jonsen, Albert R., and Stephen Toulmin
"Act and Person in Argument." *See under* Perelman, Chaïm, and Lucie Olbrechts-Tyteca
act-essence. *See under* argument
act-person. *See under* argument
adherence, 1, 3, 4, 5, 21, 23, 24, 25, 26, 27, 30, 35, 38, 109, 110, 121, 122, 124, 126, 136, 141, 143n6, 168, 177, 190, 192, 200, 220, 238
agreement, 2, 23–4, 30, 32, 33–4, 37, 40, 45, 48, 50, 52, 113, 114, 121, 123, 149, 152, 159, 168, 176, 177, 189, 204n1, 209, 225, 226. *See also* disagreement
Agricola, 43
akrasia, 165–66
Alice's Adventures in Wonderland, 61
allegory, 39, 74
Allen, James, 234n3, 235
allusion, 113–14, 116, 117, 121, 127n11, 128n15, 226, 230, 232, 233. See also *paroemiai*
ambiguity, 44, 49, 62, 67, 72, 107, 164, 168
Amelie Poulain, 226–27
American Film Institute (AFI), 231, 235
Amossy, Ruth, 6n1, 32, 54, 144, 249
analogy, 5, 26, 74–5, 137, 143, 178, 183, 206–21. See also *phoros*/theme
Anaximenes, 225, 234n2, 235; *Rhetorica ad Alexandrum*, 224, 225, 227, 234, 235
Anglo-American Committee of Inquiry, 63
antimetabole, 40, 211
anti-Semitism, 9, 58
antithesis, 115, 116, 117, 118, 128n15, 211
apodictic logic, 70, 71, 75
apothegms, 223–35
appearance/reality pair, 5, 27. *See also* philosophical pairs
"A Propos de la philosophie de M. Dupréel." *See under* Perelman, Chaïm

Arendt, Hannah, 2
argument: act-essence, 89, 184, 237, 239–41; act-person, 195, 197–99; field or domain of, 144, 186; invention of, 2, 31–2, 86, 88, 123, 183, 185–205, 207–8, 210; narrative and, 85, 88, 97–100; quasi-logical, 5, 25, 26, 40, 63, 69, 75, 141; structure of reality, based on, 5, 23, 25, 26; structure of reality, establishing, 5, 25, 26, 27. *See also* reasoning; values, argument about
argumentation, lexico-grammar and, 212
argumentation, models of, 2, 51, 58, 65, 91, 92, 97, 100, 108, 112, 135, 183, 184, 185–95, 196, 199, 200–204, 207, 212, 224–30, 231, 232, 233, 234; Toulmin model, 28n1, 173, 174, 186, 187, 189, 192. *See also* model/anti-model; Crosswhite, James; Olmos, Paula; Stati, Sorin; Toulmin, Stephen
argumentative roles. *See* Stati, Sorin
Aristotle, 3, 18, 30, 31, 46, 60, 64, 88, 101, 103, 166–8, 170, 185, 204, 207, 234n3, 235; *Art of Rhetoric*, 64, 88, 103, 168, 224, 225–29, 234n3; *Nicomachean Ethics*, 166, 167; *Poetics*, 185–6; *Prior Analytics*, 234n3; on enthymemes, 145, 167, 168, 225, 227, 234; on maxims, *gnomai*, 224–29, 234n1
Art of Rhetoric. *See under* Aristotle
association, 26, 30, 157. *See also* association/dissociation pair; dissociation
association/dissociation pair, 5, 33, 129n20. *See also* association; dissociation
asyndeton, 116, 117
atechnoi pisteis. See rhetorical appeals
Attitudes Toward History. See under Burke, Kenneth
audience, 4, 5, 6, 20, 23–7, 28n1, 31, 32, 38, 39, 40, 45, 48, 49, 50, 52, 53, 63, 67, 68, 70, 72, 73, 81, 109–26, 136–40, 142, 168, 175, 183, 184, 188–90, 192, 200, 204n1, 207–9,

audience (*continued*)
    221, 223, 225, 226, 228, 230–40. *See also* interlocutor; particular audience; universal audience
Audomari Talaei Rhetoricae libri Duo P. Rami Praelectionibus Illustrati, 46n5
Austin, J. L., 42, 46. *See also* speech act
"Authority, Ideology, and Violence." *See under* Perelman, Chaïm
auxesis, 45
axiological rationality, 134, 135, 145
axiology, 59, 82, 137

backing, 28n1, 174, 186, 187, 189. *See also* argumentation, models of (Toulmin model)
Bain, Alexander, 41
Baron, Auguste, 46n5
Bastida, Letizia Gianformaggio, 65
Belgian League Against Tuberculosis, 60
Benoit, Pamela, 160n5
Benoit, William, 160n5
Bensel-Meyers, Linda, 19, 20, 81, 145, 162–70, 183, 247
Bergson, Henri, 60, 66, 70, 78
Berlusconi, Silvio, 36–7, 46n4
Bernoulli, Daniel, 209–10
Bettelheim, Charles, 155
Bevin, Ernest, 63
Bible, the, 70, 177, 236, 239
Biesecker, Barbara, 127n5, 130
Black, Max, 41, 46
Blair, Tony, 29
Blanco, Emilio, 230, 235
Boger, George, 21, 22, 27, 28
Bogoslovsky, Boris B., 62
Bolduc, Michelle, 4, 6n3, 7, 20, 41, 47, 55–79, 127n6, 131, 145, 184, 247, 248
Booth, Wayne C., 2
Borgese, G. A., 151
Bowden, Mark, 29, 46
Britton, Karl, 46n5
Brosnan, Pierce, 231
Brunot, Ferdinand, 46n5
Brussels University, 9, 10, 11, 15, 16. *See also* Free University of Brussels
Burke, Kenneth, 2, 41, 46n5, 81, 82, 103–12, 115–26, 127n1, 127n3, 127n4, 127n5, 127–28n12, 128n13, 128n14, 128n16, 129n17, 129n20, 129n22, 129–30n23, 130n5, 130–31, 171, 180; *Attitudes Toward History*, 106, 125, 129–30n23; *Counter-Statement*, 105, 107, 115; *Grammar of Motives*, 107, 125, 127n4, 129n20; "On Persuasion, Identification, and Dialectical Symmetry," 105, 127n4; *Philosophy of Literary Form, The*, 105, 106, 108, 127n12; "Revolutionary Symbolism in America," 106; "Rhetoric and Poetics," 108, 116, 120, 125; "Rhetoric of Hitler's 'Battle,' The," 106; *Rhetoric of Motives, A*, 110, 112, 115, 116, 117, 119, 121, 122, 124, 125, 127n1, 127n4, 127n5, 128n12, 128n13, 129n18, 129n20, 130n25; "Rhetoric—Old and New," 108; "Terministic Screens," 171. *See also* identification
Bush, George W., 29, 45n1, 47

Caillois, Roger, 46n5
Calogero, Guido, 178
Canivet, Michel, 54
captatio benevolentiae, 226, 233. *See also* communion
Carbone, Ludovico, 43
Carpenter, Ronald H., 128n3, 128n16, 128n17, 131
Carroll, Lewis, 61
Casablanca, 233
Cervantes, Miguel de, 61, 74, 78
Chaignet, Antelme Édouard, 46n5
Chaïm Perelman. *See under* Gross, Alan G., and Ray D. Dearin
"Character and the Arts and Disciplines." *See under* McKeon, Richard
Charaudeau, Patrick, 143n5, 144
Chargaff, Erwin, 34
Charland, Maurice, 122, 129n18, 131
Chase, Stuart, 41
chiasmus, 211
Chlepner, Boris, 10
Chomsky, Noam, 42, 134; *Syntactic Structures*, 42
Christianity. *See* religion
Christie, George C., 51, 54; *Notion of an Ideal Audience*, 52
Cicero, Marcus Tulius, 30, 31, 47, 76, 77, 224, 226, 229, 234n1, 235; *De inventione*, 32, 226, 234n1; *De optimo genere oratorum*, 32; *De oratore*, 228
claim, 174, 186–87, 189, 192, 212, 216. *See also* argumentation, models of (Toulmin model)

classicism/romanticism, 64, 169, 230, 231, 232, 234
cliché, 45, 64, 129n22, 224, 230, 231
climax, 116, 121, 128n15, 211, 216
Cold War, the, 148, 156
Collins, Francis, 34
comic, 5, 19, 20, 43, 56, 58, 60, 66–75, 77, 78n4, 78, 184, 231. *See also* laughter; ridicule
comique du discourse, Le. See under Olbrechts-Tyteca, Lucie
comique, Le: Essai d'interprétation générale, 78n4
Comité de Défense des Juifs. *See* Committee for the Defense of the Jews
Committee Concerning the Importance of the Problem, 148–49
Committee for the Defense of the Jews (CDJ), 11, 58, 60
Committee of Experts on the Philosophical Principles of the Rights of Man, 149, 152, 154, 155, 163, 164
Committee on the Philosophical Analysis of Fundamental Concepts, 149
Communication, 46n5
communion, 5, 19, 32, 40, 45, 73, 81–82, 103–33, 184, 223–24, 225, 228, 230–31, 233, 234
communism, 12, 155, 158
Communist Manifesto, The, 149. *See also* Engels, Frederick; Marx, Karl
community, 1–3, 37, 45, 48, 65, 105, 109, 111–14, 120–26, 130n24, 141, 162, 163, 177, 179, 180n4, 187, 208, 219, 220, 231. *See also* audience; communion
Companion to Ethics. See under Singer, Peter
Concerning Justice (De la justice). See under Perelman, Chaïm
confused notions, 19, 62, 145, 147, 159
Conley, Thomas M., 2, 7, 175, 180
contact of minds, 48, 126
Cosmopolis. See under Toulmin, Stephen
"courants de la linguistique au XXe siècle, Les," 143n1
Counter-Statement. See under Burke, Kenneth
Crick, Francis, 34, 210
Critical Discourse Analysis, 34. *See also* discourse analysis
"Cross-Cultural Study of Directive Sequences and Some Implications for Compliance-Granting Research," 282n2
Crossman, Richard, 63, 78

Crosswhite, James, 6n1, 19, 51, 54, 145, 146, 183, 185–205, 247
Cunningham, F. Gary, 180n4, 181

Danblon, Emmanuelle, 48, 54, 250
Darwin, Charles, 34, 81, 83–102, 183; *On the Origin of Species*, 93, 101n5, 101n7; *Structure and Distribution of Coral Reefs*, 83–100, 89f1, 90f2, 94f3, 95f4, 97f6, 99f7, 100n2, 101n3, 101n5; *Voyage of the Beagle, The*, 97
data, 32, 46n2, 84, 174, 186, 187, 189. *See also* argumentation, models of (Toulmin model); facts
Davis, Diane, 105, 131
De Inventione. See under Cicero, Marcus Tulius
De la justice. See under Perelman, Chaïm
de Loye, Paul, 53n3
De optimo genere oratorum. See under Cicero, Marcus Tulius
De Oratore. See under Cicero, Marcus Tulius
De Vries, Hugo, 34
Dearin, Ray D., 6n2, 6n3, 7, 18n1, 19, 25, 28, 32, 33, 47, 50, 54, 56, 57, 65, 76, 78, 79, 83, 88, 101, 127n6, 127n11, 131, 145, 147–61, 169, 175, 181, 247
Declaration of Human Rights, 164
Declercq, Gilles, 229, 235
deduction, 93, 101n4, 211–13, 221
definition. *See under* argument
Deledalle, Gérard, 87, 88, 101
Demetrius, 31
democracy, 59, 145, 147–61, 164
Democracy in a World of Tensions. See under McKeon, Richard
démon du style, Le, 41, 46n5
Descartes, René, 50, 192
Descombes, Vincent, 141, 144; *Philosophie par gros temps*, 141
Dewey, John, 2, 149
dialectic, 5, 30, 43, 44, 52, 53, 64, 103, 108, 126, 127n6, 157, 165, 168, 175
dialogue, 20, 49, 52–3, 57, 73–4, 82, 119, 157, 158, 178, 183, 186, 190, 220, 232
Dialogues Concerning Two New Sciences, 215
Dickens, Charles, 231
Dionysius of Halicarnassus, 31
disagreement, 4, 27, 48, 50, 156, 175

256 Index

discourse analysis, 34, 43, 47, 82, 135, 143n1
dissociation, 5, 6n2, 25, 27, 38, 45, 66, 77, 135, 136, 138, 193, 195, 197. *See also* association; association/dissociation pair
division, 85, 107, 112, 126, 130n25. *See also* identification
Dominicy, Marc, 54
Don Quixote, 61, 74, 75, 78
Dostoyevsky, Fyodor, 166
Ducasse, C. J., 150
Du Marsais, Cesar Chesneau, 40–41, 46n5
Duncan, Hugh Dalziel, 127n5, 127–8n12, 131
Dupréel, Eugène, 59, 60, 64, 69, 108, 109, 127n6, 127n8, 131, 147; *rapport social, Le*, 109; *Sociologie générale*, 109, 127n8; *Sophistes: Protagoras, Gorgias, Prodicus, Hippias, Les*, 108; "Sur les origines de la dialectique," 109; *Traité de morale*, 109, 127n8
Dybul, Mark, 29, 47

Ede, Lisa S., 57, 78
education, 2, 3, 145, 162–67, 169, 183, 191, 193, 194, 200, 202, 223, 229, 231
eikos, 227, 234n3
Eisner, Will, 100n1, 101
Elliott, Deni, 76, 79
Emelina, Jean, 78n4, 79
Emerson, Ralph Waldo, 197, 247
Empire rhétorique, L': Rhétorique et argumentation. See under Perelman, Chaïm
endoxon, 227, 234n. See also *paroemiai*
Engels, Frederick, 149, 155, 161
entechnoi pisteis. See under rhetorical appeals
enthymeme, 145, 167, 168, 202, 225, 227, 228, 234n3
epanaphora, 116, 118
epideictic, 64, 109–12, 114, 120–26, 127n7, 127n9, 129n19. *See also* epidictic
epidictic, 110, 111. *See also* epideictic
epilogos, 228, 232
Erasmus of Rotterdam, 230
Escape to Life, 12
Estève, Claude-Louis, 46n5
Ethics of Rhetoric, The. See under Weaver, Richard
ethics, rhetoric, argument and, 2, 5, 6, 26, 44, 45, 49, 51, 57, 82, 119, 134–37, 140, 142, 143, 145–46, 162–69, 171–80, 187, 224, 225, 226–27, 229, 230, 231, 233

ethos. *See* rhetorical appeals
Études Philosophiques sur l'expression littéraire, 46n5
Eubanks, Ralph T., 127n6, 131, 165, 168, 169
eudaimonia, 164, 167, 168
Euler, Leonhard, 210
Euripides, 228
exordium, 226

facts, 17, 23–24, 27, 32, 45, 50, 82, 88, 92, 93, 95, 113, 129, 135, 136, 138, 139, 143, 143n6, 154, 163, 167, 177, 189, 190, 198, 200, 234n2. *See also* data; self-evident
Fahnestock, Jeanne, 19, 29–47, 81, 82, 128, 131, 183, 184, 207, 211, 220, 222, 248; *Rhetorical Figures in Science*, 207, 211
Fairclough, Norman, 34, 47. *See also* discourse analysis
fascism, 12, 149, 151
Feynman, Richard, 183, 206–22; *Six Easy Pieces: Essentials of Physics Explained by Its Most Brilliant Teacher*, 206, 212, 213–20
Field, G. C., 151, 153
figures of speech, 5, 19, 32, 37–40, 44, 211. *See also* rhetorical figures; *names of particular figures*
"First Philosophies and Regressive Philosophy," 66
Fitch, Kristine L., 28, 28n2
Fitzroy, Robert, 91, 92
Fleming, David, 201, 204
Fleurs de tarbe, Les, 63–64, 76
Florian, Alix, 53n1
Fonteyne, P., 61
form, psychology of, 107. *See also* Burke, Kenneth
"Fragments pour la théorie de la connaisance de M. E. Dupréel," 109, 127n8
Frank, David, 4, 6n1, 6n3, 7, 8, 20, 41, 47, 55–79, 127n6, 129n21, 131, 145, 157, 160, 184, 202, 248
Freddi, Maria, 20, 81, 183–84, 206–22, 248
freedom, 1, 3, 4, 59, 70, 135, 143n6, 145, 150, 152, 157, 159, 162, 164, 166, 176, 179, 187, 196
Free University of Brussels, 20, 57, 60, 66. *See also* Brussels University; Perelman Archives
Frege, Gottlob, 59, 60, 62, 76
Freud, Sigmund, 105

Gadamer, Hans-Georg, 3, 204n1, 204
Gage, John T., 1–7, 19–20, 81–2, 145–46, 183–84, 202, 204, 248
Galilei, Galileo, 213, 215, 222
Galvani, Luigi, 34
Gandhi, Mohandas K., 238, 239, 243
Gandon, Yves, 41, 46n5
Gendrel, Bernard, 78n4, 79
General Semantics movement, 41
George of Trebizond, 31, 45
George, Ann, 106, 127n4, 131
Georges, Pierre, 137, 144
Gestalt theory, 84, 86, 88, 90, 100
gesture-speech theory, 105, 127–28n12
Gheorghiu, Virgil, 61
gnomai. See maxims
Goblot, Edmond, 62
Godfather, The, 233
Godfather, The: Part II, 232
Golden, James L., 54, 148, 158, 159, 160
Gone with the Wind, 233
Gonseth, Ferdinand, 62
Goodman, Nelson, 87, 88, 101
Gorgias, 64
Govier, Trudy, 21, 28
gradatio, 40, 115, 116, 117, 121, 211
Graff, Richard, 19, 20, 32, 81–82, 103–33, 183, 184, 249
Grammaire et affectivité, 46n5
Grammar of Motives. See under Burke, Kenneth
granduer, De la, 61
Grant-Davie, Keith, 32
Grilli, Alessandro, 226, 235
Grootendorst, Rob, 221n7
Gross, Alan G., 6n2, 6n3, 7, 18n1, 19, 20, 25, 28, 32, 33, 47, 54, 56, 57, 79, 81, 83–102, 103, 127n6, 127n11, 131, 175, 181, 183, 207, 209, 209, 210, 220, 222, 248, 249; "Presence as Argument in the Public Sphere," 83; *The Rhetoric of Science*, 207, 209; *Starring the Text: The Place of Rhetoric in Science Studies*, 209, 210
Gross, Alan G., and Ray D. Dearin, 6n3, 25, 33, 127n6, 127n11, 175; *Chaïm Perelman*, 83, 88
Guide pour la class de rhétorique, 46n5
Guingouain, Gersende, 53

Haarscher, Guy, 54
Habermas, Jürgen, 2
hain-tenys, Les, 46n5
Halliday, M. A .K., 34, 47
Hallyn, Fernand, 210, 222
Halm, Karl, 31, 47
Hanson, Jim, 127n3, 131
Hawhee, Debra, 105, 132
Hayakawa, S. I., 41
Heath, Robert L., 105, 127n4, 132
Heidegger, Martin, 2
Hermagoras oder Elemente Rhetorik, 46n5
Hermogenes, 31
hierarchy, 25, 27, 32, 57, 77, 85–86, 141, 163–66, 171, 177, 189–91, 200
Hitler, Adolf, 8, 58, 106, 151. *See also* Nazi
Hjelmslev, Louis, 134
Hochberg, Julian, 84, 101
Hochmuth, Marie, 108, 129n12, 132
Hodge, M. J. S., 101n5, 101
Hoffman, Mark, 81, 184, 236–44, 249
Holocaust, 2, 8, 12, 59
homoioteleuton, 116, 118
Horvath, Barna, 153
Hoskins, John, 31
Houtlosser, Peter, 221n7, 222
How to Do Things with Words. See Austin, J. L.
human rights, 164
Human Understanding: The Collective Use and Evolution of Concepts. See under Toulmin, Stephen
humor. *See* comic

Idea of Justice and the Problem of Argument, The. See under Perelman, Chaïm
identification, 81–82, 103–33. *See also* Burke, Kenneth
induction, 85–6, 92, 100, 101n4, 208, 213, 221
informal reasoning. *See under* reasoning
Institutio oratoria. See under Quintilian
interlocutor, 4, 20, 21, 52–53, 85, 126, 157, 188, 208, 220. *See also* audience
Introduction to Reasoning, An, 186. *See also* Toulmin, Stephen
invention. *See under* argument
Iowa Colloquium on Rhetoric and Public Policy, 147, 152, 159
Isocrates, 190, 204

Jakobson, Roman, 43, 47, 134; "Two Aspects of Language," 43
Janik, Allan, 186, 205
Jasinski, James, 127n1, 129n17, 129n18, 132
Johannsen, Wilhelm, 34
Johnson, George, 34, 47
Johnson, Mark, 195, 196
Johnstone, Henry W., Jr., 6n2, 53n6
Jonsen, Albert R., and Stephen Toulmin, 171, 173, 174, 178, 180n5, 181; *Abuse of Casuistry, The*, 173, 180n5
Jordan, Jay, 106, 132
Jørgensen, Jørgen, 151, 155
Jouhandeau, Marcel, 61
Judaism. *See* religion
justice, 2, 3, 17, 48, 50, 56, 59, 118, 140, 148–52, 157, 159, 175, 179, 234n2, 242. *See also* under Perelman, Chaïm (*Idea of Justice*)

Kagame, Paul, 29, 45n1
kairos, 48. *See also* rhetorical situation
Kalinowski, Georges, 53n4
Kallen, Horace M., 155
kalon, 164–7, 169
Kant, Immanuel, 5, 18, 51, 53, 60, 65, 72, 77, 187
Keenan, James F., 180n5, 181
Kellogg, Brainerd, 41
King Baudouin of Belgium, 58, 147, 148
Kingdom of God Is Within You, The. *See* Tolstoy, Leo
King, Martin Luther, Jr., 118–19, 128n15, 132, 183
Klemperer, Victor, 46n5
Kline, Susan L., 25, 26, 27, 28
Kluback, William, 127n9, 132, 160, 170
Köhler, Wolfgang, 81, 84, 101
Korallenriffe: Verbreitung, Tierwalt, Ökologie, 99
Koren, Roselyne, 19, 54, 82, 134–44, 145, 146, 183, 184, 249
Korzybski, Alfred, 41
Kotarbinski, Tadeusz, 158
Kremer-Marietti, Angèle, 127n3, 132
Kress, Gunther, 221n5, 222
Kuhn, Thomas, 2, 184, 206, 207, 208–9, 217, 218, 219, 220, 222; "Remarks on Incommensurability and Translation," 209; *Structure of Scientific Revolutions*, 207, 208

Lalande, André, 62
language, 3, 19, 30–37, 41–45, 46n6, 48, 84–85, 120, 124, 126, 128, 134–44, 150, 162, 169, 171, 179, 188, 189, 198, 200, 211, 221n8. *See also* discourse analysis; figures of speech; linguistics; style
Language and Politics, 46n5
Language in Thought and Action, 41
Lasswell, Harold, 62
Latini, Brunetto, 63, 76, 77
laughter, 5, 66–75, 78, 78n4, 231. *See also* comic
Lefebvre, Henri, 155
Leja, Michael, 84, 102
Lenin, Vladimir, 150
Lévinas, Emmanuel, 2, 3, 20, 53, 54
Lewis, C. I., 151, 153
"Liberty, Equality and Public Interest." *See under* Perelman, Chaïm
Likert scale, 36
Lincoln, Abraham, 152–54, 243
Lindsay of Birker, Lord, 155
linguistics, 34, 43, 82, 85, 112, 128n12, 134–44, 164, 184, 207, 211, 212–13, 216, 220, 221n5. *See also* discourse analysis; psycholinguistics
Lischer, Richard, 128n15, 132
loci, 5, 32, 107, 115, 165–78. *See also topoi*
logic, 2–5, 21, 22, 26–27, 31, 38, 62–64, 69, 70–71, 73, 75, 77, 85, 86, 108, 112, 134–37, 140, 163–69, 173, 179, 180n3, 187, 192, 194, 211, 221n9, 224, 225, 227, 229, 233. *See also* deduction; induction
logical positivism, 1, 59, 60, 62, 64, 76, 77
"Logique et rhétorique." *See under* Perelman, Chaïm, and Lucie Olbrechts-Tyteca
logos. *See* rhetorical appeals
Longinus, 31, 39, 40, 46n5; *On the Sublime*, 46n5
Loraux, Nicole, 129n19, 132
Love Story, 232
Lunsford, Andrea A., 57, 78
Lyell, Charles, 92–93, 102

maisons fugitives, Les, 61
Malinowski, Bronislaw, 125, 129n22, 129–30n23, 132
Maneli, Mieczyslaw, 17, 56, 57, 79, 158–59, 161

Manusov, Valerie, 28n2, 28
Marchal, Joseph A., 55, 57, 79
Marshall, James, 153
Marx, Karl, 149, 155, 161
Marxist, 150, 155, 156, 157
Matthaei, Heinrich J., 210
Mattis, Noémi Perelman, 5, 6–7n3, 8–18, 25, 28, 56, 60–61, 65, 79, 145, 249
Maude, Aylmer, 243, 243n1
Mauriac, François, 61
maxims, 24, 45, 82, 110, 113–14, 116, 117, 128n15, 184, 223–35. See also *paroemiai*
McKeon, Richard, 3, 64, 81, 145, 148, 149, 151, 152, 153, 154, 161, 162, 163, 164, 165, 167, 168, 169; "Character and the Arts and Disciplines," 169; *Democracy in a World of Tensions: A Symposium Prepared by UNESCO*, 164; "Philosophic Semantics and Philosophic Inquiry," 168; "Spiritual Autobiography," 162, 164
Mead, George Herbert, 52, 105, 127n4, 132
Measell, J. S., 25, 28
Meheus, Joke, 207, 210, 211, 221n1, 222
meiosis, 45
Melanchthon, Phillipp, 3, 30, 31, 38, 40, 43, 45, 47
Meltzer, Bernard N., 129n22, 132
metaphor, 26, 39, 42, 63, 74, 195, 208, 210, 211, 215, 243
"*méthode analytique en philosophie, De la.*" See under Perelman, Chaïm
Meyer, Michel, 56, 57, 76, 79
Mickunas, Algis 158, 159
Miller, George, 43
Minter, William, 29
model/anti-model, 26, 27. See also argumentation, models of
Moran, Patrick, 78n4, 19
Morris, Charles W., 46n5
Mortara Garavelli, Bice, 221n4, 222
Mosellanus, Petrus, 31
Musolf, Gil Richard, 129n22, 132
mystère frontenac, Le, 61

Naess, Arne, 148, 160n4
National Socialism, 58
Nazi, 11–15, 58–60, 143, 148, 157, 176
Nazi-Deutsch, 46n5
Nelson, Jack K., 76, 79

New Rhetoric and the Humanities, The: Essays on Rhetoric and Its Applications. See under Perelman, Chaïm
New Rhetoric: A Treatise on Argumentation, The (*Traité de l'argumentation: La nouvelle rhétorique*), 1–5, 6n1, 15, 16, 19–27, 29–45, 46n3, 52, 53n2, 55–58, 60, 61, 65–78, 78n1, 81–83, 108–10, 112, 114, 119, 121–26, 127n8, 127n9, 128n14, 129n20, 129n23, 130n24, 134, 135, 137, 139–42, 143n1, 143n2, 143n3, 143n6, 143n7, 144n8, 145–46, 148, 160, 162, 165, 167, 169, 171, 175–79, 180n6, 183–85, 187–95, 198–204, 207, 221, 221n9, 223, 225–26, 231, 233–34, 237–40; translation issues and, 32, 60, 46n2, 78n1, 110, 125–26, 127n9, 130n24, 188. See also Perelman, Chaïm, and Lucie Olbrechts-Tyteca; *and key terms*: adherence; argument; comic; communion; dissociation; philosophical pairs; presence; reasoning; style; universal audienc"New Rhetoric and the Rhetoricians, The: Remembrances and Comments." See under Perelman, Chaïm
"New Rhetoric, The: A Theory of Practical Reasoning." See under Perelman, Chaïm
new rhetoric project (NRP), 21, 23, 25, 145, 149, 150, 157, 187, 195, 248
"*New Rhetoric's Argument Schemes, The: A Rhetorical View of Practical Reasoning*," 25
Newton, Isaac, 206, 211
Nicolas, Loïc, 20, 48–54, 183, 184, 250
Nicomachean Ethics. See under Aristotle
Nienkamp, Jean, 19, 20, 146, 171–81, 250
Nietzsche, Friedrich, 59
Nirenberg, Marshall W., 210
Norman, Timothy, 190, 204
Notes from the Underground, 166
Notion of an Ideal Audience. See under Christie, George C.
Notizbuch eines Philologen, 46n5
Nussbaum, Martha C., 2, 165, 166, 170

Ogden, C. K., 41
Olbrechts, Raymond, 60
Olbrechts-Tyteca, Lucie, 43, 47, 55–59, 66–75, 79, 132, 184; life, 15–16, 18, 60–61; *comique du discourse, Le*, 30, 66–78; "Rencontre avec la rhétorique," 62, 63, 64.

Olbrechts-Tyteca, Lucie (*continued*)
See also *New Rhetoric, The: A Treatise on Argumentation*; Perelman, Chaïm, and Lucie Olbrechts-Tyteca
Olmos, Paula, 20, 82, 184, 223–35, 250
Olson, Gary A., 186, 204
Ong, Walter, 43
"On Persuasion, Identification, and Dialectical Symmetry." *See under* Burke, Kenneth
On the Origin of Species. See under Darwin, Charles
On the Sublime. See under Longinus
ontology, 137
Orero, Pilar, 231, 235
Osiatynski, Wiktor, 158
Ossowski, Stanislaus, 155
other, concept of, 20, 48, 50, 51, 52, 53, 105, 109, 137, 173, 188, 242–43

Paechter, Heinz, 46n5
Paget, Richard, 105
Palestine, 13, 63
paradigm, 174, 178, 208–9, 217, 219, 220
paradox, 59, 128, 138, 227, 232; of substance, 107
paradoxon, 227, 228. See also *paroemiai*
Pareto, Vilfredo, 60, 61, 78n3
paroemiai, 184, 223–24, 225, 228, 229, 230, 231, 232, 233, 234. *See also* allusion; apothegms; cliché; *endoxon*; maxims; *paradoxon*; proverbs; *sententiae*
particular audience, 49, 51, 52, 73, 112, 167, 168, 177, 184
Pascual, Ricardo R., 155
pathos. *See* rhetorical appeals
Patri, Aimé, 155
Paulhan, Frédéric, 62
Paulhan, Jean, 41–42, 44, 46n5, 61, 63, 64, 76; *fleurs de tarbe, Les*, 63–64, 76; "Traité des figures ou la rhétorique décryptée," 42, 46n5
Peacham, Henry, 31, 32
Pearson, Helen, 34, 47
Peirce, Charles S., 3, 81, 84, 85, 87, 88, 90, 100
pensée et la langue, La, 46n5
Perelman, Chaïm, 6n2, 7, 28, 43, 47, 48, 54, 55–56, 57–60, 61, 79, 127n6, 132, 134, 144, 145, 161, 170, 181; "A Propos de la philosophie de M. Dupréel," 109; "Authority, Ideology, and Violence," 156–57; *Le champ de l'argumentation*, 54; *Concerning Justice (De la justice)*, 15, 59, 62, 76, 109, 137, 145, 147, 148, 150, 152, 159, 160, 175, 179; *L'Empire rhétorique: Rhétorique et argumentation*, 75, 127n9; "First Philosophies and Regressive Philosophy," 66; "Fragments pour la théorie de la connaisance de M. E. Dupréel," 109, 127n8; *The Idea of Justice and the Problem of Argument*, 6, 175; *Justice, Law, and Argument: Essays on Moral and Legal Reasoning*, 161; "Liberty, Equality and Public Interest," 157; life, 4, 8–18, 58–59, 63, 147–50, 175; *Logique et argumentation*, 54; "De la méthode analytique en philosophie," 160n2; *The New Rhetoric and the Humanities: Essays on Rhetoric and Its Applications*, 59, 157; "The New Rhetoric and the Rhetoricians: Remembrances and Comments," 21; "The New Rhetoric: A Theory of Practical Reasoning," 124, 125–26, 130n24; "La philosophie du pluralisme et la Nouvelle Rhétorique," 157; "Pragmatic Arguments," 165; "Raison éternelle, raison historique," 64–65; *The Realm of Rhetoric*, 167, 127n9; "Rhetoric and Politics," 111, 122; "Rhetorical Perspectives on Semantic Problems," 44, 46n6; "Rhétorique et philosophie," 51; "Rhétorique et politique," 111; *Rhétoriques*, 48, 49, 50, 51, 137, 140, 143n6; UNESCO project, and 147–61, 163, 164; "Value Judgments, Justifications and Argumentation," 170. See also *New Rhetoric, The: A Treatise on Argumentation*; Perelman, Chaïm, and Lucie Olbrechts-Tyteca
Perelman, Chaïm, and Lucie Olbrechts-Tyteca, 7, 28, 47, 54, 55–79, 102, 127n6, 127n7, 127n11, 133, 144, 170, 181, 205, 222, 235, 243; "Act and Person in Argument," 64; collaboration of, 15–16, 20, 23, 25, 55–79; "Logique et rhétorique," 61, 64, 109, 110; *Rhétorique et philosophie: Pour une théorie de l'argumentation en philosophie*, 64, 175. See also *New Rhetoric, The: A Treatise on Argumentation*
Perelman, Fela, 8, 10–18, 60, 63

Perelman Archives, 20, 53n3, 53n9, 58, 60
person-act. *See under* argument (act-person)
persuasion, 4, 39, 75, 81, 86, 88, 104, 108, 110, 119, 120, 121, 122, 123, 124, 127n1, 129n18, 209, 225, 229. *See also* adherence; agreement; communion; contact of minds
phatic communion, 125, 129n22, 129–30n23
philosophical pairs, 5, 27, 66, 77, 169. *See also* appearance/reality pair; association; association/dissociation; dissociation; universal/particular
philosophic semantics, 168–69
"Philosophic Semantics and Philosophic Inquiry." *See under* McKeon, Richard
"philosophie du pluralisme et la Nouvelle Rhétorique, La." *See under* Perelman, Chaïm
Philosophie par gros temps. See under Descombes, Vincent
Philosophy of Literary Form. See under Burke, Kenneth
Philosophy of Rhetoric, The. See under Richards, I. A.
phoroi, 74, 75
phoros/theme, 26, 137, 207–8, 210, 215, 217, 218, 219, 221n2. *See also* analogy
phronesis, 174
Pickwick Papers, The, 231
Pilotta, Joseph J., 54, 148, 158, 159, 160
Pinker, Steven, 84, 102
pisteis, 224, 225, 229. *See also* rhetorical appeals
Plamentz, Petro, 155
Plato, 3, 165–66, 169
ploche, 45n1
pluralism, 19, 81, 145, 149, 157, 162, 163
Poetique de St-John Perse, 46n5
polyptoton, 30, 45n1, 211
Pope John XXII, 16
Popper, Karl, 209, 222
Porzig, Walter, 46n5
Practical Ethics. See under Singer, Peter
practical reasoning. *See under* reasoning
"Pragmatic Arguments." *See under* Perelman, Chaïm
preferable, 4, 135–36, 165, 168, 176–77, 195, 207, 226
presence, 5, 19, 27, 32, 40, 41, 44, 45, 76, 81, 83–89, 92, 98, 100, 103, 119, 136, 164, 191, 198, 220; superordinate, 81, 83, 88

"Presence as Argument in the Public Sphere." *See under* Gross, Alan G.
Principles of Geology, 92, 93
Prior Analytics. See under Aristotle
probability, 5, 234n1, 234n2. *See also* probable
probable, 108, 227–28, 234n1. *See also* probability
projection/anticipation, 49, 52, 53
propaganda, 8, 62
Protagoras. See Plato
proverbs, 82, 113, 114, 116, 117, 121, 184, 223–34. *See also paroemiai*
psycholinguistics, 43

qualifiers, 34, 174, 186
quasi-logical arguments. *See under* argument
Quintilian, 31, 40, 44, 45, 171, 179; *Institutio oratoria*, 31, 40

"Raison éternelle, raison historique." *See under* Perelman, Chaïm
Ramus, Peter, 43
rapport social, Le. See under Dupréel, Eugène
rapports sociaux. *See* social rapports
rational, 8–9, 62, 63, 65, 82, 112, 122, 143n6, 148, 165, 176, 180n3, 186, 187, 194, 196
rational enterprise, 186, 194
rationalism, 9, 24, 25, 50, 58, 64, 141, 142
rationality, 49–51, 112, 134–44, 145
reality. *See* appearance/reality pair
reality, structure of. *See under* argument
Realm of Rhetoric, The. See under Perelman, Chaïm
reason: appeal to, 3, 86; defense of, 3, 5, 65; practical, 43, 108, 124–26, 140, 165–67
reasoning, 21, 23, 25, 60, 65, 67, 69, 78, 86, 112, 173–74, 175, 178, 187, 190, 192, 195, 221; analogical, 206–21, 221n4, 221n8; figures of, 42; informal, practical, or rhetorical, 1–3, 5, 43, 59, 62, 71, 75, 108, 124, 126, 166, 227, 229; probable, 228; quasi-logical, 141, 164–69, 179; Talmudic, 58; written, 173, 195, 198, 202. *See also* argument
rebuttal, condition of/for, 174, 186, 187
reductio ad absurdum, 70
religion, 180n1, 184, 198, 238; Christianity 9, 72, 174, 180n5, 236–41; Judaism: 9–13, 15, 17–8, 58–59, 60–61, 63

"Remarks on Incommensurability and Translation." *See under* Kuhn, Thomas
"Rencontre avec la rhétorique." *See under* Olbrechts-Tyteca, Lucie
responsibility, 3, 4, 24, 53, 134, 136, 139, 140–42, 145, 198
Return to Reason. *See under* Toulmin, Stephen
"Revolutionary Symbolism in America." *See under* Burke, Kenneth
Reynaud, Paul, 70
rhetoric, classical, 1, 5, 40, 41, 43, 44, 63–64, 108–9, 124, 127n6, 224, 226, 229, 233; literature and, 56, 58, 60, 61, 65, 74–76, 229, 230; psychology and, 62, 84–88, 105, 107. *See also* rhetorical appeals; *names of specific rhetoricians and works*
Rhetorica ad Herennium, 31, 40
Rhetorica ad Alexandrum. *See under* Anaximenes
rhetorical appeals, 86, 229, 238–39; *entechnoi pisteis*, 224; ethos, 86, 88, 136, 139, 227, 233; *logos*, 86, 189; *pathos*, 52, 86, 224, 225, 228, 231, 233
rhetorical figures, 5, 19, 29–47, 107, 110, 114, 115, 116, 117, 120, 121, 128n16, 184, 207, 211, 223, 226. *See also* figures of speech
Rhetorical Figures in Science. *See* Fahnestock, Jeanne
"Rhetorical Perspectives on Semantic Problems." *See under* Perelman, Chaïm
rhetorical situation, 45, 57, 58, 70, 77, 110, 186, 237, 240, 241, 243. See also *kairos*
"Rhetoric and Poetics." *See under* Burke, Kenneth
"Rhetoric and Politics." *See under* Perelman, Chaïm
"Rhetoric of Hitler's 'Battle,' The." *See under* Burke, Kenneth
Rhetoric of Motives, A. *See under* Burke, Kenneth
Rhetoric of Science, The. *See under* Gross, Alan G.
"Rhetoric—Old and New." *See under* Burke, Kenneth
rhétorique, De la, 46n5
"Rhétorique et Philosophie." *See under* Perelman, Chaïm
Rhétorique et philosophie: Pour une théorie de l'argumentation en philosophie. *See under* Perelman, Chaïm, and Lucie Olbrechts-Tyteca
"Rhétorique et politique." *See under* Perelman, Chaïm
Rhétoriques. *See under* Perelman, Chaïm
rhétoriques et son histoire, Le, 46n5
Ribot, Théodule, 62
Richards, I. A., 41, 44, 163; *Philosophy of Rhetoric, The*, 41
Ricœur, Paul, 3, 48, 54
ridicule, 5, 68, 70, 72, 75, 114
ridiculous, 69, 70
Rieger, Ladislaus, 155
Rieke, Richard, 186, 205
Rochefoucauld, La, 230
Rokkan, Stein, 148, 160n4
romanticism. *See* classicism/romanticism
Ross, Alf, 153
Rostand, François, 46n5
Russell, Bertrand, 59
Ruyer, Raymond, 53n9

Saint-Aubin, 46n5
Saussure, Ferdinand de, 84, 85, 87, 102, 134
Schiappa, Edward, 25, 28, 224, 235
science, 1, 2, 23, 24, 34, 48, 67, 82, 88, 98, 100, 143n2, 147, 165, 166, 169, 179, 183, 184, 195, 206–21, 221n2, 221n5
Science and Sanity, 41
Schopenhauer, Arthur, 36, 74
Schrödinger, Erwin, 210
Schuhmacher, Helmut, 99fig7, 102
Scott, Robert, 55–56, 57, 79
Sebeok, Thomas A., 43, 47, 87, 88, 102
self-evident, 2, 139–40, 143n3, 143n6, 187. *See also* facts
"Self Reliance," 197, 247
Selzer, Jack, 106, 127n4, 131
semiotics, 84, 85, 88, 100, 143n1
sententiae. *See* apothegms; *paroemiai*
Sermon on the Mount, 239
Signs, Language, and Behavior, 46n5
Sillars, Malcolm, 160, 161
Silverman, Stephen J., 76, 79
Simmons, Ernest J., 237, 243
Singer, Peter, 171, 172, 173, 174, 180n1, 180n2, 181; *Companion to Ethics*, 172; *Practical Ethics*, 172, 180n2
Six Easy Pieces: Essentials of Physics Explained by Its Most Brilliant Teacher. *See under* Feynman, Richard

slogans. *See* maxims; *paroemiai*
social rapports, 109
socialism, 154, 155, 156, 158, 159
Sociologie générale. See under Dupréel, Eugène
Socrates, 165, 166, 167
Some Like It Hot, 232
Sophistes, Les: Protagoras, Gorgias, Prodicus, Hippias. See under Dupréel, Eugène
speech act, 42, 43, 136
Speech Communication Association (SCA) Conference, 160
Spinoza, 60
"Spiritual Autobiography." *See under* McKeon, Richard
Stalin, Joseph, 150
Starring the Text: The Place of Rhetoric in Science Studies. See under Gross, Alan G.
stasis, stases, 32, 37, 202
Stati, Sorin, 212, 221n9
Steinberg, Lucien, 60, 79
Sternberg-Grenier, Véronique, 78n4, 79
Sterne, Laurence, 61, 70
Stern, Judy E., 76, 79
Structure and Distribution of Coral Reefs. See under Darwin, Charles
structure of reality. *See under* argument
Structure of Scientific Revolutions. See under Kuhn, Thomas
Sturm, Johann, 43
style, 19, 29–46, 82, 86, 88, 107, 112–19, 120, 123, 127–28n12, 128n14, 128n15, 128n16, 184, 197, 200, 213, 220, 227–28
substance, 107, 121
Sudden Impact, 233
superordinate presence. *See under* presence
"Sur les origines de la dialectique." *See under* Dupréel, Eugène
Susenbrotus, Joannes, 31, 32
Sweezy, Paul M., 150, 154
syllogism, 26, 167. *See also* enthymeme; logic
Syntactic Structures. See under Chomsky, Noam
Systemic Functional Linguistics. *See* Halliday, M. A. K.

Talmud, 13, 58. *See also* religion, Judaism
Talon, Omer, 40, 43, 46n5

Tarde, Gabriel, 62
Taxi Driver, 233
Technique of Controversy, The, 62
Tel-Aviv University, 6n1
"Terministic Screens." *See under* Burke, Kenneth
testimonia, 229
Testrom, John, 47
theme. *See phoros*
Thomas, Jerry R., 76, 79
Thornburgh, Nathan, 159, 161
Tindale, Christopher W., 54, 127n11, 133, 226, 235
Todorov, Tzvetan, 53n8, 54
Tolstoy, Leo, 184, 236–44
topoi, 5, 19, 25, 64, 183, 185, 192, 193, 195, 200, 201, 203, 204. *See also loci*
Tordesillas, Alonso, 127n6, 133
totalitarianism, 58, 157
Toulmin, Stephen, 2, 28n1, 28, 146, 171, 173, 174, 178, 180n3, 180n5, 180n6, 181, 183, 186, 187, 189, 205; *Cosmopolis*, 180n6; *Human Understanding: The Collective Use and Evolution of Concepts*, 186; *Return to Reason*, 173; *The Uses of Argument*, 174, 186, 180n3, 180n6. *See also* argumentation, models of; Jonsen, Albert R., and Stephen Toulmin; Toulmin, Stephen, Richard Rieke, and Allan Janik
Toulmin, Stephen, Richard Rieke, and Allan Janik, 186, 205
Traité de l'argumentation: La nouvelle rhétorique, 1, 4, 43, 46n3, 55, 58, 60, 61, 65, 66, 67, 68, 69, 70, 71, 72, 73, 74, 75, 75, 77, 110, 148, 175, 180n6, 188, 223, 226. *See also New Rhetoric, The: A Treatise on Argumentation*
Traité de morale. See under Dupréel, Eugène
"Traité des figures ou la rhétorique décryptée." *See under* Paulhan, Jean
Traité de sociologie générale, 78n3. *See also* Pareto, Vilfredo
Tristram Shandy, 61, 70, 72, 74
tropes, Des, 46n5
Troyat, Henri, 237, 243
Tucker, Robert, 32
Tufts, J. H., 109, 133
Twenty Fifth Hour, The, 61
"Two Aspects of Language." *See under* Jakobson, Roman

United Nations Educational, Scientific, and Cultural Organization (UNESCO), 58, 145, 148–60, 163–64, 168, 170. *See also* Committee of Experts on the Philosophical Principles of the Rights of Man; Committee on the Philosophical Analysis of Fundamental Concepts

universal audience, 3, 5, 19, 20, 21–26, 48–54, 56, 57, 65, 72–77, 168–69, 173, 176, 177, 180n2, 184

universal/particular, 25, 49, 51, 52, 73, 109, 112, 113–14, 145, 167–69, 176–77, 178, 180n2, 223, 225, 227, 234. *See also* philosophical pairs

Université Libre du Bruxelles. *See* Free University of Brussels

University of Chicago, 64, 105, 125

University of Oregon, 6n1, 195, 202; writing, speaking, and critical reasoning, 201

Un Monde, 61

Uses of Argument, The. See under Toulmin, Stephen

values, argument about, 2, 4, 23, 25, 27, 32, 45, 60, 62, 77, 85, 108–14, 117, 118, 120–23, 125, 126, 130, 134–37, 140, 143, 152, 158–60, 163–69, 171, 175–79, 189–91, 200, 208, 219, 227

"Vagueness: An Exercise in Logical Analysis," 41

van Dantzig, D., 160n3

van Eemeren, Frans H., 221n7, 222

Vannier, Guillaume, 54

Vega, Luis, 227, 235

V for Vendetta, 199

Vico, Giambattista, 3, 40, 194, 201

violence, 1, 3, 4, 59, 77, 78n3, 156–57, 178, 188, 199, 237–40, 242–43

vita activa/vita contemplativa, 59, 61, 71, 127n6

Volkmann, Richard, 46n5

Volta, Alessandro, 34

Vossius, Gerardus, 43

Voyage of the Beagle, The. See under Darwin, Charles

Vygotsky, L. S., 190, 205

Warnick, Barbara, 19, 20, 21–28, 56, 57, 58, 61, 66, 71, 73, 79, 145, 183, 250–51

warrant, 173, 174, 186, 187, 189. *See* argumentation, models of (Toulmin model)

Watson, James D., 34, 210

Watson, James Sibley, Jr., 105

Weaver, Richard, 2, 41, 46n5, 81, 160n5, 163, 165, 184, 237, 240, 243; *Ethics of Rhetoric*, 41, 46n5, 237, 240, 243

Weber, J. P., 53

Weizman, Chaïm, 63

Wellek, Rene, 43

wellerisms, 231

Wess, Robert, 129n18, 133

Whately, Richard, 70

White, Zachary M., 106, 133

Whittaker, Robert, 238, 243

Wiggins, David, 166, 167, 170

Williams, Walter, 29, 47

Winn, Wendy, 19, 20, 32, 81–82, 103–33, 183, 184, 251

Wizard of Oz, The, 232

Wolin, Ross, 105, 106, 107, 133

World War II, 2, 18, 35, 56, 59, 60, 124, 145, 148, 162

Wright, Mark H., 105, 133

Wunder der Sprache, pas, 46n5

Wynn, James, 221

Yáñez, Christián Santibáñez, 223, 235

Zappen, James, 105, 127n5

Zionism, 12, 13

Zyskind, Harold, 168, 170